The New Capitalism

The New Capitalism

William E. Halal

John Wiley & Sons

New York · Chichester · Brisbane · Toronto · Singapore

Library of Congress Cataloging in Publication Data:

Halal, William E.
  The new capitalism.

  (Wiley management series on problem solving,
decision making, and strategic thinking)
    1. Industrial management.   2. Entrepreneur.
3. Capitalism.   I. Title.   II. Series.

HD31.H228 1986   658.4'012   86-1643
ISBN 0-471-87472-8

Printed in the United States of America

10 9 8 7 6 5 4 3 2 1

To my children, Jason and Aurora, and
the rest of their generation; for they will build
the world that my generation can only dream about.

Acknowledgments

Acknowledgments and thanks are due many people who helped make this book a reality. Foremost is John Mahaney, my editor at Wiley, whose seasoned judgment and patient understanding were invaluable. Cynthia Kirk, a consulting editor at Wiley, served a key role by helping edit the manuscript. Melonie Parnes, Kathleen Kelly, Diane McNulty, Laurie Angel-Sadis, and Thomas Gilmartin all played important roles at Wiley in taking *The New Capitalism* from manuscript to finished book. Special appreciation is reserved for Lee Preston, Professor of Business Policy at the University of Maryland, who provided continual advice and encouragement, and for Susan Tolchin, Professor of Public Administration at George Washington University (GWU), whose support was steadfast. David Ewing, Managing Editor of the *Harvard Business Review*, encouraged me to begin the book; Lee Fritschler, Director of Advanced Study Programs at The Brookings Institution, provided a forum for testing these concepts; and Norma Loeser, Dean of the School of Government and Business at GWU, reimbursed my expenses. Many colleagues at GWU reviewed early drafts, notably Jayne Spain, former vice president of Gulf Oil and now Executive in Residence; Joe Cordes, Professor of Economics; and Jerry Harvey, Professor of Management. Robert Kuhn, scientist-entrepreneur and adjunct professor at New York University, reviewed the manuscript, as well as Harold Linstone, Editor of *Technological Forecasting & Social Change*. I am indebted to many students and organizational clients who bore such controversial ideas gracefully. Deepest gratitude goes to my wife, Carol Lynn, for providing the close support I needed to complete this project over three difficult years, as well as the counsel of her special wisdom.

Contents

PART 3: TOWARD A NEW ECONOMY

The New Capitalism

Prologue

Origins:

A NEW FUTURE FROM OLD IDEALS

Major revolutions from both the left and the right have been sweeping through the United States during the past two decades to transform the "Old Capitalism" of an industrial past into a "New Capitalism" for a post-industrial future.

Two Faces of a Single Revolution

The first of these revolutions was launched by the student revolt that rolled across the country when the Free Speech Movement erupted at the University of California in 1964. I was a graduate student at the Berkeley campus during that notorious period, although, coming from the aerospace industry to study business and economics, I was hardly a revolutionary type. But those unusual rumblings of change my attention because they seemed to mark the beginning of a new era in American life.

A maturing industrial system had become so productive that it could provide a surfeit of goods—but not without mounting economic problems such as pollution, unemployment, and dangerous products. Meanwhile, the penetrating power of television introduced a bold new frontier of information technology—to reveal deep divisions over explosive social issues like the war in Vietnam. All this was framed within the context of massive institutions—profit-

Portions of this prologue are adapted from my article, "The Second American Revolution: Redefining Capitalism for the Information Age," in *Creating a Global Agenda* (World Future Society, 1984).

centered big business and bureaucratic big government—that had swelled to dominate society.

Faced with such disturbing economic, technological, and social upheavals, it is not surprising that young people felt an urgent need for change. There was a lot of frivolous naiveté to the student protests, but too much has been made of the drugs, sex, and violence by a press bent on catering sensationalism to a leering public. The significance of that period, it seems to me, was a genuine interest in extending democratic ideals to insure that our system of political economy safeguarded the environment, served the real needs of households, recognized the rights of workers, and generally promoted the public welfare over financial gain alone. These concerns were later protected by federal legislation, and yesterday's protestors have become today's decision-makers as they move into control of major institutions.

In 1980, however, Americans were reminded how unpredictable is the path of progress when the "neoconservative revolt" threatened to sweep away such gains by returning to laissez-faire capitalism. Although many were stunned by the election of Ronald Reagan because it seemed to repudiate human values, it has now become clear that the nation was sending its leaders another urgent message rather than simply reacting to excesses of the 1960s. The Reagan victory also began a major revolution, but this one was supported by large numbers of average people who wanted to quell the stifling regulations of a complex government bureaucracy, the tax burden of an overblown welfare state, and other such indulgences that sapped the strength of the economy.

Thus, the country appeared to be caught in a bitter conflict as it swerved sharply from the left to the right; however, beneath all the emotional rhetoric the same forces of change were still thrusting us into a complex future that suddenly became far more complex.

I have been captivated by studying these issues since my encounter with the future at Berkeley, and it is evident to me that these two revolutions can best succeed if they are seen as different faces of a single, far larger revolution—John D. Rockefeller III called it the "Second American Revolution." It may not be apparent to true believers of either persuasion, but there seems to be a basic unity joining both political movements. The neoconservative revolt actually comprises the "other half" of the transformation that began during the 1960s. Then, liberals were intent on promoting democratic values; now, conservatives want to foster free enterprise. These two unfinished revolutions define a distinctive American agenda of the great needs facing the nation today.

After more than 200 years, the United States remains the most exciting social experiment in history, which is why so many people are eager to immigrate to our shores. The dark side of the American Dream, however, is a serious failing to live up to the potential of our magnificent heritage. There is an inability to truly realize the two central principles of democracy and free enterprise that form the intellectual and spiritual foundations of the nation, and therein lies the underlying cause of the recent revolutions from the left and the right.

Beneath the complacency that now lulls the land, I suspect there dwells great potential for rebellion at the chasm between our democratic ideals and the crass, authoritarian reality of everyday life in the marketplace—the contrast is rather like the way people often relegate their faith to a perfunctory observance of empty rituals at church on Sunday while sinning mightily throughout the week. Just as the rich, white males who once controlled the Republic were tested to extend political rights to the poor, blacks, and women, today we face another challenge to enfranchise employees, customers, and other powerless constituencies of social institutions. The fact is that people have very limited rights to influence decisions affecting their jobs, schools, shops, hospitals, churches, or other forums of modern life. And these are just the most obvious shortcomings. "Reaganomics" emphasizes that we live in a society fascinated with power and extravagance, existing comfortably alongside daily injustices and widespread poverty. Many work hard to remedy these faults, but, for a nation professing to hold human values in the highest esteem, there persists an enormous gap between our principles and our practices.

Likewise, the principle of free enterprise is also often extolled but rarely observed. Yes, government has grown into a big brother that inhibits entrepreneurial freedom, but the main cause of the economic crisis is that lumbering oligopolies like auto making and steel are unfit to compete with foreign firms. Some markets are being deregulated to restore competition, and vibrant enterprise thrives in new high-tech fields. However, the hard truth is that big business remains dominated by huge, inefficient bureaucracies, and mergers are causing these dinosaurs to grow even bigger. The problem is not only government and business, but also includes labor, education, medicine, and other institutions that burden modern life with giant pyramids of hierarchical control. Real independence today is limited to a few brave souls who have the courage to strike out alone, while most people struggle with a growing organizational labyrinth that threatens to engulf us all in its bureaucratic web.

Recently, however, these contradictions have begun to work out as the transition to a post-industrial era reached crisis levels. The turning point in this transition seems to have finally passed during the traumatic recession of 1980 to 1983 that broke the fever of a mounting economic crisis, and now a variety of strong trends are rapidly forming which show that a technological imperative is accelerating the United States into an information age. Enormous confusion persists, of course, but what stands out is that a central theme runs through all these trends: the ideals of democracy and free enterprise are being reaffirmed because they offer the best means of adapting to a very difficult new frontier.

We are also learning that a overreliance on either of these principles produces serious distortions. Democratic government that fosters human welfare at the expense of individual freedom has come to resemble "socialist dictatorship," and, conversely, enterprise that ignores social values can lead to "capitalist exploitation." In fact, the imbalance of stressing one over the other is responsible for the recent swings to the left and right. The challenge Americans face is to creatively synthesize these two great ideals, which would produce a new economic order that exemplifies both traditions — "Democratic Free Enterprise."

The Intent of This Book

The main thesis of this book is that strategic institutional changes are presently creating this more sophisticated form of capitalism for a post-industrial society.

But how does this book differ from the mass of similar works that have become so popular lately as the economic transformation grows imminent? The literature in management is alive with many exciting new ideas, such as those of Peter Drucker, William Ouchi, and Peters and Waterman. There is also a flurry of recent attempts to revitalize economics by authors like George Gilder, Lester Thurow, and Robert Reich. And many futurists have arisen to suggest what lies ahead, notably Daniel Bell, Alvin Toffler, and John Naisbitt, because we need guidance in a time of great change. What does this study add to these groaning shelves besides its mere weight?

This book builds on all this knowledge and my studies to show how the economic crisis is being resolved as major corporations spearhead the passage to an information age. Business is evolving rapidly into a new institutional form based on American traditions, which should transform the entire economic system, and, ultimately, Western society itself. These changes comprise the New Capitalism.

To describe this historic transformation, I have integrated data, examples, and trends covering a broad range of topics, including technological advances, organizational structures, power relations, institutional goals, strategic change, macroeconomic policy, and the world economy. The primary focus on business is extended to touch on other key institutions that make up the social order, including government, labor, education, medicine, and even religion. This information is adapted from my previous research studies and consulting projects which employ economic analyses, computer simulations, questionnaire surveys totaling about 1000 respondents, and interviews with more than 200 people. In addition to these primary sources, I have also drawn on books, periodicals, reports, and other secondary sources.

One of the most useful features of this book is to show that the New Capitalism is an unusual combination of both democracy and free enterprise, and so my emphasis is on balancing liberal versus conservative views that are often believed to be incompatible in economic thought. This approach will not convince all, but I have earnestly tried to reconcile profit with social welfare, "supply-side" and "industrial" economic policies, and other prominent conflicts. The most significant aspect of the new era now beckoning is a synthesis of opposites, and this book reflects that imperative.

In spite of a frenzy of attention on such topics recently, most persons remain puzzled over the meaning of this economic upheaval and institutions are still struggling to grasp the adjustments needed to survive. The main contribution I offer is not simply to describe a new era, changing management practices, economic trends, or other subjects that many have covered, but to integrate this overwhelming wealth of knowledge into a coherent whole, to reconcile conflicting positions, to clarify where it is all leading, and to show the way it affects business, government, social institutions, and the lives of people. In short, to explain how a very different system of political economy is emerging—a New Capitalism.

The New American Spirit

This sounds fairly logical, but there are troubling questions involved that go beyond scientific objectivity. Is it possible to "know" the future at all? Almost everybody has different notions about what they think would be best, so how can such a broad range of controversial views be reconciled? Do "optimum" solutions like Democratic Free Enterprise constitute political advocacy rather than scholarly knowledge?

In one sense, I've avoided these questions by providing objective descriptions of "alternative futures" in the last chapter defining three main choices Americans face: a scenario of "Corporate America" extending the present conservative reign of laissez-faire big business, a "Regulated America," which would be created by a liberal backlash that restores big government, and a third possibility unifying both the left and right wings—"Democratic Free Enterprise America."

It is useful to see such differences sharply, but to stop here would miss the essence of the problem. These are not equally attractive choices to be objectively weighed by dispassionate decision-makers; the future is being shaped now by a perplexing melange of new ideas, political movements, and moral values churning among diverse elements of society. And the very heart of the economic crisis centers on such deeply ingrained, emotionally charged issues. For instance, a tenacious animosity among management, labor, and government prevents the cooperation needed to improve productivity, while a perennial conflict between bureaucratic controls versus individual freedom hampers innovation. These dilemmas persist because of an entrenched belief in the efficacy of rational decisions made by those in power to pursue financial gain. But this is the outmoded logic of an "economic man" raised on the "Old Capitalism" from an industrial past, whereas today's disorders can only be solved by confronting these more disturbing, personal matters that are so resistant because they exceed sheer logic.

Now our traditional beliefs are being rejuvenated to overcome such obstacles—not out of dedication to principles or altruism—but because they are becoming the most practical way to master the challenges of the information age. Information technology is spreading like wildfire to ignite an enormously higher level of social complexity, and the need to handle this turbulence is creating one of the most significant but least understood imperatives of our time: the startling discovery is dawning that democratic participation and entrepreneurial freedom are no longer luxuries or moral niceties but the most essential ingredients for survival, especially in the high-tech fields of the future, because they are **productive**. Thus, a quiet economic transformation seems to be underway as the demands of information technology relentlessly drive these two powerful ideals to new heights and unite them into an unusual alliance.

Just a few years ago such lofty motives were considered anathema in business, but today important changes are forcing major economic breakthroughs in this direction—simply out of enlightened self-interest. As the following chapters will show, capitalism is changing. Rising like a phoenix from the ashes of a dying epoch, the New Capitalism is being invented now by creative entrepreneurs who are leading the way into the future.

The unavoidable need for a sustainable type of progress is opening up a vast frontier of "smart growth" that balances the advantages of growth versus its costs to improve the net quality of life. Sheer material consumption is yielding to an interest in small cars, lean diets, and other forms of more intelligent living. Innovative firms like Dow Corning, Armco, and 3M are developing production systems that save energy, recycle waste, and avoid pollution—while also making bigger profits. Companies like GM, GE, and Bendix are automating routine jobs in factories and offices, thereby shifting the labor force to professional work that is more productive and gratifying. Other firms are drawing on the revolution in high-technology to develop new markets for improving communications, education, health care, and other unmet social needs. To provide these personal services, a "client-driven" form of marketing is emerging that serves customers needs better. These challenges are far more complex, but cultivating this "inner" domain of "human economy" offers a wiser approach to growth that is almost unlimited.

Hierarchical pyramids are shedding their bureaucratic inertia as they become transformed into "market networks" in order to survive intense competition caused by deregulation and escalating foreign competition. This more flexible, responsive type of structure is evolving as the microcomputer, telecommunications, and other breakthroughs in information technology convert organizations into "integrated information systems" that permit an innovative form of decentralized control. IBM, for instance, took the lead in micro-computers from Apple by using a self-contained "Independent Business Unit" to provide entrepreneurial flexibility in developing the PC. Large companies like GE, TRW, and 3M are thereby becoming "confederations of entrepreneurs," launching a boom of countless small, quasi-independent ventures that bring the dynamic creativity of free markets *inside* large organizations themselves.

Within these organizational networks, a wave of "participative leadership" is rising to enlist the commitment of a new breed of employees who seek self-fulfillment. Corporations like Delta Airlines, Motorola, and Ford are developing labor-management relations that contract for performance, share profits, collaborate on decisions, improve working conditions, and safeguard employee rights. One of the most striking developments is that the need to become com-petitive forced Chrysler, Eastern, Pan Am, and about a dozen other major companies to seat employees on their boards—which would have been unthinkable earlier. A few employee directors do not make a revolution, but these early signs of a breakthrough in working relations are growing because the sharing of rights *and* responsibilities is best for both labor and management. At People Express, for instance, a vital spirit of cooperation among ticket agents, pilots, and managers made this airline so productive that it is thriving while most others are struggling.

Not only are employees becoming enfranchised, a political coalition is evolving among other business "stakeholders" to create a democratic form of governance that serves "multiple goals" while enhancing profit—it can be thought of as a better way to make money. The Europeans, Japanese, and avant-garde American companies like IBM, Dayton-Hudson, and Hewlett-Packard work closely with labor, government, customers, and suppliers to foster business success. A good example is the way Lee Iacocca saved Chrysler from bankruptcy by uniting its constituencies to work together for their common good. Even competitors are learning to collaborate, as in the partnerships that all domestic auto makers have formed with their foreign opposition. Thus, an "open-system" model of the firm is evolving in which executives become "economic statesmen" forming a "social contract" that integrates these disparate interests into a larger economic community. In effect, this broader role should expand the mission of business to create "social wealth" as well as financial wealth.

These moves along with other new strategic practices are leading toward a form of "strategic management" that is needed to cope with the escalating change of today. Most large companies and many government agencies now use strategic planning, issue management, and participative strategy formulation to gain control over their future. The result is an "organization-environment symbiosis" that uses external forces for change to devise more effective strategies—much as the oriental martial arts convert the strength of an aggressor to one's own defense.

The old adversarial business-government relationship is also being resolved as progressive corporate and civic leaders unite to convert the problems that plague society into opportunities for progress. Wang Laboratories worked with the community in Lowell, Massachusetts, to turn this decaying mill town into a model of high-tech prosperity. A coalition of banks, hospitals, and universities brought new life to Indianapolis as a cultural center. Texas, Michigan, Massachusetts, and Pennsylvania have started labor-management-government alliances to spur economic growth. At the national level, there is wide interest in forming similar alliances to improve macroeconomic policy. Moves are now underway to redefine the economic infrastructure by using taxes to internalize social costs in lieu of regulations, "privatizing" government functions, forming business-government programs to spur technological innovation, and other changes that aid the operation of the marketplace. In time these private-public sector partnerships may evolve into a powerful new economic system that combines robust competition with creative collaboration to foster healthy economic growth.

Related changes are beginning around the globe that may even defuse the tension between the USA and the USSR. Being forced to search for solutions to the economic crisis, a variety of similar experiments are underway in Europe, the Third World, and socialist states, which is producing "hybrid economies" that combine various types of democracy, state control, and free enterprise. Red China, for instance, seems intent on developing a form of "market socialism." The result should be to fill in the gap between the extreme ideologies of the Old Capitalism and the "Old Socialism." There are enormous obstacles that will take decades to overcome, of course, and a rich diversity will flourish among various nations. But such prospects offer the hope of creating a world order that may reconcile the conflict between the superpowers as the New Capitalism becomes not too unlike the "New Socialism."

All these trends are well-established, logical extensions of American principles that seem to be coming to fruition in a new form of political economy—Democratic Free Enterprise. The way this system is evolving spontaneously from the grassroots is also revealing. Our society is energized by the inspiration of common people— the strength of democracy is that the governed lead more wisely, and free enterprise is productive because it releases individual creativity. These are the origins of a viable new future: growing out of the deep tap-roots of old traditions that have enduring power to renew our economy with timeless values, and fed by the finer grass-roots to update this vision so it remains true to the changing reality of life in countless homes and offices. I've used extensive quotes in this book from a wide spectrum of viewpoints—learned scholars and powerful business leaders as well as ordinary workers and housewives—in order to capture the flavor and diversity of this "New American Spirit" that is the underlying source of the New Capitalism.

Obviously, these are controversial prospects still in their infancy, and other nations like Japan have been making similar moves for many years. But there is an especially fresh, creative, pragmatic strength to this vibrant new vision coming out of the United States because we inherited these principles, and so we are in a unique position to develop the New Capitalism. In short, I think a renaissance is beginning today because Americans are realizing that the best way to gain real economic power is to put our ideals to practical use. The legitimacy of democracy is being united with the productivity of enterprise to invent a prototype for the new frontier—a powerful blend of cooperation and competition now guiding nations toward a higher order of prosperity, freedom, and social harmony.

We should be comfortable with such ideas because they stem from our traditional values, but change always provokes strong resistance and heated controversy. So readers should be cautioned that this book may challenge popular beliefs, and some parts may even be infuriating. My intention is not to be unduly critical, nor to indulge in Utopian fantasies. It is to examine our institutions honestly, in order to show how we may harness the discordant, confusing forces of today into a more useful economy that promises to realize the exciting possibilities ahead.

There is an old saying that producing a book is like giving birth to a child. Having finally delivered these ideas I have labored over for so long, my hope is that the young but growing concept of Democratic Free Enterprise will help extend our heritage more fully into the future.

WILLIAM E. HALAL

Washington, D.C.
March 1986

Part 1

Redefining Capitalism

1
Enterprise Lost:
PASSING OF THE OLD CAPITALISM

How are we Americans to understand the bewildering storm of change that has engulfed our nation during the last two decades? The 1960s raged in a hurricane of revolution. Then, in the 1970s, we were battered by the energy crisis, the Watergate scandal, and the fall of Vietnam; while later we became awash in microcomputers, the women's movement, and an invasion of Japanese products. The 1980s hit us with a wave of conservativism that drove the country from left to right almost overnight, but now Reagan's supply-side revolt is floundering.

It's little wonder that we're confused because all of this turbulent change flows from the passage of American society between two great epochs that stand like towering land masses in history—the old industrial era fading into the past and a new post-industrial era taking shape in the future. The best way to grasp the meaning of our time is to see that this transition is roughly comparable to a similar transformation that our agrarian ancestors witnessed. Just a few decades ago, the typical family in agricultural America lived a short, brutal farm life of back-breaking drudgery and a standard of living barely above the subsistence level. The world has changed so much since then that the industrial society we take for granted now—jet travel, skyscrapers, traffic jams, the moon landing, TV, the Bomb—would have been incomprehensible to our grandparents,

---

Portions of this chapter are adapted from my article, "The Post-Industrial Organization," *The Bureaucrat* (October 1974).

and it still amazes the few old survivors of that period left among us.

Just as today's world is so foreign to our elders, so will the coming world of our children seem odd in contrast to our present way of life. Because if one steps back to view the broad sweep of these disruptive events of the 1970s, it becomes clear that the "Old Capitalism" of the industrial age is passing rapidly. The energy crisis signaled the end of a system that encouraged unconstrained growth and consumption. Watergate dramatized how authority could no longer go unquestioned. And the fall of Vietnam marked the loss of America's world supremacy.

Although such changes have sounded a death knell for the past, the other events of the 1970s portend a "New Capitalism" emerging for the future. The microcomputer heralds the beginning of an economy based on information technology. The rush of women into the workplace highlights a shift to cooperative working relations. And the recent economic prowess of Japan hints at the rising role of the developing nations in a new global order.

The swings between the liberalism of the 1960s and the conservativism of the 1980s, then, can be seen as a clash of views over how to find our way across this ocean of change. Although the neoconservative revolt represents an urgent need to steer around the shoals of liberal big government, the decline of Reaganomics now requires another major correction to avoid a sea of treacherous budget deficits lying dead ahead. But despite these wrenching lurches between left and right, on the whole Americans are redefining capitalism into a fairly balanced economic system that is needed to pioneer the frontier of a new era.

These first two chapters in Part 1 survey this remarkable passage from the Old Capitalism to a New Capitalism. Here we explain why the creative power of enterprise was lost as American business fell from its former heights into a maelstrom of crisis. Probing into key issues reveals that the problem is the outmoded management of major corporations, and at a deeper level these faults stem from dilemmas in the ideology of the Old Capitalism. Then Chapter 2 will show that a new vision of business and economics is emerging to regain the power of American enterprise—the New Capitalism.

CAPITALISM IN CRISIS

Just a few years ago the industrialized world was basking in its monumental accomplishments. During a relatively brief century or so since the Industrial Revolution, income in advanced nations rose more than ten-fold from the meager few hundred dollars per year most people once lived on to over $26,000 per household today, while the average work week declined from about 70 hours to less than 40 hours.[1] For the first time in history, the basic necessities of life were reasonably satisfied, life spans doubled, and material comfort became widespread.

This unprecedented triumph was largely due to the enormous power of the Old Capitalism—that cultural ideology prizing "growth," "power," and "profit," which sociologist Max Weber called the Protestant Ethic underlying the spirit of capitalism. Mass production technology so successfully overcame the physical needs of life that the most brilliant achievements of this period will be remembered not as great monuments or works of art, but as the factories, automobiles, and supermarkets that historian Kenneth Clark called symbols of "heroic materialism." To use this technology effectively, a tough form of modern management was developed that made great American corporations like General Motors, U.S. Steel, and Du Pont models of efficiency. And the profit-motive served as a guiding principle to coordinate the entire system because, as economists such as Adam Smith showed, free market competition harnesses self-interest to foster the broader public welfare.[2]

Of course, these gains were not obtained without serious costs. The harsh nature of industrial capitalism produced major depressions, bitter labor strife, and brutal monopolies. Our system may have many faults, but its sustaining justification lies in two great strengths: it is a prosperous form of economy and it maintains considerable freedom. Capitalism has soundly demonstrated its superiority over socialism in improving living standards, and modern business is a model of enlightenment compared to the centralized authority of planned economies.

It is not too bold to claim that the Old Capitalism made the industrial age one of the great success stories of history. Not too long ago, the acclaim for business produced such feverish enthusiasm that its virtues were hailed in the popular literature and by civic leaders. Business even became the unofficial American religion as the clergy preached that profit-making manifested moral righteousness and divine inspiration. John D. Rockefeller humbly demurred, "The good Lord gave me my money." A high point occurred when President Calvin Coolidge bestowed the very identity of the nation on capitalism with those famous words: "The chief business of the American people is business."[3] And so over the next few decades at its zenith of confidence, the United States became the industrial leader of the world, the Mecca of technology and managerial skill, the official seat of the Capitalist Empire.

Cross-Currents of Change

Today, however, this former euphoria has given way to a deep foreboding as Americans struggle to tame enormous new economic forces rushing upon them. Foreign competition, the consumer movement, a revolution in information technology, environmentalism, demanding workers, and other unusual changes have opened a gaping breach between an outmoded past and an uncertain future. Where just a few years ago the prospect of a new economic era was considered to be merely of academic interest, suddenly this turbulent transition has reached a state of crisis roughly comparable to the Great Depression of the 1930s.

In view of the gravity of the situation, it's rather puzzling to see that such paralyzing inaction often reigns. Many executives, for instance, deny that their organizations are in trouble or that there is an urgent need for change. While serving as a consultant to a major company, I was a bit shocked when their executives would not acknowledge that they were in a crisis, although the firm was suffering a loss of $1 billion.

The problem seems to be that an admission of crisis implies failure or blame, whereas it is really a manifestation of change. A crisis is not simply a catastrophe, but a sharp growing pain that is a necessary part of development. From this constructive view, crisis forcibly confronts us with the truth about our limitations that must be overcome, and the trauma that is unavoidably involved serves to guide the way ahead. Thus, the economic crisis is actually a natural, even mysterious, event that marks a passage from the past that is dying to the future being born, so it is characterized by "cross-currents of change" that present both grave dangers as well as bright prospects.

The danger was most acute during the recession of 1980 to 1983 when inflation had climbed to double-digits, unemployment soared, business bankruptcies hit an all-time peak, and the increase in poverty produced "cheese lines" of an uncanny similarity to the soup lines of the 1930s. Historian Arthur Schlesinger Jr. noted, "a spreading, haunting fear that, for the first time in half a century, a major depression is no longer inconceivable," and a cover of *Time* magazine asked, "Is Capitalism Working?"[4] Many of these problems still remain and others have since appeared. Bank and farm failures have become so widespread that they rival the crash of 1929, the nation is incurring a crippling trade deficit, the federal budget is out of balance beyond any past experience, and the Third World debt threatens the international financial system.

But, just as the Great Depression forced the United States to modernize its old economic system, so did this recession spark a similar turning point. A famous 1980 issue of *BusinessWeek* posed the challenge: "The U.S. economy must undergo a fundamental change if it is to retain a measure of economic viability."[5] The threat of economic collapse so alarmed business and government leaders that, after years of procrastination, major reforms finally began in earnest, as we shall see in the next chapter. There are many welcome signs that a restructuring of the economy is underway, however, the crisis is hardly over because this is going to be a prolonged transition that may last another decade or two as a declining past yields only gradually to a rising future. "We're not even a tenth of the way into the kind of restructuring we are going to see," warns Jim Farly, Chairman of Booz, Allen & Hamilton.[6]

These cross-currents of change explain why the supply-side revolution had such mixed success. The Reagan policies—tax cuts, deregulation, and reduced public spending—did help encourage economic growth and reduce inflation, certainly, but they were of limited value and led to other severe problems.

Any serious revitalization of growth, for instance, must occur through a profound shift to a different form of growth that is still in its early stages. This transition is clearly visible in stock market prices, which make up one of the broadest indicators of economic progress. Figure 1.1 shows the yearly highs and lows of the Dow Jones Industrial Average on a logarithmic scale to reveal trends more clearly. In 1965 the index broke out of a 35-year upward trend and moved sidewise between about 600 and 1100 points for almost two decades; whereas, if the old trend had continued the index would now be in the range of 5000 points! The same pattern can be seen in per capita income and GNP.[7]

This plateau occurred because the robust growth in consumer goods that fueled the "golden period of industrial growth" is leveling off. Many families with average income levels are still eager to

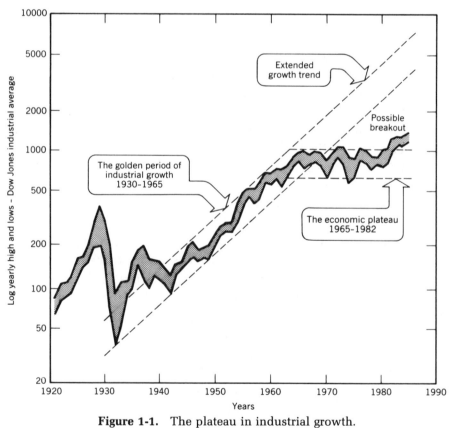

Figure 1-1. The plateau in industrial growth.
Source: New York Stock Exchange.

acquire possessions, of course, and there will always remain a need for replacement buying. But population growth is declining and many people in the upper middle class are losing interest in owning more goods like cars and appliances, so their sales peaked during the late 1970s. The following views would have been unheard of a few years ago:[8]

> *"We can live quite comfortably with what we have now," said an American professional. Another admitted, "Frankly, I've gotten to the point where I'm tired of collecting material things." A Japanese observed, "Households are saturated with goods," and a European noted, "There's no buying power anymore."*

The breakout in Figure 1.1 signals the beginning of an economic turnaround, largely because new fields such as services and information systems are thriving. This frontier may be exciting, but as yet it comprises a small portion of the economy. Meanwhile, most traditional industries remain in serious decline, despite the claim that supply-side economics would release a special "magic" of the marketplace. Change was stimulated in some sectors, but severe obstacles impede healthy economic growth that go beyond simply providing freedom from regulations and lower taxes. The real constraints stem from poor technological innovation, unwieldy corporate bureaucracies, adversarial labor-management-government relations, and other such subtle, complex problems that even hamper high-tech firms in Silicon Valley.[9]

Thus, Reaganomics failed to produce the vigorous economic boom supply-side theorists promised because it had little to do with easing this very difficult transition. True, the economy did recover strongly for the first two years after the recession, but that's because there was so much to recover ***from***. Now that more results of the supply-side experiment are in, it's clear that economic growth has not improved significantly from the Carter years that were stigmatized by "malaise." Economist Robert Dunn recently summarized the evidence:[10]

> *The supply-side revolution has been a flop . . . there has been a decline in the savings rate, private investment has not increased as a share of GNP, growth of the economy has not accelerated.*

A similar ebb and flow between the decline of the past and prospects for the future can be seen in stagflation, a critical measure of economic performance that combines both inflation and unemployment to make up an "economic misery index." Although there is normally a trade-off between these two factors, Figure 1.2 shows the sum of inflation and unemployment rates moved strongly upward since the late 1960s as both grew severe simultaneously. If the economy is thought of as a sick patient, stagflation is the major symptom of the economic malaise that still lingers on.

As Figure 1.2 also shows, the fierce discipline imposed by the recession of 1980 to 1983, deregulation, and foreign competition created a sharp breakout, so stagflation seems to have finally peaked and may be starting down to more normal levels. However, unemployment remains so high it would have been considered disastrous a decade ago, and if unreported unemployment is included,

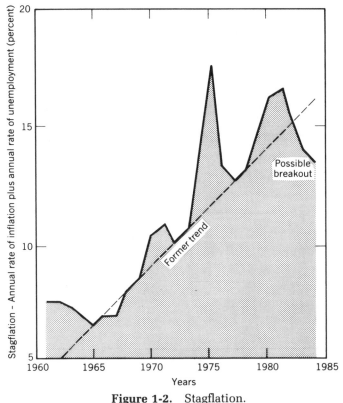

Figure 1-2.   Stagflation.
Source: Department of Commerce.

the actual level may be as high as 15 percent.[11] Thus, the decline in stagflation is more modest than Republicans boast.

Even these minor gains were achieved only because tight monetary control induced the most severe economic plunge since the Great Depression, sacrificing unemployed workers and failing businesses to reduce wage demands and product prices. Economist Otto Eckstein noted, "The fundamental thing we have learned is that if we make a recession deep enough and long enough, we can lick inflation." In terms of an illness, this remedy is like bleeding the patient. It treats the problem at a superficial level that exacerbates the malady by idling productive resources and incurring hidden social costs. The Urban Institute found that the average household lost $3300 due to the recession, and studies at Johns Hopkins University show all this hardship is causing about 400,000 premature deaths in the U.S.[12]

Not only is the decline in inflation modest and costly, it may be only a temporary lull awaiting another explosion of prices because the underlying causes have not been addressed. Many attribute stagflation to high government spending, rapid growth of the money supply, expensive energy, and other technical factors, but studies show they only play a minor role. Switzerland, Austria, Japan, and other nations maintain much lower rates of inflation and unemployment under these same conditions, largely because they are able to collaborate among labor, management, and government to restrain wage and price levels and to increase productivity.[13]

Stagflation grew serious because of these more subtle reasons. Unions demanded wage increases that exceeded productivity gains. Oligopolistic corporations passed higher costs on to customers. Government policies insulated business from competition. In short, stagflation is symptomatic of a deep cultural tendency for key economic actors to seek exorbitant rewards without making compensating contributions. It emanates from what author Christopher Lasch called a "culture of narcissism"—the endless pursuit of self-interest. With all this consumption beyond gains in productivity, the laws of supply and demand take hold and stagflation results. Journalist Joseph Kraft noted, "Our economy is in trouble because we spend more and work less hard than people in other countries."[14]

Relying on the threat of lost jobs and bankrupt firms to drive prices down is destructive and can only be maintained briefly,

while the self-interest that fuels the inflation spiral is still poised
to take off again. The economy took two decades to disintegrate
into such a dangerous state, so it will require many years to alleviate
the corrosive institutional conflict which ultimately raises prices
and undermines productivity.

And the attempt to halt the mushrooming growth of the welfare
state is backfiring due to enormous political resistance. Despite all
the outrage over heartless reductions in support programs, government spending has continued to grow, albeit more slowly, because
it is unrealistic to expect people to simply give up essential public
services they now rely on. Reagan may blame Congress, but the
inevitable result of his tax cuts was to throw the federal budget
wildly out of control. David Stockman bluntly warned just before
leaving the Office of Management and Budget (OMB), "We must
either massively cut spending or raise taxes by large, unprecedented
magnitudes."[15]

Rather than dismantling big government, therefore, the main outcome of supply-side economics was to produce the notorious federal
deficits of $200 billion which have become a major embarrassment.
Criticism is so widespread that it even comes from Republican
allies. Economist Herbert Stein, former Chairman of the Council of
Economic Advisers under Presidents Nixon and Ford, charged, "The
most distinctive feature of Reagan's economic policy . . . was the
size of its deficits." Business leaders are aghast over a "crazy federal
budget" that is "a scandal," and Republican Senator Charles Mathias
exclaimed, "We are living in an economic fantasy world." Yet the
belief that sheer financial incentives will produce a miracle of growth
is so fierce that economist Arthur Laffer, Congressman Jack Kemp,
and other originators of supply-side theory fervently propose even
greater tax cuts.[16]

The unyielding difficulty of these problems reveals that government
has become a convenient scapegoat for the ills of our society that
are due to other causes. It is tempting to believe the economy would
thrive if only those "puzzle palaces on the Potomac" could be
cleared away, but this is an empty illusion. President Reagan is
rather like a modern Don Quixote, fruitlessly attacking the windmills
of government that grind on while the real dangers lie all about in
the prosaic problems of an obsolete economic system we battle

daily. The mayor of a small town said about the crisis: "It's not simply Congress and it's not simply the previous administrations. It's business. It's the economy."[17]

The economic crisis cannot be corrected by solutions like supply-side economics because they merely address symptoms. Declining growth, stagflation, budget deficits, and other such disorders are simply the visible outcroppings of a fundamental shifting in economic foundations, all knotted together in an interlocking jumble that is so incomprehensible it may produce even more difficult problems, such as *de*flation, which are impossible to anticipate. The challenge of revitalizing the economy remains so illusive, therefore, because our policies are out of touch with the realities that have actually caused the economic crisis—outmoded industries, bureaucratic corporations, labor-management conflict, the lack of feasible alternatives to big government, and other more basic problems that have led to a loss of enterprise.

These disorders are so deeply rooted in the economic system that the heart of the problem cannot be addressed simply at the national level. Indeed, the economic crisis has no "heart," or central focus, but is scattered throughout the nation in multitudes of business corporations, government agencies, labor unions, and other institutions that make up a failing social order. The true causes of the crisis are to be found at this **institutional** level lying below the macro level where government guides the entire system and above the micro level where small entrepreneurs operate a free market. This stratum has been called the "***meso***-economic" level by business economist Lee Preston,[18] while I think of it as the "***mega***-economic" plane. The mega economy is composed of the large institutions that set the general direction for the economy—particularly corporations like the Fortune 500 that comprise the principal actors in modern economies—so it is the primary source of the economic decline.

The Outmoded Institutional Infrastructure

With the maturing of the industrial era, a huge layer of complex institutions has sprung up to permeate our lives. Most of us work in a large organization; business firms produce our goods and services; contact with our government occurs through various agencies; we are educated by schools and colleges; our health is entrusted to hospitals; we rely on television networks for information; and we even worship in the bureaucracy of organized religion. Further, these organizations have joined together to form an interlocking system that comprises the structure of society itself, and so the most critical challenge today is the humble but everpresent task of managing this "institutional infrastructure" that forms the context within which we define our relationships, problems, decisions, and other common elements of everyday life. Sociologist Daniel Bell observed, "This is an 'organization society' in that the organization rather than the small town is the locus of one's life," and Joseph Kraft noted, "[Today] the agonizing problem is living with organizations."[19]

As institutions have grown into a vast organizational thicket, they have also declined in effectiveness. Figure 1.3 shows how the portion of the public expressing high confidence in all institutions suffered a severe decline during the same period when the economy struck a plateau in growth, chronic stagflation, and other symptoms of economic malaise.[20] Although 1984 figures suggest a breakout, confidence remains far below normal levels.

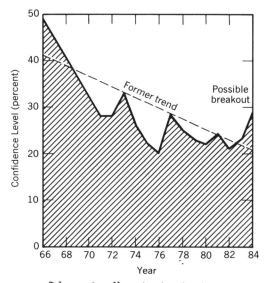

Figure 1-3.   Average confidence in all major institutions.
Source: Harris Survey. Percentages indicate the portion of a national sample of the public expressing a high level of confidence in the leadership of all major American institutions.

The problem is not the fault of individuals, but is more deeply rooted in the outmoded nature of today's massive organizational systems which acquire a life of their own, exceeding the power of ordinary people. Present institutions were successful during a simpler past when the great need was to increase industrial production; where work consisted of routine physical tasks performed by un- educated, docile people; and so on. But now a complex new frontier looms ahead as the explosive growth of information technology makes the computer the central tool of a knowledge-based society. Thus, the creative power of enterprise has been lost because insti- tutions cannot cope with this complexity, and it will only be restored by heeding the imperatives of a vastly different future. Fletcher Byrom warned when he was CEO of Koppers Company, "We have pre-1940 institutions trying to deal with post-1980 concerns," and Harvard professor Robert Reich nicely summed up the problem:[21]

> The same factor that previously brought prosperity—the way the nation organizes itself for production—now threatens decline.

Table 1.1 disaggregates the average trend in Figure 1.3 by specific institutions for three key periods—the previous high in 1966, the low during the recession of 1980 to 1983, and the upturn in 1984. The following discussion examines institutions primarily responsible for the economic crisis—government, business, and labor—and Chapter 11 extends this analysis to include the other quasi-economic institutions.

The decline of confidence in the federal government, for instance, occurred because of widespread disenchantment over various in- trusions into the pocketbooks and freedoms of Americans. For decades now, high taxes, bureaucratic regulations, and poor public service grew increasingly at odds with a culture that values individual self- reliance.[22] Supply-side economics was appealing because it offered some hope of regaining the power of the citizenry, leading to a sharp rise of confidence in 1984. However, the public's faith remains low because even Reagan's charisma has not been able to resolve the persistent problems described above, and supply-side economics is often seen as the old trickle-down theory disguised to enrich the nation's elite.

TABLE 1.1.   CONFIDENCE IN VARIOUS INSTITUTIONS

	1966	1980 to 1983	1984
Federal government (Congress and The White House)	42%	20%	34%
Major companies	55	17	19
Organized labor	22	11	12
Universities	61	34	40
Medicine	73	35	43
Legal system (Supreme Court and attorneys)	45	21	26
Military	61	31	45
Public media (television news and the press)	48	21	23
Organized religion	41	22	24
Averages	49%	23%	29%

Source: Harris Survey. Percentages indicate the portion of a national sample of the public expressing a high level of confidence in the leadership of these various institutions.

Liberals also seem unable to help. The Democratic party remains captured by politicians who want to tax business and the rich in order to support government programs, and even the new concept of an "industrial policy" is distinctive mainly in proposing aid to troubled but promising industries. This made sense in a past era of unlimited growth, but now it is easily attacked as a luxury that cannot be afforded during hard times. Neoliberals are struggling to redefine the Democratic platform, yet they seem trapped in emulating neoconservative market solutions that are a dull imitation of supply-side economics, which is why Gary Hart's "new ideas," for instance, were so quickly dismissed.

What is there about government that causes its continued growth against the strong demands of the public and the best efforts of politicians? And why is it that competent civil servants who genuinely want to serve the public interest have earned such a reputation for mediocre performance?

A large part of the problem, of course, is the notorious ineptitude of large government bureaucracies. However, the more fundamental cause is that the role of government is not defined by lawmakers and the wishes of the public, but by business. The history of business-government relations shows that government has grown as a countervailing force to offset increasing corporate power. Social analyst Irving Kristol noted, "If one thing is certain, it is that the more 'big business' we have the more 'big government' we shall get."[23]

Big government arose in three main periods of reform. At the turn of this century, Theodore Roosevelt led a populist uprising against business monopolies that created the present antitrust laws. Then, the Great Crash urged Franklin D. Roosevelt (FDR) to develop deposit insurance, unemployment compensation, fiscal and monetary controls, and other forms of regulation to stabilize the economy. In the 1960s, the interest in quality of life produced a new wave of "social legislation" to protect against pollution, consumer fraud, worker injuries, and other such problems.[24]

Even today Americans pay far lower taxes than most modern nations because the United States is without public services that are badly needed to compensate for various limitations of the private sector, such as a national health system, relocation programs for the unemployed, and the like. And the much detested federal regulations remain intact because the public demands a clean environment, safe work conditions, wholesome products, and other basic necessities of modern life. These unwieldy bureaucracies may be a serious problem, but the rise of big government is largely due to abuses of big business and the lack of better alternatives for resolving critical social issues.

This intimate, symbiotic relationship between big business as the primary actor in society versus government as an overseer of business conduct also explains why Washington has acquired such a well-deserved reputation for mediocrity. Apart from agencies like NASA and the Department of Defense perform a valuable function in their own right, most government work consists of issuing regulations, responding to complaints, enforcement, and so on. This is a thankless, uninspiring role with little sense of purpose, so the ineffective tone of the federal bureaucracy largely results from the onerous mission it has been assigned.

Not all aspects of government are affected by business, of course, but the main cause of the problem cannot be overstated: big government is sustained by the shortcomings of big business. As corporations continue growing to create more messy externalities, the need for still more government aid insures that earnest attempts to reduce the public sector are doomed to fail unless the role of the private sector is redefined as well.

As Table 1.1 shows, even now only 19 percent of Americans feel confident about the leadership of major companies. One cause is that the traditional focus on profit-making has led to'widespread scandals that have created hostile relations with a cynical public. Environmental disasters by chemical companies involving the Love Canal, kepone, and asbestos poisoning have stiffened pollution controls and laws protecting workers. Ford's faulty Pinto gas tank, the defective Dalkon Shield contraceptive of A. H. Robins Company, and other notorious cases of consumer injuries have brought a surge of product liability claims. Distrust over the management of the Three-Mile Island meltdown helped close down the nuclear power industry. David Ewing, Editor of the *Harvard Business Review*, noted, "Public anger at corporations is beginning to well up at a frightening rate."[25]

In a time of economic crisis, however, the main problem is a pragmatic concern over the loss of economic strength. Opinions differ, but typical studies show widespread declines in most industries. In steel-making, for instance, David Roderick, CEO of U.S. Steel, warned, "Steel is now in its deepest crisis since the Depression of the 1930s." Although such struggles have directed attention to the plight of the "smokestack" industries, John Young, President of Hewlett-Packard who chaired President Reagan's Commission on Industrial Competitiveness, reports that 8 out of 10 major high-technology industries have been losing world market share. As a result, inflation-adjusted accounting shows that corporate profits were almost wiped out by inflation during the past decade. While American firms are failing, Japanese business is moving in to take over large parts of the American economy. Japanese investment in U.S. subsidiaries spurted 130 percent from 1981 to 1985. *BusinessWeek* summed it up: "U.S. industry's loss of competitiveness over the past two decades has been nothing short of an economic disaster."[26]

Thus, in contrast to the adulation business enjoyed only a short time ago, the heroes of enterprise have been stunned to realize they are no longer loved because they are failing to serve the needs of customers, employees, the nation, or even their own investors. Why have firms that were so successful only recently fallen from grace so sharply? In an age of "robber barons," the problem could be blamed on the rapacious greed or the ignorance of tycoons. But modern managers are well educated, dedicated professionals who are trying very hard to carry out their obligations to society and to succeed economically.

The old form of management did not suddenly turn bad, it is simply no longer appropriate. One executive put it succinctly: "Business hasn't changed—society has." Present corporations were designed for managing routine manufacturing work in a stable industrial past. That period is gone forever, and now firms are struggling with an unfamiliar world of large organizations, complex technologies, foreign competition, critical consumers, government controls, a new breed of workers, and a general questioning of their role in society. In the early 1980s, when Reginald Jones was CEO of General Electric, he warned that business was suffering from a widespread "management malaise"—poor product quality, adversarial labor relations, a short-term focus on profits that excludes long-term strategy, and a general tendency toward bureaucracy rather than enterprise.[27]

Enlightened managers are searching for remedies, and the heady popularity of books extolling management excellence has directed a rush of attention to new solutions. Chrysler was rescued from the brink of bankruptcy through an unusual pact between management, labor, and government, highlighting major moves underway in smokestack America. The rejuvenation of IBM into a flexible, innovative giant reflects the prowess of the sunrise industries. But these islands of hope are limited to a few isolated cases as yet because the economic crisis has barely passed a turning point. Most large firms in auto making, steel, textiles, appliances, and other major industries remain almost crippled by outmoded management practices, and even the so-called "excellent companies" that Peters and Waterman studied are still struggling with the same difficult adjustment to a new era.[28]

Labor unions bear their share of the blame as well. Table 1.1 shows that organized labor is the least respected institution, primarily because it remains trapped in an adversarial role that is now obsolete. There are some effective unions, of course, especially the new ones thriving in service fields, but they generally seem unable to adjust to new economic realities. Despite a massive loss of jobs through automation and foreign competition, most unions continue to pursue the goals expressed by Samuel Gompers decades ago—"more." Because few unions are realistic enough to share the responsibility for increasing productivity in order to help their troubled employers, wages were frozen or reduced in 40 percent of recent labor contracts, and membership is down to almost half of its former peak. Even their own members are critical. A poll found that two out of three union workers believe unions are more to blame for inflation than business.[29]

Organizational Gridlock

Obviously, this is only a brief survey of a broad range of complex activity, and it has focused on limitations rather than a balanced assessment of both good and poor performance. Most of these institutions carry out their role with at least modest success, and there are many instances of excellence that we will examine later. Once again, we should stress that such problems are not primarily the fault of politicians, executives, or other individuals, but stem from outmoded technological systems, organizational structures, and institutional goals.

However, the unavoidable conclusion is that our institutions do not work very well. People are often discouraged at seeing these overwhelming problems, but perhaps it is better to feel their full weight in order to begin solving them. The unyielding truth is that the economic crisis is not attributable to some vague, disembodied entity like "the economy" or "society"—it is directly traceable to specific institutional causes. As this evidence and Chapter 11 show, poor growth, stagflation, and other economic disorders are the result of burdensome big government, corporate bureaucracies, adversarial labor unions, endless military spending, skyrocketing medical costs, and complex legal proceedings that all encourage waste, decrease productivity, and stifle innovation. Such habits are encouraged by public media that romanticize extravagant lifestyles. We remain confused over all this because the educational system has left us bereft of understanding in a time of great change. Even religion has contributed by failing to provide a sense of purpose.

Further, these institutional faults are intimately related in a complex web of relationships centering about the role of large corporations. Big government has risen to counter the limits of big business. The hostile behavior of labor unions is a predictable result of an adversarial tradition with management. These and other institutional connections described in Chapter 11 form the interlocking structure of society itself, with major corporations strategically located to control central points of this megaeconomic suprasystem. Harold Geneen acknowledged when he was CEO of ITT: "Large corporations have become the primary custodians of making our entire system work."[30]

Thus, the economic crisis is best diagnosed as what economist Mancur Olsen calls an "institutional sclerosis" and what futurist Hazel Henderson identifies as the "entropy state."[31] The crisis is the result of an interlocking complex of institutional systems that blanket the nation in such a snarl of excessive technology, labyrinthian structures, and self-serving interests that the economy threatens to slowly grind to a stop under its own weight as it becomes seized in a sort of "organizational gridlock."

Most professionals urge the need for change, which is confirmed by my experience working with organizations. I meet with a variety of people in my work, and they are almost always suffocating in complexity, mediocrity, red tape, coercion, and irresponsibility. Unfortunately, they have a painful time acknowledging the situation openly, much less knowing what to do about it, because of a sort of "unspoken conspiracy." The "organizational problem" today is rather like sex before it was "liberated." We are all involved and it is the source of great confusion and despair, yet the topic is usually taboo for open discussion. The obstacles to a reasonable mode of organizational behavior seem to be so enormous, so pervasive, and so beyond the ability of mere individuals that most people have given up hope. To maintain a semblance of sanity and peace, we have come to accept what approaches a modern form of madness as simply an inevitable part of life that cannot be changed.

So the reason policy makers cannot resolve the economic crisis is subtle, illusive, and insidious. The economy is in crisis because the entire social order is itself in a state of crisis. The challenge modern societies face is not to develop more effective forms of taxation, monetary control, or other macroeconomic solutions. Sound national policies are essential, but the main need is to redefine major institutions, especially the large corporations that dominate the economy.

Bringing about such fundamental change is going to be very difficult because sensitive matters are involved that provoke a deep level of resistance. It's also clear that institutions have been declining for years, and many people have shown that a different form of management is far superior, so why has so little change occurred? And why is the problem so pervasive among so many diverse institutions? In short, what is the underlying force that sustains institutions and that seems unmoveable?

Institutions do not appear out of thin air, but are manifestations of the ideas, beliefs, and values a society holds sacred. In the final analysis, the problem runs even deeper because organizational behavior flows from some type of conceptual model, ideology, paradigm, or other abstract matters of intellect, custom, and faith that people need to interpret reality. Institutions today tend to adhere to the same outmoded management because most of us are still hooked on the old values of growth, power, and profit. So the economic crisis cannot be fully understood without going to the ideological crux of the problem—the beliefs we hold about business and economics.

THE UNDERLYING DILEMMAS OF DECLINE

The ideology of the Old Capitalism that successfully powered the industrial past is rapidly becoming exhausted. It is still useful, but the approaching information age exceeds our existing concepts, thereby leading to confusing dilemmas that underlie the previously mentioned problems. Obstacles have appeared that limit physical growth. Hierarchy and authority produce ineffective bureaucracies. Self-interest diminishes the interests of us all. These pervasive disorders are the source of a gripping fear that society is out of control. Pollster Patrick Caddell's studies show, "We're finding substantial numbers of people who believe the future is slipping away," while typical Americans report:[32]

Too much has been changing lately . . . there's a great uncertainty, a lack of order, nothing's working. . . . The basic fabric of society has broken down. . . . Somehow everything has to be brought back under control.

Ultimately, then, modern economies are in a state of crisis, not because their performance is especially poor, but because the old familiar way we view the world no longer makes sense as a bewildering new era looms ahead. Daniel Bell and Irving Kristol called it "The Crisis in Economic Theory," while journalist Robert Samuelson noted the cause of this disorientation:[33]

The economic problem today is, broadly speaking, that Americans live with ideas and assumptions forged in another era that are no longer suitable.

The issues surrounding the economic crisis may stem from outmoded institutions, but we now move to a deeper level of analysis beyond action and social structure to examine the underlying logical dilemmas from which the economic decline finally emanates.

The Dilemma of Growth: Materialism versus Quality of Life

Physical growth has always been important, but it became a central goal of modern economies because the *raison d'etre* of capitalism is to expand economic development. This was useful earlier when it was necessary to mechanize farms, build manufacturing plants, and create other parts of the physical infrastructure to tame a new continent. Total capital investment in the United States increased 30-fold since the turn of the century and now represents about $250,000 for every farmer and about $50,000 for every factory worker. Growth was so urgent that politicians were pressured to inflate the economy prior to election, producing a pattern of business cycles that coincides with the 4-year political cycle.[34] This imperative of "more is better" is still manifested in the behavior of institutions: corporations strive to increase the sale of goods, governments enlarge programs, and labor unions demand higher wages.

With the famous *Limits to Growth* study, however, the feasibility of continuing this relentless drive for still more cars, appliances, and now electronic gadgets has become a heated debate. Proponents of "hard growth" claim science can overcome any constraints, and some optimists believe the world should reach a "super-industrial" state of development supporting 30 billion people at American levels of consumption. But others contend this would interfere with the quality of life, so they advocate "soft" technologies reminiscent of the agrarian past. This view of "no growth" argues for a "steady-state" economy, a decentralized system of self-sufficient households, and cultivating human values rather than material consumption.[35]

Both of these positions are sound in important ways, but they are diametrically opposed to one another, and that is the dilemma of growth. It is hard to see how the world can realize its potential as an advanced civilization without the development of sophisticated technologies. Yet it is also true that a new age of limits and higher values challenges the old view of unlimited physical growth and material consumption.

The inevitability of further growth is self-evident. Even cautious estimates indicate the world population should double over the next few decades before stabilizing around 10 billion people. Further, industrialized nations (mainly the United States, Europe, and Japan) only account for about 1 billion people, so the other 9 billion will come from undeveloped nations with exploding populations that are only beginning to industrialize. Although the idea of soft technology is tempting, is it reasonable to believe these people will not want automobiles, supermarkets, comfortable homes, and the other things we consider indispensable? The World Bank claims, "Growth is vital to reducing all aspects of absolute poverty. . . especially in [the] poorest countries."[36]

The inescapable conclusion is that the growth in industrial plant, material consumption, pollution, and resource usage is likely to increase by about a factor of 10 during the next few decades, producing very difficult social stresses that will require far more sophisticated economic systems. This growth may concentrate in the Third World, but it will aggravate rising externalities like costly energy and environmental controls that even now impose serious disincentives on the "throw-away economy" of the United States. One study estimated that energy use and pollution would triple if present patterns continue.[37]

Values are changing as well. People in advanced economies are becoming disenchanted with growth as an end in itself, material consumption is often unsatisfying, many distrust the complexity of technology, and they fear the insidious effects of pollution. Instead, they are becoming interested in social relationships, satisfying jobs, and other aspects of the quality of life. Daniel Yankelovich's studies conclude, "There is a deep-seated conviction in the public that we overdid the materialist thrust of consumer society," and Pope John Paul II cautioned, "We must find a simple way of living."[38]

Thus, an immutable challenge has been raised to the old concept of growth. The industrial epoch of conspicuous consumption may soon become an aberration in history, a brief, wasteful window in time that will seem as rare as the indulgent lifestyles of the feudal monarchs. There will be further growth, but of a different type that can solve tough new problems facing a mature society. Everyone wants to enjoy material comforts, so how can we handle the rising costs that attend manyfold increases in consumption? Can the interest in quality of life be reconciled with business' need for profit? What would be a feasible relationship between the developed and under-developed nations?

The Dilemma of Power: Control versus Freedom

The routine nature of hard growth urged institutions to develop rational, mechanistic structures using a specialized division of labor coordinated by a hierarchy of administrative levels. Manufacturing offers the most obvious example, but white-collar work is usually performed the same way. Although this idea is old stuff to us today, it was hailed as a great social innovation defined as "scientific management" and the "theory of bureaucracy" during the rise of industrialization.[39] What could be more reasonable in an age of machines than to simply construct institutions themselves as "social machines"? Even now most people intuitively understand that organizations work as pyramids of influence because hierarchy has become a standard feature of everyday life, one of the myths of Western culture.

Lately, however, these structures have become so large and unwieldy that they now pose a major barrier to economic performance. A large body of research shows that hierarchical organizations invariably decrease productivity, inhibit innovation, and lower morale. The difficulty of coping in these cumbersome environments is so great that job stress and burnout are the characteristic malady of our times, and there are poignant accounts by disillusioned people of the crippling effect on prestigious, once powerful institutions.[40]

The most prominent example is the hierarchical structure of government. Despite continual attempts to manage government in a more rational manner, federal agencies have doubled during the past few decades and now administer about 2000 programs. Congress operates a total of about 200 committees and subcommittees with such overlapping jurisdictions that 44 bodies supervise the Environmental Protection Agency (EPA) alone. The resulting maze is virtually unmanageable, wasteful, and paralyzed by inaction, creating a Kafkaesque nightmare of red tape that swiftly entangles anyone who gets close to it. Elliot Richardson, an administrator for many presidents, claimed that the federal bureaucracy "is a system out of control," and J. Peter Grace said after conducting a presidential study of government: "You can't tell who the hell is doing what."[41]

But large companies exemplify the same problems. "American government may be bureaucratic and inefficient," said economist Lester Thurow, "but American industry is just as bureaucratic and inefficient." Big corporations employ hundreds of thousands of people, contain scores of specialized jobs, are engaged in worldwide activities, and produce a wide array of products—all stacked up in a hierarchy that may reach 15 levels. The challenge of managing this complexity exceeds the abilities of even the most competent executives who must unify all efforts at that pinnacle where the chain-of-command finally converges. As a result of this hardening of the organizational arteries, large companies are struggling to survive while small firms are creating most new inventions and jobs. What is truly alarming is that mergers and a consolidating world economy means even larger **global** corporations are inevitable, which will further magnify such problems.[42]

The most revealing sign of this dilemma is that, although the term "bureaucracy" originally implied rational order, it has now become a perjorative meaning exactly the opposite qualities: irrational adherence to petty rules, disorder, unwieldy systems, and the like. The most damning thing one can say about an organization today is to call it a "bureaucracy."

These hierarchical dinosaurs arise fundamentally from an authoritarian form of decision-making. Although democratic nations like the United States pride themselves on being bastions of freedom, on closer examination we have to admit that the democratic process is limited to symbolic rituals that take place at intervals of four years or so for electing government officials. Whereas most of the institutions that intimately affect our lives—corporations, schools, hospitals, and so on—are governed as dictatorships. They may be benign dictatorships in which orders are usually couched in gentle tones, but nonetheless they are still dictatorships ruled by a chief executive.

The results are apparent in business where being a tough boss was once thought to be efficient. Not all employees have the talent or interest for sharing decisions, and many situations require firm action. But the general lack of labor-management collaboration is one of the greatest causes of the economic crisis. During the last decade the growth of U.S. productivity has been lower than that of England, where a similar labor-management problem is so bad it amounts to a class war.[43]

Authoritarian supervision was needed to manage the routine tasks and uneducated workers of the past, and it is true that democracy is a messy, risky, time-consuming process thought to be incompatible with the pragmatic mission of organizations. However, changing attitudes are making the old reliance on unquestioned power unacceptable. During the Watergate crisis, for instance, the nation first challenged a president for the misuse of his power; and in business, a corporate executive told me, "Young employees represent a quiet revolution from within the firm." These new realities have made an institutional form of coercion one of the most debilitating aspects of work today because it clashes with the democratic values of American life. Political scientist Arthur Miller noted, "The gap between the democratic theory and reality is enormous."[44]

Thus, the old mechanistic model of organization is rapidly becoming outmoded since it is based on the obsolete idea that sheer power is necessary to maintain order, thereby creating a major conflict between the institution's need for control versus its members' need for freedom. We have a hard time conceiving of alternatives because hierarchy and authority have been used effectively in large organizations for centuries, so it is all most of us really know. But modern nations are challenged to invent more flexible organizations to free themselves from an entrenched habit of relying on power that may have been useful in the past but is now a barrier to economic vitality. It is a great irony that the United States once led the world in creating free markets and democracy, yet it now lags behind most other nations in extending these concepts to the workplace. And because institutions are becoming larger, their environment more turbulent, and competition more intense, this need is increasing dramatically.

The Dilemma of Profit: Self-Interest versus Community

The pursuit of wealth has been so deeply ingrained in the American psyche that most of us cannot imagine how business could be managed otherwise. Profit is the lifeblood of the corporation and the most essential concept in the entire economy because, theoretically at least, profit maximization should optimize the public good. Even the Soviets calculate profitability of industrial sectors to manage their economy. In the drive to increase profit, business should strive to satisfy social needs in order to increase sales, and it should use land, labor, capital, and other scarce resources effectively to reduce costs. This constitutes such a self-guiding criteria for industrial efficiency that the profit motive should automatically produce the greatest social benefits. Medieval alchemists never learned to transmute lead into gold, but capitalism did to a great extent convert greed into social welfare.

This central function of the profit motive made it the keystone in the architecture of the Old Capitalism, justifying all other concepts and linking them into a coherent intellectual system. For instance, profit also fosters economic growth. Higher profit means more capital can be invested in producing more goods, thereby employing more workers, and so on. The beneficial effects of profit were drummed into us by leaders like President Nixon to instill respect for its central economic role:[45]

All Americans will benefit from more profits. More profits fuel the expansion that generates jobs. More profits mean more investments which will make our goods more competitive in America and in the world. And more profits means there will be more tax revenues to pay for the programs that help people in need. That's why higher profits in the American economy would be good for every person in America.

The problem, of course, is that the messy realities of economic life do not fit very well into this tidy theory. Former Federal Trade Commission (FTC) Chairman Michael Pertschuk observed, "Simplistic faith in the benign workings of the unfettered marketplace has an Alice in Wonderland quality about it."[46]

For one thing, the elegant perfection of profit-seeking works only when large numbers of small firms compete against one another, whereas the struggle for economic survival tends to concentrate corporate power. Auto-making, steel, oil, chemicals, electronics, and most other industries are so oligopolistic that the largest 200 corporations own two-thirds of all industrial assets—and a growing wave of mergers is increasing this concentration even further.[47] True, foreign competition has introduced tough competition recently, but in time the emerging world economy should go through a shake out that will leave most industries dominated by *global* oligopolies of massive multinational corporations, producing centers of economic power that are as yet undreamed of.

Another deviation from the ideal is that there is poor information to guide buyers' purchases and little receptivity to serving their genuine needs. These imperfections limit the client's ability to influence the products and services that firms provide, making the doctrine of "consumer sovereignty" more of an empty myth. Similar imperfections hinder "labor markets."

Competition exists, of course, but the old ideal—efficient markets in which numerous small entrepreneurs compete to serve genuine social needs of well-informed people—is pretty remote from the growing reality of a few global megacorporations selling flashy products to increase sales. A study in the *Harvard Business Review* reports that most managers themselves believe profit is poorly related to social benefits.[48]

When business really does compete, the fight for profit produces harsh conflict and disorderly markets that are unacceptable in a modern society to the public and even to business. As Milton Friedman reminds us, capitalism is a profit **and loss** system in which weak firms are destroyed. This brutal truth explains why, in spite of all the rhetoric preached about the virtues of the marketplace, business has **invited** government regulation in order to insulate itself from the threat of competition. Those supporting capitalist ideals anguish over the way business is protected by federal laws that set prices, limit imports, impose tariffs, provide subsidies, or otherwise curb the risks of a free market. It is estimated that 40 percent of all U.S. goods are protected by various import barriers.[49] J. P. Morgan noted why we try to avoid this primitive struggle for survival that underlies the glib ideal:[50]

> *Most businessmen hate competition. . . . A man's competitor is the fellow who holds down his prices, cuts his profits, tries to seize his markets, threatens him with bankruptcy, and jeopardizes the future of his family.*

Air travel offers a good example of the chaos that results from unfettered profit-seeking. Deregulation allowed airlines to lower fares and select their routes, which did succeed in drawing new lines and more travellers. But this was gained at the cost of dropping service to some cities, crowding passengers, jeopardizing safety, slashing wages, forcing dozens of firms into bankruptcy, and creating a bewildering maze of ticket prices. Even an archconservative like Barry Goldwater was disappointed: "I thought the deregulated airline industry would . . . arrive at sensible ticket prices," he complained, "Instead, you can fly to the same place for 10 or 12 different prices." Ed Daly, President of World Airways who once advocated deregulation, now says it is "disastrous and completely irrational," and Thomas Plaskett, Vice President of American Airlines, is also disenchanted: "We find it difficult to reconcile such destructive behavior with the overall public interest."[51] The industry may become orderly in time, but only because it will be concentrated into another tight oligopoly as small firms are forced out; control of the airways will then have shifted from big government to big business. Some lawmakers want to "reregulate."

A similar situation occurred when "Ma Bell" abandoned the most convenient telephone system in the world for a maze of access fees, rental charges, repair costs, and other "free market innovations" that may double customers' bills. Polls show 64 percent of Americans think breaking up AT&T was a "bad idea." An exasperated real estate broker exclaimed after struggling to get phone service, "Here I am a capitalist and I wish they would nationalize the telephone industry."[52]

Even if the ideal could become a reality, profit has lost its original purpose because the mission of business is changing. A sharp focus on finances was once the prime criterion of sound management because the most critical need of the industrial age was to accumulate capital for building manufacturing plants. While managers have been fussing over the bottom line, however, a more sophisticated society has emerged that is primarily concerned with improving the quality of life: employees expect rewarding jobs if they are to provide committed efforts, customers demand genuine product value and good service to continue their patronage, and so on. Gaining the support of these groups now comprises the *social* mission from which any enterprise derives its economic strength because it is the *source* of profit itself.

No one would argue that it is imperative to be profitable, of course, in order to cover costs, attract investors to risk their capital, and reward managers for good performance. But under these new conditions, the old devotion to profit has become a pathological obsession in which managers regard the interests of their constituencies as *obstacles* intruding on the primary goal of making money. The common impression is that corporations are economic buccaneers, roaming the high seas of finance in pursuit of monetary gain. Here's how William Best described it based on his experience as a consultant to major companies:[53]

> In recent decades, America's dedication has been to the fast buck—individual wealth without any basis for it. We live in a society populated by slippery con men, wheeler-dealers masquerading as financial entrepreneurs.

This myopic, misplaced priority has created a chronic inability to serve the real needs of customers, which has led to the growth of the consumer movement and the successful invasion of foreign competition. Reginald Jones warned, "The biggest problem in

American business today is the sharp decline in the quality of U.S. produced goods." And dissatisfaction of workers with their jobs is largely responsible for the decline in productivity. The average American's paycheck has barely kept pace with the rate of inflation, so per capita income in the United States has fallen below about a half dozen other nations.[54]

In what is the supreme irony, this zealous emphasis on profit has not even been successful in producing **profit**. Return on common stock has averaged only 3 percent during the past two decades. If inflation is considered, the loss in real stock values is so great it was described by economist James Lorrie as "The Second Great Crash," notwithstanding the bull market of 1983 which is a mere blip on this longer trend, as seen in Figure 1.1.[55]

Contrary to the cynicism that is so popular, therefore, the problem is not that managers are sacrificing their obligations to employees, customers, and other constituencies in order to maximize profit. Rather, companies are no longer very productive in all respects, **including** their financial responsibility to investors, because the profit-motive has become a limited goal that produces poor performance for both society and the firm. Profit has taken on an exaggerated life of its own among financially oriented managers who have elevated the role of money from an instrument for serving human needs into an end in itself—a sort of holy grail that cannot be questioned. Akio Morita, CEO of Sony Corporation, cautioned, "American companies are trapped by their drive for quick profits."[56]

Obviously, profit will always remain essential, but it has lost its utility as the **central** goal of economics for the strictly practical reason that the information age demands collaboration to succeed. Removed from its original purpose in an industrial era, the once great force of the profit motive now stands as a dysfunctional anachronism that obscures a crucial paradox: **enlightened** self-interest lies not in being selfish but in serving the needs of the broader economic community that corporations depend upon for their very existence. The dilemma of the profit motive is that a slavish adherence to self-interest harms the interest of all—including the profit-maker.

The pervasive nature of the problem can be seen in the fact that most other institutions also succumb to the same temptation. For instance, government has become so insular that the means of the bureaucracy have replaced the ends of public service in a manner that is legendary. Although the official goal may be to serve the public, in fact, an agency's clients often justify budget appropriations to increase the power of administrators. Journalist Nicholas von Hoffman observed, "The client is less the customer than raw material for servicing the system."[57]

The myth of the profit motive persists because corporate executives are under enormous pressures that force a narrow pursuit of self-interest with single-minded tenacity: financial analysts focus on short-term profit, corporate boards expect it, a drop in earnings poses the threat of takeover, and it is an easily measured criteria of performance. However, executives are willing parties because they share in the firm's gains—although with unfortunate consequences even for themselves.

Compensation of CEOs in big firms runs about $1 million annually, which amounts to about 70 times the average worker's income compared with a multiple of about 10 to 20 in Europe and Japan. Yet, executive pay continues to increase more than twice the rate of workers. This is so inequitable that the annual ***increase alone*** amounts to hundreds of thousands of dollars, which is roughly a factor of 10 greater than the ***total*** pay of workers. During the economic decline in 1983 when workers had to "giveback" wages or lose their jobs, a 13.7 percent increase for CEOs caused such outrage that there were calls to restrict executive pay through federal law.[58]

Rather than buying happiness, however, such gains are an empty victory since the pursuit of profit inherently alienates the profit-maker from the rest of society, creating an isolation that is ineffective and often intolerable. Very few business executives are public figures because they cannot defend their positions when facing ordinary customers, employees, or public citizens. In the fabled Silicon Valley, Judith Larsen and Everett Rogers report how the prevailing culture of "single-minded devotion to self-interest" has caused managers to burn out, while creating rampant marital problems, estranged children, a cultural desert, and exploited workers. Even their wealth is often a burden. Studies by Professor John Kotter of Harvard Business School graduates showed, "The more money they were making, the unhappier they were becoming."[59]

It is obvious that corporations must be profitable, and it is equally obvious that everyone must look after their own self-interest. But the dominant role accorded profit now presents the main barrier to a more civilized and prosperous economy: it encourages ruthless conflict; creates disorderly markets; necessitates big government; does not serve customers, workers, investors, or the public welfare; places business in an untenable role; prevents productive collaboration; fosters stagflation; causes needless pain for business executives—and it even fails to produce good profits. In a modern interdependent era of more subtle challenges, greed will simply produce a few unhappy big winners and a restless horde of small losers.

A GAP BETWEEN MYTH AND REALITY

These dilemmas reveal how the Old Capitalism is suffering from an escalating gap between the mythical ideals of the industrial past versus the realities of a post-industrial future. The result is an enormous loss of social energy as the ineffective institutions of today produce wasteful chaos instead of constructive guidance.

One sign of the problem is that the higher, official levels of most institutions are out of touch with the complex reality of organizational life that is driven underground in the form of various bootleg activities.[60] A famous illustration is the movie and television show M.A.S.H., in which the military bureaucracy is hopelessly unable to cope with the bizzare confusion of army life that somehow has a perverse rationality of its own. Gossip feeds a grapevine that is more useful than office memos and information systems. Shortcuts and cheating circumvent unrealistic performance standards. Informal leaders provide the guidance that actually runs the system contrary to formal authority.

A similar shadow organizational culture exists among executives. The Watergate scandal, for instance, revealed the vast extent of illegal relationships among corporate and government officials. In big business, oligopolies circumvent market competition, and interlocking directorates provide a form of tacit collusion. Former

General Motors (GM) executive John DeLorean revealed how the reality at GM headquarters was not too unlike working life at the bottom: "The [executive suites] abounded in rumors, gossip, and role playing which contradicted the implied atmosphere of precise and calculated management."[61]

At the macroeconomic level, this same gap between the myths of "public America" versus the more complex realities of "private America" is responsible for white collar crime, which amounts to about $200 billion annually, and the "underground economy" that is estimated to be as large as 20 to 30 percent of GNP.[62]

This illicit realm constitutes the real life of institutions lurking beneath the official facade of modern society. It is analogous to the dichotomy between the conscious level of human thought, which purports to be rational and organized, versus the fertile realm of the subconscious mind which Sigmund Freud showed to be the disorganized but creative source of consciousness itself. Just as individuals become mentally ill when there is an imbalance between their conscious and subconscious levels of existence, so too are modern economies suffering because of a similar gap between the primitive ideology we have inherited from the past versus the rich complexity of modern life that escapes institutions.

The endless growth of physical technology and material consumption have produced a nightmare of smog, congestion, pollution, an energy crisis, and stressful living—while people yearn for simple pleasures like clean air and water, satisfying jobs, and community ties. Dictatorial bureaucracies have assumed independent lives of their own which imprison employees, clients, and even managers—while a difficult new frontier demands freedom for entrepreneurial innovation. The legitimate pursuit of reward has turned into greedy self-interest—while survival in an interdependent economy is almost impossible without collaboration that fosters social welfare.

These are the real sources of the economic decline—living within our minds in the outmoded beliefs we cling to because we cannot grasp the dictates of a new era. The fact is that an unprecedented evolutionary shift is in progress, and so the economic crisis ultimately is caused by the shallow way we have defined the problem. In short, it is not the **economy** that is in crisis, it is the economic **system**—the Old Capitalism—that is in crisis. As Peter Drucker put it, "The present crisis in economics is a failure of the basic assumptions of the paradigm."[63] This loss of faith in traditional beliefs is the main reason enterprise has been lost, and it will not be regained through miracle cures like supply-side economics, industrial policy, or other popular attempts to restore the past.

Although we may be lulled into euphoria during upturns in the business cycle and plunged into gloom at downturns, the dominant trend is that a very long but upward struggle is just beginning to restructure the economy for a remarkably different future. The underlying strength of the turnaround seems to be moving the nation to higher ground, which is confirmed by breakouts in the stock market, stagflation, and confidence in institutions. But the recovery to full economic health will take many years, it is being jeopardized by excesses of the neoconservative revolt, and it will only succeed if big corporations adopt a modern philosophy of business. Robert Anderson, CEO of Rockwell Corporation, warned, "The resurgence in the economy may mask the real problems we have."[64]

The old philosophy seems unlikely to handle the unusual problems that will plague the nation during the next decade or two. High technology industries are thriving, but the smokestack industries remain in serious trouble. Unemployment is likely to continue at unacceptable levels for many years, especially as automation eliminates jobs. The underlying structural factors that produce stagflation are improving only slowly so prices are likely to move upward again. Sophisticated new technologies are creating a revolution that will transform product markets, organizations, and society itself. The public remains adamant about environmental protection and other quality of life issues, so a backlash is brewing over deregulation policies. Corporations will be confronted with increasing competition from vital economies like Japan that are able to collaborate among business, government, and labor. The consumer revolt may intensify because buyers are becoming more critical. Labor unions are growing hostile over the loss of pay and jobs, so bitter labor-management conflicts seem inevitable. Women and young people are entering the work force, bringing new demands for higher pay, challenging work, and sharing power.

A short time ago, Americans had developed the most powerful economic system the world has known, glorying in what seemed to be unlimited progress and such skillful command that economists believed they could turn their science to "fine tuning" the business cycles. Today, the very intellectual foundations of the system are in shambles. The industrial epoch was a great success that brought the West to its present high point of prosperity, but now there is an urgent challenge to turn our attention to the development of a different economy for a new era.

2

Enterprise Regained:

EMERGENCE OF THE NEW CAPITALISM

The gloomy malaise that haunted the past two decades has been waning since the traumatic recession of 1980 to 1983 forced a surge of vitality to begin flowing through the economy again. Deregulation and foreign competition have instilled a healthy respect for productivity, lower prices, and enterprise. Capital is being poured into research on computers, biogenetics, and other revolutionary fields. Powerful information systems are creating a rush of innovation that is automating factories, modernizing offices, and opening new markets.

Possibly the greatest source of change is the example being set by a vanguard of progressive firms like IBM, GE, TRW, 3M, MCI, and many others which are developing an exciting new model of business to free institutions from the impasse of organizational gridlock. These innovative corporations have begun to rethink their entire approach to management—lean and flexible organizations, improved product quality and service, and labor-management-government collaboration are becoming a reality.

This economic renaissance is also beginning to sweep through other nations, notably West Germany, France, and Italy, where inflation is decreasing, growth is increasing, and innovation is spreading. Business is picking up so strongly in Italy that an executive claimed, "the dark days are behind us." Most of the world's stock

Portions of this chapter are adapted from my article "The Life Cycle of Evolution" (forthcoming).

markets hit all-time highs in 1985. Even Red China's economy has been surging more than 10 percent per year.

What is most remarkable is how sharply this new sense of optimism contrasts with the grim mood that prevailed just a few years ago when various signs of decline seemed inevitable. As we saw in the last chapter, chronic stagflation, pollution, the energy crisis, and other dismal prospects appeared to limit further growth. Big organizations seemed to produce bureaucracies that inhibited productivity and innovation. A host of difficult new social demands politicized major corporations. But the recent adjustments to these hard realities are dispelling the brooding anxiety of the past. Author George Gilder noted the turnabout:[1]

> No longer is it plausible to speak of the zero-sum society, the limits to growth, the death of productivity. . . . No longer is it tenable to talk of the exhaustion of energy and resources, the enduring loss of American technological leadership.

Both the "old pessimism" and the "new optimism" may be a bit extreme, of course, and the changes under way are still limited to a small corporate avant-garde so it will take years before they fully enter the mainstream. But this dramatic change in mood signals that a major shift in ideology is evolving that should in time resolve the economic crisis. The paradigm of the Old Capitalism became outmoded because it could not project our former way of life into a more complex future, while now creative entrepreneurs are developing a new perspective that can solve these dilemmas. Leon Keyserling, former Chairman of the Council of Economic Advisers, urged, "We now need a veritable revolution in economic thought," while George Cabot Lodge of the Harvard Business School observed how a new paradigm of economics has been replacing the old one:[2]

> The U.S. is in the midst of one of the great transformations of Western civilization. What is happening is that the old ideas and assumptions which once made our institutions legitimate, authoritative, and confident are fast eroding. They are slipping away in the face of a changing reality and are being replaced by different ideas and different assumptions which are as yet ill-formed, contradictory, and shocking.

This chapter describes how the economic transformation now underway should complete the passage from an industrial past into a post-industrial future. After showing how the revolutionary power of technological change is driving modern economies into an information age, I outline trends emerging at the grassroots to form a vision of the New Capitalism that promises to regain the power of enterprise we have temporarily lost.

THE INFORMATION AGE ARRIVES

This transition can be better understood by seeing that economic systems are natural organisms, constantly changing through an extraordinary process of social evolution that has been building slowly for thousands of years. From this long-term perspective, it becomes evident that societies grow and mature through various well-defined stages in their life cycle, just as humans do, and now information technology is accelerating this process so rapidly that a knowledge-based society is imminent.

The Evolution of Higher-Order Technology

In the modern world of today, technological progress has superceded biological development as the principal mechanism for evolutionary change. Technology is defined here in a broad sense to include not only the more familiar "lower-order" technologies, such as agriculture and physical hardware, but also the new "higher-order" technologies, or what are commonly called "high-tech": "social technology" used to provide services and to improve the functioning of social systems, and "information technology" which facilitates education, communications, scientific research, and other forms of knowledge. As these various technologies progress, they alter the type of work people do, the structure of institutions, and central values. In short, the relentless advance of technology has become the driving force for social change. Economist Barbara Ward expressed it best:[3]

> We are living in what is, by all odds, the most tumultuous type of historical epoch . . . the fundamental cause of our century's upheavals is the steady, continued . . . working out of the world's technological and scientific revolution.

From this perspective, one can see how different social orders emerge as science and technology expose new frontiers. Figure 2.1 presents a model I developed that shows how civilization evolves through a series of increasingly powerful stages.[4] A new technological form rises to become the dominant basis for the social order, and it then recedes as the next wave of technology repeats the same process again. As scientist Jacob Bronowski described it, the frontier of society progresses along the crest of successive waves of technological advance.[5]

Figure 2.1 shows we've already passed two highwater marks made by these waves of social evolution, the "agrarian" and "industrial" eras. The first relied on human labor to maintain the agricultural estates that formed the feudal societies of Europe, the Orient, and the plantations of the New World. By the 1800s automatic machinery began decreasing farm employment to the astonishing point where only 3 percent of the work force is now needed to operate the entire agricultural system of the United States. Physical technology then dominated the social order during the industrial era early in this century.

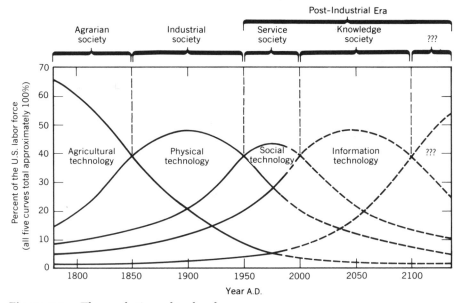

Figure 2-1. The evolution of technology.

Source: "The Life Cycle of Evolution," *Technological Forecasting and Social Change* (forthcoming).

As shown, the most recent wave began in the United States at the twilight of industrialization following World War II; for the first time in history, a critical point was reached at which the service sector became more prominent than manufacturing. Just as the number of agricultural workers receded earlier, automation has reduced industrial employment to about 20 percent of the labor force, and soon less than 10 percent of the working population will be needed to maintain the manufacturing system. Industrial capacity remains essential, of course, just as agriculture continues to be important now. However, the agrarian and industrial eras have become lower rungs on the ladder of evolution leading to a higher level that is rapidly emerging. This new frontier was identified by sociologist Daniel Bell as the "post-industrial" era—a broad provisional concept that encompasses the entire period following industrialization.[6]

As Figure 2.1 also shows, this post-industrial phase seems to involve a sequence of two subordinate stages corresponding with the advance of social and information technology. These stages are unique in subtle but crucial ways, so each is producing, in turn, a "service society" and a "knowledge society," or what is also commonly called the "information age."

Western nations are now in the midst of the service society phase. Their economies comprise an elaborate network of complex social institutions employing various types of service workers—clerks, teachers, salespeople, managers, and others performing socially oriented work that serves people. "America is becoming a white collar bureaucratic nation," says economist Lester Thurow.[7]

Just as in previous stages, service economies are now in the process of being automated as well. The computer revolution is eliminating clerical work (word processing, automatic bank tellers), teaching (programmed instruction), sales (computerized marketing systems), middle management (management information systems), and other service tasks that can be programmed, freeing people for bigger challenges that are just emerging. Many believe information technology now dominates, but this results from confusion in lumping service and information jobs together. Information technology is gaining very rapidly, however, the crossover point should not be reached until about the year 2000. Dennis Kneale, a journalist reporting on computers, noted, "Even the industry's most enthusiastic visionaries now admit it will take decades . . . to fulfill the promise of the computer."[8]

Within the next decade or two, the present transition should restructure the economic order to clear the way for a full flowering of information technology to begin in earnest. Today's surge of computerization is but a faint glimmer of what is to come when most people will use computer stations in their office and/or homes, connected to powerful information systems that span the globe with telecommunications networks. The result will be to create a vastly different type of social order, a "knowledge society," which focuses on the systematic collection, integration, and distribution of knowledge on an unprecedented level.

It is hard to exaggerate the significance of this development. As the information age makes it possible to control the growing complexity of the future, facilitate the advance of science, and serve other unimaginable purposes, it should create a "central nervous system" for the planet, thereby unifying the economic and political units of the Earth into some type of coherent international order that we cannot yet understand.[9]

An even higher level of evolution seems likely because the information age should mature eventually and give way to a succeeding stage of development, just as all earlier stages have done. So something beyond a knowledge society appears almost inevitable, but it is so distant that little purpose would be served by raising such speculative possibilities.

In a sense, none of these developments is really new because "high-technologies" have always been used to a lesser extent. Information systems, for instance, have existed since ancient times, although they were simple clay, stone or paper systems, rather than the enormously powerful electronic systems being developed now, and they only occupied the efforts of a small elite of "scribes." The higher stages of development are distinguished in that one of these technical functions develops into a more sophisticated form, becomes the principal task for the majority of the work force, and thereby dominates the social order. In short, the evolution of these higher functions matures. Because each successive stage provides higher order gains in human capability, the power of fully developed societies must be enormous.

A Passage to Maturity in the Life of Nations

It is important to note that the long-term trend formed by these stages accelerates very rapidly by almost any measure of change: world population, the speed of travel, energy usage, and countless other indicators all rise steeply over the past few centuries. This pattern is apparent in the rapidly decreasing time intervals between stages: 4 MILLION years passed before humans developed an agrarian society; roughly 10 THOUSAND years later the industrial revolution began to form an industrial society; about 2 HUNDRED years after that a service society emerged; and approximately 5 DECADES are needed until a knowledge society develops at about the turn of this century.

The result is that the present period represents a critical transition during which civilization is virtually being rocketed from an endlessly long, fairly quiescent past into a fully developed state in a very short time. That is why the past few decades seem so especially hectic and rife with change. Our present understanding of this process is possible only because the explosive growth of information technology is thrusting us rapidly into higher phases, and so the nature of evolution is becoming apparent as an orderly process of organic planetary growth. Marshall McLuhan described this new sense of awareness in a vivid analogy:[10]

> Today, it is the instant speed of electric information that, for the first time, permits easy recognition of the patterns and the formal contours of change and development. The entire world, past and present, now reveals itself to us like a growing plant in an enormously accelerated movie.

What are we to make of this miraculous "unfolding"? Does the evolution of "higher" stages mean that life will become far better, approaching a Utopia? Is this progress inevitable?

Social evolution seems to be an existential process of overcoming present challenges, which then lead to still greater challenges. Most people in developed nations today live in physical comfort that would have been considered opulent for royalty in the past, as reflected in the fact that average life spans have doubled over the last century alone. But the price of these advances has been the growth of pollution, resource shortages, complex institutions, and other such problems that did not exist before. Although social and information technologies may alleviate these problems, they in turn are causing the hectic stress of rapid change, information overload, and so on. Rather than ushering in a Utopia, therefore, the power of high-technology will be desperately needed simply to contain this chaotic explosion of life.

One useful way to grasp the significance of the post-industrial transformation is to compare the evolution of civilization to the life cycle of a human being. Although the differences in size and complexity are huge, the planet is now playing out essentially the same sequence of developmental stages that each human passes through—on an infinitely larger scale—and the present economic crisis is roughly comparable to the traumatic growth crisis that unavoidably faces every youth. The typical adolescent has reached almost complete physical growth but has not yet developed the more subtle social, intellectual, and moral abilities to function in complex situations. This is precisely the state of advanced nations today, which are rather like gangling teenagers. These societies have developed physical technologies that can dominate the world, yet they desperately need collaborative institutions that work, they lack information systems to control their complex economies, and they urgently require shared values to guide the use of this awesome power. In short, just as puberty ushers the child into adulthood, the transition to an information age represents a passage from adolescence to maturity in the life of nations.

It is easy to be cynical about such prospects, and it is certainly possible that we may not complete this passage, but instead slide into a new dark age through nuclear war, economic collapse, or blissful apathy. But the principal barrier to the future is that we are limited by our existing conceptions of the present. Industrial society is the only social order we can comprehend because it is all we have known, and the information age promises to be as different from the industrial era as that period differed from agrarian society. Most of us are still committed to the industrial paradigm because it is an accepted part of our culture, so why should anything change? Paradigms are not enduring truths but simply temporary islands of rationality, which form ideological stepping stones that civilization places in an ascending evolutionary path rising from one era to another. If the earth itself is constantly changing as continental plates drift over the globe, why should our beliefs remain stable?

Information Technology Becomes the Cutting Edge of Science

The central fact of our time is that the cutting edge of science is developing the technology to harness the flow of information and thereby create a knowledge-based society—just as the assembly line utilized physical technology to power an industrial past. Jean-Jacques Servan-Schreiber, a French intellectual, noted the significance: "Information is destined to hold the place that energy once held in yesterday's industrial society." Where earlier the most critical factor of production shifted from labor to capital—now it is knowledge. Thus, labor-intensive and capital-intensive industries are yielding to a new sector of "knowledge-intensive" industries that are primarily driven by the power of information. Trends show that this newly discovered ability for manipulating knowledge is rapidly becoming the most valuable resource commodity in modern economies:[11]

Computer Sales increased from only a few large machines sold to laboratories and major corporations a few years ago to 10 million computers sold in 1985 alone. Now big organizations often order computers in quantities of thousands. Sales value increased from $10 billion in 1980 to about $30 billion in 1984, and is estimated to reach about $400 billion before the year 2000. A survey shows that 80 percent of the public believes that computers will soon be as common as telephones, television, and dishwashers.

Computer Makers in the United States alone now number 150 firms, most of which did not exist a few years ago. Apple Computer Company grew from a garage operation in 1977 to become the first company to join the Fortune 500 in five years.

Software development is one of the largest growth fields with 3000 software firms slashing prices to compete. The market is increasing by more than 30 percent per year and should reach $30 billion in 1988.

Electronic Memories will become the cheapest means of storing information in about a decade, emptying out files, libraries, and other collections of old paper we have laboriously collected and shuffled through over many years.

Teleconferencing is being used in more than 200 organizations now, and is likely to increase dramatically as the technology improves, the costs of travel increase, and the need for long-range communication grows.

Computer Publications have skyrocketed to 46 magazines and 2400 books within the past few years alone.

Computer Stores first opened in Los Angeles in 1977. Now dozens of them operate in every major city, just as auto dealerships proliferated a few decades ago when industrialization began. Nation-wide there are now about 10,000 such stores.

Computer Blue Books that list market prices for used computer equipment are now published, just as blue books organized the market for used cars in an industrial era.

Computer Repair is also growing into a major industry, the way service stations grew to take care of autos.

The Entire Information Industry is estimated to exceed $1.4 trillion by 1992, becoming the largest segment of the economy.

We may not be able to grasp the full significance of these trends, but they can be best viewed as blips on the futurist's radar screen of time signaling the passage to a new era. Agriculture formed the first great model of civilization that persisted from antiquity, then industry created the second paradigm that lasts today. Now computerized information systems are creating a revolutionary leap that constitutes the third great paradigm in social evolution. All of the bold, disruptive predictions that experts have been warning of for decades—the rapid advance of science and technology, a major shift in cultural values, restructuring of the economic system, and so on—are coming dramatically to life in the everyday experiences of middle-class America. The long-heralded transition to an information age has finally arrived.

Barring unforeseen disasters, this transition should be completed around the end of this century as the spreading power of information technology coalesces into a rich web of intelligence spanning the planet. It may take another decade or two until this full potential is realized, but the breathtaking speed of the above trends show the revolution is pushing relentlessly on.

Redesigning the "Economic Automobile"

The challenge presented by this transformation can be summed up using the popular analogy of comparing the economy to a car. Present economic policies fall into two groups that focus almost exclusively on financial factors: those that *increase* the flow of money to stimulate economic activity—lower taxes, increased money supply, higher federal spending, and so on—are comparable to "stepping on the gas." Policies that *decrease* the flow of money to depress economic activity—higher taxes, decreased money supply, lower government spending, and so on—are analogous to "stepping on the brakes." Most nations employ various combinations of these two approaches: stepping on the gas to keep the "economic automobile" moving briskly (growth), while using the brakes occasionally to avoid reckless speeding that could cause a breakdown (a recession).

Using this analogy, the problems now facing modern economies can be seen to have multiplied dramatically. With the onset of a more complex era that is not understood, the car is forced to travel over uncharted terrain that is winding and rough. There are several "passengers" in the vehicle (public officials, business executives, labor leaders, etc.) who are all wrestling for control of the wheel. Fuel has run low so there is danger of stalling, and polluting exhausts are causing poor visibility. Meanwhile, other cars are racing alongside (Japan, England, France, etc.) so at times they collide. To control these problems, government has set up a traffic system that is so complex it further interferes. As if it were not hard enough to simply keep the vehicle running and on the road, there are various alternative routes branching off, and we do not know where they all lead or where we would like to go.

From this perspective, the economy is performing poorly—not because we have failed to discover the right combination of tax breaks, growth rates in the money supply, fiscal spending, and other traditional policies—but because society itself has entered a very difficult new phase of development. Traditional solutions do not address the heart of the problem, which is the outmoded structure of major institutions; they merely shuffle it around among inflation, unemployment, budget deficits, and other trade-offs. What is needed is not a better way for running the economic auto more effectively. Rather, the car has to be redesigned, its occupants have to learn to work together, and the road system has to be improved. In short, we need a more effective transportation system.

The challenge of travelling this difficult new economic journey is so great that it is tempting to rush to the conclusion that the "old economic auto" of the industrial past has collapsed. One economist frankly declared, "Our craft is bankrupt. Economists have nothing more to say."[12] But this is overstating the problem. The Old Capitalism remains useful, however it has limited power to handle a more complex frontier, much as the horse-drawn carriage became outmoded in an age of the automobile. One can still travel in a stagecoach, but it is awfully slow and rough.

This analogy helps illustrate how the new ideology emerging now should resolve the economic crisis. The New Capitalism comprises a blueprint for an improved auto design (major corporations) and a roadmap of the entire transportation system (other institutions making up the economy). In other words, we need to junk the old gas guzzler with tail fins that ran pretty well in the past, and replace it with a sleek, compact, high-tech, more efficient, powerful model of the future, to be handled by a sophisticated driving team, and cruising along superhighways.

A NEW VISION FROM THE GRASSROOTS

In fact, this modern equivalent of the Old Capitalism is emerging now in a variety of bold new trends that have been forming during the past few years. This view is not derived from any traditional monolithic perspective, but from a rich blend of diverse ideas and innovations that are being synthesized into a far more sophisticated whole. And it is not being invented by any one group with a monopoly on the truth, but is evolving spontaneously from countless managers, workers, customers, public citizens, government officials, intellectuals, and corporate executives.

Some of the more influential leaders who have shaped this vision include Reginald Jones, former CEO of GE Company, who called attention to the widespread "management malaise"; Lee Iacocca,

Chairman of Chrysler, who saved his firm from bankruptcy by creating a political role for business; William Norris, founder of Control Data, who started the first research and development (R&D) consortium in the computer industry; Thornton Bradshaw, CEO of RCA, who pioneered in integrating the financial and social goals of business; Ruben Mettler of TRW and John Welch at GE, who are inventing a network model of organization that spurs innovation; Steve Jobs, the founder of Apple Computer, who began a new industry; Esther Peterson, a prominent consumer advocate, who singlehandedly changed the relationship between business and its customers; Douglas Fraser, the first union leader to sit on a major corporate board; and many, many others described later who comprise a new breed of modern entrepreneurs. *BusinessWeek* noted, "The Organization Man is dead . . . a new business elite has emerged, and its power and influence [has] altered, irradicably, the business landscape."[13]

Although these individual contributions may be limited, the broader perspective they collectively form seems to converge into a remarkably consistent new vision we have been awaiting to guide the way ahead. Table 2.1 summarizes this transformation in ideology by comparing the features of the industrial paradigm—the Old Capitalism—with the contrasting features of the post-industrial paradigm—the New Capitalism. As the next sections show, the seven concepts in this table are groupings of approximately 40 or so major trends, which are in turn illustrated with several hundred examples in the next seven chapters of Part 2. The following discussion shows how these strategic principles of the New Capitalism resolve the dilemmas of the Old Capitalism. Others may organize these ideas differently, and, obviously, some examples, trends, and concepts will change as the transition to a new era moves on in uncertain directions. But some framework roughly like this is emerging now to offer an exciting new vision of business and economics.

Smart Growth: The Inner Domain of Unlimited Progress

Earlier we showed how "hard" growth is no longer feasible because pollution, energy shortages, and other social costs should grow dramatically as material consumption increases roughly 10-fold. The advance of technology is resolving these problems as the au-

TABLE 2.1.   THE TRANSITION TO A POST-INDUSTRIAL PARADIGM

	Industrial Paradigm: The Old Capitalism	Post-Industrial Paradigm: The New Capitalism
Frontier of progress: (Chapter 3)	Hard Growth	Smart Growth
Organization structure: (Chapter 4)	Mechanistic Hierarchies	Market Networks
Decision-making power: (Chapter 5)	Authoritarian Command	Participative Leadership
Institutional values: (Chapter 6)	Financial Goals	Multiple Goals
Management focus: (Chapter 7)	Operational Management	Strategic Management
Economic macrosystem: (Chapter 8)	Profit-Centered Big Business	Democratic Free Enterprise
World system: (Chapter 9)	Capitalism vs. Socialism	Hybrids of Capitalism and Socialism

tomation of production shifts the strategic factors that drive modern economies to more subtle social and intellectual technologies that can manage these impacts. Chapter 3 describes how the following trends foreshadow the shape of this frontier of "smart growth":

Quality of Life.   As the economy matures, rising costs of consumption are making the old "consumer ethic" less desirable, and higher values are becoming more attractive. The result is a growing interest in more useful goods, social relations, personal development, and other quality of life interests.

Balanced Choices.   Continued growth is inevitable, so balanced choices are becoming unavoidable in which the benefits of consumption are weighed against social costs to find that optimal point where social welfare is maximized. The GM downsizing decision is a prominent example that marks an historic event in which industry first realized that "less is more."

Automation. Industrial robots and other forms of automation are being perfected by the Japanese, Germans, and U.S. firms like GE, GM, IBM, Bendix, and Deere such that less than 10 percent of the labor force will work in blue collar jobs at the end of this century. Office automation is growing even faster. Soon office, shop, and field operations should be integrated into a single computerized system.

Energy Management. A more sophisticated approach to the energy problem is evolving as homes, towns, organizations and states selectively use fossil fuels, nuclear plants, solar cells, biomass, and other energy sources to reduce consumption by roughly half of existing levels.

Environmental Control. Firms like Hercules, 3M, and Dow Corning are developing new techniques to recover lost energy and raw materials from waste products, while producing lower costs and less pollution.

Service Markets. New industries are being formed to provide better communication, education, health care, housing, and other services by corporations like Control Data, Hyatt Legal Services, Kinder Care, and Rouse Company, which are converting social problems into profitable ventures.

Scientific Breakthroughs. The information age is accelerating the progress of science and technology, thereby producing breakthroughs in physical science, bioengineering, social science, and information technology.

Information Technology. Information science is making revolutionary advances in superchips, a fifth generation of computers, laser printers, fiber optics, and telecommunication satellites. As more powerful information systems move into factories, offices, homes, and schools, they are uniting individuals, institutions, and nations into a central network for the planet.

Customer-Driven Business. Progressive firms like IBM, Western Union, Giant Food, Johnson & Johnson, Avis, McDonald's, GE, and Hewlett-Packard (HP) are developing more effective marketing and consumer affairs functions that serve genuine customers' needs better in order to compete. The result is a shift from the old emphasis on "selling" to a new "client-driven" focus on "serving."

Obviously, we will always remain dependent on physical technology, and smart growth is difficult to grasp because it is subtle and intangible. However, the dilemma of limited growth appeared unsolvable only because growth was defined in physical terms. As higher-order capabilities make it possible to judiciously realize the benefits of physical progress while minimizing the costs, growth should become accepted as simply a means to a higher end of improving the quality of life. Beyond physical growth, a vast unexplored frontier of improved services and scientific advances offers future prospects for elevating human welfare that are almost unlimited.

Market Networks: The Flowering of Creative Enterprise

Mechanistic hierarchies were well suited for an industrial past but they are no longer feasible in a new era of change, diversity, and disorder. Chapter 4 shows how the quantum leap in environmental turbulence brought on by the onslaught of computers is transforming organizational structures from a hierarchy of decision-makers into "market networks" of small, self-managed enterprises—"confederations of entrepreneurs":

Environmental Complexity.   A growing world economy is creating new business competition and demands for more effective management of resources. The baby-boom, working women, the aged, and people pursuing a self-fulfillment ethic are spawning a diverse range of subcultures that should increase in the decades ahead. In addition, rapid scientific advancement is forcing major structural changes throughout modern economies.

Multidimensional Structures.   Corporations like GE, TRW, Dow Corning, and Digital Equipment (DEC) are creating matrix systems of two or more organizational dimensions to focus on different product lines, management functions, and markets.

Decentralized Control.   Distributed information systems are encouraging decentralized decision-making. The result is that firms like GE, HP, Tandem, 3M, Esmark, Xerox, and TRW are being transformed into flexible networks of small, self-managed units, thereby converting bureaucracies into internal markets.

The Entrepreneurial Boom.   Thriving young firms like MCI, Microsoft, Computerland, and Genentech have kindled a boom in new ventures that is moving now into large corporations like IBM, Exxon, TRW, and GE.

Intrapreneurship.   A new role of the "intrapreneur" is evolving at companies like Levi-Strauss, Control Data, Arthur D. Little, TRW, 3M, and Xerox Rank that allows employees to define their own jobs both within and without the organization.

Inter-Institutional Networks.   Corporations in auto making, the computer industry, and other fields are forming collaborative alliances abroad,

R&D consortiums with competitors, and other external linkages to create an international network of cooperative organizations.

These changes are producing a different type of structure which is based on principles of "self-organization" rather than hierarchy. The dilemma of bureaucracy persisted because control was defined in mechanistic terms suitable for an industrial age. Now these hierarchical pyramids are becoming living, fluid systems that achieve a more powerful form of control by allowing wide-ranging freedom to handle the exploding complexity of the information age. This flexibility is gained at the cost of tolerating greater organizational complexity and ambiguity, but most institutions and the structure of society itself are evolving into an interwoven, organic fabric of changing ventures that brings the ideal of free markets to flower.

Participive Leadership: Extending Democracy to Daily Life

Authoritarian command was useful in an industrial era of dependent employees and simple tasks, but now people are becoming empowered by a new sense of independence, and a more complex environment demands their active involvement. The result is that collaborative problem-solving is becoming an accepted part of working life. Chapter 5 will show how the following trends are moving the use of power toward "participative leadership":

The New Breed of Workers.   Attitudes toward work, authority, and careers are changing dramatically, especially among young adults. Money and other benefits remain important, but most people are primarily motivated by achievement, social significance, autonomy, creative work, and self-fulfillment.

Pay-for-Performance.   Companies like Crown-Zellerbach, GM, Ford, and Delta are creating incentive systems that link pay to work performed rather than to seniority or job classifications. This trend is affecting not only workers, but executives and other professionals as well.

Employee Ownership.   Profit sharing plans are spreading and now include 340,000 firms, while employee-ownership is being used at 6000 companies like Weirton Steel, MCI, AT&T, and at auto-making, airline, and cab companies.

Quality of Work Life.   Alternative forms of work involving self-managed assembly lines, job redesign, work sharing, quality circles, flexi-time, labor-management committees, and autonomous work teams are being used at Ford, GM, Motorola, Aetna, Prudential, Delta, J.C. Penney, Lincoln Electric, and Procter & Gamble. The concept is also spreading to government, medicine, and the church.

Employee Rights.   Workers are gaining rights to job security, privacy, due process, access to sensitive information, and pay equity at companies like IBM, Aetna, AT&T, Control Data, Du Pont, Prudential, Polaroid, Xerox, Dow Chemical, and Delta.

Participative superior-subordinate relationships are difficult and they are not appropriate for all situations, but managers and employees are being forced to work together if they hope to compete in a world economy. The contradiction between democratic ideals and an authoritarian workplace persisted because coercion was thought to be the only means of maintaining discipline. That dilemma is being resolved as a more sophisticated workforce shares both responsibilities and rewards with management. As this form of leadership becomes widely accepted, we should find that the principle of democratic governance can be extended to manage jobs, schools, local communities, and other aspects of daily life more effectively.

Multiple Goals: The Strength of Economic Community

Participative problem-solving is also spreading to form a broader institutional role that serves "multiple goals" involving labor, customers, and other economic actors whose collaboration is crucial to the health of any enterprise. The following trends described in Chapter 6 show how business is adopting this "open-system" perspective to incorporate these diverse stakeholders into a larger economic system:

Social Reporting.   A discipline of social reporting that extends financial principles to the measurement of social impacts is being used at GM, ARCO, Toyota, BankAmerica, and Aetna.

The Social Contract.   A two-way contract linking profit and social objectives is developing at Aetna, 3M, Dayton-Hudson, Giant Food, HP, Sony, Wang, Westinghouse, and Control Data.

Stakeholder Coalitions.   A more productive role for business is being developed at IBM, HP, Sony, and Kollmorgan that unifies customers, employees, public communities, and other stakeholders into a political coalition.

Social Investing. Billions of dollars in investment capital are now controlled by investment funds, universities, churches, communities, and other groups that regard social responsibility as being inseparable from financial performance. Social investing is estimated to be growing at 150 percent per year.

Democratic Governance. Corporate boards are adding outsiders, public directors, labor leaders, consumerists, women, minorities, and others to broaden the constituencies they represent.

Some of these trends are not yet well-developed, but the long-term prospects are striking. By integrating stakeholders into a coalition of interests, the goal of large corporations should broaden to create not only financial wealth, but *social* wealth as well. The dilemma of the profit motive that created a perennial conflict between business and society was the result of a limited concept of enterprise as a strictly financial institution. As we accept the reality that financial success is inextricably tied to various groups that are part of any organization, it is becoming clear that profit-making and social welfare are inseparable. There are risks involved, but this more powerful role promises to foster the sense of community that is indispensable to healthy enterprise.

Strategic Management: Converting Threats into Strategy

Just as the Old Capitalism inherently focused on maintaining stable, efficient operations, these concepts of the New Capitalism explicitly foster change—"strategic management." Progressive organizations work with elements in their environment to create smart growth, they use market networks to implement decisions, resolve obstacles through participative leadership, and bring external interests into policy-making. Chapter 7 describes how these and the following additional trends lead to the development of a "strategically managed organization" that is able to cope with the discontinuities of a new era:

Strategic Planning. Most large corporations like GE, IBM, and Exxon have developed various approaches to strategic planning over the past two decades, and this methodology is being adopted by government agencies and other institutions.

Creating the Future. Rather than simply "forecast" future impacts, approaches to managing environmental relations are being used to "change" the future at the life insurance industry, AT&T, the Communication Workers of America, the U.S. Congress, Ford Motor Company, Shell Oil, GE, and entire cities and states.

Issue Management. Capabilities for identifying and resolving strategic issues have been formed at ARCO, BankAmerica, TRW, DEC, IBM, Nabisco, and many other institutions to focus directly on the most critical long-range problems.

Participative Strategy Formulation. A participative approach to strategy formulation is being used to change attitudes and reach commitment at corporations like GM, ComSat, IBM, AT&T, and Xerox.

Strategic management promises to transform the insular organizations of today that were designed to manage internal operations into adaptive enterprises that are symbiotically integrated with their environment. Resistance to change persists because of a belief that institutions are self-sufficient and capable of unilateral control. Strategic management recognizes that self-control is a fiction because all energy and resources flow from outside groups that provide the very life of any institution. Strategic organizations convert this external power into constructive forces for change, creating a vital, resilient enterprise that is an integral part of its surroundings.

Democratic Free Enterprise: A System of Both Cooperation and Competition

The old economic system of "profit-centered big business" that led to an adversarial relationship with big government may also be transformed by macroeconomic applications of the New Capitalism. The following trends are underway, as shown in Chapter 8, to redefine the present system of political economy by unifying the free enterprise values of the political right with the democratic values of the left:

The Role of Big Business Becomes a National Issue. Just as big government erupted into a heated debate in the 1980s, pollsters, politicians, consultants, public interest groups, and intellectuals predict the role of business is likely to become a national political issue during the 1990s.

The Decentralization Strategy. Centrists advocate a political bargain that would decentralize control of major economic responsibilities to a self-regulating private sector. The right would urge major corporations to develop a form of enterprise that incorporates social impacts, and in return, the left would use government collaboration to foster economic growth.

Democratic Economic Policy-Making. Bodies composed of leaders from business, government, labor, consumer, and community groups are forming to address major economic issues at state, industry, and national levels. The concept is supported by liberals, conservatives, the public, and business.

Collaborative Business-Government-Labor Relations. Partnerships are evolving among business, government, labor, and other groups in cities like Lowell, Massachusetts, Indianapolis, Indiana, and the states of Texas, Michigan, and Pennsylvania to pursue joint ventures that combine economic growth and community welfare.

Redefining the Economic Infrastructure. The economic infrastructure is being redefined using market supplements that replace regulation, by privatizing government functions, developing business-government programs for fostering technological innovation, and other structural changes that create a more efficient economic system.

Such trends reflect an unusual combination of cooperation and competition which forms the central strategy for managing economies in the information age, as exemplified by the Japanese. Firms were protected from the harshness of competition in the past by oligopolies, regulation, and poor market information, and the prospects for widespread cooperation would be dismal if we were to rely on the inclinations of people. But technological advances are changing all that. The industrial era fostered brutal conflict because physical resources are finite, thereby urging a "zero-sum game"—I gain at your expense. However the social and information technologies that are gaining prominence *increase* value when shared, so they form "positive-sum games" of collaborative problem-solving—all can win.

These are not simply theoretical distinctions because numerous examples are appearing, as noted in the preceding trends. Corporations are uniting in joint research consortiums, domestic companies are forming partnerships with their counterparts abroad, while a surge of collaboration is occurring among labor, management, government, and other formerly antagonistic parties. *BusinessWeek* recently noted, "For companies big and small, collaboration is the key to survival."[14] Meanwhile, free enterprise is flowering as oligopolies yield to deregulated markets, world wide competition, and internal corporate ventures. Thus, the startling realization is setting in that different parties may compete with one other in a more benign fashion that includes mutual collaboration as well.

This blend of cooperation and competition could in time resolve the old conflict between free enterprise versus democracy to form a unique system of political economy—"Democratic Free Enterprise"—that marks the dominant character of the New Capitalism.

Hybrid Economies: A World Order Bridging Capitalism and Socialism

At the global level, the New Capitalism offers interesting possibilities for resolving the clash between the opposing ideologies of capitalism and socialism. As trends described in Chapter 9 will show, a variety of economic experiments are underway around the world, particularly in the emerging economies of Third World nations, which may lead to a coherent world order:

Rise of the Third World. Undeveloped nations in the Orient, South America, and Africa are industrializing rapidly to become a major force in the growing world economy.

An Integrated World Economy. Global corporations like IBM, Phillips, Gulf & Western, and Sears are creating international ventures with less developed regions, thereby establishing economic relations that integrate East with West and poor nations with rich nations.

Variations on Capitalism and Socialism. A variety of economic systems is forming as capitalist nations like Japan, Egypt, Greece, Spain, Hong Kong, and France adopt some features of socialism while socialist nations like China, Vietnam, Hungary, and even Russia embrace elements of capitalism.

The USA and the USSR maintain their mutual hostility largely because they view each other's system as the antithesis of their own. But as the center of the economic-political spectrum becomes filled by hybrid economies joined in a global network of economic relationships, the Old Capitalism and the Old Socialism should be increasingly seen as simply the two extremes of a richer set of variations making up a complex world order. The obstacles are enormous, of course, but the result could unify the Earth into a single coherent but highly diverse system.

THE ECONOMIC HIGH FRONTIER

These 40 or so trends span an enormous range of difficult issues and raise many complex, profound implications. How then can we understand the broader meaning of such changes, their historic significance, and their impact on business and the economy?

It seems to me that the New Capitalism can be best understood as presenting a higher intellectual vista that signifies the passing of the old "industrial" domain which focused almost exclusively on the material, physical dimension of economics; now the need to master the "social" domain of business activity is becoming urgent, although it has always comprised the forces that actually drive any economic system—institutions, knowledge, values, and other higher-order matters. The Old Capitalism was often puzzling because financial statistics simply mirror all this more subtle, complex behavior, and the economic crisis is finally forcing us to acknowledge that business is intrinsically a human phenomenon that cannot be understood apart from its social and political origins.

Thus, a higher ground of economic life is being discovered as the passage to a new era draws near—as though a vast "economic high frontier" has been opened up which today's entrepreneurs are just beginning to settle. Although this is a more personal level of business and economics, it cannot be successfully cultivated with good intentions alone but requires more sophisticated institutional structures, powerful information systems, and enlightened self-interest. So to really solve the economic crisis, Americans must successfully pioneer this higher, mountainous plateau of challenging economic problems that lies unavoidably ahead—which would then lead to all the elements of the New Capitalism.

Difficult undertakings such as this do not succeed because of logical, intellectual reasons, but when a new set of ideas becomes a living part of American culture because it can solve the disorders of our time. That is precisely the value of the new paradigm. This vision not only has the power to overcome the dilemmas of the Old Capitalism, it offers a broader view that is able to contain the exploding complexity of a turbulent future. All of the old ideals — physical growth, authoritarian hierarchies, self-interest, and so on— are still valid in this higher region, however they are inadequate from a practical perspective and unsatisfying from a personal perspective. In precise terms, the Old Capitalism remains necessary, but it is no longer sufficient because a New Capitalism is becoming more important.

Physical technology and growth are useful, although they are a limited part of an inexhaustible inner domain that offers boundless opportunities for a more intelligent form of progress that improves the quality of life. Authority and hierarchy may be necessary, however, commitment, individual freedom, and entrepreneurial innovation require market structures and participative leadership. And beyond self-interest, greater economic success is possible by extending the role of business to create a community of interests that is beneficial for all. In short, the New Capitalism does not repudiate the Old Capitalism but absorbs it into a broader synthesis — just as Einstein's theories incorporated Newton's laws into a more powerful paradigm of physics.

Realizing these advantages, however, requires a profound reconceptualization of business into a more benign and creative posture that would constitute a revolution in economic thought, although in keeping with traditional values. Peter Drucker predicted, "The next economics will require a radically different microeconomics as its foundation."[15] The essence of the Western approach to political economy is far more than growth, power, profit, or other principles associated with the industrial past. The genius of the West is that free enterprise is a self-organizing system that promotes entrepreneurial innovation to serve human needs in a democratic society. That is what differentiates it from state-controlled socialism, and that is what creates its unique strength. But to really serve such ideals, business must mature to embrace a broader set of goals that correspond with the public welfare in a democratic fashion, and it must permit the freedom that allows the marketplace to function effectively.

Some may feel these ideas are Utopian. However, a recent survey showed that two-thirds of the leaders in business, government, labor, and academia believed "the U.S. economy is undergoing a structural revolution."[16] The very fact that the present is commonly called the "information age" would have been unbelievable only a few years ago, and an enormous wave of experimentation is leading to an economic renaissance in modern nations, although it may go unnoticed. Furthermore, the trends outlined above attest to the growing recognition that enlightened management practices are becoming attractive, not because of benevolent motives, but because human values and entrepreneurial freedom are **efficient**. It also seems clear that a similar vision is forming in other fields. Nuclear scientist Fritjof Capra at the University of California described the paradigm shift in physics this way:[17]

> The 1980s will be a revolutionary time because the whole structure of our society does not correspond with the world-view of emerging scientific thought. . . . In modern physics, the image of the universe as a machine has been transcended by a view of it as one indivisible, dynamic whole whose parts are essentially interrelated. . . . The vital social choices we face [involve] principles of self-organization— centralization or decentralization . . . hard technology or soft technology—that affect the survival of humanity as a whole.

Regardless of what it is called or the form it may take, something roughly similar to the New Capitalism is badly needed on the basis of hard economic considerations, it is logically indicated by our traditions, and numerous trends suggest it is becoming a reality. This transformation began two decades ago and should be completed roughly about the year 2000, so the midpoint in this long, confusing journey seems to have finally passed. With the destination in sight, many different people are catching a glimpse of the more productive, responsive form of economy that could lie ahead, and this vision is starting to regain the power of enterprise needed to master an unexplored new frontier.

Obviously, these are sensitive, historic moves that always have to overcome enormous obstacles. Such change will meet continual resistance, it will not be made quickly nor out of altruism, it will provoke painful anxiety as the familiar past yields to an uncertain future, it is not going to be adopted universally, and there is no assurance it will succeed at all. Modern nations have been struggling through a storm of change for two decades now since this upheaval began, and more grief is almost certainly in store.

All these obstacles should be overcome, however—not by trying to recapture a golden past, as some urge in a maudlin spirit of false optimism—but because we are being forced to come to grips with a very difficult transition as the old era fades away and a new era governed by fundamentally different principles relentlessly carries us on—Alvin Toffler called it "The Third Wave" of great social change.[18] Traditional industries are in decline, while unlimited prospects are being opened up by sophisticated new technologies. Business, government, and other major institutions may be in a state of crisis, yet the grassroots of families, communities, and small enterprises is throbbing with vibrant new ideas and bold optimism. Dickens described this same rich blend of conflicting historic forces during the Industrial Revolution: "It was the best of times, it was the worst of times."

So the passage to an information age seems likely to be completed despite all these turbulent cross-currents, although slowly and with much turmoil. And while it may finally resolve the faults that plagued the Old Capitalism, other problems will undoubtedly arise. But in a decade or so, the New Capitalism emerging now should tame this high frontier of economic life, leading eventually to such a more civilized, albeit challenging, world that our children will wonder how we tolerated the crude industrial past—just as we muse sadly at the harsh plight of the early pioneers, farmers, and our other American forebears.

Part 2

Strategies for the Future

3
Smart Growth:
THE INNER DOMAIN OF UNLIMITED PROGRESS

The foundations of the American economy are shifting today as traditional industries decline and a new wave of enterprise rises. Not long ago, the Mahoning Valley in Ohio was the productive heart of the nation where blazing steel furnaces poured hot metal to be formed into cars rolling off the GM assembly line in nearby Youngstown. "Now, a visitor can drive [through the valley] and see silent, empty steel mills stretching mile after mile," reported the *Wall Street Journal.*[1] The collapse of this industrial might has laid off more than 100,000 workers in this valley alone, leaving entire communities dazed as a way of life they had depended on for generations suddenly evaporated. An older steelworker expressed the shock he shares with millions of other unemployed Americans: "I don't know what's going to happen to me. Where am I going to go? What am I going to do?"

This decline was caused by an onslaught of foreign competition that has left auto making, steel, appliances, and other industries which were thriving just a few years ago operating well below their former levels. Steel, for instance, is roughly at 40 percent of its old peak and shows little sign of improving. The popularity in American households of brands like Toyota, Cuisinart, and Sony attests to the victory that foreign makers achieved as domestic goods lost their competitive edge. In addition to the threat from Japan and Europe, there are many vital young nations in Asia and South

America that have passed the industrial "take-off point" recently, which will heighten competition even further. Some economists claim the decline in basic industries is creating a "*de*industrialization of America" that will enfeeble the economy for years to come.[2]

But the only real obstacle is a tendency to view this situation as a problem, whereas Americans are beginning to find that such difficulties actually represent great needs crying out for solution. There is an old saying that crisis is an opportunity in disguise, and the economic crisis offers especially great possibilities precisely because it is so unusual and poorly understood. As we will soon see, the type of symptoms outlined in Chapter 1—stagflation, slowing technical innovation, costly energy, pollution, and big government—may be converted into bold opportunities, just as entrepreneurs turned the problems of the industrial past to advantage. For instance, stagflation is yielding to a vastly more productive form of growth as firms "reinvent the assembly line" into automated factories and offices, while opening up new industries in services, information systems, biogenetics, and other fields spawned by the acceleration of high-technology.

This demise of an aging "Smokestack America" alongside a surging young "Sunrise America" shows that the biggest source of progress today lies in an unsuspected direction—virtually all of the massive problems that plague our society can be turned into equally massive benefits by creative entrepreneurs. Peter Drucker admonished, "The first job of a business manager is to convert social needs into profitable opportunities."[3] To realize these possibilities, however, corporations must relinquish the conventional wisdom of the past—"hard growth"—and develop sophisticated new technologies to serve a growing demand for improving the quality of life—a form of "smart growth." Modern economies are undergoing a traumatic process of "creative destruction" to revitalize their industries, so older companies that cannot serve this new imperative will inevitably be swept away by young ones that can, just as great oaks must someday fall. And despite the abundant gloom that fuels the economic crisis, the opportunities for those who can grasp this dictate of the future are boundless.

This chapter describes how such a more sophisticated form of growth is opening up a vast "inner domain" of progress in a mature society. We first review the cultural changes now leading to a new American dream of "less is more," then we explore how the economic problems of today may be converted into the profitable opportunities of tomorrow, and finally we survey the consumer-oriented practices being developed to serve these needs.

THE CHANGING AMERICAN DREAM

Historians will probably record that 1973—the year the smoldering energy shortage erupted into a major oil crisis—was a critical turning point dividing one era from another. The former industrial age was driven by what appeared to be limitless physical growth, while now the United States faces the end of the myth that "more is better." One dramatic impact of this change was the General Motors "downsizing" decision, which Joseph Downer, an executive vice president at ARCO, called "a major event in industrial history." Elliott Estes, who was president of GM at that time, explained the significance:[4]

> [The corporation] had to change the direction of everything it had been telling itself and telling the customer. The old message was more for more. Bigger is better. It had to change to smaller is better. Less for more.

What has happened to the "Great American Dream" when GM no longer advocates "bigger is better"? At the risk of oversimplifying a very complex period, it seems that the U.S. is passing through a cultural transition consisting of three phases: the student revolts of the 1960s challenged the old concept of unlimited material progress; then a discovery of self-worth followed in the 1970s to seek a superior lifestyle; and today an adjustment to the hard realities of the 1980s is leading people to value still higher "inner" satisfactions. Thus, the American dream is evolving toward a more thoughtful view that balances the advantages of growth against its social costs in order to optimize the net quality of life—from "more," to "better," to "less."

The 1960s: Questioning the Old American Dream

This cultural change began during the two golden decades of prosperity following World War II when the old familiar world worked
beautifully: business thrived, jobs were plentiful, the stock market
rose steadily, and energy was cheap. As one wag put it, "the air
was still clean and sex was still dirty."

In such a surfeit of physical well-being, the first "post-industrial
generation" moved beyond the material interests of the past because
they knew little of the deprivation suffered in the Great Depression.
They also developed a sense of independence as the gentle counsel
of Dr. Spock urged their parents and teachers to treat them with
indulgence. The power of television entered living rooms everywhere,
opening up an endless new world of information that caused a
quantum jump in the general level of awareness. Higher education
became so accessible that almost half of high school graduates attended college.[5]

This quiet shifting of cultural foundations erupted when the baby
boom matured during the late 1960s to challenge the status quo.
They may have been young and naive, but they were first to raise
alternatives to the prevailing ideology of unconstrained physical
growth: respect for the environment, disdain for excessive materialism, self-fulfillment of the individual, simpler lifestyles, and
other hallmarks of the notorious "counterculture" now often con-
temptuously remembered as the "flower children." These values
were so unusual that many feared they were revolutionary. However,
even some business leaders were supportive, indicating that this
was not a violent revolution from below but a "humane" revolution
from above.[6] Studies of Daniel Yankelovich concluded:[7]

> The [1960s] point to vast changes in the complexion and outlook of
> an entire generation of young people. Indeed, so startling are the
> shifts in values and beliefs . . . that social historians of the future
> should have little difficulty in identifying the end of one era and
> the beginning of a new one.

A few years later similar ideas were absorbed by older, middle-
class Americans as the hard edges of the counterculture were tempered with a sense of responsibility. Harris polls showed a consensus

that the quality of life had grown worse, and that "The American people have begun to show a deep skepticism about the nation's capacity for unlimited economic growth." Another poll indicated "an aversion to the competitive rat race . . . a deep concern about the environment, an aversion to 'bigness,' and a suspicion, rather than an automatic acceptance, of technology as a solution to all problems." Harris noted:[8]

> *After the turbulence of the '60s, mainstream America seems to have adopted many of the views that once were regarded as the exclusive province of the younger generation, which seemed disillusioned with conventional values.*

Thus, a more questioning, painful time of social catharsis had shattered the old American dream of affluence that proved so hollow and opened up a Pandora's box of serious misgivings about the industrial system. A significant low point in all this doubt occurred when the children of rich families rebelled against the trappings of their parents, as in the bizarre case of Patty Hearst. One member of a revolutionary group bragged, "It used to be a joke in the movement that you can't get into [the] Weathermen unless your parents are millionaires."[9]

The 1970s: The Me-Generation Discovers Itself

As these old myths were purged from the American character, powerful new energies were unleashed as well. During the "me-decade" of the 1970s people found an irresistible need to develop their latent abilities, succeed in a career, achieve something of importance, and otherwise fulfill their potential.[10] The 1960s may have provided a needed period of self-examination, but during the 1970s America began to discover its inner strength as it became clear that reforming society must begin by reforming oneself.

The focus on self-fulfillment became overindulgent and hedonistic at times, but, as Nobel Prize winner Saul Bellow pointed out, this was simply another facet of modern life that reveals the diverse, creative energy within the most ordinary human being.[11] Television commercials, that bellwether of social change, affirmed this outpouring of self-esteem by urging us to obtain only the best because we deserved it: "Nothing's too good for Daddy and me" (Del Monte), "You, you're the one; we do it all for you" (McDonald's), and "What's good enough for other folks ain't good enough for me" (RC Cola).

At the very time of all this self-indulgence, however, the economy was suffering from stagflation and other aspects of the "malaise" that marked the late 1970s, largely because of the narcissism that prevailed. But while the external world continued in decline, this internal progress of personal growth was setting the stage for the economic advances that began in the 1980s.

The 1980s: Acceptance and Fulfillment

Now this maturing process is moving through a more pragmatic phase that should reconcile the self-interest of the me-decade with new interests in the quality of life, social harmony, and, ultimately, a liberating simplicity.

The major theme is striking a balance between consumption and higher values to improve the overall quality of goods, services, and living conditions—to "live well" rather than simply consume more. Harris polls show that the public opts for "cleaning up the environment . . . breaking up big things, and getting back to more humanized living." Yankelovich reports that people are reluctant to give up basic comforts, but they are cutting back on energy, meat, and clothing, and recycling waste materials because of rising costs in an era of limits. Inflation is perceived to be the result of wastefulness, and so "A new antiwaste morality is gaining momentum." Conspicuous consumption is yielding to conspicuous *conservation* as small families, solar energy, compact cars, lean diets, town houses, generic brands, and other forms of practical living become admired.[12]

There is also a hunger for fuller personal relationships and commitments to one's family, place of work, community, and nation. Harris reports: "Significant majorities place a higher priority on improving human and social relationships . . . than on raising the standard of living."[13] Once again, television ads tell the story. A Pepsico executive explained how the company's new advertising strategy is to capture the mood of a "*we*-decade": "If the '70s were the decade of self, the '80s will be a season for sharing, an era of emotion, relationships."[14]

Beyond quality of life and community values, there are signs of growing interest in simple life styles that free people to experience "transcendent" satisfactions. Studies of Duane Elgin show that much of the nation feels the complexity of modern society is too demanding.[15] Even affluent two-income "yuppie" families often find it hard to maintain the lavish lifestyle dictated by the old American dream. An ethic of "voluntary simplicity" is spreading that strives to reduce life to its more rewarding human essentials, thereby fueling a surge of demand for travel, adventure, the arts, religiousity, and other interests that provide a sense of meaning and purpose. Marketing analyst Nelson Foote described this movement in American culture using an apt phrase: "From more to better to different to less."[16]

Of course, these trends are generalizations that do not apply to many individuals, especially now that the neo-conservative revolt has made wealth and extravagant living attractive again for some. Still, American society as a whole is undergoing a remarkable change since the transition to a new era began. Where once the youthful interest in unconstrained growth, material consumption, and hard technology was unquestioned, now the country is moving toward a more pragmatic, mature ethic that accepts the reality of limits. Americans are beginning to realize simpler but deeper satisfactions as they draw on philosophical roots sent down long ago by early American philosophers like Emerson, Thoreau, and Whitman who saw that the solution to our lives of "quiet desperation" lay in cultivating a calm simplicity that liberates the spirit.

TODAY'S PROBLEMS ARE TOMORROW'S OPPORTUNITIES

These new interests pose far more subtle, complex challenges than the relatively simple problems of the industrial era that focused on building factories and distribution channels to increase the supply of consumer goods. But the need to improve the quality of life is more than a tough problem. Chapter 1 showed that the problematic issues surrounding the economic crisis are merely symptoms of the transition to a different type of growth, so the following analysis describes how these problems of today can be converted into the opportunities of tomorrow.

Stagflation Forces the Transition from Goods to Services

Just a few years ago large corporations were so effectively insulated from competition that almost all major industries were operated as oligopolies that could, in effect, "administer" their prices. The result was high profit margins, increasing labor costs, meager productivity gains, and other forms of industrial "fat" that were passed on in higher prices to customers, leading to inflation and low growth— stagflation. Now that foreign competition has forced these firms into a fight for survival, some dramatic changes are in progress.

Stagflation sends a strong, clear message that industry needs to become more productive, even in high-technology fields like the computer industry where the driving force now is lowering manufacturing costs.[17] Firms that can master this imperative for improved productivity will win the fight for survival being waged now, and the primary weapon in this battle is the revolution in various forms of automation now underway.

Automatic machinery has been used for decades, but now **computerized** machinery presents a breakthrough. Smart robots, for instance, comprise a new breed of "steel collar workers" that can be programmed to perform an infinite variety of complex tasks. The National Bureau of Standards claims this "flexible manufacturing" would "raise productivity by hundreds of percent."[18] Some typical applications suggest the potential:[19]

Japan's Fanuc Corporation built "the first factory totally operated by robots." Manned essentially with only service employees and no blue collar workers, this plant brings the forecasts of science fiction to life as its robots work around the clock in dark silence flawlessly making other robots.

General Motors formed a joint venture with Fanuc to build 20,000 robots in the United States. By eliminating routine jobs, the proportion of skilled workers in GM plants should rise from the present level of 16 percent to about 50 percent.

General Electric automated an existing factory in Erie, Pennsylvania, improving efficiency by 240 percent, increasing output, and **creating**

jobs because the plant is more competitive. The company calls the development of this "factory of the future" the "most important undertaking of the century."

John Deere & Company built a flexible manufacturing plant in Iowa that can produce 5000 different configurations of vehicles.

Apple Computer created the first automated computer production line in Fremont, California.

Computerized information systems are also automating routine white collar jobs. The consulting firm of Booz, Allen & Hamilton estimates the cost of office work in the United States totals about $1 trillion now and will reach $1.5 trillion in 1990. Automation of this work will save $300 billion within a decade as computerized word processing, mail, data files, sales records, and inventory control systems change the old "paper-pushing offices" into sophisticated information networks. Investments in office automation are twice as profitable as factory automation because these are virgin applications, so the growth of office technology doubled in 1982 alone. Further, the combination of both factory and office automation should transform corporations into total information systems operating in real time. *BusinessWeek* claimed:[20]

> *U.S. companies are on the verge of achieving a dream: manufacturing enterprises where push-button factories and executive suites, no matter how physically remote, become parts of the same integrated entity.*

The effects on management will be profound. A study conducted at Carnegie Mellon University concluded, "Some time after 1990 robot capabilities will . . . make all manufacturing operatives replaceable." It is estimated that the use of robots, computer-assisted design and manufacturing (CAD-CAM), and office automation will affect roughly 45 million jobs in the United States—about half of the entire work force. The virtual elimination of most routine work will greatly increase the proportion of employees with highly trained skills, and the responsibility for decision-making will spread downward. Obviously, these massive structural changes are creating severe union-management tensions and a need for retraining programs. But progressive union leaders know the best way to save jobs is by remaining competitive. "We don't look at automation as job elimination," said Gary Watson, a local UAW president.[21] After much disruption, automation should ultimately provide huge productivity gains, improve quality, eliminate boring work, and create new technical and professional jobs.

Flexible manufacturing is also changing the relationship between the manufacturer and the customer. By making it possible to set up jobs automatically, short production runs are feasible to tailor-make products. Companies in Japan, Europe, the United States, and the Soviet Union are now able to produce lots of a few hundred items, and the Rand Corporation claims it should soon be as easy to custom-produce a product as to mass-produce it. The result will necessitate a closer involvement with clients, who may even in some cases directly control automatic, "continuous-flow" production systems to serve their own needs.[22]

These developments can only be seen as a revolution in the nature of work that is merely beginning, but which will soon replace most routine mental tasks with information technology. "We're in the Model T days of the robot," says Fred Geier, an executive in robot manufacturing, while Walter Abel, Vice President for R&D at Emhart Corporation, claims, "We are at the start of a new era where [production] will be almost fully automated. That's the new ball game."[23]

As fully automated factories are developed over the next few decades, resources and labor should be freed up to serve higher-order functions in a post-industrial era—just as the automation of agriculture allowed us to move on to industry a century ago. Some people fear automation will cause mass unemployment, but the history of technological progress shows the reverse. Eliminating routine work simply allows humans to address tougher challenges. Management consultant Irving Canton points out that the key to making this transition is a "shift in management's point of view from selling a product to selling the solution to a customer's problem."[24] Consider how the following range of more sophisticated, diverse life styles is creating the need for a host of important new services.

The baby-boom cohort seeks fulfilling experiences rather than material possessions, so they are opening up huge new markets for travel, sports, and entertainment. Women have moved into the workplace, thereby requiring child care, convenience foods, household help, and other time-saving services. An aging population poses special demands for health care, transportation, and housing. The hectic pace and stressful problems of today create a need for exercise, healthy diets, and leisure to maintain well-being. There is an awakening interest in personal development through education, various psychotherapies, and spiritual disciplines. Add to all this the need for affordable homes, protection against crime and disaster, and other common problems people struggle with, and it becomes clear there are myriad new challenges in meeting the demands of modern living. Here are some examples of how creative enterprise is developing this growing market for services:[25]

McDonald's now employs more people than U.S. Steel. The need for convenient fast food is growing so fast that revenues now total $44 billion and are expected to double by the end of this decade.

Kinder Kare is the nation's largest day-care chain—the McDonald's of child care—operating 750 centers and expanding to 2000 centers by 1990. There are 270 other firms in the field, while the entire childrens industry runs about $15 billion and is growing at about 30 percent per year.

Home Health Care using kidney dialysis, chemotherapy, IV feeding, and other treatment self-administered by patients in their homes is so attractive, especially for 32 million older Americans, that the market now amounts to $2 billion, and is expected to reach about $9 billion in 1986. One medical supplier said, "It's just absolutely exploding . . . It's the future."

Hyatt Legal Services has opened about 200 legal clinics since its founding in 1977 to serve the growing demand for low-cost, convenient counsel. Hyatt is now the largest law firm in the nation.

Quality Inns developed a factory-built "room of the 1990s" with luxury features that rents for only $40 a night, highlighting the growing use of mass-produced housing systems composed of a few basic modules that can be assembled into a wide variety of sizes and shapes.

Sylvan Learning Corporation was started in 1980 to provide individualized instruction in basic skills. The concept has been so effective that the firm now runs 100 learning centers which produce sales of $5 million. The founder claims, "We're just scratching the surface of the market."

Control Data's Plato computerized training system serves customers like GM, Du Pont, Motorola, Procter & Gamble, General Mills, and American Airlines to produce $200 million in sales and is attracting scores of competitors. The company's CEO claims, "We're looking at an infinite market."

TeleLearning Systems is an "electronic university" that offers 170 courses through home computer. It expects to expand to 500 courses soon employing thousands of teachers to reach a million students (20 million homes now have computers) to become the world's largest educational institution.

These are just a few examples of the vast range of new industries that are emerging at the frontier of economics to provide improved financial transactions, communications, information systems, medical care, shopping, home maintenance, education, leisure activities, and so on. Obviously, this transition from manufacturing to services is going to take decades, and its implications cannot be fully understood yet. But it's clear that the problem of stagflation simply masks great new possibilities. There is no lack of opportunities for imaginative entrepreneurs who see that the problems plaguing society can be converted into attractive new ventures. Stagflation is simply a temporary symptom of the transition to a more automated, sophisticated level of economic development—smart growth—that will vastly improve the quality of life.

Slow Technical Innovation Obscures the Acceleration of Science

The decline in technical innovation is another apparent problem that actually obscures a far more opportune frontier. In the past few years, a slow-down in R&D funding, patents, new commercial applications, and other indicators has provoked a fear that America has lost its former technological supremacy. U.S. expenditures on civilian R&D dropped to 1.7 percent of the GNP in 1984, compared to 2.4 percent for West Germany and 2.6 percent for Japan. The Japanese threaten a "second Pearl Harbor" by surpassing Americans in auto design and electronic equipment, and they may be winning the race to develop a fifth generation microcomputer.[26] Even the American fortress of high-technology will employ only about five percent of the workforce for many years, so this young economic sector offers little hope of absorbing the shrinking industrial base of the nation.[27]

But these fears are misleading because the slowdown in technical innovation and the limited size of new hi-tech fields does not reflect the unusual influence of the computer revolution that is just beginning to transform science, technology, and society itself. As the last chapter showed, technological change is the driving force of social evolution, and now the move to an information age is dramatically increasing our ability to amass knowledge—the very heart of all innovation. J. Fred Bucy, President of Texas Instruments, points out that technology is not hardware, but "know-how. It's knowledge of how to make things." Most innovations of the relatively simple industrial age were created by clever applications of technical common sense, as in Thomas Edison's cut-and-try approach to inventing the electric light. Today's advances emanate from sophisticated scientific research, like the revolution in biogenetics, that yesterday's most brilliant inventors could not have discovered without the computers that now support science. The result is that scientific knowledge is accelerating at an unprecedented level, driven by the frenetic pace of the computer revolution.

The rate of advance in information technology is so great that it is hard to grasp its full impact. When the computer was born a few short decades ago, the original machines were so bulky and expensive that IBM estimated the future market to be less than 10 computers. Now 10 **million** computers are sold **annually**. Common microcomputers have become more powerful than these early models but cost less than $1000 and can be carried in a portable case about the size of a typewriter. The computational power of today's machines is roughly equivalent to the brain of an ant, but as it continues to increase by a factor of 10 every 5 to 7 years with each new generation of systems, by the end of this century computers should be as powerful as the human brain—the most complex entity in the known universe. This remarkable progress can be appreciated by an analogy that appeared in *Computerworld* magazine: comparable advances on the automobile would have produced a Rolls Royce costing $2.50 and operating at 2 million miles per gallon of gas.[28]

One of the least visible outcomes of this new capability is its effect on the way science works. Modern scientific research would be impossible without powerful computers that process huge amounts of data. The computer also permits systematic storage, retrieval, and application of the wealth of underutilized scientific knowledge previously hidden in libraries. A good example is Control Data's automated system for the transfer of technology called *Technotec*. And as homes and offices are connected into information networks that will soon form an "information utility," the data obtained from financial and social transactions on these systems are creating new methods of studying economic, social, and political behavior.[29]

An especially great impetus for scientific progress is occurring as scientists, engineers and managers use these information networks to work together over great distances. I was fortunate to participate in a project sponsored by the National Science Foundation which used a "computerized conferencing" network to link together 500 professionals from the United States, Canada, and Europe over a period of several years. The sharing of knowledge among so many people around the world was an amazing new experience—an expanded dimension of communication transcending time and space— yet these systems are becoming commonplace. Comtex Scientific Corporation now disseminates scientific knowledge through "electronic journals." Such networks should speed up the publication of research results from years to days as this form of communication spreads through the scientific community.[30]

Thus, powerful information systems are opening up a world of heightened understanding that accelerates the rate of scientific and technological progress enormously. The philosopher Alfred North Whitehead observed that the invention of the scientific method was in itself the greatest invention of the 19th century; now the creation of information networks uniting a growing class of professionals working around the world carries the method of science to its logical conclusion. An entirely new social order is being formed that focuses its energies on nothing less than the progress of knowledge. It is estimated that about 6000 scientific articles are published each day, and the total sum of information doubles every few years. As many scholars have shown, this increase in knowledge is the very stuff that fuels technological advancement, productivity, economic growth, and other gains in human welfare.[31] The following examples highlight advances now underway in physical science and technology:[32]

Earth Science has achieved a breakthrough in the tectonic theory of continental plates by computer analysis of data from space satellites, seismic instruments, and international monitoring teams. This new paradigm provides a powerful understanding of volcanos, earthquakes, weather, crops, mineral deposits, and other geological factors.

Materials Research is developing light steels, tough plastics, flexible ceramics, superconducting metals, composites with special properties, and other customized materials that permit a variety of new applications.

Medical Science is advancing rapidly through the invention of sophisticated diagnostic machines like nuclear magnetic resonance, new medicines like interferon, artificial and replaceable organs for virtually every part of the body, and a better appreciation for the social factors affecting health.

Genetics has achieved an intellectual victory through the discovery of the structure of DNA, which is leading to prediction and control of birth defects, cures for a variety of diseases including cancer and aging, and the design of useful new microorganisms. There are now about 600 genetic counseling centers in the United States and $2.5 billion has been invested in 100 biotech companies. The market is expected to grow to $100 billion in the year 2000.

Brain Research has progressed as new instruments, drugs, and computer analysis now permit probing the origins of emotions and thought itself. Dr. Herbert Weingartner of the National Institute of Mental Health notes, "We're sitting on the edge of a revolution that rivals quantum physics in the 1920s."

Space Exploration is moving rapidly now that the space shuttle is operational, making permanent orbiting research stations feasible. Fairchild Industries is planning to build space factories to be leased for industrial ventures.

A major technical frontier lies in the social sciences because of the pressing need to redefine major institutions. As we saw in Chapter 1, "social technology" is often ignored because organizational problems are so endemic that most people have despaired of resolving them. Yet these relationships comprise the prosaic matrix within which modern people conduct their lives, so they are the principal barrier to further progress. Although contributions of this field are as yet meager because rigorous attempts to understand the social world are still new, significant capabilities have developed within the past few decades since the social sciences have begun to blossom:[33]

Behavioral Science is becoming a mature discipline through the use of computer analysis, group process studies, and clinical research, leading to important new insights and techniques for modifying behavior. For instance, computerized instruction is moving so fast that half of all corporate training should soon be automated, including sensitive areas like supervising employees.

Organization and Management has become such an important social science in its own right that scientist Olaf Helmer claimed, "The next great breakthrough in the sciences, comparable in significance to such physical breakthroughs as the creation of life and the control of thermonuclear energy, may be the construction of a theory of organizations."

Social System Modeling is advancing to the point where the behavior of individuals, juries, organizations, political races, and the entire world can be modeled with good accuracy. About 100 behavioral scientists now provide advice in jury selection.

Conflict Resolution has been developed into such a useful discipline that the U.S. Congress recently approved a "National Peace Academy" to resolve international disputes. The field claims, "There is now a science—tested and proved in actual practice—that can help make war obsolete (and) this science can be taught, learned, and applied."

Modern societies have always used social technology, as in the invention of democracy, the modern corporation, and other "social mechanisms." Now, however, it is urgently needed on a far wider basis to control the complexity of modern institutions. Social interventions are poorly understood, and they often fail. But those who learn how to master this newly developing ability to manage social systems more effectively will realize powerful advantages in the years ahead.

The main frontier of progress, of course, is information science—the key force driving the evolution of a new era. Although the technical achievements being developed now are too vast to be described fully, a few highlights will convey the scope of new capabilities that are becoming available:[34]

Superchips are being developed that will contain as many as 1 million devices on a single chip. Chips with 1 billion devices are predicted by the year 2000, which could store the contents of the Library of Congress in a space and at a cost comparable to that of a single book today.

Fifth-Generation Computers will be far more sophisticated machines that use powerful microchips in arrays of 100 or so; they will compute with light signals; use an internal data base of "expert systems" containing specialized knowledge; and work with people in a more comfortable type of interaction.

Artificial Intelligence and Expert Systems are being developed that "learn" and "think" roughly as humans do. Dozens of expert systems are available to solve many common problems now, and about 50 companies and labs are working on more sophisticated versions using as many as a million chips operating in parallel.

Laser Printers are becoming available that will overcome the biggest obstacle in computer technology—printing out hard copy quietly, quickly, and with the flexibility for handling text and graphics.

Information Networks are being developed by IBM, Xerox, and AT&T to link together computer systems in factories, offices, and homes, with applications expected to reach $1 billion in sales by 1988. "Integrated Services Digital Networks" are also being developed that make it possible to transfer information among telephones, computers, and any other device.

Glass Fiber Optics offer transmission systems of such efficiency that a single cable can carry 1.8 million messages simultaneously and so cheaply that they can connect all households and offices into an integrated societal system. AT&T has installed its first continental hook-up, and the British are installing a national network that leapfrogs the old cable TV systems.

Telecommunication Satellites carry roughly 1 million times as much information as the old land lines, and direct broadcast satellites can transmit to small antennas located on homes and offices. With more than 100 satellites in use and the number growing, it should soon be possible for most individuals to communicate around the world using portable devices, like the new "cellular phones," in both audio and video modes.

Information Centers integrating computers, video systems, and other information equipment are evolving to provide a complete set of capabilities.

Smart Applications of information systems are proliferating, including the smart credit card, smart autos, smart buildings, smart appliances, and so on.

The BioChip is a "biological computer"—a molecular electronic structure that stores information in extremely high densities of as much as 10^{19} bits/cm^3, approximating the natural powers of human brain tissue.

Even now, this rapidly developing capability is creating a transition to electronic financial transactions, computerized education, on-line news service, teleconferencing, recorded legal proceedings, electronic town meetings, unlimited access to entertainment, and even televised medical and psychiatric treatment. The unique character of these applications seems likely to provide the driving impetus for widespread structural and attitudinal changes, similar to but far greater than the enormous effects of television a few decades ago. There are serious problems involved, of course, such as the invasion of privacy and computer crime that have received much attention. But the net effect is that the world is being transformed into a knowledge-based society as individuals, organizations, and nations form a central nervous system that may eventually unify into a single "global organism" exhibiting an unprecedented level of intelligence.[35]

This outline of emerging breakthroughs illustrates that there really isn't a decline in technological innovation but rather a shift in emphasis. Americans tend to think of technology in terms of hardware: machines, automobiles, weapons, and so on. Physical science and technology remain essential, just as a mature adult must remain physically fit. But the frontier of progress now lies in this subtle but more powerful domain of high-technology: biogenetics and medicine that allow humans to control life, social science that can alter individual behavior and create more effective institutions, and information systems that offer sophisticated new tools for managing economies and expanding our understanding. As the knowledge-generating power of the information age accelerates advances in these fields, a vast range of more intelligent modes of growth should appear which will defy the imagination—just as Americans pioneered the frontier of physical science in an industrial era. Peter Drucker summed it up:[36]

> We clearly face a period in which the demands and opportunities for innovation will be greater than at any time in living history.

Environmental Constraints Become Resources

Economic progress also appears to be limited by the increasing depletion of energy, water, and rare minerals, and by the pollution from industrial effluents, cars, and household wastes. The rosy opinions of optimists notwithstanding, trends show that the rapid spreading of industrialization around the world will increase the demand for scarce resources and the load on the ecological system by many orders of magnitude, as we saw in Chapter 1.

But just as in the cases of stagflation and technological innovation, such issues are troublesome only because we focus on the constraints they pose rather than the gains they offer. The "energy shortage," for instance, exists primarily in our minds. If one looked about the natural world carefully, it becomes clear we are surrounded by various forms of energy that are almost inexhaustable; the sun, wind, tides, volcanos, biomass, and other forces in nature could provide far more energy than needed if harnessed effectively. Barbara Ward put it this way:[37]

> *When social historians look back on our day, they will be astonished at our almost obsessive concern with sufficient supplies of energy. Our planet, is, after all, one vast system of energy.*

For instance, the energy crisis occurred because we waste two-thirds of our fossil fuels and we have not learned to use other sources. This problem is now being corrected with startling results as Americans change their consumption habits. An oil glut has appeared primarily because higher gas prices encouraged the move to smaller autos that save fuel, and more expensive electricity and heating oil caused power utilities to scrap their old expansion plans as homes and offices were insulated. Polls show the strong majority of people say they will use less energy even if prices **decline**. Most studies conclude such trends could save roughly half of present consumption in a decade or two. Thus, conservation represents the **best** source of energy available, and it is also creating profitable new industries and jobs.[38]

Americans are not only using less energy, they are also using different types of energy. One of the most promising but underestimated sources is solar energy, particularly the use of photovoltaic cells (PVCs) which are ideally suited for the dispersed, low power needs of electronic equipment in the information age. Silicon PVCs were once prohibitively expensive for all but space flights because they cost about $1000 per watt, but the price has been lowered to about $5 to 7 per watt and will reach the point of broad economic feasibility at $1 to 2 in about 1990. As costs have declined their use has increased by 50 percent per year, or by a factor of five in the last three years. There are now 6000 homes in the United States using PVCs, and proponents claim half of all homes will use such systems within 20 years. A Gallup poll showed, "Solar is the energy source that Americans prefer," while an executive exclaimed, "The market is exploding." Here are a few examples of the 60 or so companies now in the field:[39]

> **Atlantic Richfield** built a 1.6 megawatt power generation plant using PVCs in California that will be operated by Pacific Gas & Electric to supply power to 6400 customers.
>
> **Solarex** developed the first "solar breeder" plant in Maryland that uses a PVC power generating system to manufacture more PVCs.
>
> **The Japanese** are using a less expensive type of "amorphous silicon" for PVCs which is expected to increase capacity from the present 6 megawatts to 50 megawatts in 1986. The enormous potential of amorphous silicon is often compared to the breakthrough created by the transistor.

Conservation and solar energy will be far more useful than has been commonly credited, however it would be a mistake to believe any single approach is going to prove sufficient, especially as worldwide industrialization increases energy demands tenfold. Oil should remain available in the short term, but the energy crisis is likely to come back with a vengeance in a decade or so as economic growth picks up, causing supplies to tighten with a hard snap. Coal is plentiful and it is convenient for industries located in coal-producing regions. However, studies show that the pollution of coal exhaust causes 50,000 deaths per year, so huge costs are involved to clean it up. Nuclear energy is attractive, but it must be located in communities that are prepared to accept the risk of a nuclear catastrophe. Although solar is very desirable, it may only be economical where sunshine is abundant. Allen Murray, President of Mobil Corporation, recently warned of the consequences:[40]

> We're headed for another round of energy shortages. Certainly by the end of this century. Possibly well before that.

A far more sophisticated view of "energy management" is emerging now which recognizes these strong and weak points of all energy sources to develop those best suited for different users and local regions. The resulting diversity of energy forms produced by many small, decentralized suppliers should be more efficient and less susceptible to massive failures than the present reliance on big, centralized fossil fuel plants. Consider some examples of how business firms and communities are creatively managing their "energy assets" to develop the most feasible solution to their needs, with power companies acting as "facilitators" of this "energy market" rather than monopolies:[41]

Dow Corning invested $35 million to build its own power plant and now saves $2.5 million per year. There are estimated to be 2000 such "energy entrepreneurs" today, producing about one quarter of all electricity used.

IBM is experimenting with new energy technologies, such as a "cold storage system" at Tucson that is saving $140,000 per year on a $500,000 investment.

Dade County, Florida built a garbage-powered generating plant to provide electric power. About 200 such projects are now planned in the United States.

Oregon and New England are heavily forested so their citizens now derive roughly half of their energy from wood.

Springfield, Vermont refurbished local dams to generate electricity.

Iceland and Western American States are using geothermal energy to heat water and homes and for industrial use.

Pacific Gas & Electric invested $64.5 million in wind farms at Altamont, California, that operate 400 wind turbines; it has 600 contracts to buy the surplus of small power producers and manufacturing plants co-generating electricity; and it offers four rate schedules for different times of day.

Pennsylvania Power & Light offers engineering consulting services to advise customers on selecting energy sources and improving energy efficiency.

Virginia's Power Company is developing solar PVC systems, fuel cells, wind turbines, fluidized-bed coal combustion, and other hi-tech energy forms.

Environmental pollution is also a thinly disguised opportunity, even though the problem is now reaching crisis levels. After years of progress in requiring scrubbers to remove pollutants from industrial exhausts, the rash of toxic dump sites like Love Canal has shown that the problem is far more endemic—even in hi-tech areas, like Silicon Valley, that were once thought to be free of pollution. Pollutants were simply being returned to the environment at 17,000 to 22,000 dumpsites that are slowly poisoning 80,000 bodies of water which half of the American population relies on. More people are being killed from pollutants than by auto accidents. The recent head of the EPA, William Ruckelshaus, warned, "Life now takes place in a minefield of risks."[42]

This realization of the profound nature of the problem is leading to a more fundamental solution: the redesign of manufacturing systems to avoid creating pollutants and/or to recover waste material for recycling into useful products—what Joanna Underwood, founder of the Inform research group, called pollution control at the "front end." The beauty of this view is that—contrary to the claims that business must be allowed to pollute to remain profitable—sound pollution **control** is becoming **profitable**, simply because pollutants are **resources** in the wrong place. Alice Tepper Marlin of the Council for Economic Priorities states, "The most important way to offset the initial expense of installing pollution controls is through revenue from the recovery of by-products."[43] Examples of modern "pollution management" programs demonstrate the advantages in using less raw materials and energy, lowering operating and maintenance costs, and recovering valuable waste materials:[44]

3M Company developed a "Pollution Pays" program over the past 10 years that has saved $200 million in the cost of energy and production, the value of recovered materials, and less expensive pollution control equipment. A company spokesperson described their view: "Pollutants are resources, and creating the right technology can put them to productive use."

Uniroyal once dumped a dangerous by-product, nonenes, at great risk to employees and the community, but began burning it in a steam generating plant. The company gained pollutant-free energy, avoided the dangers of handling this chemical, and saved $183,000 the first year on an investment of $48,000.

Hercules Powder invested $750,000 to remove waste it once dumped in the Mississippi River and now saves $250,000 per year in lost material and water.

Dow Corning spent $2.7 million to recover chlorine and hydrogen from a manufacturing process at a savings of $900,000 per year in operating costs for a 33 percent annual ROI.

Westvaco Corporation began converting paper wastes into useful products a few years ago, and now this operation occupies four plants and could double sales to $45 million per year.

Exxon saved over $1.5 million in solvent costs at a New Jersey plant by putting floating covers on tanks to prevent evaporation of compounds.

U.S. Steel reduced its hazardous waste by almost 50 percent in four years by selecting pollutant-free materials and developing new recovery methods.

Aluminum and Steel Manufacturing now uses 50 percent recycled scrap metal.

The Town of Machida, Japan, has a recycling program that recovers 90 percent of the city's waste for useful purposes.

Organic Farming is spreading rapidly to an estimated 50,000 commercial farmers who want to minimize the use of chemical fertilizers and insecticides to save expenses and avoid damaging their land.

Additionally, the design, manufacture, and service of pollution control systems now constitutes a profitable industry in the United States, growing at 20 percent per year, producing $50 billion in annual revenues, and creating about two million jobs. Former EPA head Russell Train said:[45]

> *We have all heard it suggested that environmental programs will slow down economic growth. Just the opposite is true. It is pollution, not its control, that limits growth.*

These examples show that natural constraints really represent opportunities for a more intelligent form of environmental control. A complete view of the complex cycle of nature is becoming unavoidable now as costs escalate at the input and output of the industrial system: extracting new supplies of resources is becoming expensive, while disposing of waste products is creating unacceptable levels of pollution. As a result, the National Academy of Sciences argued that all material processes should be managed as a "complete material cycle."[46] Only this "total system" concept will permit the future growth that seems unavoidable without sacrificing a reasonable quality of life.

Big Government Offers Big Opportunities

A major reason for the disenchantment with big government is that, although the public sector serves urgent needs, it exercises a monopoly that avoids the discipline of the market. A major solution

is evolving now as the antigovernment revolution provides an unusual opportunity for visionary entrepreneurs to claim these social
functions for the private sector. Not simply to "do good"—although
that might be one justification—but to realize profitable gains by
providing useful service. Here are a few examples:[47]

IBM, DEC, Westinghouse, and Control Data have profitable computer
facilities operating in the nation's worst ghettos to provide jobs, training,
and a sense of community pride that reduces crime and other social
costs.

Giant Food started a supermarket in the most depressed part of Washington, D.C. using concepts of joint business-community control.

Aetna is revitalizing ghetto neighborhoods in Chicago, and **Dayton-
Hudson** is sponsoring community renewal projects in Minneapolis.

Citicorp has invested $1 billion to rehabilitate 35,000 homes in New
York City.

Control Data, Apple Computer, and IBM are pioneering in the use of
computer systems to provide cost-effective, efficient education.

James W. Rouse, developer of the planned community of Columbia,
Maryland, and Faneuil Hall Market in Boston, has started Enterprise
Foundation to assist residents of slums in owning and renovating their
old homes. Projects are under way in 12 cities now and future plans
are to expand the operation to 100 cities. Says Rouse, "We're going to
make a major impact on the life of the poor in the U.S."

The possibilities for imaginative firms interested in combining
profitable business with public service are vast, precisely because
there are so many difficult social problems in modern societies that
badly need solving. Chapter 8 will describe other approaches being
undertaken through government-business partnerships. William C.
Norris, founder of Control Data, sees the prospects this way:[48]

*Business has for too long been living in the past . . . While business
has been mainly ignoring the major problems of society, the government has demonstrated its inability to cope successfully with
them alone, and they are growing to disastrous proportions . . . The
list of needs is long . . . cheaper energy; the rebuilding of cities;
environmental protection; lower food costs; less costly health care;
higher quality education; better availability of technology; and most
important of all, a greater number of jobs, especially skilled jobs . . .
What is required is a fundamental change in which business takes
the initiative and provides the leadership in planning and managing*

the implementation of programs meeting these needs, in cooperation with government, labor unions, universities, churches, and all leading segments of society . . . The best approach is to view them with the strategy in mind that they can be profitable business opportunities.

CLIENT-DRIVEN INSTITUTIONS

This new frontier of smart growth may convert the economic crisis into great opportunities, but it also exacts tough new demands, particularly in the relationship between institutions and their clients. Automation shifts attention from routine tasks to the difficult job of serving subtle client needs using sophisticated technologies that deliver complex services. Managing energy and pollution in a closed material cycle involves the integration of technology into community living patterns. Performing public functions requires demonstrating a concern for the social welfare. In short, there may be great opportunities ahead, but they can only succeed if commensurate responsibilities are assumed as well.

To address these challenges, progressive companies are developing "consumer affairs functions" and a form of "social marketing."[49] The result is a "client-driven institution" that provides genuine value and service rather than simply selling goods, it evaluates how well the customer's interests are served, and uses participative working relations to bridge the gap between management and customers. Enlightened business has always advocated placing the client foremost, so these concepts represent a fulfillment of the marketing functioning.

Revolt of the Sovereign Customer

One of the cherished myths of the Old Capitalism is that, although corporations are obligated primarily to serve their stockholders, this arrangement is actually in the best interests of the customer. Because business must compete to win customer patronage, in this best of all possible worlds it is not the stockholder or the executive who actually controls corporate decisions—but the buyer. By selecting among options available in the market, the client dictates what types of products and services will be offered, at what price, their design and quality, and so on. In other words, the consumer is sovereign—or, as businessmen used to say, "The customer is always right."

Such convenient beliefs may be comforting, but they also blind us to unpleasant realities that may grow to catastrophic proportions before being acknowledged. Buoyed by their faith in insightful market research, persuasive advertising, slick public relations, clever government lobbying, and other means for manipulating the market, American business was stunned when customers began switching to foreign products in droves because their interests were ignored at home. Louis Harris warned:[50]

> The country is in the throes of a deep-seated consumer revolt that is likely to grow and have a greater impact in the years ahead.

The growth of the consumer movement can be gauged by the fact that there are now more than 1400 professional consumer advocates in the United States, and a great structure of consumer regulations has been erected since the 1970s. Many business executives believe consumerism is largely provoked by the self-interest of overly critical consumer advocates, but these critics are influential only because there is a huge mass of dissatisfied customers urgently seeking their help.

One indication of the problem can be seen in the rate of product injuries. When the Consumer Product Safety Act was being considered, hearings before Congress revealed that more than 20 million Americans were injured by defective products annually; of these, 110,000 persons were permanently disabled, and 30,000 lost their lives. To seek redress, the number of lawsuits skyrocketed from 50,000 in 1960, to 500,000 in 1970, and to more than 1 million by the mid-1970s. These injuries cost customers more than $5 billion per year, and corporations have incurred an equivalent level of product liability losses. In some industries, insurance premiums increased as much as 700 percent.[51]

Surveys also show that a strong majority of the public feels the value they get for their money has "gotten worse," the quality of goods and services has deteriorated, they receive poor market information, advertisements are misleading or deceptive, they have few meaningful alternatives, they find it difficult to get complaints corrected, and they feel most firms are primarily concerned about profits rather than customers. Buyers are equally disillusioned with federal regulation, but they reject the belief that "consumers don't need any help in looking after their interests." Even a pro-business conservative, journalist James J. Kilpatrick, lost his patience:[52]

> [I am] fed up to the teeth with American business [for providing such shoddy merchandise and poor service that] is not far removed from the long ago cry of "the public be damned."

The problem is made worse because shoppers in advanced nations like the United States have become extremely sophisticated, demanding in their expectations, and cynical about the claims of advertising. Faced with an increasing variety of competing goods from all over the world and with declining real incomes, customers are aggressively seeking low prices, good service, and lasting product value. A marketing study reported that Americans are interested primarily in "integrity buying" that offers "real product benefits," and "products that last longer," emulating the European buying habits that spurred high quality imports now flooding U.S. markets. There will always be some demand for cheap products, but the trend is away from short-lived goods that fueled the throw-away economy of the past, and toward what E. F. Schumacher called the "economics of permanence."[53]

Some firms have improved their ability to serve these changing needs, but most have not. For instance, a major study by Professor David Garvin found that great differences persist between American and Japanese product quality.[54] Rather than feeling "sovereign," therefore, disenchanted shoppers have often felt more the victims of American business, and the consumer revolt can be best seen as a reassertion of their lost power.

From Selling to Serving

In an attempt to woo back the customer, innovative firms are finding a variety of creative ways to genuinely serve the client's needs. The spirit of this new orientation was set by Esther Peterson, who was appointed the first consumer affairs executive at Giant Food in 1970.

Ms. Peterson made it clear she was creating a new business function that advocated the buyer's interests foremost when she shocked corporate executives and delighted the public by cautioning customers **not** to buy products that were overpriced or harmful. Since then consumer affairs departments have become common in large corporations, but on the whole the concept has not lived up to its promise. Critics point out such departments are often simply window dressing that serves as an extension of marketing and public relations, consumer affairs executives usually are not powerful people, they may not have access to the chief executive, and they are generally unable to influence corporate policy.[55]

As we saw in Chapter 1, the cause of this halfhearted performance is deeply rooted in the ideology of profit. Although business managers may give lip service to serving customers, in fact, the prevailing myopic focus on short-term profit urges most firms to serve their own convenience rather than the client, with the problem being especially severe in marketing. Marketing units are usually accountable for meeting sales goals established by higher management, so marketing personnel are not primarily interested in the needs of customers but in maximizing sales revenue. That's why almost all advertising consists of ostentatious displays of consumption intended to entice the customer with exaggerated claims and outright misrepresentation, rather than useful information. The recent chairman of the FTC, James C. Miller III, acknowledged that legal action against all untruthful ads would be unrealistic because, "virtually any advertising can be found to be deceptive." This reflects a relationship with the customer that is fundamentally "adversarial" because the true goal of the firm is not to serve the customer but to make money—the welfare of the customer is simply a means to that end, and may even be an obstacle to that end. Scholars writing in the *Harvard Business Review* report many firms regard the complaining customer as "the enemy," while *BusinessWeek* claimed some companies think of the customer as "a bloody nuisance."[56]

This flaw in our business culture explains why so many corporations perceive the heightening demands by customers as foreign and unsettling—even though the failure to meet these new realities threatens the firm's existence. Firestone refused to acknowledge defects in a series of radial tires, ultimately resulting in very costly claims and a severely tarnished reputation. Ford resisted redesigning the Pinto gas tank, costing huge sums in unnecessary legal fees, a notorious lawsuit that damaged customer loyalty, and hundreds of needless deaths. After 20 years of studies showing a definite link between smoking and 340,000 deaths per year from lung cancer, the R.J. Reynolds Tobacco Company recently shocked the medical world by claiming yet again that the proof is not conclusive.[57]

Thus, a self-defeating rush for success has caused many managers to lose sight of the central fact that sound business must serve genuine needs if it hopes to win the client's lasting patronage. A satisfied customer spends $142,000 on autos over his or her lifetime, $2500 for appliances, and $22,000 in groceries.[58] Executives face a great challenge in reorienting their companies to this purpose, or the marketplace will make the changes for them. The problem is especially formidable because the organization faces a paradox of subverting its immediate self-interest in order to concern itself with the welfare of the client, whose satisfaction is not very apparent, fluctuating, and difficult to evaluate.

A growing number of firms are changing their posture to produce an organization that is "customer driven"—rather than profit driven, sales driven, or technology driven. These high performing companies have a strong commitment to customer value, service, product quality, and reliability. They make a point of holding frequent meetings to instill these attitudes in their employees. Executives act in sales roles to set an example, and they reward these qualities in others. Here are a few examples of firms that have created outstanding reputations:[59]

> **IBM** is a monument to the success that results from placing client welfare foremost. IBM salespeople are constantly impressed with an emphasis on service. Their role is **not** to sell, but to find the least expensive solution that will solve a problem as if they were "on the customer's payroll."
>
> **L. L. Bean** has such a reputation for quality and service that 97 percent of its clients give it top ratings. The firm guarantees 100 percent satisfaction or a cash refund, field tests its merchandise, tracks all complaints, and claims, "A customer is the most important person in this office."
>
> **Hewlett-Packard** recently introduced a "do it right the first time" program to reduce failure rates by a factor of 10, which is reinforced by division-

wide meetings. The program has realized major quality gains along with a $200 million savings from lower inventories and a boost in morale.

Procter & Gamble quickly moved to study their Rely tampon for toxic shock syndrome and then removed the product from the market, gaining the company inestimable gains in customer confidence.

Johnson & Johnson brilliantly managed two crises resulting from the poisoning of Tylenol capsules by withdrawing the product, establishing a toll-free hotline for customers, exchanging old capsules for tablets, keeping retailers fully advised, and cooperating with the press. As a result, potential economic disaster was avoided and the product's share of the market has recovered.

Lanier has top executives make sales calls once a month and answers all complaints within four hours.

McDonald's achieved unusual success because of its goal to provide "Quality, Service, Cleanliness, and Value."

Digital Equipment defines its primary goal as providing quality rather than sales, which will then lead to growth and profit.

Campbell Soup is reorganizing into autonomous product groups to encourage a reputation with customers as a firm that "looks after the buyer's well-being" by developing products that "consumers perceive to be in their best interest."

Holiday Inn offers a money-back guarantee and finds this policy encourages disgruntled customers to report their complaints and to patronize the chain again.

These excellent companies succeed in maintaining a client-driven-orientation by using firm organizational discipline to resist a natural tendency of serving one's immediate self-interest. Managing this tension is so difficult that it often requires executives, consumer affairs specialists, quality control personnel, and others to oversee operating units. But in a society of more discriminating buyers, only institutions with the self-control to place their client's need foremost will survive. An American Express executive expressed it best: "Service is our most strategic marketing weapon."[60] The old era of selling is over, and a new era of serving has begun.

Measuring Customer Value

Another major need is to develop effective information systems that enable the customer to evaluate the product in order to make meaningful buying decisions, and that tell the firm how effectively the customer has been served. Salvatore Divita, a professor of marketing, noted, "The difficulty with present measurements is that only the seller's satisfaction is measured, that is, sales and profits." Without this type of "user-oriented" information, the concept of consumer sovereignity is simply an empty piety. One shopper who was trying to evaluate life insurance complained, "I try to be an intelligent consumer," but the maze of incomparable rates is "inscrutable."[61]

A good example is provided by the automobile business. The traditional approach of simply selling "a machine" ignores the car owner's concerns, so foreign competition has taken over a third of the U.S. market by designing autos as a transportation *system* that includes "soft" factors: fuel economy, maintenance, safety, insurance, and quality. The average car now costs more than $10,000 and these other costs amount to about $4000 per year, making the total investment almost $50,000 over a 10-year product life—only exceeded by the purchase of a home. Also, car accidents kill roughly 50,000 people per year and injure hundreds of thousands. Yet American car manufacturers have paid little attention to these factors, so it is little wonder that they are puzzled at the decline in sales. One executive lamented, "We need to find out what will make the consumer buy."[62]

This vital need was corrected when the federal government required fuel economy ratings, crash tests, and other consumer data, which was subsequently published in the *Car Book* in 1981 by the National Highway Traffic Safety Administration. The book was such a great success that 1 million copies were distributed in three weeks. Jack Gillis, the official responsible for this publication, explained:[63]

> . . . the public is starved for useful information on cars. We're entering the era of the enlightened consumer. They are crying out for comparative information. . . . we were establishing a new basis for comparison—safety and performance instead of styling . . . if American manufacturers don't think safety, they are missing the boat. The Japanese are going to do it, just as they produced the popular fuel efficient small cars.

Although one would think that American car manufacturers would stampede to provide this data to demonstrate the superiority of their vehicles, old ways die hard in Detroit. Under pressure from business, former Transportation Secretary Drew Lewis discontinued this publication because it embodied "an anti-industry kind of position . . . (and) too much of a bias in the direction of just taking pot shots at these people." He said, "people don't need a consumer guide to buy a car."[64] The most generous interpretation is that these are old beliefs based on ignorance, because the worst thing we can do to anyone is to not provide useful feedback that urges improving performance.

These soft factors are no longer questions of "social responsibility" in the moral sense—they have become the most crucial determinants in the success or failure of a product and, ultimately, of the firm. We all tend to avoid facing the painful truth about our failures, yet being confronted with the criticism of clients is precisely the strong medicine needed to instill a healthy dose of reality into business voluntarily rather than through lost sales. Paradoxically, a better strategy would be to pay *less* attention to sales levels, financial figures, and so on in order to focus on evaluating the benefits the firm delivers to clients. If we really hope to understand and serve customers better, this information is far more useful because it is the very source of business vitality, while traditional measures simply reflect the gains that result later.

Excellent corporations are designing systems to collect and interpret customer feedback using periodic surveys that evaluate the firm's product and services and that elicit suggestions. Complaints are also carefully monitored to spot trends and ideas for improvement. Operating units are audited periodically on the performance of personnel, attitudes toward clients, and the like. Consider the following examples:[65]

> **IBM** once again leads the way by measuring the attitudes of its employees and customers on a monthly basis.
>
> **L.L. Bean** conducts surveys and interviews to evaluate customer satisfaction, and it gathers data on complaints for analysis and follow-up.
>
> **Caterpillar Tractor** conducts two customer surveys at different time periods following a sale, it analyzes service reports, and conducts quality audits.
>
> **Western Union** conducts audits of its offices, it tracks complaints, and monitors client satisfaction through surveys.

McDonald's surveys customers for complaints and suggestions about the quality of its food, service, and so on, and it audits its stores for performance.

Developing better techniques for evaluating these intangible factors presents a big challenge. All existing financial information systems had to be invented, and the task now is to extend these old methods to measure the soft factors that have become critical in a new economic frontier. But enlightened institutions that can master these skills should be rewarded handsomely. Mary Gardiner Jones, Vice President for Consumer Affairs at Western Union, summed up the need:[66]

Consumer affairs offices must develop realistic performance standards which go beyond revenue goals and expense budgets and which clearly embrace the quality of performance measured in terms of service quality and customer satisfaction.

Bridging the Producer-Consumer Gap

The most important way to create a client-driven institution is to simply put the corporation into direct touch with the customer in order to revive the traditional attentiveness of small business to its clients. A variety of new techniques are being used to recreate that personal seller-buyer relationship which withered away with the growth of large multinational institutions remotely controlled by distant executives. Progressive firms form "consumer advisory councils" composed of typical customers who meet periodically to evaluate products and services and to offer advice. Toll-free "cool lines" allow disgruntled clients to voice their grievances directly. Executives make a point of periodically patronizing their own outlets to gain a firsthand impression of how customers are served—the way benevolent sultans and kings roamed their empires incognito to stay in touch with their subjects. Managers, engineers, and sales personnel work directly with clients to get their point of view first hand. Peters and Waterman note that excellent companies stay "close to the customer." Following are some typical examples:[67]

IBM has been unusually successful because almost all of its products are developed in such close collaboration with customers that the client and IBM organizations overlap. The firm also maintains a 24-hour client hot line.

Apple Computer gained its early lead in microcomputers by perfecting design features on its first machine in close collaboration with users.

Hewlett-Packard invites customers to make presentations to its engineers, pointing out strengths and weaknesses in the product.

Citibank has backroom operators visit customers and account officers to coordinate the solution of problems directly.

General Electric recently asked its design engineers to visit customers and dealers to seek advice on product design and performance. A GE executive said, "Engineers are getting their directions from customers."

Avis, Marriott, Southern Airways, and McDonald's executives randomly patronize their own retail shops to sample the service provided by employees.

Avis, American Express, GE, Sony, and Whirlpool use toll-free numbers to monitor complaints, provide information, get suggestions, and learn about customer's needs. Procter & Gamble puts its phone number on all packages.

Esteé Lauder is becoming the leader in cosmetics because it conducts sound research in skin care, uses trained salespeople who can provide useful advice, and encourages customers comments, often directly to the CEO.

Kroger Company conducts 250,000 consumer interviews per year to understand the needs of its buyers more precisely.

American Express has worked to develop close working relations under the policy of running the company "like a huge mom and pop drugstore."

The most powerful strategy would be to appoint independent consumer advocates to the corporate board of directors to share in policy making. American business has resisted such ideas ferociously, and there are good justifications. The vision of Ralph Nader lecturing automobile executives within their board rooms does not inspire confidence. However, these fears have prevented seeing the great advantages that would result. Our critics are usually the people we should pay closest attention to precisely because they are most keenly aware of our weak spots—that is why they can infuriate us so badly. This does not mean that corporations must invite disruptive confrontations, but it would be useful to cautiously but earnestly form working partnerships with responsible consumer advocates in order to hear those difficult but constructive messages about what the customer really wants, how the company has failed to provide it, changes that are needed, and the like.

Collaborative corporate-client relations can not only serve existing client needs better, they also offer an unusually advantageous edge in learning how to develop products to serve new needs. Studies show that almost all successful product innovations originate from customers, rather than from the organization. In response to client requests, League Insurance Company developed a program to offer infant car seats to its policyholders free of charge, thereby reducing the rate of car injuries, which enabled lower premiums as well as higher corporate profits. The president, Robert Vanderbeek, said:[68]

We put public service right in the mainstream of our operations— partly because it is good, bottom-line business.

A variety of other trends are rapidly appearing as information technology makes it possible for sellers and buyers to conduct transactions using computerized information systems. Videotext television is being developed by Sears, Penney, Grand Union, General Mills, ITT, and other companies to allow customers to shop using remote viewing. Sales personnel are being assisted by computers that provide product performance data, operating instructions, prices, and other information for the client. Computer networks are connecting airlines with institutional passengers, distributors and their outlets, and manufacturing firms with suppliers and dealers.[69]

Whatever blend of methods are used, corporations are bringing their customers into the workings of the organization because of a growing realization that the interests of both buyer and seller are congruent. Contrary to conventional beliefs that it is necessary to be something of a cut-throat in business, the evidence shows that companies providing products of high quality and good service also have lower costs, higher productivity, and better profits. This closer relationship will be uncomfortable to some extent, particularly for internal organizational units that are usually insulated from the environment. But maintaining this exposure to the realities of the market should create a keener ability to respond to the clients whom organizations must serve to justify their existence. Harvard's Theodore

Levitt compares this intimate new buyer-seller relationship to a marriage:[70]

> *The era of the one-night stand is over. [Now] the sale merely consummates the courtship, at which point the marriage begins.*

THE EMERGING HUMAN ECONOMY

These trends can be best understood as opening up a complex new economic frontier. In a relatively simple past manufacturers merely sold goods, but now the maturing of Western economies is leading to far more difficult tasks. Automation, service markets, scientific breakthroughs, a closing ecological system, the growing need for public services, and demanding customers are steadily evolving within a social order based on information technology, a diversity of life styles, and an emphasis on improving the quality of life. To complicate matters, a shrinking global marketplace and the spreading of industrialization is escalating all these pressures even further. Soichiro Honda, founder of Honda Corporation, pointedly summed up the fate of institutions unable to adapt: "They shall all perish."[71]

This massive complex of intangible factors constitutes an "inner" dimension of economic life that is emerging rapidly—what sociologist Severyn Bruyn called "the social foundation of the economy that is so fundamental to its very existence."[72] In this more difficult "interior" domain, modern economies cannot hope to achieve the "hard" growth of a super-industrial society—nor can they revert to the "no" growth of an agrarian-like steady-state economy. The only feasible approach to managing a 10-fold increase in industrialization within tightening resource constraints and a decaying ecological system is to balance all these subtle factors wisely using the growing capabilities of high technology—"smart" growth.

The main criterion that will guide us through endless such dilemmas in the years ahead is the radical idea that the goal of modern economies should be to maximize human welfare. By acknowledging that the purpose of growth is not sheer physical expansion but to improve human well-being, growth is placed in perspective as a means to this higher end. The concept of smart growth, then, unifies a variety of related terms proposed by others—"human" growth, "optimal" growth, "clean" growth, "soft" growth, "quality of life," and "less is more"—by showing that their common focus is to intelligently direct all aspects of growth to serving human needs. Thus, smart growth shifts attention from material advances in the external world to a more useful, almost boundless form of social progress in this inner world of "human economy."[73]

The concept of smart growth reconciles the worker's conflict between struggling to maintain jobs in declining smokestack industries while fighting demands to reduce labor costs in order to meet competition—automation can shift people to fields that are more productive and that offer more satisfying work.

Likewise, smart growth quells management's need to urge more cars, appliances, and other goods on a public innundated with the fallout of excessive consumption or we will suffer economic stagnation—vast new markets are being created that provide vitally needed services fulfilling higher-order social needs.

Smart growth also resolves the issue of using jet travel, medical equipment, computers and other hard technologies versus the interest in self-contained communities, holistic health care, human skills, and other soft-technologies—a judicious balance among these capabilities can produce an optimal way of life.

Smart growth avoids the impossible choice between nuclear reactors, synthetic fuels, limited oil reserves, and other "hard" energy sources in contrast to conservation, solar power, biomass, and other "replenishable" supplies—it includes all of these energy forms used selectively to fit diverse needs.

Smart growth requires neither material prosperity at the expense of a dying environment nor accepting a frugal lifestyle within a pristine wilderness—benign production and pollution control systems can recycle materials to create a comfortable life while maintaining a harmonious natural world.

The complex, personal nature of this imperative requires a closer, more participative working relationship between organizations and society, and especially with clients. An impersonal marketplace may continue to be adequate for many simple functions. But for most important economic areas in the future—medical care, education, and other personal services—the need will be to expand the role of the institution so as to integrate the customer as an active member. As this closer relationship is established, we should find that the interests of both parties are better served when the purpose of enterprise encompasses the welfare of the client in addition to sales, growth, and profit. This broader mission will not be restricted to business but should include all major institutions. For instance, universities will confront tough new demands as students increasingly question the value of what they are taught and their relationship with faculty, and the medical profession will face unusual challenges as patients become active participants in their treatment.

If these changes can be further developed, the troubling decline of smokestack industries could be transformed into vast new opportunities as institutions learn to use resources more productively to serve lasting needs, thereby raising the standard of living dramatically while also improving the quality of life throughout society. Buckminster Fuller refuted the "terrible misperception that scarcity is inevitable," and Professor George Steiner claims, "We are a few years away from assuring that everyone can have a minimum level of goods and services."[74] This skillful management of the economy would then allow modern nations to turn their attention to the great challenge of truly realizing the human potential—which represents a virgin frontier of unlimited possibilities.

4
Market Networks:
THE FLOWERING OF CREATIVE ENTERPRISE

When *Time* magazine chose the personal computer as "Man of the Year" in 1983, suddenly it became clear that computers were no longer esoteric devices used by scientists, corporations, and whiz kids but common tools entering millions of ordinary offices and homes. Now this proliferation of computers is transforming institutional structures from the machine-like hierarchies of the industrial past into organic networks that are compatible with a new era based on the flow of knowledge.

The hierarchical pyramid has been the primary form of social structure since ancient times, while later it was modernized into what Galbraith called the "technostructure" of experts who run the "New Industrial State."[1] Hierarchy is such a basic American concept that a "pyramid of life" appears on the $1 bill capped by the eye of God, and most of us believe success is reached by climbing to "the top." Socialist countries have carried the idea even further because planned economies are managed by a single hierarchical system, as if Exxon were to run the entire United States.

But recent events indicate that the great pyramids of business, government, and other major institutions are collapsing, The economic crisis forced corporations to lay off blue-collar workers and middle managers whose work can now be done by robots and com-

Portions of this chapter are adapted from my article "Information Technology & the Flowering of Enterprise," *European Management Journal* (Winter 1982).

puterized information systems,[2] portending the elimination of the bottom and middle layers of the pyramid. Droves of brilliant young people like Steve Jobs, the founder of Apple Computer, are shunning big companies to start their own firms. Great empires like AT&T are disaggregating, many large corporations are threatened with extinction, and even the biggest hierarchy in America—the U.S. Government—is under fire, proving that size alone is no longer an asset but a liability.

So after centuries of faithful obedience to the rule of hierarchy, institutional pyramids everywhere are tottering, their lower halves are vanishing, and the remainder is breaking up into small pieces. "Rigid hierarchical structures have begun to crumble at the best-managed companies," noted *BusinessWeek*.[3] In a decade or so, the organizational monoliths that once formed the foundation of the industrial epoch may seem like ancient, decaying monuments of a vanishing culture that worshipped machines.

This chapter describes how information technology is dissolving hierarchical organizations into flexible market networks composed of loosely connected ventures. The large bureaucracies of the Old Capitalism produced concentrations of power that made a fiction of the ideals of individual freedom and market competition. But now, the principles of creative enterprise are finally coming to flower as progressive corporations restructure modern economies to provide the innovation for pioneering a difficult new frontier.

COMPLEXITY IN THE INFORMATION AGE

The computer could not have arrived at a better time because it is badly needed to manage the complexity of today. As the last chapter showed, an emerging frontier of smart growth promises to alter the technological base of modern economies as computerized factories and offices convert corporations into automated systems embedded within an intricate complex of economic, social, and political problems. Now a more skilled work force must be supervised using new forms of leadership. A growing ethic of less is more requires careful control of environmental pollution and energy usage. Clients come from an increasingly diverse population that includes working women, the maturing baby-boom, a melange of races, and older people, all interested in higher values. Major industries are emerging to develop sophisticated information systems, better health care, more effective education, and other services that improve the quality of life. Political demands are growing among labor, customers, investors, and the public. Continuing scientific breakthroughs will add even further to these difficult changes. And a burgeoning world economy is heightening competition and escalating resource demands manyfold.

In short, we are facing an extremely complex social order that is going to be very difficult to manage harmoniously in the years ahead, and the most critical challenge is to integrate institutions into the larger society from which they derive their very life.

Computers Replace Automobiles

The significance of this change is symbolized by the replacement of the automobile with the computer as the primary machine, or instrument, of modern economies. *Time* noted, "The enduring American love affair with the automobile is now being transformed into a giddy passion for the personal computer."[4]

Because the automobile was the principal focus about which the industrial age was organized, its influence on life has been pervasive. Automaking once used roughly one-fifth of the labor, capital, and other resources of the United States to produce an equivalent portion of the GNP, which is why the decline of this industry alone is a major cause of the economic crisis. Cars have also produced a sprawl of roads covering vast portions of the landscape with concrete and asphalt, sprinkled liberally with gas stations, billboards, and shopping centers—making pollution and traffic congestion a way of life.[5]

Automobiles will continue to be used in the information age, of course, but car sales peaked in the 1970s.[6] Where before autos were indulged as an alter-ego for Americans, now in an era of limited energy most people simply want a practical means of transportation. As the auto fades, computers are rising in importance, thereby altering the very structure of the economy. In an industrial order that focused on physical objects, the lives of most people revolved about cars because this "industrial tool" facilitated a series of moves to conduct business and personal affairs: from home—to work—to shops—to schools—to hospitals—and so on. In an age of the computer, the information contained within these institutions will instead **come to us** through powerful computerized systems. "Now, increasingly there will be alternative ways to meet and 'share a common experience,'" says Peter Drucker, "The first impact will probably be a sharp drop in business travel."[7]

As a result, institutions will no longer be discrete collections of persons working in a fixed place, but fluctuating communication networks that connect people in myriad economic and social exchanges. Alvin Toffler compared this transition to the earlier move from an agrarian to an industrial era:[8]

> Watching masses of peasants scything a field 300 years ago, only a madman would have dreamed that the time would soon come when the fields would be depopulated, when people would crowd into urban factories to earn their daily bread. . . . Today it takes an act of courage to suggest that our biggest factories and office towers may, within our lifetimes, stand half empty, reduced to ghostly warehouses or converted into living space.

It should be noted that the vacancy rate in office buildings has been increasing ominously during the past few years, which may be a sign that such changes are already occurring.[9]

A Shift from Internal Operations to External Relations

The consequence is that the frontier of economic activity is shifting from the old "internal" focus on routine operational tasks like the manufacture of goods to a new "external" focus on the use of sophisticated information systems to manage complex institutional relations. Consider, for example, the following signs suggesting an enormous increase in diversity among consumers. It is estimated that there are now more than 700 different models of cars in the United States, 200 brands of cigarettes, 4000 magazines, and 9000 radio stations. A mass mailing firm offers 55,000 different lists to its clients. The computerized U.S. Census is broken down into 250,000 distinct groups of people.[10] As cybernetician Stafford Beer noted, "the old world was characterized by the need to manage things—the new world is characterized by the need to manage complexity."[11] Journalist Russell Baker captured the result a few years ago when modern work life began changing from production to handling information, albeit still largely in the form of paper:[12]

> In the common everyday job, nothing is made anymore. Things are now made by machines. . . . Consider the typical 12-story glass building in the typical American city. Nothing is made in this building and nothing is repaired. . . . Still the building is filled with people who think of themselves as working. At any given moment of the day, perhaps one-third of them will be talking into telephones. Most of these conversations will be about paper, for paper is what occupies nearly everyone in this building. Some jobs in this building require men to fill paper with words. There are persons who type neatly on paper and persons who read the paper and jot notes in the margins. Some persons make copies of paper and other persons deliver paper. There are persons who file paper and persons who unfile paper. Some persons mail paper. . . . Some persons confer about paper. In the grandest of offices, men approve of some paper and disapprove of other paper. The elevators are filled throughout the day with . . . vital men carrying paper to be discussed with other vital men.

In an age when science is rapidly developing the means to acquire, process, store, retrieve, and disseminate virtually any form of information using communication networks that span the globe, the implications are enormous. A revolution is imminent in the way organizations work as the power of information technology makes it possible to manipulate this knowledge electronically from almost anywhere rather than shuffling paper in an office.

There persists a fear that this technology will reduce work to its simple, inhuman basics by driving out the skill of the craftsman. But a long-term perspective shows this is not true generally. The main change has been the level of "abstraction" in work. In an agrarian society the vast majority of people worked at menial tasks on farms, in an industrial era they tended machines, and now in an information age they handle knowledge. Some of this new "knowledge work" is also menial and boring, of course, but routine tasks are precisely what computers are good at, leaving humans free to handle more demanding jobs. Almost half of young people attend college today, producing for the first time in history a society composed mainly of a professional class. George Beitzel, a senior vice president at IBM, estimates that "by 1989 there will be 60 million office workers, comprised of 40 million managers and professionals."[13]

The long-term trend is fairly clear. Working life was once characterized by physical labor and repetitive routine, but today most jobs are fraught with difficult interpersonal relations, information overload, and other stressful, confusing problems that defy our crude institutional mechanisms. These needs are creating a modern equivalent of "economic man" who is not primarily occupied with physical concerns but with social and intellectual interests—what could be thought of as a new prototype of "intellectual man." "Where once we stood simply on the edge of the production line," said social critic Douglas Davis, "we stand now on the edge of consciousness."[14]

The Revolutionary Power of Information Technology

Obviously, it will take decades for these events to unfold, and nobody fully understands how they will work out. However, one thing is certain: information technology is a revolutionary force that is introducing a vastly more turbulent society which could easily fly apart into uncontrollable disorder—yet it also offers the main hope for managing this spiraling growth of rich complexity. Even now the growing power of computerized information systems is converting scores of corporations into a modern equivalent of the factory—"knowledge-manufacturing systems" that focus their efforts on collecting, analyzing, and distributing huge amounts of data. As a result, the role of executives in large institutions is shifting toward the management of an organization as a large, complex information network, operating in real time to create new knowledge.[15]

One major effect of this structural transformation will be to radically alter the types of jobs and enterprises in modern economies. Adam Osborne, creator of the portable computer, claims: "Of all jobs in the industrial world today, perhaps half will be eliminated during the next 25 years . . . Entire industries . . . have been severely crippled or wiped out by competition from a quarter they never anticipated

. . . . That is the consequence of revolution." Ironically, Osborne himself became a victim of this revolution when his own firm failed.[16]

Because information forms the invisible links that bind a society together, this new technology has the power to dramatically shift our sense of reality and accelerate all other forms of social change. Computerized telecommunications networks enable people to interact faster and more widely, they speed up the rate of technological innovation, amplify our ability to control events, enrich our environment with more accurate information, offer broader choices, extend our range of experience, provide greater knowledge, and heighten awareness—thereby contributing to the forces that drive social evolution. Clive Sinclair, the English entrepreneur who invented the first pocket-sized electronic calculator, believes, "The 1990s will differ from the 1970s as profoundly as the 19th century from the 18th."[17] An essay in a Berkeley underground newspaper dramatized the meaning of this new form of power:[18]

> Communication systems will spread like a raging fire, out of control, beyond prediction, the mirror image of a bursting comet. Every man, every woman will soon be able to be a star in the heavens and will of his own mind, and as free to spread his own message as the limits of the imagination permit. Freed from the technological constrictions of antiquated communication structures, the mass will vanish, the individualistic appear, and a renaissance of the creative spirit will dawn.

Such unsettling prospects present a warning that modern economies have entered an era of unusual, difficult, constant change that cannot be mastered using hierarchical structures. That's why contemporary institutions are pervaded by a sense of ineptness, a chronic aridity of thought, and an emptiness of the spirit that has produced widespread declines in productivity, innovation, and commitment, along with grumblings of rebellion and despair. But a quiet trickle of fresh ideas is flowing from creative entrepreneurs that may swell into a wave of change to wash away these obsolete pyramids. The existing organizational infrastructure was built on the foundations of the assembly line, and now the computer is creating an upheaval in the economic order that should alter the structure, behavior, and texture of society as a whole. *BusinessWeek* warned:[19]

> *. . . considering the impetus behind the electronics revolution, these early changes may represent only the first tremors of an earthquake.*

CONFEDERATIONS OF ENTREPRENEURS

This complexity of the information age demands its own structural form, just as the industrial age produced an inevitable fit between physical technology and the monolithic pyramids that governed the past. The task of creating efficient production systems required centrally controlled hierarchies, but in a post-industrial era organizations must provide myriad quick, flexible responses in order to handle the exploding turbulence that comprises the central challenge of today. Philosopher C. West Churchman expressed it best: "The spirit of our age is to hit complexity straight on, taking it for what it is."[20]

Various intellectual fields all indicate the same technological imperative. In management science, scholars agree on the principle that organizations—like all other organisms—must adapt to a more turbulent environment by developing "organic" structures. In general systems theory, a "law of requisite variety" holds that the degree of environmental complexity any system faces must be matched by an equally more powerful control system. In information science, it is widely accepted that the more diverse the social system the more information that must flow between its constituent parts.[21]

How can we hope to create such sophisticated institutions? By bringing the principles of free enterprise that govern the external marketplace right into organizations themselves. Thomas Gilmore of the Wharton School posed the challenge this way:[22]

> *We can no longer control people by authority and bureaucracy. Ways must be found to create real entrepreneurial opportunities for managers who want them within corporate frameworks. I see that as a major challenge for the American economic system.*

The model that is emerging now to provide this flexibility is an organizational equivalent of the dominant structural form of the future—the networks created by information systems. In place of rigid hierarchical control, networks are organized on organic principles that permit changing interconnections, thereby offering a more powerful form of control able to manage a turbulent environment. "The network is the institution of our time," observed Marilyn Ferguson, Editor of *The Leading Edge Bulletin*, and John Naisbitt predicted, "In the future, institutions will be organized according to a management system based on the networking model."[23]

Networks are growing all about us as they become the icons of a high-tech society. Financial networks are forming as electronic transactions connect banks, shops, and clients. Radio and television networks have created a global village. Personal networks are evolving through linkages of people sharing common interests. As a result, the United States is becoming what scholars Starr Roxanne Hiltz and Murray Turoff describe as a "Network Nation": "In place of a society as a collection of communities . . . now it is a complex set of overlapping networks." Even in Russia, a Soviet computer scientist claims, "Communications networks, data banks, and information systems make necessary an administration which differs completely from what has gone before . . . international, nonhierarchical cooperative systems."[24]

First Steps: The Multidimensional Matrix Arrives

Business began the move away from hierarchies and toward networks years ago with the development of a matrix form of organization. The matrix is defined as a "multiple command system." It comprises "a new species of business organization" that "represents a sharp break with traditional forms of business," said Walter Wriston when he was CEO of Citicorp.[25]

As Table 4.1 shows, about two-thirds of 25 firms in a study I conducted were structured along more than one organizational dimension: functional areas, product divisions or project teams, client or marketing groups, and geographic regions. The matrix is controversial, but it is an established fact today because most large

TABLE 4.1.   MULTIPLE HIERARCHIES IN LARGE CORPORATIONS

	Hierarchical Dimensions of Organization			
	Functional Areas of Expertise	Products or Projects	Clients or Markets	Geographic Regions
Exxon	*			*
General Motors	*	*		
Texaco	*	*		*
IBM		*		*
General Electric	*	*		
Atlantic Richfield		*		
Dow Chemical		*		
United Technologies	*	*	*	
Boeing	*	*		
Xerox		*	*	
TRW		*		
Texas Instruments		*		
Crown-Zellerbach		*		
Mead		*		
Hewlett-Packard		*		
Digital Equipment	*	*	*	*
Clarck Equipment		*		
Rexnord	*	*		*
Bankamerica			*	*
Citicorp			*	*
Mariott		*		*
Comsat	*	*		
Walt Disney		*		
Hoffman-LaRoche	*	*		

Source: William E. Halal, *Strategic Planning in Major US Corporations* (General Motors Report, 1980). Also published in "Strategic Management: The State-of-the-Art & Beyond," *Technological Forecasting & Social Change* (May 1984).

organizations must of necessity operate different types of units that cut across one another. One company in this study, GE, summed up the rationale this way:[26]

> We've highlighted matrix organization (because it's) a bellwether of things to come . . . all of us are going to have to learn how to utilize organization to prepare managers to increasingly deal with higher levels of complexity and ambiguity in situations where they have

*to get results from people and components not under their direct
control . . . where so many complex, conflicting interests must be
balanced.*

The Paradox of Power: Achieving Control through Freedom

But there are many approaches to matrix organization. Early applications were "centralized grids" in which two command systems
simultaneously controlled operating units, producing—not greater
flexibility—but greater rigidity by compounding problems through
two overlapping bureaucratic hierarchies. Texas Instruments, for
example, was recently forced to free its profit centers from the
stifling effects of a two-dimensional grid controlled by both "strategic"
and "operating" executives.[27]

The centralized grid failed to provide the flexibility that is so
badly needed because it exemplifies the worst features of the old
"rational," or "mechanistic," model of management. By having two
hierarchies rather than one, the grid highlights the perennial dilemma
facing all institutions: reconciling the conflicting demands of providing freedom for innovation—while maintaining control against
disorder. Some executives abdicate their responsibility and permit
anarchy to go unchecked, but the more typical response is a confining,
even dictatorial, overuse of power that strangles the very life out
of institutions. Robert Levison, an operating executive at a major
company, described the result:[28]

*As a businessman I am sick and tired of the waste . . . that our present
highly centralized forms of management create. . . . big companies
have become almost socialistic in their policies and practices . . .
the division manager is summoned to corporate headquarters every
so often for an "indepth review." Typically, you have 25 corporate
executives [questioning] your operation like drama critics called in
to review a tottering Broadway production. . . . The payoff? Humiliated
division managers, who learn once more that their job is to execute
orders, not to make decisions . . . and a hodge-podge of numbers . . .
to juggle [in order to] make them come out the way the experts
thought they ought to come out. . . . management people throughout
the United States [should] rise up in rebellion.*

The problem seems to be that the old concept of hierarchical control is so entrenched in our society that most executives find it hard to allow people the freedom to do things on their own; there is a sort of myth of the "macho" manager who guards against disorder by maintaining detailed knowledge of everything in his organization. But as the difficulty of coping with escalating turbulence in a large complex organization increases, these threats are dealt with by redoubled efforts to impose still more controls, creating an impossible situation in which the executive tries vainly to gain a Godlike omniscience in knowing "each sparrow that falls." Peters and Waterman describe the underlying beliefs of this old philosophy that produces rigid complexity, time-consuming committees, deadening analyses, and endless approvals from higher authority:[29]

> *Big is better ... make sure everything is carefully and formally coordinated ... the manager's job is decision making ... analyze everything ... produce fat planning volumes ... get rid of the disturbers of the peace ... control everything ... keep things tidy ... specify the organization structure in great detail ... write long job descriptions.*

This old type of control is so overwhelming that managers become bottlenecks impeding action, and the chief executive is usually the biggest bottleneck. Additionally, the organization is doomed to mediocrity because all "unapproved" behavior becomes suspect, leading to a sterility of thought that is anathema to innovation. One of the most debilitating features of institutional life today is that most large organizations suppress creative dissent, causing executives to be surrounded by "yes-men" while those with new ideas are regarded as critical malcontents. Peter Drucker quipped, "So much of what we call management consists in making it difficult for people to work."[30]

A centralized control system at Xerox was so stifling that engineers could not modify design details (like the size of a light bulb in a copier) without complicated approvals; "What should have taken two weeks to a month took two years," a typical Xerox manager lamented. Ford was laboring under 15 levels of management—while Toyota used 6; a Ford supervisor described his response: "If we had to go through channels, we would never get anything done." At Levi-Strauss a groaning organizational behemoth became so unwieldy that an executive admitted: "We had enough staff and organization to run General Motors." James Affleck, CEO of American Cyanamid, summed up the problem:[31]

> We will have to recognize that no chief executive or management team can or should attempt to manage the activities of thousands, or hundreds of thousands, of individuals under their nominal control eight hours a day. That cannot be done any more than their thoughts can be managed.

It is becoming clear that the solution is a new "business contract" combining tight control of **performance** with freedom of **operations**—what Peters and Waterman call "simultaneous loose-tight properties." Thus, both control and freedom are enhanced by defining assignments on a contractual basis: holding business units accountable for agreed-upon goals, while also allowing almost complete freedom to achieve results as they see fit. "The basic orientation of the entire organization must be psychologically attuned to results," said William Coggin, an executive at Dow Corning.[32]

A wealth of research evidence shows that people are very capable of selecting their assignments, defining their work roles, and choosing their coworkers to produce "bottom-up" structures that have been called "self-designed systems." Large organizations are thereby broken up into a flux of smaller units able to govern themselves, which then instills a vital spirit of commitment and innovation. Professor Peter Vaill, who has pioneered in the study of high-performing systems, observed, "Clarification of purposes is a prominent feature of every high performing system I have ever investigated," while Peters and Waterman found that the most creative projects in big firms are usually small illicit "skunk works" run by a few eccentric but highly motivated geniuses.[33]

By maintaining central control over results but decentralizing operations, the paradox of control versus freedom is being resolved to achieve a superior form of control—not at the expense of freedom, but **through** freedom—by allowing large numbers of self-managed enterprises to nibble away at complex problems. Richard Cornuelle, a former executive at the National Association of Manufacturers, described the result as "Demanaging America . . . the process is self-managing. It works without authority, and it works sensibly, creating order out of potential chaos."[34] Although the idea may seem different, it simply represents an extension of the trend that began decades ago when growing corporations found it necessary to decentralize into semi-autonomous product divisions.

Major forces are now relentlessly restructuring big corporations in this direction. Competition is producing great pressure to reduce administrative overhead and permit greater freedom for innovation, while powerful new information systems are making it possible to automate middle management functions. As a result, it is estimated that 90 percent of the top 100 firms have reorganized to eliminate middle management jobs. Companies like Firestone, Crown-Zellerbach, Chrysler, Brunswick, and Xerox have cut their management ranks by as much as 40 percent, and many have dropped entire management levels so that product managers report directly to the CEO. Some establish a rule of thumb limiting the hierarchy to no more than six levels between the CEO and any employee. W. James Fish, Manager of Personnel at Ford, claims, "We're looking at a total restructuring of American business." *BusinessWeek* summed up the change:[35]

> As top managers see that much of the information once gathered by middle managers can be obtained by computers, they have begun to view many middle managers as 'redundant.' . . . They look on the very fiefdoms they have created as vast cost centers . . . Corporate structure is changing to let data flow from shop floor to executive suite without the editing, monitoring, and second-guessing that had been the middle manager's function. . . . corporate pyramids are flattened, with fewer levels . . . [CEO's] are frantically trying to push [decisions] down to those who are closest to the marketplace, giving more autonomy to plant managers, sales people, and engineers . . . creating environments in which compensation depends on performance, and freedom to improve performance provides the psychic reward.

These reorganizations are not temporary, nor are they minor adjustments. They reflect the beginning of an historic restructuring of large institutions that was anticipated long ago by management scholars like Herbert Simon who foresaw the automation of middle-management, Warren Bennis who proposed the use of organic organizations, and executives like Peter Townsend who rejuvenated Avis by reducing its encrusted bureaucracy.[36]

Beyond the Grid: Decentralized Networks

Thus, the grid seems to be an intermediate stage between the traditional hierarchy and a full-fledged network, and the critical element that transforms the matrix into this flexible system is freedom. In its mature form, the matrix is decentralized to allow units and individuals to move through the system freely, taking on responsibilities as they choose and drawing on the organization's capital, facilities, personnel, and information to accomplish their task. The responsibility of executives is to define the framework of the system, set up a basis for accountability and incentives, and encourage an "internal market" to allocate resources spontaneously rather than through administrative fiat. Additionally, an advanced matrix may incorporate three or even four dimensions, which increases the variety of units and the degrees of freedom. Digital Equipment and Dow Corning are structured as four-dimensional matrices, and these firms are known for their sound management. William Coggin at Dow Corning described his organization this way:[37]

> The single most pressing problem that faces any industrial organization is how to cope with change. The multidimensional organization is designed to combat that problem . . . We perceive our organization to be a dynamic one, and to date, our experience indicates that we do indeed have the ability to manage change rather than be managed by it.

Figure 4.1 illustrates a matrix network for three dimensions incorporating product, functional, and geographic command structures. The productive heart of the system is composed of small business units spun off product divisions as innovative ventures. These ventures operate as profit centers, developing and distributing new products and services. Functional units typically recruit, train, and release specialists to work on products and geographic units. They are usually cost-centers, but may also sell their advice and assistance to other units using internal transfer prices to become profit-centers. Geographic areas may also be profit centers, buying products from

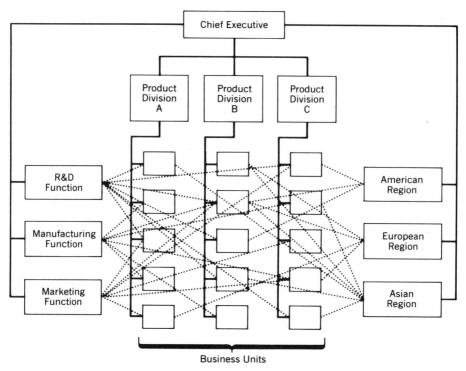

Figure 4-1.   Network formed by a 3-dimensional decentralized matrix.

product divisions and distributing them to clients in their region, thereby providing the closer, more integrated service that single product divisions cannot. This dynamic flow of market relations constitutes the fluid, organic quality that is uniquely advantageous about a network. From this view, the organization is no longer seen as a one- or two-dimensional hierarchy, but as a web of tensions that may pull in different directions, yet held together by pockets of productive collaboration. Numerous examples indicate that decentralization is catching on.[38]

Hewlett-Packard holds employees accountable for project results but gives them wide operating latitude. The firm has created a "striking new managerial style with a uniquely American entrepreneurial spirit," as one executive described it. "The financial controls are very tight—what is loose is how (people) choose to meet those goals."

Tandem Computer has an entrepreneurial environment that is easy going but demands results. "Most companies are overmanaged," said an executive, "We give [people] a lot of responsibility and tell them where we want them to go. The one percent who abuse the freedom we fire. It's that simple."

Interlake sold its failing steel plants to new owners who permitted plant managers local control over all major decisions. The newly organized firm, Newport Steel Corporation, sparked a renaissance of entrepreneurial behavior and commitment that produced a striking turnaround.

TRW has achieved success using a philosophy of management autonomy. A vice president explains, "We don't legislate anything out of corporate headquarters," while a division manager says, "It's my responsibility to find ways to grow this business—not the president's."

Xerox has decentralized control of its 24 strategic business units to grant operating managers authority to select the products and technologies they feel are most promising, speeding up the process of getting a product to the market from years to months. Even support units, like the company's Logistics and Distribution Group, are being converted into profit centers selling their services to Xerox product units and to outside firms.

GE has decentralized to allow business units to do their own planning, it has doubled the level of expenditures not requiring authorization, and extended its incentive system to cover 5000 managers. The CEO, John Welch, expressed his philosophy this way: "If you pick the right people and give them an opportunity to spread their wings—and put compensation as a carrier behind it—you [almost] don't have to manage them."

Eagle-Pitcher claims, "Decentralization is a virtual religion with us." The company provides capital to operating managers, but gives them complete control over budgets, profits, capital investments, marketing, product development, and salaries.

Curtice-Burns has a central staff of only 12 people because it allows its seven divisions to operate autonomously. The chairman says of the risks entailed: "We, as managers, have to have failures to learn."

This new organizational freedom is also fostered by a number of variations on the traditional nine to five, five-day a week job, such as the use of flexitime schedules, part-time jobs, temporary work, and job sharing. It is estimated that half of the workers in West Germany use some variation of flexitime, as well as roughly 20 percent of all Europeans. In Switzerland, 95 percent of the workers favor the concept. In the United States temporary help is growing at 20 percent per year and includes 4 million workers, while 30 percent of American employees use various forms of flexible scheduling.[39]

These moves may soon pale in comparison to what will occur as the growth of computerized information systems "short-circuits" the traditional hierarchy. Distributed information networks linking individual microcomputers together, all hooked up nationally through teleconferencing systems, should revolutionize the way institutions behave. White-collar workers will then be able to conduct their jobs virtually anywhere, rather than in the confines of the office, becoming what Alvin Toffler called a new breed of "teleworkers" who operate "electronic cottage" industries. About 5 million Americans work out of their homes now, most of whom are "telecommuters" employed by 450 companies experimenting with the idea, mainly because productivity gains can reach 50 percent. Studies at the University of Southern California estimate that 10 million people will be telecommuting by 1990, and Toffler claims half of the population could do so now.[40] Consider the following:[41]

Microcomputers are predicted to become the organizing focus of the work habits of 65 percent of all workers by 1990.

Fortune 500 Companies are almost all implementing systems that provide computerized data files, teleconferencing, electronic mail, and other such capabilities.

Texas Instruments has installed an information network that links 50 plants in 19 countries in a corporate-wide network that sends 100,000 messages a day at an average cost of eight cents.

Bank of America executives in different cities have been holding regular teleconference meetings since 1968, and **Aetna** has done the same since 1981.

Atlantic Richfield has installed a $17 million teleconferencing system that connects its Los Angeles headquarters with offices around the nation. The company expects to save $10 million per year in travel expenses while providing faster communications.

Ford Motor Company recently held a video conference showing new car models to 18,000 dealers and sales people at 38 sites.

Sears, Roebuck is planning a video network linking offices in 26 cities.

Public Teleconferencing Networks are being established for commercial use by AT&T, VideoNet, Hilton Hotels, and Intelmet.

As these trends develop, a new electronic freedom may soon become a reality in large organizations. Murray Turoff, the developer of one of the first computerized networks, points out: "The beauty of [an electronic information system] is that it does not impose to any great degree a social structure but lets people develop their own." At Bell Research Laboratories, a trial of computerized conferencing shifted communications from working through headquarters to direct lateral contacts. The chairman of AT&T at that time, John DeButts, said, "The Bell System's main aim in seeking to apply the computer to our operations is not efficiency; it is freedom." Terrence Deal and Allen Kennedy, authorities on changing corporate cultures, predict:[42]

> [Information technology will produce] an "atomized organization" in which individuals will be connected by the information network and a common culture rather than the organizational chart.

The Entrepreneurial Boom

A decentralized network is more than a "flexible structure," but an "entrepreneurial **system**" that uses its flexibility to encourage innovative ventures. Mergers are concentrating economic power into a few global corporations dominating each industry world-wide, so there is an urgent need to find a way of taming the threat of bureaucracy as organizations grow ever larger. The solution is evolving now as market networks spawn multitudes of semi-autonomous "internal" enterprises. Peters and Waterman found that excellent companies are all good at "chunking"—breaking a complex system into self-contained units that are manageable in size.[43] Here are some examples:[44]

IBM used a self-contained, autonomous "independent business unit" (IBU) to develop its successful personal computer, and the same concept is being applied to 15 other new ventures.

Apple developed its revolutionary Macintosh computer using an "A team" strategy that emulates the original "garage" operation which launched the company; the concept allows a small handpicked group almost complete freedom to work within the corporation.

Hewlett-Packard spins off new divisions when they exceed 1500 people to sustain the sense of small, autonomous units. "If we're going to improve productivity," argues an executive, "workers have got to care."

Texas Instruments has created thousands of small problem-solving teams to improve various aspects of their operations, and is decentralizing into small autonomous profit-centers.

GE scattered production of aircraft engines from a former centralized plant into eight "satellite" plants.

3M Company's 52,000 employees are divided into smaller units that average 270 people to produce a total of 50,000 products. A vice president said, "We make a conscious effort to keep our units as small as possible because we think it helps keep them flexible and vital. One consistent request we get from our people is that they be allowed to run a business of their own."

Dana Corporation created the "store manager" concept to give 90 factory managers almost complete autonomy for all aspects of their operations.

Procter & Gamble uses the brand manager role to encourage entrepreneurial control of each product in their line.

Crown-Zellerbach has integrated credit, labor, marketing, and sales functions at 16 container plants, producing higher productivity and lower costs.

Kollmorgan, a hi-tech company of 4500 employees, consists of 13 divisions further decentralized into autonomous product teams. The company strives to create a "spirit of freedom, equality, mutual trust and respect," which has been so successful that sales have doubled every 3½ years.

Covergent Technologies creates a "strike force" to take on new ventures as a "company-within-a-company."

Nucor Corporation operates mini-steel mills using teams of 20–30 employees who work at lower fixed pay but receive bonuses that may double their income. Ken Iverson, the CEO, claims, "We're trying to eliminate the hierarchy."

This trend toward small-scale enterprise is destined to grow because the high technologies that will dominate the future do not require large amounts of capital and economies of scale. Providing services, the development of software, R&D, information handling, and other aspects of smart growth lend themselves to small ventures. As the above examples show, even manufacturing plants can become smaller "focused factories" that minimize bureaucracy because automation permits economies of scale as low as a few hundred units. Average size of new plants decreased from 644 employees in 1970 to 210 in 1980. The new "mini-steel mills," for instance, have enjoyed such strong growth that their share of domestic steel production has increased to almost 20 percent. New "mini-photo labs" that operate locally to provide 1-hour color film service are springing up by the thousands to capture a growing share of the market from giants like Kodak. Beer is being made increasingly in "microbreweries" that can produce small runs of more expensive brands for special market niches. Dr. Koji Kobayashi, Chairman of Japanese Electronics Company, predicted:[45]

> [The information age] will lead to the demise of today's large centralized factories [to be] replaced by networks of relatively small, widely distributed, and extremely versatile factories that can build individual products to individual orders.

Chapter 3 showed how the opportunites for smart growth are virtually limitless, which can be seen now in a rising tide of startup ventures that represents only the beginning of a great wave of high-tech innovation to come in the years ahead. The number of new ventures increased from 93,000 per year in 1950 to more than 600,000 in 1984. During this same time, half of the Fortune 500 firms disappeared through mergers or failures. Investment in venture capital has also increased dramatically as 900 new companies raised $13 billion in stock equity during 1983, about ten times the amount raised in previous years. Terrence McClary, head of venture investment for GE believes, "We are at the tip of the iceberg in the exploitation and application of technology."[46]

Big corporations are starting to respond to this boom not only to take advantage of a good thing, but simply to combat the threat these new ventures pose. Goliath IBM was forced to move quickly to regain its dominant position after the David of Apple Computer took the lead in the exploding future of personal computers. Other large corporations like GE, TRW, Exxon, GM, and Xerox are frantically searching for ways to establish a claim on new businesses that are popping up like spring flowers by using licensing deals, capital investment, and joint ventures. GE invested $100 million in 30 promising startup companies.[47]

But these are attempts to cash in on the success of independent entrepreneurs, whereas the real challenge facing big corporations is to make their own organizations hospitable to innovation. Exxon finally had to divest its Information Systems Group after its heavy hand stifled the creativity of that young enterprise. Xerox drove away its promising Diablo Systems and Schugart Associates divisions because of highly centralized controls. A former Intel manager, who left to start out on his own, recalls, "If I wanted to do a new product at Intel, I had to visit all those committees." James Brian Quinn at MIT observes:[48]

> *Many corporations fail to tolerate the creative fanatic who has been the driving force behind most major innovations. . . . [he] is obnoxious, impatient, egotistic, and perhaps a bit irrational in organizational terms.*

On the other hand, entrepreneurs need the company as much as it needs them. Starting a new business is fraught with risk, filled with agonizing doubt, and overwhelming in its demands on individuals who go it alone. People like Steve Jobs, who founded Apple Computer, represent the few who survive such an ordeal. For every Steve Jobs there are at least two to three other creative and dedicated people who fail and are left financially and emotionally bankrupt, while scores more are simply afraid to take the enormous risk. Americans regard the entrepreneur as a hero, but this glorifies the harsh truth that the Herculean challenge of starting a business is so difficult that most of our society's creative talent goes unused.

The problem is being resolved now as progressive corporations learn to provide an entrepreneurial environment in which talented people can develop their ideas into successful new ventures. GE's McClary claims, "Some people are stifled in a corporate environment. We want to get them into one where they can be more creative." Gordon Moore, Chairman of Intel, described how to avoid losing good talent: "our best defense is to keep this an exciting place to work." To really put some teeth into these intentions, companies like TRW are offering stock equity and other incentives that give a piece of the action to engineers, technicians, and even secretaries for helping a startup succeed. William Miller, President of SRI, believes, "This may be a permanent change in the way we do business."[49]

Conversely, small entrepreneurs are learning that big corporations are useful for providing venture capital, risk assuming capacity, access to technology and facilities, and colleagues to collaborate with. A manager who started a new venture at Convergent Technologies credited a major part of his success to the fact that, "We had a healthy company behind us, with the financial resources to help things happen;" senior managers acted as "kind of an informal board of directors."[50]

The consequence is to redefine the very nature of big business. Rather than the traditional concept of a bureaucratic hierarchy of decision-makers, large organizations are rapidly becoming what Norman Macrae, an editor at *The Economist*, called "confederations of entrepreneurs." Executives at GE expressed the new strategy this way:[51]

> *Our philosophy is to encourage talented managers to act as entrepreneurs expert in their businesses, markets, and communities with direction and support from the corporate headquarters. . . . We're trying to reshape GE in the minds of its employees as a band of small businessess . . . to take the strength of a large company and act with the agility of a small company.*

If more corporations can foster this new mode of internal enterprise, the culture of business should shift away from the hierarchical fetish for controls, rational analysis, and paperwork toward that single ingredient that marks the successful entrepreneur—action. Discipline and accountability remain essential, of course, but organizational excellence today is distinguished by fluid environments that offer opportunities to experiment, to take risks, to try out new ideas.

The Intrapreneur

The role of employees in an organizational network is similar to the professional model of self-employed physicians, engineers, and attorneys. People are free to move within this organic field, contracting for various responsibilities to create, in essence, their professional "practice." Norman Macrae foresees even clerical tasks being contracted for by self-managed units that compete with one another within the organization—ushering in the age of the ***intra**preneur* —in order "to give ordinary people more scope for becoming tycoons."

Management scientist Jay Forrester envisions future working relations this way:[52]

> In the new organization, an individual would not be assigned to a superior. Instead he would negotiate, as a free individual, a continually changing structure of relationships.

A large "intrapreneur movement" is gathering momentum in Sweden, other parts of Europe, and the United States. The focus now is on implementation, and with fleshing out the concept by defining "intracapital" and other management practices to form the internal equivalent of an external market. There is such strong interest in the possibility of transforming bureaucracies into innovative enterprises that *The Economist* called intrapreneurship, "a major social invention." Following are a few examples:[53]

3M Company allows personnel to choose their assignments, and any one with an idea for a new venture may shop around at various divisions to obtain capital and support. The result has been described this way: "[The company] is so intent on innovation that its essential atmosphere seems not like that of a large corporation but rather a loose network of laboratories and cubbyholes populated by feverish inventors and dauntless entrepreneurs."

Arthur D. Little is an international consulting firm that has been managed as an organic network for years. The autonomy of self-managed teams of professionals is so keen that the old superior-subordinate relationship is reversed and the responsibility of management is to support its employees. A company document states: "Most high-ranking administrators consider their roles to be that of facilitating the work of the professional staff."

Levi-Strauss put up $3 million in venture capital to fund six internal projects, one of which, "Two-Horse Jeans," has been the firm's "single most profitable product." The funding has been increased now to $4 million.

Control Data has started 80 small ventures in the past few years.

McCormick & Co. has developed a bidding system that allows employees to compete for better jobs.

Advanced Technology is a new firm built on the principle of fostering entrepreneurial ventures among its employees. The company "reorganizes as it grows" organically, and after five years it now employs more than 1000 employees that produce almost $100 million in sales.

AT&T has starting a campaign to promote high-technology ventures backed by $20 million in investment capital to support the ideas of employees, which has thus far produced six projects.

One healthy outcome may be to legitimize internal competition. There is a terrible fear among "organization men" that competition may detract from the efforts of other units, which is a bit strange in a society that professes the free enterprise ethic. Interesting cultural studies show that the degree of individualism a nation permits is strongly related to its wealth-producing capacity. The United States is a highly individualistic nation, yet we have severely restricted the freedom of employees in large organizations, thereby failing to use this cultural trait very effectively.[54]

Whereas successful corporations like IBM, Hewlett-Packard, 3M, Texas Instruments, and Procter & Gamble have long had a policy of encouraging internal competition for the same reason it is fostered in the economy as a whole: in a world of unmanageable complexity, competition allows the best solutions to emerge. P&G encourages "a free for all among brands with no holds barred" because "creative conflict . . . is the only way to keep from becoming too clumsy." IBM favors parallel projects until a competing review—a "shoot-out"—is held to determine which approach is to be further developed.[55]

As intrapreneurs gain greater freedom to break down the old "industrial" concept of work, an even greater variety of working arrangements should emerge that we can only guess at. One possibility is to relinquish the idea that people should devote their allegience to a single organization. Professional employees are increasingly taking on assignments for different institutions, expanding the intrapreneur model to become true entrepreneurs who cultivate a professional practice that cuts across—not just departments—but entire organizations. Xerox Ltd. in England encourages managers to work as "outside consultants" operating out of their homes so they can take assignments for other firms as well. Various authorities in the field offer some startling visions:[56]

Home based businesses are growing and they are going to expand terrifically. . . . Over the next 10–20 years, most people in all levels of business will work at home at least two or three days a week. . . .

The way we work in this society is going to be transformed. . . . The 9–5 era is over.

The result could not only benefit individuals, it could prove a boon to institutions by providing access to a far greater range of talent than they could employ on a full-time, permanent basis, and by increasing flexibility in the work force during times of expansion and contraction.

Interorganizational Networks: The Global Suprasystem

Such linkages between organizations are expanding to form *inter*-organizational networks that connect entire organizations to one another. The most traditional examples are between organizations in the same field, such as trade associations and real estate brokers jointly listing property. A modern example is the Briarpatch Network, consisting of almost 200 small shops that have formed a loosely connected cooperative in the San Francisco area to assist one another.[57] Another common form of cross-institutional network is the Japanese tradition of Zaibatsu in which a variety of firms join together for their mutual benefit, roughly equivalent to the American conglomerate. Small firms also cluster as satellites to a large "host" manufacturer, a common practice among major corporations, their suppliers, and distributors in industries like auto manufacturing and aerospace. These arrangements are going to increase dramatically as information technology fosters a proliferation of small scale ventures, such as the "mom and pop" hi-tech cottage industries that are springing up as software and small part suppliers, forming a network of feeders to large host companies.[58]

The more unusual arrangements are hybrid associations, such as the partnerships that all American auto makers have formed recently with their counterparts abroad. While GM, Ford, and Chrysler compete against Toyota, Fiat, Renault, and other foreign auto firms, they are also cooperating with these adversaries in making and selling auto parts and entire cars for one another. This phenomenon is also flourishing in hi-tech fields where a dozen or so joint ventures and research consortiums have been consummated. Even IBM and its new rival, AT&T, are beginning to share some computer products.[59] Thus, the economy is developing startling new structural forms that exceed what would have been considered bizarre fantasies just a few years ago.

This intermeshing growth of interorganizational networks is making it difficult to tell where one organization stops and another begins. There are estimated to be some 1.3 million corporations in the United States today, 90,000 schools and universities, 330,000 churches, and myriad other miscellaneous institutions, all interacting with one another to weave a rich tapestry of social structure.[60] Some of these links were always in place, of course, but now they are expanding as information systems increasingly connect organizations into working relationships that constitute the organic structure of the economy and society itself. The entire real estate industry, for example, is merging into a single national market operated by information exchanges that list all property in the United States. Academics are studying the growth of this new phenomenon, which has been identified as "interorganizational relations," "coalitional structures," and "transorganizational systems." Social scientists specializing in this field summed up the implications:[61]

> Patterns of linkage and dominance between large-scale organizations are basic features of social organization in [advanced] societies. . . . Progress in research on interorganizational relations will very likely pave the way for analytically linking the study of organizations with the study of total societies.

At the world level, international networks like the Law of the Sea Conference, political blocs like the Common Market, multinational research programs, and other such collaborative efforts among nations are growing exponentially. Jessica Lipnack and Jeff Stamps, who have pioneered the study of networks, report the number of international organizations increased from 1000 in 1950, to 4000 in 1970, and to 20,000 in 1982. Thus, global networks are rapidly coalescing into an institutional suprasystem for the planet, with nation states, transnational corporations, and other major organizations acting as nodes in this system. As theologian-anthropologist Teilhard de Chardin speculated long ago, the conclusion should be a tightly knit constellation of human organization covering the entire globe which interacts as a single unified organism. Marshall McLuhan foresaw this prospect at the beginning of the information age: "It is a principal aspect of the electric age that it establishes a global network that has much of the character of our central nervous system." And Alvin Toffler updated the vision:[62]

> What appears to be emerging is neither a corporation-dominated future nor a global government but a far more complex system similar to the matrix organizations we saw springing up in certain industries. Rather than one or a few pyramidal global bureaucracies, we are weaving nets of matrices that mesh different kinds of organizations with common interests. . . . In short, we are moving toward a world system composed of units densely interrelated like the neurons in a brain rather than organized like the departments of a bureaucracy.

FROM PYRAMIDS TO LIVING SYSTEMS

Naturally, this brave new world of computer based organizational networks has its drawbacks. Many people do not like the idea of working with complex, impersonal information systems, and others abhor being isolated in one's home as a place of work. Some managers are nonplussed at the notion of controlling employees who work away from the office. "We're trained to supervise people who are sitting there and who look like they're working," said one worried manager. These problems may be alleviated as teleconferencing becomes commonly available to provide some sense of personal contact. Certainly, nobody advocates replacing normal human contacts with exotic information technologies, but simply to augment face-to-face relationships.

Of course, many organizations cannot rely on market structures but will remain committed to the traditional "command and control" approach. Large, highly precise projects like military operations and space launches demand the close coordination of thousands of people in split-second timing. It is hard to envision a military commander asking his unit if they would like to "take that hill" when and how they see fit. As IBM reminds us in its ads, information is power, and this power can be used either to create decentralized networks or to improve centralized control. So there will be a rich growth of different structural forms that suit the unique needs of differing institutions. If we were to think of mechanistic versus organic structures as a continuum ranging from 0 to 10, most bureaucratic organizations today would be at about 2 to 3 on this scale, while the adaptive ones would be located at about 7 to 8. These are differences of degree, and even the most organic institutions will retain a basic hierarchy as a rudimentary skeleton supporting the networks that form their living tissues.

One of the most controversial aspects of market systems is that multiple reporting relationships blur the lines of authority. This problem raises a common fear that unmanageable conflict will result from violating an ageless belief going back to the Bible, "No man can serve two masters," as well as the traditional injunction of scientific management insisting on "unity of command." But the reality today is that most individuals typically work on several projects, so multiple allegiances are increasingly a fact of life. Danger arises only when these various interests are denied to form hidden conflicts, rather than being addressed openly in a productive manner. William Ouchi reports that in Japanese companies, "Every employee, from top to bottom, is simultaneously a member of as many as eight or a dozen work groups, each with a different task." Digital Equipment is a successful company which encourages such freedom that one manager remarked: "Damn few people know who they work for." Studies show that people working on several projects of their own choosing perform better than those on a single assignment, they develop wider knowledge, improve interdepartmental coordination, and are more committed.[63]

Those raised on the chain-of-command also worry that the new freedoms will result in losing organizational control. The key to understanding networks is that they offer a different form of control that is more subtle. In place of today's unrealistic responsibility for knowing "each sparrow that falls," network managers focus on controlling only a few strategic factors that really count: the design of systems that measure performance, development of new technologies, resolving conflict, and providing help to operating managers.

It is also necessary to squarely face the fact that market structures are messier than the tidy bureaucracies many prefer. To an extent this is an unavoidable price we must pay for the creative productivity of free enterprise, but such problems actually represent signs of useful change that were squelched by the use of authority. In general, the behavior of networks can always be understood in terms of free markets. Is a supervisor unable to staff his/her unit with voluntary transfers? In a market this means that working conditions are unattractive. Are some units suffering chronic losses? Again, the marketplace would allow them to fail because they are not providing a valuable service. Do wide differences in income exist? These disparities may disturb a sense of equity, but they provide incentives to reward good performance and avoid the need to discipline poor workers or even to fire people. Thus, what may appear to be disorder in a network is really vital information to be heeded.[64]

A Horizontal Outlet for Young Professionals

The biggest problem posed by organizational networks, however, stems from the very advantages they offer. Freedom is a difficult thing for most of us to handle, and many find the challenge of defining their own working roles an overwhelming burden. The responsibility of balancing a variety of conflicting assignments, managing multiple working relationships, braving the uncertainty of an ambiguous future, finding the will to be self-reliant, and other challenges facing the intrapreneur are not for everyone. Many will prefer the safe haven of a secure traditional job working for one boss who tells you what to do.

But these problems have always confronted people who want to carve out their own niche in life, and the proportion of such independent persons is growing dramatically now. Educated young people tend to be bored with the narrow specialization of jobs in a bureaucracy, which is why one-third of them are switching careers. They are also reluctant to define their worth along the scale of a hierarchy, where, by definition, most of us are left competing at lower levels for some meager measure of identity and meaning. A study by my graduate business students showed almost unanimous attraction to the idea of intrapreneurship because it would permit the freedom to use their best talents at work, and the concept was regarded as a key solution to the revitalization of modern economies.[65]

Networks also offer a solution to the frustration over career advancement. The sheer number of baby-boomers threatens to overwhelm diminishing opportunities for promotion now that middle management ranks are being automated, so young professionals are feeling trapped in limited career paths. "Hierarchy is their enemy," claims Yale business professor Rosabeth Moss Kanter. One young manager said, "I feel blocked—completely, totally, and utterly. The only way around it is out."[66] The trough of the "baby-bust" following the baby-boom may sop up this surplus of employees in a decade or so, but only at entry levels, leaving a bulge of maturing professionals stuck in the system.[67] Meanwhile, the general labor shortage that should result will force employers to compete for personnel by striving to offer attractive working conditions.

If organizations are redefined as networks offering intrapreneurial roles, however, this stifled energy of young people can be channeled into endless **horizontal** outlets instead of dissipated fighting their way up a hierarchy.

Using the Hidden Realities of Organizational Life

One of the greatest advantages of networks is that granting employees their freedom would alleviate the debilitating coercion which cripples most institutions today. Forcing people to work for a particular superior at assignments they do not choose is a crude carryover from an earlier age that has serious dysfunctional results. The belief that authority imparts control is increasingly seen as an illusion which only leads to stifling bureaucracies; the fact is that authority invariably drives the true behavior of subordinates underground, insulating managers from the subtle realities of organizational life and causing them to actually lose control. Studies show that the ubiquitous "informal organization" is far stronger in authoritarian institutions, whereas in an organic culture it is allowed to surface and become absorbed with the formal management system as a legitimate, useful function.[68]

This situation persists because the ideal of a free labor market is largely another of our cherished myths that obscures a harsh reality. Employees cannot usually move to other organizations because they would lose their seniority rights, pension benefits, and other rewards that often lock people into their present jobs, and most people lack opportunities for other positions. Internal transfers are often prevented to serve the convenience of managers. These factors cause all but the most intrepid individuals to become virtual slaves of their employers rather than free agents. The *Los Angeles Times* reported, "The unhappy fact remains that many people today work for abusive, domineering, and erratic bosses."[69]

Eliminating this coercive use of authority would turn bureaucracies into ***free*** enterprises. One benefit would be to wipe out the messy cabals that are rife in institutions. A hot undercurrent of interpersonal tensions smolders beneath the surface of most workplaces today, occasionally erupting into an explosive conflict, and outright political wars are as common as the headcold in America. This is likely to become an even greater problem as the increasing diversity of the work force throws persons of different sexes, races, ages, and values together, making it almost impossible to preselect a compatible work team. How will we manage such sharp differences when people have so much trouble getting along under the best of circumstances? The magnitude of the problem was best expressed by Robert Shrank, an academic who has studied working life by holding ordinary jobs:[70]

> *Humans seem to have an almost limitless ability to solve mechanical problems and at the same time show an enormous inability to understand how to live with . . . each other.*

These difficult realities could be greatly alleviated by recognizing that those who can't get along should simply be free to go their own way by voluntarily selecting another assignment. Allowing people to choose their work units will then permit these troublesome differences that hamper bureaucracies to become constructive forces that are part and parcel of the strength of free markets. The net result should be to allow a tough but playful form of entrepreneurial management to emerge out of the illicit informal organization that has to bootleg and connive to accomplish anything. Peters and Waterman describe this rich, informal creativity in excellent companies:[71]

> *In company after company, we found 10-person skunk works that were more innovative than fully equipped R&D and engineering groups with casts of hundreds. We found example after example of people experimenting and pointing with pride to their useful mistakes. . . . We observed less standardization of procedure and a con-*

comitant greater willingness to "let them do it any way they want if it makes sense and works."

Thus, market networks offer the promise of permitting the realities of organizational life to surface and become a useful source of energy and talent, instead of an unacceptable deviation to be suppressed by authoritarian bureaucracies, as we saw in Chapter 1. The result can only make organizations more free, more human, and more productive.

The Metastructure of Living Systems

As old hierarchical pyramids evolve toward this fluid new species of networks, institutions should develop the organic features that characterize all living systems—whether natural organisms or social organisms. Actually, excellent organizations have always behaved this way, so we are simply getting closer to the truth that others have seen:[72]

William Ouchi, author of *Theory Z*: "My ideal of a completely efficient and perfectly integrated organization is one that has no organizational chart, no divisions, no visible structure at all. In a sense, a basketball team that plays well fits this description. . . . The problem facing a basketball team is huge in its complexity, and the speed with which problems occur is great. Yet an effective team solves these problems with no formal reporting relationships and a minimum of specialization of positions and tasks."

John Sears, manager of President Reagan's 1980 campaign: "The campaign has a life of its own; it's a living, breathing thing that you no longer can control. The candidate and a few of his close advisers sit atop this creation, holding on for dear life as it plunges toward Election Day."

Lewis Lapham, editor of *Harper's*: "If we could imagine the biological processes of civilization being held together by systems of trade and credit and thought, certainly as fragile and as beautiful as the ecological systems that bind together the chains of life in a pond or estuary, then . . . maybe we could conceive of structures infinitely more creative and diverse."

From a strategic view, this organic quality fosters an unending stream of adaptive strategic changes, making market networks uniquely suited to the complexity of a new era. Virginia Hine, who coined the network concept, claims:[73]

> A network is built for change, beautifully adapted to change and the transformation of an established unchanging structure. I suspect that's why it's becoming the paradigm of the New Age.

Modern organizations cannot be understood or managed using the older perspective of structure as a relatively fixed and enduring arrangement, but as a **pattern** that emerges out of the constantly evolving, self-directed behavior of people. Thus, a market network can be thought of as a "**meta**structure"—it is a living, natural system of changing structures, rather than a structure itself. Within this fluid organizational framework, individuals and units comprise the self-arranging modular components or cells that interlock in an infinite variety of unpredictable ways to meet changing institutional needs.

A good example is provided by the way Rubin Mettler, the CEO of TRW, is creating a new corporate structure that exemplifies this organic model. Mettler has discovered that merely mandating policy is ineffective, so his goal is to reshape TRW's culture, pushing line managers to look for innovative ways of improving their businesses, either alone or cooperatively. He is setting up committees to encourage cross-fertilization of ideas, devising financial incentives, productivity and quality programs, communication networks, an index of the company's technological capabilities, and a data base that allows professionals working on some 250 independent R&D projects to share knowledge. The result is that TRW is no longer a traditional hierarchy but a flexible system for producing innovative strategies.[74]

Market networks offer a unique form of power as self-directed individuals collectively act in an open-ended way, producing an uncanny ability to adapt to environmental uncertainty and complexity. Nobody need predict the future or direct the organization; it feels it's way along like a giant superorganism with a life of its own. In a future that should see more change than we can imagine, the advantages are incalculable.

Network Leadership

The role of corporate executives should change markedly in these new institutions. Managing a traditional hierarchical pyramid was

similar to operating other "mechanisms" in an industrial age—
rather like running an automobile or a turret lathe. The operator
has to make critical decisions to keep the machine running smoothly,
to insure an adequate supply of energy and parts, and to perform
repairs during breakdowns. In terms of managing an organization,
this would translate into making all important business decisions,
hiring people and buying raw material, and resolving conflicts and
crises. But in an information age of organic networks there is no
such machine—just a fluid tangle of individuals and units going
their own way in a larger web of societal connections. Harlan Cleveland, a former federal official and now Director of the Aspen Institute,
captured the essence of networks a decade ago:[75]

> *The organizations that get things done will no longer be hierarchical*
> *pyramids with most of the real control at the top. They will be . . .*
> *interlaced webs of tension in which control is loose, power diffused,*
> *and centers of decision plural.*

This model raises difficult new questions about the role of executives and the very nature of institutions. If an organization becomes
simply a collection of autonomous units, what distinguishes it from
the outside marketplace? What gives it an identity, and makes it
more than the sum of its individual parts? In short, what is the
executive really managing?

Fundamentally, there seem to be two main strengths that executives
must nourish carefully because they constititute the basic identity
of modern institutions. The first is the store of technology, information, skills, and other "hard" resources shared by members of
the network. For instance, conglomerates with widely differing units
have diluted this common body of technical capabilities, and so
the meager benefits from their union often do not justify the added
costs of maintaining a larger institution. Studies show that diversified
companies do not perform better economically, so now a trend is
underway to divest conglomerates of unrelated acquisitions to realize
their higher "break-up" value. Trans World Corporation is being
sued by stockholders who want the firm to sell off Trans World
Airlines, Hilton Hotels, and Century 21 Real Estate because they
believe holding these subsidiaries has actually reduced their net
worth.[76]

Executives of the future should encourage adding to the firm's store of technical skills in order to increase the value of this critical resource. Because the new information technologies have the unique power to multiply knowledge when shared, this function comprises the heart of modern organizations. Peter Drucker noted, "The 'organization of the future' is a structure in which information serves as the axis."[77] Thus, the high-tech corporation is becoming, not a production system or a social system, but a knowledge-generating information system managed more like a research laboratory or a university. In an industrial age organizations manufactured goods, but now in an information age they "manufacture" knowledge. Those that can accomplish this task best will outperform others.

A good example is the way McGraw-Hill is managing a diverse range of capabilities in publishing, information services, and electronic systems. The CEO, Joseph Dionne, is using task forces, incentive systems, training, and liaison personnel to unify these various units into an "intellectual community" that "adds value" in order to make "the whole more than the sum of its parts." A key element of his strategy is the development of a computerized "information turbine" that would comprise a central data base, fed by all units and drawn on to serve various clients, to drive the entire corporation.[78]

The other major leadership focus is the set of beliefs, values, and other "soft" qualities that make an institution a community. A virtual revolution in thought has finally acknowledged the crucial importance of these subtle, cultural aspects of management that characterize outstanding organizations: the need to unify the firm into a cohesive whole, to distinguish it from others, and provide the motive force that drives it to success. Successful executives avoid the temptation to get immersed in the intricacies of day-to-day operations in order to concentrate on these "spiritual" needs that only they can provide. They inspire by offering a vision of the future, they are skillful at communicating shared beliefs, they know how to encourage others to realize their own talents, and how to move large organizations into action. Many people do not share the values of President Reagan and Prime Minister Thatcher, for instance, but almost all will acknowledge their great strength lies in a keen ability to use their charismatic talents for this end.

These new leadership responsibilities are time-consuming and can only be attended to if routine operations are under control.

However, information technology should liberate the modern executive from most operational drudgery as robotics and computerized office systems integrate factory, office, and field operations into an automated enterprise. Managers report the change this way:[79]

> The computerized system has eliminated 95 percent of my emergencies
> . . . Now I spend my time planning, not reacting . . . Before you had
> a vice president in an ivory tower sending out directions. Now the
> factory manager can make many decisions unilaterally. . . . Managers
> now have more time to participate in planning and forecasting, and
> more time to manage people.

Such capabilities are freeing executives to focus on the two main tasks of managing networks just described: designing a flexible organization that fosters innovative problem-solving, and then using their personal influence to create a tightly-knit intellectual community. Industrial psychologist Michael Maccoby's studies show modern managers exbibit more "flexibility about people and organizational structure, and a willingness to share power." Thus, rather than acting as a traditional "boss" or "decision-maker," leaders are becoming more like a coach, teacher, or catalyst, assisting their confederation of fellow entrepreneurs in assuming responsibility for creating smart growth in the system they manage jointly.[80]

This same concept applies to the problem faced by national leaders in managing the economic macrosystem, as we shall see in Chapter 8. Free enterprise economies are themselves network systems, albeit they are often overly rigid, leaderless networks, which is largely why they are in a state of crisis. The solution to these problems is not to hope that sheer laissez-faire conditions will suffice, nor to implement some form of state planning. The key is to redesign modern economies so they behave as more effective markets systems, which is to say better networks. These ideas for leading market networks, therefore, apply to all levels of management in the approaching information age: a supervisor managing a team of subordinates, a large organization managing a confederation of entrepreneurs, or a nation managing a free enterprise economy.

The Flowering of Enterprise

Although the image of organic institutions has often inspired people, it has been seldom realized until the crisis in economics and the explosive growth of information technology required it. Theorists of change point out that systems remain stable for long periods until a vast increase in complexity creates such disorder that they suddenly make an evolutionary leap in a very quick, discontinuous structural transformation.[81] After two to three decades of slowly building momentum, the post-industrial transition finally seems to have reached a critical mass where the economic system is rearranging itself into a new structural state within a few years. Now the major corporations that comprise the nexus in a complex institutional infrastructure are breaking out of the bureaucracy that has paralyzed modern economies in an organizational gridlock, releasing reservoirs of energy that have been long suppressed.

This transformation is also taking place in other institutions, such as universities, hospitals, and churches. The Catholic Church revised its code of canon law in 1983 to redefine the church from a traditional hierarchical society governed by the clergy into a community of believers endowed with rights and obligations. Universities and hospitals increasingly are organized along the lines of a matrix with disciplines cutting across program offices for conducting research, degrees that are offered, and other activities. As John Naisbitt observed:[82]

> Centralized structures are crumbling all across America. . . . The people of this country are rebuilding America from the bottom up into a stronger, more balanced, more diverse society.

The same trend is also taking place in other Western nations. England is encouraging new venture formation as their staid old financial markets are deregulated to permit very ungentlemanly competition. The socialist government in France is moving toward free enterprise concepts to rejuvenate their stagnating economy. Even the Japanese tradition of lifetime loyalty to one employer is breaking down now as talented professionals switch jobs.[83]

As this imperative of the information age unfolds, institutions should become loosely connected webs of internal ventures that pass resources, employees, and information freely throughout the organization and across its permeable external boundaries. The resulting economic conditions—numerous small competing enterprises, freedom of entry and exit into contracts, and, above all, the widespread availability of more accurate market information—constitute the requirements that economists have long defined for the operation of "perfect markets." Large institutions are thereby becoming part of the open marketplace, bringing the advantages we have always attributed to the free enterprise system directly into the internal operation of organizations themselves: flexibility for adaptive change, easier management of complexity, entrepreneurial freedom for innovation, and other advantages for coping with a turbulent environment.

Thus, the development of organizational networks seems likely to raise to life the classical laws of economic theory. Rather than simply being unrealistic textbook ideals, these elegant, precise principles may begin to approximate actual economic behavior as the organic decisions of near-perfect markets replace the elitist dictates of bureaucratic corporations and governments that produced crude forms of control fraught with limited vision and rebellion. Instead, an economy composed of interwoven market networks should slowly but steadily draw on the collective ingenuity of countless individuals to devise more brilliant solutions than any leader could ever dream of. The organic system that results will liberate talented people, reconcile the conflict between freedom and control, unify the mythical beliefs of organizational life with its richer hidden realities, and combine the power of large economic concentrations with the innovation of small enterprises. Politically and geographically, it will link together major institutions in the private and public sectors to form a coherent global order.

This structural transformation should realize the original vision which Adam Smith and others saw only dimly at the start of the industrial revolution. Before this century ends, I suspect that today's stagnating giant institutions are likely to become alive with myriad small, creative, constantly changing ventures offering an endless variety of sophisticated goods and services. A great deal of disruptive change will be involved, and there will always be a need to retain some traditional controls. But in time the relentless force of information technology should cause free enterprise ideals to bloom into full flower as a vastly more productive and liberating foundation for the New Capitalism.

5

Participative Leadership:

EXTENDING DEMOCRACY TO DAILY LIFE

All across the United States a quiet revolution is gathering strength. In Smyrna, Tennessee, Japan's Nissan Corporation has started an automotive plant that successfully manages the same employees who create so much trouble for U.S. car producers. It's a little jarring to hear a typical American auto worker beam: "We're one big happy family here at Nissan."[1]

In Kansas City, Eastern Airlines recently gave its employees part ownership of the firm, including four seats on the board of directors, in return for accepting lower wages.[2] The company then reaped a public relations bonanza as pilots, stewardesses, ticket agents, and other "employee-owners" appeared on television commercials convincingly inviting the public to use the superior service on **their** airline.

While in San Francisco, that leading edge of the avant-garde, women hold a majority of public offices, including mayor, president and 6 of 11 seats on the board of supervisors, four of seven seats on the board of education, and two representatives to the U.S. Congress. Supervisor Doris Ward described the impact: "We have taken a softer approach to the issues. We are doing things with less conflict."[3]

Portions of this chapter are adapted from my papers "Toward a General Theory of Leadership," *Human Relations* (April 1974); "The Legitimacy Cycle: Long-term Dynamics in the Use of Power," Andrew Kakabadse and Chris Parker (eds.), *Power, Politics, and Organizations* (London: Wiley, 1984); "Participative Management: Myth & Reality," *California Management Review* (Summer 1981).

Such examples highlight changing realities that are altering the basis of power in modern societies. The onslaught of foreign competition, new management practices, women entering the work force, the maturing of the baby-boom generation, different attitudes toward authority, and more complex jobs are causing a profound shift in the relationship between leaders and followers.

This chapter describes how a form of participative leadership is evolving that promises to invigorate institutions with new life. Americans have long prided themselves as being democratic people, yet for centuries the Old Capitalism was based on harsh authority. Now the economic crisis is forcing employers to enfranchise employees in the governance of their work, not out of a sense of justice, but because the productivity of worker participation makes this historic move necessary. In time, the principle of democracy should be extended to include myriad other such humble but immediately important aspects of daily life.

THE SHIFTING ILLUSION OF POWER

The attractive features of market networks described in the last chapter—flexibility for innovative change, greater individual freedom, and so on—are of little use if these systems are not used effectively. Institutional structure only serves to guide behavior; it is a field on which organizational life is played out. What we call structure is really an enduring pattern that is constantly being shaped by the interplay of key actors as they carve out relationships with one another.

Whenever people address such matters, I have found that the central issue invariably seems to revolve around the use of power. The question of "Who controls whom?" is of central importance in human affairs, and for ages the answer has generally been the same: the strong control the weak. From the brute force wielded by stone age cave dwellers, to the imperial might of medieval monarchs, to the economic clout of industrial tycoons, those with power have usually subjugated those without it. Some scholars even claim that humans adapted to a primitive environment by evolving genetic traits that cause aggressive behavior, just as animal species instinctively create dominance hierarchies, so our present authoritarian institutions simply reflect a biological urge to dominate.[4]

Indeed, if one examines the way people treat each other today, the "dominance theory" still looks pretty valid. Yale psychologist Stanley Milgram conducted a famous set of experiments which showed that average Americans will obey orders instructing them to punish others to the point of death.[5] Combative heroes like John Wayne often stir a warm feeling of security and an exciting flutter of patriotism because they embody our ideal of a "strong" leader.

In the world of work, this same coercive use of power generally prevails despite many forces that have urged change. One justification for a move to more benign leadership is that the extension of democracy to the workplace was originally intended by the founding fathers. Albert Gallatin, Secretary of the Treasury for Thomas Jefferson and James Madison, stated, "The democratic principle on which this nation was founded should not be restricted to the political process but should be applied to the industrial operation as well." Later, the U.S. Industrial Commission appointed by Congress and President McKinley affirmed, "The tradition for freedom is strong in the minds of working people . . . for a measure of self-government."[6]

Because participation offers many advantages, the Europeans, Japanese, and other nations have taken the lead by developing various approaches over the past few decades. In the 1970s, The Conference Board reported that worker participation was well-established in Europe, while the London *Economist* warned, "Like it or not, it's coming."[7] Today, a dozen or so countries enjoy well-established, productive systems of labor-management cooperation that have gained them a crucial edge in global competition.[8]

Like local wines, participation does not travel very well, so the United States has tried to find its own way as many of America's biggest corporations experimented with the concept. A list of their names reads like the *Who's Who of American Business*: GM, Ford, AT&T, Syntex, Corning Glass, Prudential, Monsanto, Texas Instruments, McCormick, General Foods, Motorola, Procter & Gamble, Delta Airlines, and many, many others. These projects have produced numerous research studies on the subject, usually showing that participative management offers considerable gains.[9]

Yet, despite our traditions, the examples of other nations, countless encouraging experiences of U.S. companies, a wealth of accumulated knowledge, and many business leaders who have preached the virtues of participative management, American practices have changed very little. Important steps are being taken by progressive firms like those noted above, which we shall examine later, but for the bulk of Americans such moves remain beneath the surface waiting to erupt. During the economic crisis of 1980 to 1983, BusinessWeek identified this as a major cause of economic decline: "Companies continue to impose an authoritarian style of management on an increasingly educated and independent work force."[10] The fact is, after proclaiming the strength of democracy for over 200 years, the United States has yet to extend this cherished ideal to the management of institutions.

Changes in the use of power are difficult because any institution demands some form of control to survive. "Whatever else organizations may be . . . they are political structures," said management psychologist Abraham Zaleznik, "in which a dominant coalition of key executives is necessary to create order." Studies of another psychologist, David McClelland, show that effective managers are characterized by a strong need for power.[11] The hard truth is that the essence of any leader's job is to get people to do things, so effective leadership must unavoidably focus on the skillful use of power.

In view of this long history of coercion, the difficulty of introducing worker democracy, and the inevitable need for control, is it really possible to govern institutions in a more benign fashion? If changes are occurring in the use of power, how likely are they to continue and what are the implications?

Power Acts Down but Legitimacy Flows Up

To answer these questions we must first begin by understanding the nature of power relationships. There may be a need for power, but the evidence shows this need is primarily a cultural phenomenon that can take many forms. Power is derived ultimately from a subtle illusion that is created by the intangible beliefs of both the follower and the leader. Even those who do not approve of President Reagan admit he is a supremely skilled leader because he has an abiding faith in himself, and he has honed his skills as an actor to convey this conviction to others. "The power structure of any institution is a complex network of forces, both seen and unseen," as management consultant Robert Greenleaf put it. This power structure is built upon psychological traits that are deeply ingrained during the formative years of childhood by our first authority figures—our parents. Zaleznik pointed out how this intimate relationship is maintained in later life:[12]

> The personalities of leaders take on proportions which meet what subordinates need and even demand. . . . the chief executive is the central object in a coalition because he occupies a position analogous to parents in a family.

From this view, power emanates from child rearing practices, social conditions, and other cultural factors imprinted on human personalities. In the past, economic hardship, widespread ignorance, and a generally harsh society created a sense of insecurity that fostered dependence on strong authority figures. The need to be aligned with someone bigger than ourselves is vividly apparent at rare moments. A few years ago, a Japanese soldier was discovered hiding on a Pacific island since World War II. Still neatly dressed in his original uniform and faithfully defending his island, he was at last relieved after dutifully serving his Emperor all alone for more than 30 years without the slightest quavering of doubt. Likewise, the great power of FDR came from his ability to provide the assurance of a kindly, wise father to comfort a nation frightened by the Great Depression. This reverence for symbolic power figures still exists, as author Theodore White revealed in his relationship with modern presidents: "The president is a high priestly figure . . . I'm always scared when I speak to a president . . . I always have that sense of awe."[13] Dostoyevsky described how the basic need for security and meaning causes most people to yield their freedom for the support of strong leaders:[14]

> . . . nothing has ever been more insupportable for a man and human society than freedom . . . man is tormented by no greater anxiety than to find someone quickly to whom he can hand over that gift of freedom with which the ill-fated creature is born . . . for the secret of man's being is not only to live but to have something to live for. Without a stable conception of the object of life, man would not

consent to go on living, and would rather destroy himself than remain on earth, though he had bread in abundance.

So power is not simply imposed by coercive leaders who wish to dominate; it is granted eagerly by followers who want the various types of support that leaders can provide: maintaining order, creating a ceremonial sense of social harmony, employing knowledge to solve problems, providing inspiration, offering a vision of the future. Not only can power be benign, but these more useful forms of influence are usually far more powerful. Witness the great power that was accorded FDR, John F. Kennedy, Winston Churchill, Gandhi, Pope John Paul II, and other charismatic leaders. In sum, modern societies cannot simply order people about but must strive to develop the intangible bonds that gain genuine commitment.

Thus leadership is most effective when it is perceived to be **legitimate**, when followers accept a leader's power because they believe it to be sufficiently just, rightful, or desirable to comply willingly, rather than to submit begrudgingly or to oppose the leader. Legitimacy is essential to successful leadership over the long-term even in what some like to think of as "totalitarian" societies like the Soviet Union. Can 300 million people have been suppressed against their will since 1918? Power may appear to flow from higher authorities, but true power ultimately is gained from the support of subordinates. In other words, power may be exercised from the top down, but its legitimacy is drawn from the bottom up. When legitimacy is lost, the influence of the leader will inevitably wane, as dramatically illustrated by countless revolutions throughout history, and even by the Watergate crisis in the United States. Former Secretary of State Cyrus Vance stated this axiom in the use of power: "[Once] a government has lost its legitimacy in the eyes of its people, no amount of outside intervention can secure its long-term survival."[15]

A Historic Trend Toward Freedom

This psychological basis of power has changed markedly over the broad sweep of history. Figure 5.1 illustrates these long-term trends by showing how the forces of social evolution outlined in Chapter

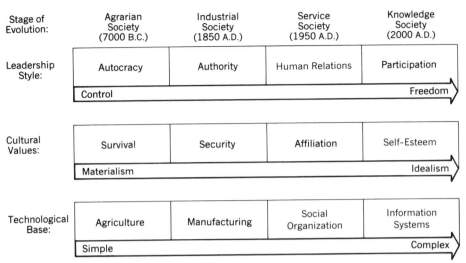

Figure 5-1.   The evolution of leadership.
Source: William Halal, "Toward a General Theory of Leadership," *Human Relations* (April 1974), and "The Life Cycle of Evolution," *Technological Forecasting and Social Change* (forthcoming).

2 gradually shift the dominant form of leadership toward "higher" levels.[16] Advances in the technological base exert the most impelling impetus for change because they alter the tasks that leaders must get their followers to accomplish. Generally speaking, simple, well-structured tasks (farming, manufacturing, etc.) require little discretion so they can be dictated, whereas complex technologies (service and knowledge work) demand freedom for collaborative problem-solving. Because the work we do determines the conditions of life that shape our outlook, prevailing cultural values then change the type of power considered legitimate. Just a few decades ago most people lived at the margin of subsistence with little education, so dictatorical leaders emerged to meet basic needs. Contrast that with the me-decade!

This evolutionary perspective helps explain how power has changed over various eras. The agricultural stage was marked by autocratic leadership because the simple task of tilling the soil could be dictated, and a primitive culture of peasant farmers struggling for survival fostered dependence. It is no coincidence that traditions of submission to the absolute power of parents, feudal lords, and monarchs were passed on unquestioned throughout history, and even today autocratic governance persists in almost all agrarian societies.

With the move to industrialization, formal authority was used to hire and fire "economic men" for performing routine physical tasks to gain financial security. Thus, factory foremen and industrial bosses did not rule on the basis of brute force or sheer whim, but relied on a rational form of authoritarian control made legitimate by the needs of the economic system.

Following World War II the assembly line gave way to a service society of white collar office workers who used various social skills to operate a complex organizational infrastructure. At just about that time, Freudian psychology revolutionized Western culture, spreading a new-found sensitivity to emotions and social relations. This concern for "affiliation needs" reached its climax during the 1950s when sociologist David Riesman observed the rise of an "other-directed" national character so intent on being "liked" that popularity became a powerful Madison Avenue tool for selling anything from cars to toothpaste.[17]

Because work was now predominantly concerned with social relationships, a human relations form of leadership emerged. The leader was still in command, but he could rarely use his authority to give blunt orders for fear of offending social harmony as people became sensitive to being "bossed around." Now the leader had to rely on social skills to create the feeling of a unified family workers wanted and to foster the warm atmosphere needed for running service organizations. Thus, the "organization man" was born and persists today as the dominant style of leadership. The last of the outspoken U.S. Presidents was Harry Truman, who has been followed by a succession of "human relations experts": Eisenhower, Kennedy, Johnson, Nixon, Ford, Carter, and Reagan all felt compelled to present a facade of polite solicitousness, while maneuvering behind the scenes for control.

The 1960s and 1970s witnessed wave upon wave of liberation movements among blacks, students, women, and other relatively powerless groups as the inexorable growth of information technology and the values of the me-decade produced another major shift in the use of power. A study conducted by my associates and I confirms that a crucial change recognizing new rights for individuals occurred between 1962 and 1975.[18] Results show that it is no longer considered proper for supervisors to rule on tangential aspects of employee behavior, such as the type of clothing worn at work, company social functions, getting along with coworkers, and the like that were once the prerogative of management. Even issues directly related to work itself, like relocation to a new job, use of working time, and criticism of the company, are frequently questioned and employees seem likely to gain control over such concerns. Overall, the data show that the power of organizations to control their members has declined significantly during the past two decades.

Although the study may have covered a somewhat unusual period of change, it bears out the long-term trend of Figure 5.1. Indeed, if one examines the history of industrial relations, it becomes clear that almost **all** forms of behavior were once controlled by employers at the beginning of industrialization, including the most highly personal functions like church attendance and family life. A quaint sign from an old New England factory once warned: "The company will not employ any one (sic) who is habitually absent from public worship on the Sabbath, or whose habits are not regular and correct."

Over a very long time, therefore, the development of complex technologies and idealistic cultural values have slowly urged more enlightened forms of leadership. Such movements are not apparent from our usual short-term perspective spanning a few decades, but they are clearly visible if one examines the way power has evolved from the brutal rulers of antiquity, to the divine right of medieval kings, to the industrial boss, and to the human relations expert today. This orderly progression has ocurred not because of the benevolence of leaders, although many have showed great heroism in liberating their people, but because changing conditions made a more benign form of power mandatory.

I conclude there is a long-range trend in which people gain increasing freedom as they acquire the ability to perform difficult tasks responsibly. At early stages of social development, insecure and uneducated subordinates are almost fully constrained by their superiors, much like the relationship between child and parent, and the simple nature of the prevailing technology makes dictatorial control possible. However, people have a persistent attraction to freedom in order to realize their potential, and increasing technical complexity necessitates greater discretion. Thus, historic forces exert a powerful tendency toward human "liberation," individually as each person matures, and collectively for organizations and society as a whole. In the famous words of Warren Bennis, "Democracy is inevitable."[19]

The Participation Gap

Today, the failure to adjust to rapidly changing conditions in this long-term trend has produced a crisis in leadership. Figure 5.1 illustrates the imminent shift to an economy based on information technology and cultural values favoring self-esteem. However leadership remains largely unchanged, producing an incongruence in the prevailing mode of power. Psychologist Michael Maccoby warned, "The old models of leadership no longer work," and Jerome Rosow, Director of the Work in America Institute, noted why: "Changes in American moral and social values have been rapid and penetrating over the past decade. In contrast, large organizations are slow to change. Thus an institutional lag persists." The result is that modern societies are poised at the brink of an historic upheaval in the power structure underlying the entire social order. Robert Greenleaf described it this way:[20]

> The model of a single chief sitting atop the hierarchy is obsolete, and consequently we are at a point of crisis for want of trust in our major institutions. . . . Now, as I read the signs, we are in a period of radical transition regarding power, authority, and decision everywhere.

The coming mode of leadership clearly seems to be "participation," which can be thought of as a mild, introductory form of democracy. Most managers have become supportive and considerate in recent years, but much of this is "human relations" or "industrial courtesy" and rarely comprises true participation in which subordinates actually share an important degree of decision-making power. Just beneath the casual appearances, both parties well understand that the superior retains almost sole control over their relationship. Professor Mason Haire expressed this discrepancy pointedly: "Almost all managers talk in Theory Y terms (participation) but act in Theory X terms (authoritarian)."[21]

Table 5.1 summarizes the results of a survey my associates and I conducted concerning the present use of 16 common types of participation and the preference for their future use. Contrary to many popular claims, the study found that only about one quarter of employees are involved in matters affecting them. Former Avis executive Robert Townsend estimates that a few thousand firms out of about 1 million American companies now practice some form of participation.[22] As a result, there is a considerable "participation gap" because the proportion of those who believe they **should** participate is more than twice as great as the level of current practices. Almost two-thirds of those responding favor all types of participation on average, so wide interest exists that is not being channeled effectively.

The participation gap has created a host of problems which contribute to the economic crisis: low job satisfaction, lack of employee commitment, declining productivity, poor quality of work, high personnel turnover, absenteeism and tardiness, and labor conflict. These effects are so numerous and complex that entire libraries have been devoted to their study, but a few highlights stand out to help grasp the nature of the problem.

The issue of work today divides on two opposing viewpoints. A "progressive" view claims that American workers are dissatisfied with present work practices and proposes sweeping changes in job design, while the "conservative" view points to well-documented survey data showing the proportion of satisfied employees averages about 80 percent and has changed little over the past decades.[23] These two sides to the argument are not really incompatible since the truth lies somewhere between a complete rejection of the status quo versus its blind affirmation.

As the data show, a majority of workers claim to be "satisfied" with their jobs because they are reasonably well-off in comparison to their friends and coworkers, especially during hard times when having a job at all is a precious asset. The success of industrialization has bestowed great blessings on the working lives of most Americans. They are fairly well paid, working conditions are decent, they are treated with at least reasonable dignity, and there is always some hope of advancement.

However, this is only part of the story because other concerns are hard to evaluate, much less admit, on a simple questionnaire.

TABLE 5.1.   PARTICIPATIVE PRACTICES VS. P0REFERENCES[a]

Type of Participation	(A) Now Practicing	(B) Should Practice	(B − A) Participation Gap
Work processes			
Self-pacing	56%	51%	−5%
Autonomous work teams	47	69	22
Problem-solving committees	40	87	47
Flexitime	24	50	26
Job rotation	19	55	36
Mean	37%	62%	25%
Communication			
Consultation meetings	35%	88%	53%
MBO	34	80	46
Counsellors or ombudsmen	30	75	45
Attitude surveys	24	84	60
Representation on policy-making bodies	18	73	55
Mean	28%	80%	52%
Compensation			
Stock distribution plans	10%	19%	9%
Incentive systems	33	70	37
Profit sharing	19	44	25
Mean	21%	44%	24%[b]
Personnel actions			
Selection of new coworkers	22%	66%	44%
Wages, promotions, and so on	11	49	38
Selection of supervisors	1	27	26
Mean	11%	47%	36%
Grand Mean	26%	62%	35%[b]

[a] Calculations in this table exclude ambiguous residual categories such as "uncertain," "not possible," and "no response," so the basis for these figures ranges between 70 and 94 percent of the total sample.

[b] Due to rounding error, these figures do not exactly equal those in column B minus column A.

Consider what author Studs Terkel discovered talking to hundreds of people: "When I'd interview, very often, at the beginning, people would say, 'Oh, I like my job, I like it.' . . . [but I would find later that] the great majority of people don't get any satisfaction from their work." Such responses show that the prevailing satisfaction is often superficial, but it is maintained because most workers are reluctant to acknowledge casually that a lifetime invested in some field has been wasted and their working lives lack meaning. As a recent University of Michigan study showed, people are not satisfied in terms of a "higher" set of standards coming to the fore now. Those who report being "satisfied" are really saying, in the concepts coined by psychologist Fred Herzberg, that they are "not dissatisfied."[24] The best explanation is that U.S. society has met the basic needs of most people with the maturing of the industrial era, and now greater expectations have appeared as a new era approaches.

In-depth studies show that job satisfaction varies with one's position in the organizational hierarchy, and the majority of people feel trapped in jobs near the bottom. They envy those at the top who have greater rewards, freedom, and social significance in their careers, in contrast to the meager pay, low status, and meaninglessness of their own work. They have had to accept the harsh reality that they will never realize the Great American Dream of independent wealth, and are forced to adjust to a dreary, boring life in the pits of the bureaucratic machine. Often, the result is a sense of alienation that is manifested in a variety of social problems, including mental illness, alcohol and drug abuse, and poor adjustment in life generally because work is of such central importance in our culture.[25]

Workers would like more money, obviously, but too much is usually made of the importance of material rewards. Countless studies show the most critical issue is the lack of control people feel over their working conditions. The problem is highlighted by the contrast with Japan. U.S. managers have actually overpaid their employees in some industries like auto-making, but they continue to insist on an outmoded principle of unilateral control, thereby creating a "labor underground" that actually undermines their control. Although Japanese managers pay their employees less and work them harder, they receive far more skilled, highly motivated effort because they urge worker involvement to create a sense of "ownership" that is essential to enlist the committed support of any labor force. *Work in America*, a classic study conducted for the U.S. government, highlighted the need:[26]

> *What the workers want most, as more than 100 studies in the past 20 years show, is to become masters of their immediate environment and to feel that their work and themselves are important.*

This widening participation gap largely explains why productivity in America increased by only 0.7 percent during the past decade, compared with 4.1 percent for Japan, 6.1 percent for France, and 5.0 percent for West Germany. Workers themselves admit they could greatly increase productivity, and results of countless innovative programs show productivity could be raised 50 percent or more. Employee turnover in the United States is estimated to average four to eight times that of Japanese companies, and may reach as high as 50 percent annually in some cases, requiring the replacement of half of the entire work force every year. Absenteeism is so bad in some industries that the assembly lines must be shut down on Mondays because of insufficient workers. Time lost in industrial disputes in the United States is three times as great as France and Japan, and about 30 to 50 times greater than Sweden and Germany. Poor labor-management relations are also responsible for the grisly toll in industrial accidents, which injures 3 million workers and kills 100,000 others each year.[27]

What is more alarming is that these problems have been spreading upward to include professionals. The continued growth of large, complex organizations has required a huge cadre of middle-managers to control a cumbersome, maze-like institutional infrastructure that fulfills the dark visions of Kafka and Orwell. Studies show that most managers find their jobs unsatisfying, stressful, overwhelming, and filled with ambiguity and conflict. Many are considering switching to another field of work, and a majority anticipate they will become unionized. Recent surveys by Opinion Research Corporation show the proportion of managers rating their companies favorably dropped from 70 percent to 46 percent during the past decade. One such study concluded:[28]

> *A new generation has come along that has become increasingly dissatisfied with the companies they work for. . . . Faith in top man-*

agement has declined among employees, including managers. De-
cision-making is perceived as becoming more top-down . . . stress
on the job is increasing, particularly among managers . . . the entire
work force is becoming vulnerable to unionization.

The same frustration is largely behind the recent strikes by highly
paid elites like air-traffic controllers and professional athletes in
football and baseball. These groups appear to be simply asking for
more money, mainly because the press has made news of their
extravagant salaries. But their dissatisfaction primarily stems from
a paternalistic relationship with the FAA in the case of air-traffic
controllers, and with club owners in the case of sportstars. The
underlying issue is, once again, the need to gain control over working
conditions.

Thus, the inability to adopt badly needed changes has produced
a widening gap between archaic leadership practices and the new
realities of work life. Robert Townsend summed up the problem
nicely:[29]

The folks in the mailroom, the president, the vice presidents, and
the steno pool have three things in common: they are docile, they
are bored, and they are dull. Trapped in the pigeonholes of orga-
nization charts, they've been made slaves to the rules of private and
public hierarchies that run mindlessly on because nobody can change
them.

What's Holding Up the Revolution?

If this revolution is overdue, the obvious question is what's holding
it up? After all, many other nations have practiced various forms
of worker participation for decades, so why should the cradle of
democracy find it such a foreign idea to extend these rights that
were hard won in the American Revolution to include our place
of work?

The shift to a new power structure is of such profound significance,
so disturbing to both leaders and followers, and so fraught with
painful obstacles that it will take years before Americans can develop
their own unique form of industrial democracy. Much of what
passes for wisdom on both sides of this volatile issue consists of

unfounded myths and prejudices. Staunch advocates of participation often paint an unrealistically glowing picture of the benefits that are sure to accrue when "human resources are tapped," and they urge democratization of the workplace on moral grounds. There is also no shortage of opponents who regard the concept as an infringement on the prerogatives of management, too risky and time consuming, impossible to reconcile with the need for control, and posing the threat of disruptive conflict. Clearly this is uncharted territory. Should everyone participate in management decisions? On which decisions? What approaches and techniques are best? How do we get started?

The study results in Table 5.1 indicate that participative management is far more complex than commonly believed. Participation is neither a panacea that will magically release huge reservoirs of untapped human potential, nor is it a dangerous threat to management. Rather, it involves a poorly understood central issue in the changing nature of leadership that has resisted analysis because of the sensitivity of power relationships and the lack of useful knowledge. These findings, then, help replace Utopian fantasies and unfounded fears with facts and constructive suggestions.

Although the data show that there is great potential for participation, they also indicate that almost half of Americans do not favor the concept. Many motivated people are interested in the challenge of actively managing their own affairs, and they can make important contributions if encouraged to do so. Others have little desire or ability for a demanding role, and may be quite content and better employed in a more traditional situation working under authoritarian leaders, at least temporarily. The wise leader recognizes that subordinates may differ greatly in their capacity for self-control, so people should participate to their individual capacity. Professor James O'Toole, an authority on work, noted:[30]

> There are workers who are ambitious and dedicated, and others who are sullen and uncooperative. There are those who hate work, and those who would rather work than play. . . . Some workers are selfish and concerned only with guarding their "rights," but many are committed to their employers and as dedicated to their jobs as any Japanese or German worker. This diversity is the single most important fact about the American workforce.

Not only is there great diversity among individuals, there is also wide diversity in the feasibility of different forms of participation. The data in Table 5.1 show that participation in communications and work processes are generally attractive. However, participation in compensation and personnel actions—particularly the selection of superiors—is often undesirable because these are sensitive issues. The great majority of employees are responsible people who think it is best for superiors to maintain control over such critical decisions to avoid disruptions. Thus, participative management is not a monolithic concept applying to all aspects of work because there appear to be well-defined preferences for different approaches.

These results reveal the futility of simple answers. There is a great need for a major shift to participation, but not for everyone and not in the same manner. As "contingency" theories contend, different forms of leadership are best in differing situations, so participation may not be useful in some organizations, and possibly it should not be implemented throughout the organization. Some units may be led by traditional authoritarian managers and be quite successful, while others may employ unorthodox methods and be equally successful, depending on the needs of subordinates, the personality of the leader, and the tasks to be performed. An eclectic, flexible approach is best in which individual units should be encouraged to develop their own type of management, forming pockets of collaboration in a diverse organizational network.

We conclude that Americans have realistic attitudes toward the use of authority and they want to proceed earnestly but cautiously. The overwhelming majority of persons we studied favored participation in communications most strongly because the great need presently is to discuss these thorny issues. People want to understand what is possible, the pros and cons of the concept, and how to proceed further, if at all. The best way to begin is to start a dialogue among employees and managers and to be guided by the collective judgment of all those involved.

This all sounds very logical and rational, but the main obstacles are hardly logical or rational—they involve highly charged fears and destructive habits that are deeply ingrained in American culture.

One of the most poignant signs of trouble occurred when Warren Bennis himself, one of the gurus of the participation movement, found that he couldn't implement his ideals very well as head of the University of Cincinnati: "A year's trials as president of a large university make me even more certain that a viable managerial strategy does not lie in consensus," he said.[31] Many organizations have begun such programs only to abandon them for various reasons. The General Foods plant in Kansas had been considered a model of participative management for years, but serious signs of failure appeared. One manager reported, "The system went to hell. It didn't work." Employees had a somewhat different view: "Economically it was a success, but it became a power struggle. It was too threatening to too many people." Some executives seem unable to gain commitment even from their own managers. Listen to the frustration of one CEO:[32]

> My managers—even the top ones—don't seem to care about their work anymore. There is no real dedication, no commitment, no sense of obligation. I've tried giving them everything—money, long vacations, big bonuses—but nothing seems to motivate them like it used to— how long can the nation keep going on like this?

The heart of this problem is that the Old Capitalism has produced great contradictions toward authority which have yet to be acknowledged openly, much less resolved. The chief obstacle to the sharing of power is that both leaders and followers remain immobilized in what I think of as a tacit "conspiracy of dependence." Leaders find it hard to relinquish their control—and conversely followers are reluctant to assume responsibility. This conflict persists not because people are perverse or ignorant, but because our culture discourages collaboration.

Some people in positions of authority will not voluntarily yield their power for selfish reasons, of course, but the problem is far more complex. Most managers have an exceedingly difficult time learning how to make participation succeed. They dislike the extra work involved, they are unsure of how to handle such an undefined new role, and they are fearful of the risk of disruptive conflict, ridicule, and criticism. There is a persistent belief that participation is soft or permissive, and this looser form of control would permit anarchy. In fact, there is a keen realization that the economic crisis requires **higher** standards of productivity and **tighter** control. "The

battle cry of the Eighties and Nineties will be the demand for performance and accountability," noted Peter Drucker.[33] Most executives
are also adverse to sharing power because they came from an earlier
era when power was glorified and offered a cherished illusion of
superiority. Business executive Robert McMurray put it best:[34]

> Very few members of top management are by nature sympathetic to
> the "bottom-up" philosophy of management. They are hard-driving,
> egocentric entrepreneurs who have come up . . . in careers where
> they had to keep the power in their own hands . . . veterans of the
> give-and-take, no-quarter in-fighting for positions of power.

The followers' part in this "conspiracy" shows up in a reluctance
to face up to the necessary link between rewards and responsibility.
On the one hand, American workers are demanding better benefits,
interesting work, and the right to influence decisions. The genie of
employee freedom has been released from its bottle, and it is unlikely
to be imprisoned again. But as sociologist Amitai Etzioni and many
others point out, employees often refuse to be held accountable for
performance. Even after widespread layoffs due to noncompetitive
labor practices, most unions continue to resist change. The problem
of those without authority is the counterpart of those holding it:
employees find it hard to relinquish their former dependence in
order to assume serious responsibility for the enterprise. William
Winpisinger, a prominent labor leader, expressed this demanding
attitude:[35]

> Better wages, shorter hours, vested pensions . . . promotions based
> on seniority and the rest . . . That's the kind of job enrichment that
> we will continue to fight for.

This cultural impasse over the use of power is highlighted by
the exaggerated ambivalence Americans feel toward symbolic figures
like the President of the United States. At one extreme, people can
be so critical that unrealistic demands are placed on competent but
imperfect men to prove they merit our trust, which invariably dooms
them to failure. Most recent presidents left office with a majority
of the public feeling they performed poorly, and some like Truman,
Johnson, and Carter were vilified. The other extreme is equally
problematic. Many Americans are content on faith alone to vest

huge amounts of power in people like FDR who are regarded as omniscient beings free of human failings. Recently, for instance, President Reagan seems charming and self-assured, so many have eagerly swung to his support in a flight of hope, allowing the nation to be led into dangerous territory like massive budget deficits and the threat of war.

The fervent need to see the President as either a "devil" or a "messiah" stems from unrealistic expectations that cannot be met by mere mortals.[36] But still, every four years we elevate some poor soul to the impossible task of meeting our shifting, diverse moods, thereby acting out a Greek drama in which this heroic-tragic figure is doomed to either be destroyed by his ordeal or to destroy us. When a competent nation of 230 million people in an advanced society of awesome complexity continues to believe that one person will save them, it becomes clear that the conspiracy of dependence emanates from deep mythical origins in the human psyche—a sort of modern tribal ritual by which we attempt to exorcize the evils that seem beyond us.

Participative leadership will become a widespread reality only when American culture has matured to the point where both leaders and followers accept their responsibilities for a more constructive working relationship. In the interim, most institutions will continue to suffer from an outmoded human relations approach that may have been useful when the nation was coasting on its past accomplishments, but this palliative form of authority can no longer be afforded today. Human relations has become an ineffective and demeaning ruse by which superiors maintain almost complete control while manipulating employees behind a thinly veiled facade of politeness, creating a hazy fog blanketing most organizations that muddles both rights and responsibilities. One study revealed that two-thirds of managers "have no idea what their standing is."[37] The result is that institutions are unable to confront the two central issues that dwell on most minds today, but which we avoid daily: the inadequacy of performance that leaders grapple with, and the inadequacy of freedom that followers want.

The Information Age Escalates Pressure for Change

These are profound obstacles, but the move to participative democracy is an undeniable historic step that is not going to be stopped any more than one could stop an earthquake. Now as robots and information systems automate factories and offices, typical jobs increasingly require skilled professionals who must handle complex relationships, solve intellectual problems, and explore the frontiers of a new economic era. TRW expects its blue collar workers who now make up 40 percent of the company's employees to be almost fully replaced by "knowledge workers" in the year 2000. These new jobs are quasi-scientific in nature, and scientists are notorious for resisting authority because their work cannot be dictated but requires independence of thought and action.[38]

Not only are jobs becoming more complex, a new breed of people is moving through the ranks to perform them. A generation ago most employees were generally content with "lower-order" rewards, such as pay and benefits, pleasant working conditions, and congenial coworkers. Now, higher education levels, the sophistication fostered by electronic media, and greater affluence have created a new work ethic. Daniel Yankelovich's studies show, "nearly 80 percent of the population is now engaged in the search for self-fulfillment." These people still want money and social satisfactions from their work, and in fact, they feel entitled to these rewards as their due. But they also want "higher-order" rewards involving opportunities for career advancement, job interest, challenge, autonomy, and the right to influence decisions. Studies of behavioral scientists like Gordon Lippitt reveal the following profile that increasingly represents the typical American worker:[39]

Young.   The greatest bulk of employees were born during the post World War II baby-boom and is now between 20 and 40 years of age.

Highly Educated.   Roughly half of these people attended college, and they are pursuing professional careers.

Socially Aware.   Because of the influence of television and enlightened upbringing by their parents, employees today are socially sophisticated. They are not cowed by people with high status, and they understand intuitively the subtle informal dynamics of social interaction.

Cosmopolitan.   They are not "organization men/women" dedicated to one employer. Most people have traveled widely, so they have a mobile perception of their role in society, and they feel free to move if they choose.

Diverse.   The white, Anglo-Saxon, Protestant male is now the minority in the work force, outnumbered by women, people from other races, various cultural backgrounds, and different religions.

Fulfillment Seeking.   People typically have a high sense of self-esteem and are primarily interested in self-development and challenging careers offering advancement. They also want leisure time and meaningful life experiences, rather than simply working hard to accumulate possessions.

Nonauthoritarian.   The most critical feature of the new breed of employee is that they are nonauthoritarian so they want personal freedom.

This last trait points up an important distinction between **non**authoritarian versus **anti**authoritarian views. Most people acknowledge there is a fundamental need for social control, so they are not opposed to authority because they know its use is essential. But they are not automatically disposed to obedience because they feel those in positions of authority must be competent, and they must use their influence for the benefit of others. In other words, authority must be earned—it must be legitimate. Numerous opinion polls consistently show a strong and growing interest among employees— even a demand—that they be allowed to participate in decisions affecting them:[40]

John Miner has conducted longitudinal studies showing a marked decline in the type of "authoritarian" personality required to maintain bureaucratic institutions.

Daniel Yankelovich's polls showed a decade ago that 53 percent of young people want to participate in decisions on their job.

Jerome Rosow finds that the number of workers who feel they should challenge an illegitimate order increased from 30 percent in 1969 to 70 percent in 1979. In 1977, 62 percent of employees said they have a **right** to take part in decisions affecting their jobs.

These are generalizations, of course, and it is obvious that many people do not fit this profile because they are older, come from rural areas, or other reasons. But the bulk of the labor force now aspires to achieving the type of professional autonomy formerly limited to a small elite of entrepreneurs, scientists, and statesmen, thereby posing a serious challenge as they move into influential positions. And lest we forget, these are the same people who started the campus riots of the 1960s! Although their strident rhetoric has mellowed, the conforming behavior of the past is gone so they are not likely to accept the dictates of authoritarian leaders. Reginald Jones noted when he was chief executive of GE: "The counterculture is not a passing phenomenon." It may take a while until they gain control, but the initial impact is being felt now. *BusinessWeek* recently reported: "The baby boomers, grown to maturity, have finally arrived, and they are pushing for power."[41]

Thus, new demands created by the onset of the information age are rapidly escalating the pressure for change. Tasks are becoming too complex to manage without the active involvement of employees, and a more sophisticated breed of people wants to share critical decisions affecting their careers. A study conducted by AT&T highlighted the difficult challenge now being posed by these unyielding trends:[42]

> *Coming from an age in which humans were to serve the organization, it is heresy to suggest that organizations serve the people within them.*

PARTICIPATIVE DEMOCRACY COMES OF AGE

Spurred by these growing pressures and the threat of foreign competition, now the original promise for participative democracy finally seems to have come of age. Americans are practical people, so after long delays while debating the effectiveness of the concept, when the economic crisis hit home in 1980 a remarkable change in attitude swept over the land:[43]

> **BusinessWeek** observed in 1981: ". . . a new industrial relations system with a fundamentally different way of managing people is taking shape in the United States. Its goal is to end the adversarial relationship that has grown between management and labor and that now threatens the competitiveness of many industries."
>
> **The U.S. Department of Labor** has started to promote worker participation. In 1981 the Secretary of Labor, Raymond Donovan, announced, "A new era has begun that requires new approaches to old problems . . . Every experienced worker knows things about his job that . . . no management design can capture. It's an invaluable asset that American business has been ignoring for years."

A poll of leaders in business, labor, and government conducted in 1982 showed that more than 70 percent favor collaborative labor-management relations, and more than 50 percent believe this change will occur within the next few years. One company president said: "If we're going to improve productivity in this country, workers have got to care about their company."

This newly discovered receptivity is particularly apparent among the younger cohort of managers from the baby-boom generation. One survey found they tend to be, "Flexible in their management style, people-oriented rather than numbers-oriented, willing to share decision-making . . . inviting participation and handing down authority as their predecessors never did." William George described his leadership style when he was the 32-year-old president of a division of Litton Industries: "We get together as peers. It doesn't matter if you're president or an engineer. Authority goes to competence."[44]

Participation also seems favored by a wave of women managers now advancing within organizations that promises to ameliorate the use of power. The proportion of females in corporate management increased from 18 percent in 1970 to 30 percent in 1980, and is growing even faster now because women have comprised roughly half of all business students in recent years. The number of female politicians has doubled in the past decade, and should double again in four years, putting women in control of 25 percent of all public offices. Some have emulated the old "macho" qualities of men in order to succeed, but the new breed of female leader is beginning to discover unique talents. Rachel Flick, a Republican speechwriter and journalist, noted, "Uncoerced, woman has rediscovered the Feminine—the charitable, conciliatory, ministrative Feminine—and she has pronounced it not just equal to the Masculine, but morally superior."[45] Provocative studies show these traits are better suited for the needs of a new era, so power is shifting from the authoritarian men of the past to the nurturing, collaborative female leaders of the future, as exemplified by the women running San Francisco.[46]

Another sign of change is that the popularity of participation has spawned numerous research and consulting groups to promote the concept: the Work in America Institute, the New School for Democratic Management, the Federation for Economic Democracy, the National Council for Alternative Work Patterns, the Association for

Self-Management, the Society for Human Economy, and many quality of work life centers across the nation.

As the following sections will show, the most important sign that participation has arrived is that a boom of innovative applications is now spreading rapidly among progressive organizations. Although many scholars have defined principles for successful participation, these examples are most remarkable because they avoid doctrinaire theories but reflect a healthy American pragmatism and diversity. Our study tried to summarize the range of possibilities in the 16 types of participation outlined in Table 5.1, but we have seen time and time again how people can devise myriad types of useful working relations that are almost impossible to capture in any list.

The New Employment Contract: Pay-for-Performance

The conspiracy of dependence that was holding up this transition is breaking up now as it becomes clear that management control and employee freedom are not incompatible. In the past we were preoccupied with controlling employees through specifying work hours, directing assignments, supervising their work, and the like. But these controls are increasingly seen as arbitrary and unrelated to performance. It means little if people are at their desks punctually from 9–5, how they behave, and so on, if they don't accomplish much. Individuals with different talents may perform as well as others in their unique way, and a variety of approaches can always be used to accomplish most tasks. Not only are old controls ineffective, corporations are also facing up to the fact that pay increases were usually awarded automatically on the basis of seniority, job description, social compatibility, and other factors which have little to do with performance.

The last chapter showed how such problems are being resolved at the level of ventures through a new "business contract" that holds units accountable for **performance** while permitting greater freedom of **operations** or **behavior**. Similarly, at the level of individual employees, a new "employment contract" is emerging to produce a more direct, business-like relationship in which rewards are based on performance. One manager at the Nissan plant in Tennessee put it as follows: "This is participatory management, but it is not permissive management." With such controls agreed on, people may then be permitted the autonomy to carry out their responsibilities as they see fit with the assurance they will be rewarded fairly for their contribution. The *Work in America* report summed up the strategy:[47]

> Both human goals (autonomy and independence) and economic goals (increased productivity) can be achieved through the sharing by workers in both the responsibilities of production and the profits earned through production. Most workers will willingly assume responsibility for a wider range of decisions (and by so doing to increase productivity and profits) if they are also allowed to share in the profits.

This sharper focus on the crucial link between reward and responsibility has caused firms to begin measuring actual contributions realistically using sensible evaluations by peers and supervisors, setting up incentive systems, and other such methods for insuring accountability—and then making pay conditional on results. A recent report by Hay Associates, the nation's largest consulting firm in personnel matters, advised its clients that "Organizations must return to the basic 'pay for performance' principles," while journalist Norman Macrae finds there is "a movement away from paying people for mere attendance at the workplace and towards paying people for modules of work done." This insistence on accountability is not restricted to workers, but is also redefining executive pay to tie it more closely to long-term company performance. Neither is it limited to business because government is replacing seniority with performance standards, and there is a growing trend toward rewarding outstanding teachers with merit pay.[48]

Many firms are initiating new programs specifically based on a formal contractual agreement in which people are paid for their output. For instance, Crown Zellerbach placed 600 loggers on a plan that rewards an autonomously managed work crew for the amount of timber they produce per day. The result has been to eliminate the need for job classifications, work rules, performance evaluations, and other complex systems formerly used to control workers. Loggers are strongly motivated because they are earning an average of $3 more per hour, so their pay as well as corporate productivity is up strongly. As company managers described it, the new plan produces "a joint effort to attain a common goal. Everywhere we tried it, it worked well."[49]

A more prominent case is the "giveback" bargaining forced on major industries to compete internationally. For example, the 1982 settlements between the UAW and auto makers exemplified most key elements of the new employment contract: management received decreases in wage rates, fewer paid holidays, more flexible work rules, and other concessions that saved $6 billion. In return, the union received profit-sharing, a plan for lifetime job security, and participation in management decisions from the shop to the board-room. The airlines and bus companies are redefining their labor-management relationship along similar lines, and the concept is spreading to European firms because they face the same economic pressures.[50]

As a result of these unyielding economic forces that are likely to increase with further competition, no-nonsense business executives who abhor any whiff of democratic values are almost unwittingly moving toward the democratization of capitalism simply because it is productive. Employee directors are now seated on the boards of Chrysler, Eastern, Pan America, and about a dozen other major firms. BusinessWeek reported in a special issue, "A Work Revolution in U.S. Industry":[51]

> Union concessions reflect something deeper: the growing suspicion that the body of theory and practice developed in the early years of this century to shape the structure of the workplace has long ceased to fit a society in the throes of technological upheaval . . . A revolution in the way workers do their jobs is beginning to take hold throughout America's basic industries . . . moving the workplace away from rigid labor practices created by authoritarian management and institutionalized by narrowly focused unions.

Dramatic change of this sort may offer great opportunities, however, it also presents new responsibilities. There is a strong possibility of explosive confrontation if labor does not perceive its sacrifices as being equitable and if management cannot follow through to achieve lasting business success—especially now that workers have begun to assume the risk of profit sharing. For instance, the hope for permanent labor-management harmony was dealt a severe blow when the givebacks of labor were followed in 1984 with extravagant executive bonuses. Understandably, many workers who gave up pay increases are bitter.[52]

Although such setbacks remind us that redefining the old adversarial labor-management relationship will be tough, they merely obscure the long-term trend. International competition and a growing realization that the interests of labor and management are interdependent should inevitably move modern economies from the conflict of the past toward a collaborative future. Peter Pestillo, Vice President of Labor Relations at Ford, acknowledged: "The wave of the future . . . is greater participation by our work force in the business process."[53]

Profit Sharing and Worker Ownership

Various profit sharing plans are now being used in 340,000 American firms employing 17 million workers, and have been effective in improving capital formation, employee commitment, and productivity. There are also estimated to be 6000 "Employee Stock Ownership Plans" (ESOPs) in the United States today, including those at Sears, AT&T, Chrysler, Eastern, and MCI. The formation of ESOPs has spurted recently, although part of the interest is due to new legislation granting favorable tax breaks.[54]

These concepts were denounced as "socialism" just a short time ago, but now their dramatic growth reflects the attractive advantages they offer as the economic crisis forces business executives, labor leaders, and politicians to find unconventional ways of saving jobs and restoring productivity. When the Weirton Steel Mill in Pennsylvania was closed, its 10,000 workers bought the business for $200 million to create the largest ESOP in the world. A year later in 1984, employees were actively involved in running **their** company, producing a vital sense of commitment that is credited with big gains in productivity, higher quality, and lower costs. Now calling itself "America's Steel Mill," Weirton is picking up new customers and boasts the highest profit rate per ton of steel in the industry. Its earnings were $48 million in 1984 while most steel firms lost money.[55]

Such success is fairly typical. A study of 350 high-tech companies conducted by the National Center for Employee Ownership found that firms using worker ownership grew two to four times faster than those which did not. U.S. Senator Russell Long reported that a survey of ESOPs showed sizable increases in sales, employment, and profits after converting from traditional forms of management. The Senator declared:[56]

> We have to find a way to see to it that the rank and file have a chance to own and participate [in their place of work]. That's what ESOPs are all about. It works.

If the present rate of adoption continues, 25 percent of all U.S. employees should share ownership of their companies by the year 2000. This rapidly emerging concept of "worker capitalism" could then cover a viable sector of the American economy, comparable to "self-management" in France, "codetermination" in Germany, Mondragon "cooperatives" in Spain, "industrial democracy" in Scandinavia, Kibbutz "industrial cooperatives" in Israel, "worker self-government" in Yugoslavia, and other equivalents around the world. Here are a few recent cases:[57]

Airlines are moving toward various forms of profit sharing and/or stock ownership to hold labor costs down and encourage a productive sense of employee ownership. Eastern, Western, Air West, Republic, and TWA have plans in various stages of development. One pilot noted, "The real appeal is that all employees know that the harder they work, the more money they'll make."

A&P sold a failing grocery store to a worker-owner team that has turned it into a great success. Employees are now called "associates" and share in decisions on advertising, inventory, and store hours. A new employee-owner was enthusiastic: "It's something you dream about."

San Francisco Yellow is a cooperative cab company taken over from Yellow Cab by its drivers, and has been so successful that the concept has spread to Denver and Sacramento. Denver Yellow has the lowest accident and insurance rates in the nation, and turnover runs 25 percent compared to an industry average of 300 percent.

W. L. Gore & Associates is a chemical company whose 3000 "employee-associates" own stock through an ESOP and share management responsibilities, which is credited for a 25 percent annual growth rate.

One Gore associate said, "We manage ourselves here. If you waste time, you're only wasting your own money."

But worker ownership does not easily translate into worker **management**. At the Herkimer Furniture Factory, one employee-owner said: "I don't see any change. Things go on exactly as before." It's a difficult challenge to operate a successful business, especially in a culture that traditionally teaches people only how to take orders. In many cases, however, workers do gain sound control of their firms to run them successfully, as seen in many older ESOPs. The Puget Sound Plywood Company is controlled by 300 worker-owners who each have one vote in electing a board of directors. They describe the atmosphere thiw way: "At all the private companies I've worked in you're only interested in getting your eight hours and taking home the check. But here it's altogether different—it's like working for yourself. The more effort you put into it, the more you'll get out of it." As a result of this commitment, each owner's share has increased from an initial $1000 investment to about $50,000 presently.[58]

Quality of Work Life

The most prominent approach is the "Quality of Work Life" (QWL) concept, which Eugene Rosow claims is now being used among a quarter of the U.S. work force. The idea eschews any particular method, but relies on developing a sound labor-management relationship to devise various "alternative work patterns." Ted Mills of the American Center for Quality of Work Life calls QWL "a new social technology" to improve both employee welfare and company performance. Growth of the movement reached a critical new stage recently when 900 union, company, and government officials attended the first national conference on QWL—an event that would have been unthinkable just a few years ago. In 1983, the Labor Department budgeted $2 million to establish 20 regional labor-management committees promoting QWL programs.[59]

It is impossible to do justice to the full range of creative arrangements that are being developed, but the following examples convey a sense of the rich potential that lies ahead:[60]

Self-Managed Assembly Lines have been set up at Ford's Edison plant where workers can shut down the line in the event of problems, reducing defects from 17 to 1 per car. The foremen, who serve as "coaches" or "advisers," claim: "It's surprising how much an employee can see that's wrong with a job . . . now, it's like we're all one family."

Problem-Solving Committees are used at GM's Packard Electric plant, where 65 committees of employees and managers work together. One manager said, "There's a lot of electricity . . . you can't tell who's management and who's labor."

Job Redesign is encouraged by employees at Prudential Insurance Company to make assignments more interesting and productive, thereby producing great savings, improved service, and decreases in errors, absenteeism, and turnover.

The Task System is used at Harman International, patterned after the British concept called "job and home," in which workers are free to leave after completing their daily level of production.

Labor-Management Participation Teams are being used in the steel industry to solve operating problems. Three hundred teams of 15 members each are in operation at six to seven plants, saving millions of dollars through creative solutions.

Skill-Based Pay is being used at TRW to reward workers for learning to operate a wider range of equipment.

Labor-Management Training Sessions were held at the GM Tarrytown plant, producing improvements in morale and cooperation along with a massive decline in grievances.

Attendance and Safety Bonuses are paid at Parsons Pine Company to reduce absenteeism and accidents.

Autonomous Work Teams are established at Romac Industries by co-workers who determine their own salaries, select their supervisors, and control other aspects of their own affairs.

Work Sharing is used at Motorola to spread a limited number of jobs among the work force to avoid layoffs and retain a more loyal, ready-trained workforce when expansion resumes. The company's slogan is "Quality and Productivity Through Employee Participation in Management."

Job Sharing is practiced at Boston banks in which mothers hold jobs during school months and students take them during summer vacations. Some universities and other institutions often hire two persons, such as a husband and wife team, who jointly assume the responsibility for some position.

Quality Circles are estimated to operate at more than 6000 plants. Firms like Westinghouse have led the movement.

Flexitime Schedules permitting wide control over daily, weekly, and monthly working hours are in use by more than 30 percent of American workers.

Labor-Management Safety Teams are being used at firms like Bechtel to take the place of OSHA regulations and inspections.

Job Rotation is practiced among 2000 teams of assemblers at GM. At People Express, executives pitch in during rush periods to help out in baggage handling, running the ticket counter, and serving passengers.

Labor-Management Lay-Off Committees are used in Canada to help laid-off employees adjust by retraining, finding new employment, and relocating to new jobs. In 1980 alone 365 companies used the concept to assist 200,000 workers.

Employee Rights

Participation is moving beyond voluntary action to insure employee rights. Just a few years ago, it would have been considered frivolous to question the old paternalistic notion that the boss can treat workers as he or she chooses under the doctrine of the "servant-master relationship." But now, "We are seeing a new kind of innovation in industry—an innovation in rights of a constitutional nature," contends David Ewing of the Harvard Business School. So many disgruntled people are successfully challenging unjustified firings, for instance, that one attorney reported, "The trickle of suits by nonunion employees fired from their jobs is turning into a flood." To head off such costly and destructive conflicts, reforms are being initiated:[61]

Privacy Policies that insure employee files are treated confidentially are in force at about 500 companies, including IBM, Cummins Engine, Aetna, AT&T, Control Data, and Du Pont.

Due Process systems are used to resolve disputes fairly. Control Data's system of "Peer Review" employs a panel of coworkers to settle grievances, and has been so successful it is now the largest program in the country.

Employment Security is assured at Control Data, IBM, Ford, and scores of other firms through planning stable work loads, job sharing, and use of overtime.

Protection Against Firing is being enacted in several states to prevent one million unjustified firings each year. Forty states have passed or are considering laws requiring that workers receive advance notice and benefits for plant closings. Michigan State legislator Perry Bullard argues, "Someday the idea that an employee can be fired at whim will be viewed as uncivilized."

Open Discussion is encouraged through public meetings at Delta, IBM, Xerox, and Dow Chemical for airing complaints and providing information. Polaroid employee confer with management through a democratically elected committee.

Pay Equity is being assured in corporations and states to remedy discrimination against those paid less for comparable jobs. Six states have appropriated money for this purpose: Washington—$42 million, Los Angeles—$12 million, Minnesota—$40 million, Wisconsin—$9 million, New York—$36 million, and Connecticut—$5.6 million. Twenty other states are studying the concept.

Executive Participation

Participation is not only restructuring the labor-management relationship but changing the way all decisions are made, including the most critical strategies devised by executives, managers, and corporate staff. These people experience many of the same problems that have received more attention at the operating level; the chain-of-command often allows inferior policy to be dictated by powerful executives, and political maneuvering is common in the upper realms of any organization. The result is that decisions are usually based more on the power of competing interests than on careful deliberations. In addition to encouraging participation for workers, therefore, executives are challenged to use this powerful new idea themselves. Chapter 7—Strategic Management—will examine this issue in depth.

Other Institutional Settings

Not only is participation used at all levels, it is also being used increasingly in almost all types of institutions:[62]

High Technology firms are among the leaders in participation. For instance, MCI Corporation, the firm that challenged the Bell System on long-distance calls, is an ESOP. Top management said: "We compete every day with the biggest company in the world—AT&T—and you want to make sure the workers and the chairman of the board are on the same side."

Government Agencies are starting to adopt participative practices. The Department of Transportation and the General Services Administration are encouraging employees to share in decisions and dealing with problems openly.

Retailers like J. C. Penney have used participation to reduce overhead and increase earnings while other retailers were in a severe slump. The "Penney Idea" is based on "bona-fide participation, an openness in the organization that many large companies don't seem to achieve."

Restaurants have thrived on the concept. The manager of Bilbo Baggins in Alexandria, Virginia, claims, "If this works in the restaurant business, it will work anywhere."

Public Schools are using a participative system in which teachers select principals, and faculty and parents meet to make policy decisions.

Police work can be conducted using incentive systems. In Orange, California, the heartland of West Coast conservatism, local police get higher pay for producing lower crime rates, resulting in an 18 percent decrease in crime.

Courts in California used participation when a judge allowed jurors to question witnesses.

Medicine is developing the concept of the "active patient" in which patients share the responsibility with their physician for making critical decisions affecting their health.

The Catholic Church is moving toward a new concept of "shared responsibility." One parishioner noted the change: "I used to think the church belonged to the clergy ... I now think the church is the lay people."

Legislation is being influenced more widely by referendums, initiatives, and other actions at the grassroots level, as in the case of the Nuclear Freeze Movement and Proposition 13 in California. Some critics even advocate that budgets be allocated by citizen votes to functions they feel are most useful.

How It Feels from the Inside Out

To really understand the profound personal implications of these changes it is essential to hear the deeply felt views of the people involved. Listen to the enthusiastic leaders who are creating such possibilities:[63]

Corporate Executives: "It's a real fundamental change in the way we manage people"; "There's such a thirst among the workers for this process, it's amazing"; "When we give shop-floor workers control over their work, they are enormously thoughtful. Costs go down, fewer supervisors are needed, you get better quality, a problem solving atmosphere."

Labor Leaders: "I'm absolutely convinced that the future of collective bargaining is in QWL"; "Workers need and deserve a voice in determining their own destiny . . . before decisions are made, rather than afterward."

A Small Business Manager: "It's the most exciting thing that happened on the American scene. It's a fantastic, incredible thing to do—imagine what your attitude would be if your company would do the same thing for you."

Here's how the workers and their supervisors see it:[64]

A Coal Miner: "Suddenly we felt we mattered to somebody. Somebody trusted us. And in a week or two we were busting our hump."

A Production Line Foreman: "We had a lot of trouble . . . I was a policeman a year ago. Now I'm an educator, a communicator."

A Shop Steward: "Being recognized as people who can make creative suggestions has given the men a certain dignity."

A Factory Worker: "You mean they are really going to let us talk about what is going on even if we think they are doing things wrong? What a welcome change!"

A "Liberated" Supervisor: "Now, at last I feel like a manager. Before I was merely chief clerk around here."

A Personnel Manager: "It is tremendously rewarding to work with people and have them come to the same decisions as management."

A Member of a Work Team: "As long as we make our production goals, we are self-managers. We're more free."

A General Plant Foreman: "I used to feel things had to be done my way. But when you give workers an input, attitudes change and productivity goes up."

Even the logical social scientists can get a bit excited:[65]

Authors of a Classic Text: 'It is paradoxical that the standard justification for autocratic practice in industry is its alleged efficiency, since the empirical research results do not support that conclusion."

A Sociologist: "There is hardly a study in the entire literature which fails to demonstrate that . . . beneficial consequences accrue from a genuine increase in worker's decision-making power. Such consistency of findings . . . is rare."

An Authority on Quality of Work Life Studies: "If you want to think large thoughts, you could say that it is a whole new phase of human existence."

Creating a Participative Spirit

As these examples suggest, effective participation embodies a subtle quality that goes far beyond creating incentive systems, engaging subordinates in problem-solving, permitting freedom to achieve goals, or other "mechanics." The most crucial factor involves instilling a participative culture: a cooperative philosophy of shared control, genuine commitment to excellence, stressing human values, a sense of community, and other intangible qualities that form the "spirit" underlying truly participative leadership. In the final analysis, employees cannot be fooled with technique alone because they understand the real intent of those in authority. Many scholars have observed that effective organizations embody such transcendent values:[66]

Peters and Waterman find: "Virtually all of the better performing companies we looked at . . . had a well-defined set of beliefs. . . . rich tapestries of anecdote, myth, and fairy tale. . . . the stronger the culture . . . the less need was there for policy manuals, organization charts, or detailed procedures and rules . . . the language in people-oriented companies has a common flavor. Words and phrases like Family Feeling, open door, Rally, Jubilee, Management by Wandering Around . . . show people that the orientation is bone-deep."

William Ouchi describes how Japanese firms comprise a "tribal clan" claiming the type of devotion Americans attribute to the Marine Corps: "The basic mechanisms of control in a Japanese company [are] embodied in a philosophy of management [that] is communicated through a common culture [which] consists of a set of symbols, ceremonies, and myths that communicate the underlying values and beliefs of the organization to its employees."

Terrence Deal and Allen Kennedy's study of organizational cultures found: "the way we do things here" is possibly the most dominant force affecting the behavior of people and the performance of the system. In strong cultures everyone knows the goals of the organization . . . Weak cultures have no clear values or beliefs about how to succeed in their business. The ethic in strong cultures is 'we'll succeed because we're special.'"

Peter Vaill, who coined the concept of "high-performing systems," says their members use a "private language and set of symbols." They have "explicit values and ideologies" which are so private that they feel "there's no way I can explain it to you." They "live, eat, sleep, and breathe" their work, which creates a sense of "rhythm." They enjoy what Maslow called "peak experiences" and an "aesthetic sense of motivation" as "thrill seekers."

Participation Is Efficient

Contrary to a prevailing cynicism that regards participation as "nice" and "moral" but a burden that has little to do with running a successful business, the real strength of participative leadership is its enormous potential for fostering economic success. Consider some final examples of outstanding performance that demonstrate how a human orientation in the workplace is extremely practical and the source of lasting power:[67]

Lincoln Electric is a classic case in which worker participation raised productivity 100 percent over that of its competitors, making the company one of the most successful firms in its industry, and rewarding employees with their 50th consecutive bonuses averaging more than $15,000 apiece.

Sony took over the Motorola plant in San Diego and installed a Japanese management system, after which productivity of the same American workers increased markedly, product defects plunged, complaints fell, and turnover almost stopped. The CEO, Akio Morita, says, "Profit is generated through the cooperation of all people. . . . In Japan we don't pay a bonus to the management, we pay the bonus to employees."

Delta Airline employees are so committed to the firm's enlightened management that they donated a $30 million Boeing 767 to the company: "I've never been so excited in my life about giving back a portion of my salary," said a mechanic. In return, executives took a voluntary pay cut.

People Express uses participation and stock ownership to produce the lowest operating costs in air travel, which has sent sales, profit, and the stock price soaring as the company became the fifth largest airline almost overnight. Revenue increased from zero in 1980 to $1 billion in 1985. Donald Burr, the CEO, says, "This is a very democratic company. . . . We want people to be motivated by feelings of ownership and trust . . . People Express is developing the base upon which long-term profitability can be built."

Procter & Gamble's plant in Lima, Ohio, gives workers almost total control in a form of "industrial democracy." A manager says: "It has the most outstanding quality record of any plant we have—it is virtually perfect."

Volvo has developed a reputation for quality cars that last 20 years largely by virtue of pioneering in labor participation. Pehr Gyllenhammar, the CEO, claims, "When products are made by people who find meaning in their work, it is good for the products, good for the business, and good for the people."

These examples hint at the enormous gains that lie ahead if Americans can learn to really use the talents of their work force. Sidney Harman, president of Harman International, a firm that has led the way in participative management, summed up the potential:[68]

If [workers] believed they were genuinely respected for what they know, were truly part of the action, they would jolt our economists, our pundits, and our savants with what they would produce.

POWER INCREASES WHEN SHARED

Although these examples focus on accomplishments, obviously there are many problems as well. The ideal of participative leadership may strike some as unworkable or distasteful because it breaks from the traditional authoritarian relations that remain an ingrained part of American culture. Even Fred Herzberg, originator of the "job enrichment" concept, is not impressed: "The authoritarian pattern of American industry will continue despite the propaganda for a more democratic way of life."[69] One does not easily reverse what has taken a lifetime to learn, so many will find the concept unacceptable for years.

It must also be acknowledged that some experiences with participation have not produced lasting success. A classic failure occurred at Non-Linear Systems that almost bankrupted the firm. The company president later admitted, "I assumed day-to-day operations would take care of themselves. I found out differently." When autonomous work teams were introduced at the Rushton Mines, the plan was overturned because of conflict with the union.[70] Like all other innovations, there will be times when participation does not work, at least until it is used enough to understand its strengths and weaknesses better.

Even if people accept the concept and it succeeds, participation requires a major investment in time and effort before it can produce compensating gains. And those who think participation is a way to "get people to accept decisions" are going to be disappointed because mock participation is easily seen through and likely to backfire. Sound participation actually changes the way decisions are made, so the outcome may surprise and possibly even disturb the leader's preconceived notions.

There is also a tendency for some disorder to emerge as the informal organization surfaces, which may be uncomfortable to those who "like to run a tight ship." Democracy is inherently messy because freedom may draw out creative ideas and energies, but it also releases conflicts that authority has repressed.

Managers are often fearful that participation will infringe on their prerogatives. When a steel plant did away with separate dining facilities, one executive said, "That upset a lot of people. [Some managers] perceive this as a loss of their power, status, and authority."[71] But very few privileges have to be given up, and even these sacrifices should be amply compensated by productivity gains and more satisfying inner rewards.

As noted earlier, participation will not be appropriate for everyone nor will it be useful in all situations. However, "industrial" democracy should be easier to implement than "political" democracy because the growth of market networks permits people with different views to simply move to other parts of the system.This spreading tolerance for diversity will allow some units to be managed jointly by those who prefer to share power while others may continue to use traditional forms of leadership. In short, we don't have to agree on these sensitive issues to proceed.

Despite all these complications, democratic forms of leadership seem almost certain to become widely used because new economic conditions demand it. As we saw in the beginning of this chapter, participation is not another passing fad but presages an historic shift in the power structure of society. One of the most important new ideas to have registered on the national psyche recently is that adversarial conflicts must give way to collaboration if Americans hope to have a robust economy. The growing evidence in favor of participation is no longer being ignored because it has become starkly clear that the potential gains are badly needed to compete internationally: more carefully planned decisions, less resistance to change, avoidance of costly mistakes, greater productivity, improved quality, better service, job satisfaction, employee commitment, higher morale, organizational flexibility, and possibly other advantages.

If enlightened self-interest is not a sufficient motivator, fierce political changes are beginning to force organizations in this direction. The self-confident young employees of the maturing baby-boom are becoming adamant about gaining control over their jobs. Women are winning lawsuits to enforce their claim for comparable pay, which a Federal judge called "pregnant with the possibility of disrupting the entire economic system." Clerical office workers are organizing into powerful unions that one antiunion consultant likens to "ticking time bombs waiting to go off." The large industrial unions hold such vast potential power in pension funds that they could gain control of major corporations. And now that the jobs of middle managers are being eliminated, they too are becoming alienated. *BusinessWeek* reported: "Middle managers who played faithfully by the old rules feel betrayed . . . [they] have traditionally been politically conservative, but may become radicalized under pressure." These sources of discontent are fueling political movements for what some call a "transformation to economic democracy—the transfer of economic decision-making from the few to the many."[72]

It is hard to see how such a fundamental shift in power can avoid provoking a lot of resistance among people in positions of authority who will be sorely tried by deep and disturbing adjustments. Douglas Sherwin, an executive at Phillips Petroleum, posed the options to his fellow business executives:[73]

> We have a choice: we can defend every inch of the way to conserve what economic power remains—in the end losing it anyway to angry and indignant employees. . . . Or we can accept the decline of organization power and start developing a concept that lets us accomplish things without the threat of arrogated power. I advocate the latter . . . a concept of leadership.

Many executives, like Sherwin, propose the same challenge of relinquishing a reliance on formal authority to develop instead a more powerful form of personal leadership based on the leader's knowledge, problem-solving skills, sense of purpose, charisma, and vision. James MacGregor called this "transforming" leadership that is able to lift both leader and followers to higher levels of accomplishment.[74] Considering the unusual nature of the economic transition and the enormous obstacles to be overcome, some form of more inspiring, collaborative approach is going to be essential if we hope to instill productive attitudes, find creative solutions, and generally create the more vital institutions needed to compete in a revolutionary new era.

Even great leaders are not sufficient because such difficult matters are bigger than any of us, so they are best grasped by drawing on our traditions. The United States has lagged in this political sphere, but it could take the lead very quickly once we see the special meaning this transition bears for us as the founder of modern democracy. Western nations have supported democratic ideals steadfastly, not out of some romantic sense of justice, but because they are the most practical means yet devised for solving the problem of governance. Although we may complain about the disorder of democratic processes, we also know that tolerating these disadvantages is the best way to insure sound decisions and to gain the commitment of the governed.

It should help to anticipate the huge potential that lies ahead by extending the principle of democracy to include workplaces, schools, churches, and other arenas of daily life—rather than being simply an occasional ritual of voting. In most organizations today, people typically continue to squander their energy in fighting authority, forcing opinions on others, neglecting their responsibilities, avoiding differences with one another, enduring unrealistic tasks, and other realities we do not often acknowledge that create a general state of depression at work. But if Americans can learn to use their democratic heritage to address such problems in a cooperative spirit, then employees, managers, and others involved in authority relationships could convert the old conspiracy of dependence into badly needed productive efforts and a more satisfying way of life.

It may appear that authoritarian officials are standing in the way, holding back the powerless, or that there is a lack of enlightened leaders who can provide the help needed to move ahead. But institutions, like nations, get the leaders they deserve. The right leaders are here now, as they have been all along, waiting, trying, and usually being ignored because the time was not yet ripe. But some day soon, surely before the century is out, a critical mass of people will see through the illusion that they are dependent on those who control their institutions. Then they will begin to share the power over their lives—which has always been theirs for the taking.

Contrary to many conventional fears, those in power may benefit the most. Participation would allow managers to shed themselves of an unrealistic responsibility for getting things done in spite of others, and instead, to develop a more defensible position of working together in a practical mode of joint problem-solving. Douglas Fraser believes, "Making corporations more democratic will benefit not just the labor movement but all Americans," and management consultant Jack Falvey claims, "If managers would begin thinking of doing things *for* people instead of *to* them, we would see productivity increases off the scales."[75] This constructive new view should produce more effective, stimulating institutions, and those who develop the subtle skills to lead them will possess even greater power than before, although it will be a benign form of power.

What we are about to discover is that all parties gain when followers share the rights and responsibilities of leaders. There is a crucial paradox in the use of power that eludes most people today: real power is not some fixed amount of control exerted by one party over another, but an empowering sense of *capability* that can grow to provide more control for everyone as authority is widely distributed. That is the great attraction of participation that makes its adoption almost inevitable in the information age—it offers the means by which all can win. As Americans come to see this reality in a decade or two, the time should come to realize the full potential of democracy by sharing the power to control most decisions of everyday life.

6
Multiple Goals:
THE STRENGTH OF ECONOMIC COMMUNITY

One of the great turning points in American business began in 1970 when a public interest group headed by Ralph Nader launched "Campaign GM"—an attempt to "democratize" the nation's largest corporation by requiring its board to address social concerns and to add directors representing the company's employees, customers, dealers, and the public. GM management responded with full page ads in 150 major newpapers claiming the proposal was an "attack" intended to "harass the corporation" that "would do serious damage to General Motors and to its stockholders, and, in fact, to the general public."[1]

This frontal assault on the citadel of Corporate America was repulsed, but it opened a gaping breach through which a wave of critics poured. Even some of the firm's institutional investors thought Campaign GM raised legitimate new issues. For instance, the Rockefeller Foundation announced: "There are constituents other than

Portions of this chapter are adapted from my papers, "A Return-on-Resources Model of Corporate Performance," *California Management Review* (Summer 1977); "Beyond the Profit Motive," *Technological Forecasting & Social Change* (June 1978); *A State-of-the-Art Survey of Corporate Social Reporting* (General Motors Corporation, 1978); "The Corporation Evolving," Presented at the 1978 Meeting of the Society for General Systems Research (Washington, DC); "An Open-System Model of the Corporation," George Klir (Ed.), *Applied General Systems Research* (New York: Plenum, 1978); "Free the Fortune 500!," Frank Feather (Ed.), *Through the '80s* (World Future Society, 1980).

stockholders to whom corporations are also obligated. [The proposals] serve the public good."[1]

It is especially revealing that the ideas being fought so fiercely soon turned into assets. As the Nader group proposed, GM's board later formed a "Public Policy Committee" to address the firm's social impacts and it began publishing an annual *Public Interest Report*. GM also appointed the first black, the Reverend Leon Sullivan, and the first woman, Catherine Cleary, to its board. These steps proved so useful they came to be regarded as a model for large corporations.

Other objectives of Campaign GM were accomplished by different parties or in different ways. The nation's first union leader gained a seat on the board of a major corporation when GM's competitor, Chrysler, asked UAW President Douglas Fraser to become a director. Americans began switching to foreign cars in such numbers that all auto makers formed consumer affairs groups to look after the interests of their customers. And the public's needs were felt in GM policy when the U.S. Government enacted legislation to regulate auto exhaust systems, fuel efficiency, safety, and other such "social" concerns.

With the broad goals of Campaign GM largely realized because of their merit, it became clear that the company may have won the battle but it lost the war. In 1980, GM management ruefully acknowledged, "If business has learned anything from the '70s, it is that economic success is not enough."[2] GM lost because it was resisting huge social forces that rolled inexorably over the business landscape. A host of such demands has effectively "politicized" large corporations, raising provocative new issues that are altering the role of big business. Phillip Blumberg, a professor of law at Boston University, noted:[3]

> The increasing politicalization of the large American corporation ... is primarily the product of changing concepts of the role of business in society."

This chapter examines the goals that guide major institutions, that higher realm where management values define the mission of any enterprise. Just a few decades ago, the idea that business should simply make money for its shareholders was unquestioned. But now in an age of powerful interest groups primarily concerned with improving the quality of life, organizations are becoming "open-systems" that fulfill "multiple goals" involving employees, customers, and the public, as well as investors. Progressive firms are expanding their role to encompass these groups, not for altruistic motives, but to survive tough competition by developing a stronger form of enterprise that combines serving social needs with making bigger profits. The result should be a revolution in economics that recognizes social impacts as an intrinsic part of business, thereby incorporating the interests of society into the essence of corporate operations.

If business leaders can grasp the complex, irresistible new forces moving in this direction, they could emerge as far more powerful and more respected figures. Most corporations are struggling to contain what appears to be a disruptive overthrow of the present system, whereas, the system is simply being extended into a new frontier. Just as the feudal manor was replaced by the manufacturing firm when the agrarian era was transformed into an industrial society, so should the old profit-centered enterprise be reconstituted as a "multipurpose institution" to serve the needs of a post-industrial era. One of the deans of business education, Igor Ansoff, believes, "a redefinition of the firm's role in society is underway."[4]

THE DECLINING CENTRALITY OF CAPITAL

In simpler times business was expected just to make money—nothing more, nothing less. An acute measure of the distance we have traveled from that heyday of the Old Capitalism is the quaint idea that Adam Smith's philosophy extolling the virtues of profit was originally considered revolutionary because it was so *humanistic*—it freed people to seek their unabashed self-interest, comforted in the belief that some "invisible hand" would guide their actions to serve the broader public welfare.

Free Enterprise Remains Affirmed—but Profit Becomes Immoral

Those halcyon days drew to a close during the past two decades as a highly educated, materially successful society issued a groundswell of new social demands that went beyond sheer physical comforts. Americans still wanted a high standard of living, however, they became disturbed that corporations polluted the environment, discriminated against women and blacks, sold hazardous merchandise, used misleading advertisements, and employed workers in boring and dangerous jobs.

The idea that social values should be treated equally with economic values seemed so alien when it first erupted that many dismissed it as being frivolous, troublesome, or a threat to the capitalist system. Irving Kristol spoke for conservatives by condemning such ideas as the product of a "New Class," consisting of professors, journalists, and other members of an "elitist mediocracy [who are] basically suspicious of, and hostile to, the market precisely because it is so vulgarly democratic—one dollar, one vote." Some executives simply attributed social demands to the public's ignorance, but a survey showed 70 percent of CEOs wondered, "We have reason to doubt whether the corporation as we know it will survive into the next century."[5]

The strength of such views reflects the fact that profit is an emotionally charged issue in our culture. All nations have mythical symbols which are believed in so implicitly they acquire powers beyond logic, the sacred cows of society. The British revere their royalty, the French worship l'amour, while for Americans, the sacred cow is profit. The myth of the profit-motive is so loaded with meaning that it rivals hallowed images such as the American flag, apple pie, and motherhood. Because of this enormous symbolic power, the issue of profit often serves as a cultural screen on which people display their allegiance to business or vent their anger at it. Bring up this volatile subject to a group of Americans and you will get some awfully extreme reactions, both pro and con, like "just reward" versus "greed," "efficiency" versus "exploitation," and the like.

However, opinion polls show that this intense conflict between business and society is neither an attack on capitalism, elitist, nor the result of ignorance. The "mediacracy" simply reflects the fact that Americans strongly support the free enterprise **system**, but recently they have also come to believe that the profit dominated behavior of big business is no longer legitimate. Consider the following poll results on this touchy subject:[6]

Daniel Yankelovich finds that 60 percent of Americans would sacrifice if necessary to preserve the free enterprise system.

Lipset and Lipset report that 81 percent of professors agree, "The private business system in the United States, for all its flaws, works better than any other system devised for advanced industrial society."

The Business Roundtable reported that 61 percent of the public thinks the most important cause of inflation is excessive profits.

Hart Research Associates learned that 61 percent of the public believes "There is a conspiracy among big corporations to set prices as high as possible."

Opinion Research Corporation found in 1983 that average people believe profit comprises 37 cents of sales, while the true figure was 3.8 cents.

Lipset and Lipset report that those who believe firms "should be allowed to make all the money they can" fell from 61 percent in 1946 to 34 percent in 1979.

Opinion Research Corporation found in 1965 that only 24 percent of Americans felt business makes too much profit, while in 1981 51 percent thought profits were too high—at the height of the recession. In 1983, 51 percent of Americans believed profits should be limited by the government, down slightly from 60 percent in 1979.

The Union Leader, a conservative newspaper in Manchester, New Hampshire, discovered in 1983 that 80 percent of high school students disagree that profits are the best measure of how a business serves its customers, while 40 percent feel profits are excessive and should be limited by law.

Roper Reports showed in 1983 that 83 percent of the public thinks oil companies make too much money, 64 percent feel this way about insurance, and 53 percent about auto makers. On average about half of Americans think business is too concerned with profit.

This provocative data reveals strong but mixed reactions. Polls like those of Yankelovich and Lipset consistently show that the vast majority of Americans consider the ideal of a decentralized form of free enterprise far preferable to a centrally controlled economy of the type we associate with "socialism," and even critics (like professors) do not doubt the value of the system in principle. This basic support was affirmed by the recent flood of neoconservative values that has breathed new life into business, but still serious reservations remain.

As the Business Roundtable and Hart polls show, Americans mistrust the actions of corporations, rather than the free enterprise system, in which business is often viewed as placing profit goals above the welfare of the society. People have a distorted view of the size of profits, as the Opinion Research poll reveals, but these estimates may be exaggerated out of distrust over corporate motives and they may simply reflect confusion over the technical concept of profit: whether it is calculated as gross return on sales, ROI, and other details.

The main conclusion which consistently emerges is that the profit motive has declined sharply in public legitimacy over the past decade or two. Even today, in the thick of neoconservativism, the last polls show the majority of Americans no longer approve of the old emphasis on profit and many favor price controls. Businessmen themselves acknowledge the problem. One admitted: "There is reason for us to be criticized. We have been too preoccupied with profit." In sensitive industries, there are remarkable instances where the fear of angry public reactions made firms reluctant to announce high earnings, so they fudged their financial reports to look **less** favorable. A recent editorial noted the irony:[7]

> There was a time when successful companies hired public relations experts to tell the world about their soaring profits and their brilliant prospects. Now [they] want you to understand that their earnings are at best modest when viewed in proper perspective.

The problem is that many Americans have come to see profit as immoral because a focus on self-interest excludes the public welfare. Most people are emminently practical, so they do not have to be lectured about the need to cover costs and reward investors for risking their capital, which is obvious and well accepted. By defining profit as a **supreme** goal, however, the interests of the profit-maker are inherently alienated from those of whom profit is made. Business managers are thereby caught in an adversarial role in which they are perceived as "enemies" of society. Harvey Bunke, Editor of *Business Horizons*, wrote:[8]

> What really comes across is that the objective of the firm is to make money . . . There is virtually no hint of idealism . . . no suggestion that money is only a way station on the road of hope . . . To the extent that business is depicted as an institution established for the "exploitation of man by man" . . . business can expect only skepticism and even hostility from the public.

The uncomfortable truth is that there is a deeply rooted contradiction between the concept of profit versus the ethical-religious beliefs we profess in a Judeo-Christian society dedicated to human ideals and democracy. Any philosophy based on an ethic of "selfishness" and "taking" is in direct conflict with the values of almost all religions that unequivocally urge "giving" and "serving." That is why Catholic bishops in Canada and the United States are issuing pastoral letters arguing that human needs take precedence over business profits and economic growth.[9]

Apologists for the Old Capitalism claim the system is redeemed because it creates important social benefits. But this remains a hollow platitude in the view of a public which daily observes greedy individuals and corporations pursuing their narrow self-interest without regard for others. The following reactions of a housewife reflect the deeply felt antagonism that smolders, not just within academia, the press, and religion, but among ordinary people throughout society:[10]

> We have become a nation of sheep—and we are being screwed at every turn. We, the people, are letting go unchallenged atrocities that should warm the hearts of totalitarian leaders everywhere . . . I am tired of being hopelessly debt-ridden while the rich and the super-rich and the politicians go skiing . . . We are fools because we have uncomplainingly let the big-money interests take over the country . . . We have gone along for years accepting the rich getting richer, toys that can maim, built-in obsolescence, unsafe cars, medical costs that threaten bankruptcy, air that chokes us, and special interest lobbies in Washington. . . . There is insanity all about us.

Although a conservative mood has muted such criticism recently, social concerns are not a passing fad but a changing set of values prompted by the transition to a new era. Rippling quietly beneath the surface of American culture now, this new sentiment favoring socially responsible behavior should break into public controversy again as it rises in importance over the long-term. Profit-centered capitalism arose during an industrial past when the difficulty of satisfying basic needs in a time of scarcity made material values most urgent. Now the shift to a post-industrial era is bringing higher-order needs to the fore. Obviously, people will always safeguard their own interests. However, cultural norms are slowly but surely moving toward a New Capitalism in which money assumes a limited role as a means of satisfying human needs, rather than an end in itself. Drucker summed up the significance:[11]

> The new demand is . . . that business and businessmen make concern for society central to the conduct of business itself. It is a demand that the quality of life become the business of business.

Social Responsibility Arrives—but Becomes an Empty Piety

Spurred by such stinging criticism and the threat of government regulation, business made great concessions to the public interest during the past two decades. Many companies voluntarily created programs to upgrade working conditions, improve consumer relations, assist local communities, and other such initiatives. These efforts reflected a major shift in ideology that was voiced by business leaders like Thornton Bradshaw, CEO of RCA:[12]

> The issues are clear. Fairness to employees and customers, freedom from shortages and pollutants, products of good quality, prudent use of natural resources, equitable conditions of employment, a healthful workplace, and many more. These issues must be dealt with fairly and directly and to the satisfaction of American society.

This is rather strong stuff for an institution that can't seem to shake its old "robber baron" image. Even now graduates of leading business schools are still being sent into the world with the conviction that amassing a fortune is their due, and the neocapitalist revolt is widely seen as favoring the rich. Has anything really changed?

The gospel of social responsibility did sensitize business to these new demands, but the idea proved too vague and confusing to provide a viable redefinition of the role of the firm. How great a contribution must a responsible corporation make? To the extent of detracting from the profitability owed to its investors? Should corporations perform "social welfare" functions beyond their area of expertise? The list of difficult questions seemed endless because, as professors Lee Preston and James Post pointed out, the concept contains "a fatal flaw—an absence of boundaries to the scope of managerial responsibility."[13]

It was also an unrealistic view that ignored the practical need of business to perform its economic role effectively: to obtain venture capital, increase productivity, produce sales revenue, and so on. That's why managers, under the pressure of adapting to difficult new competition in a time of crisis, came to view social responsibility as mere philanthropy. The idea is tainted with the pious wish that managers should "do good," but this is a luxury that has little to do with running a successful enterprise. Underneath all the rhetoric, business still considered its main role to be profit-making while social needs were simply an unavoidable nuisance.[14]

The new social ethic represents higher expectations of a mature society that wants to improve the quality of life, and this basic change in values has forced business to develop an awareness of social concerns. However, the concept of social *responsibility* fell far short of its original promise. It has become an empty piety that was never believed by some, given lip service by many, and easily dropped by all in hard times.

The Business Versus Society Conflict Rages On

With social responsibility essentially discredited now, many companies continue to treat such concerns as simply troublesome demands. A recent poll showed most executives still believe people remain critical because they do not understand how the economic system works, so business must "educate" them.[15] The initial battle between corporations and their critics may be over, but the underlying business versus society conflict rages on.

One of the most serious concerns is the indifference to massive unemployment and its social costs that often destroy lives and entire communities. A classic example was the closing of the Youngstown Sheet and Tube Company, which left 5000 workers unemployed and indirectly laid off an additional 4000 people in related fields, devasting the entire economy and social fabric of this town. Journalist David Jenkins showed how this aspect of American life is regarded abroad:[16]

Europeans are struck by the brutality of economic life in America—the swiftness with which mass layoffs are carried out, the job insecurity that even high-level employees suffer from, and . . . the low level of assistance to those in need . . . the use of unemployment as an instrument of economic policy. The coolness with which economic planners push unemployment up a few notches in order to combat inflation is a process of almost unbelievable cruelty, since the burden is borne by those least able to do so.

Workers may be in a weak position now, but they are starting to fight back, and they possess great power to disrupt the economic system. Unions joined by the clergy are confronting the prestigious Mellon Bank in Pittsburg for investing $6 billion overseas at the very time that a decline in steelmaking caused skyrocketing unemployment in the local area. The high-powered tactics that Amalgamated Clothing & Textile Workers invented to break union opposition at J.P. Stevens are now spreading to combat dozens of other corporations. Robert Harbrant, an AFL-CIO executive, claimed, "It's a strategy whose time has come . . . There's a day of reckoning ahead." In 1980 union leaders began meeting with representatives of major brokerage houses to consider how to use the latent power of their 6500 union pension funds. This sum is expected to reach $3 trillion by 1990 to become the largest single pool of capital in the world, and could be used to gain control of major firms.[17]

Customers have threatened the survival of American firms by shifting patronage to foreign brands, but more aggressive, direct actions are being used now. The successful campaign to bring back the Old Coke, for instance, illustrates the enormous power of disgruntled patrons. Customer revolts have recently taken over control of utilities in New Orleans and New York City to give "power to the people," while a group of outraged citizens in New Mexico won a $106 million lawsuit over unfair rates of their local power utility. Following the criminal trial brought against Ford in the Pinto case, manslaughter charges are becoming more frequent in corporate liability cases. Purdue law professor Phillip Scaletta warns, "We're going to see more of [this]."[18]

City and state governments are also becoming more assertive in protecting themselves against business abuse. Dow Chemical was convicted by its home state, Michigan, for continued dumping of Dioxin in contaminated bodies of water even though an internal corporate memo decribed the chemical as "extremely toxic." The California Supreme Court ruled in favor of the city of Oakland in a suit charging the owner of the Raiders football team with violating the community's "social and cultural" identity by moving the team to Los Angeles. David Self, the Oakland City Attorney claimed, "We want the Raiders for a public benefit, not merely for private gain." A similar case was filed after the Colts were moved from Baltimore in the dead of night.[19]

Hostility is even growing between corporations and their stockholders. California may be setting a trend in which institutional investors are being organized to assert their vast collective power over management. Because the number of critical shareholder resolutions is at an all-time high, journalist Tim Carrington reports that annual meetings have become "one of the most spectacularly useless events in American business . . . that seem to accomplish little beyond a ritual humbling of executives." Reporter Jerry Knight described them this way:[20]

> Stockholder meetings are a capitalist farce . . . investors who show up either fall asleep or pelt the podium with trivial complaints . . . Elections of officers and directors of American corporations are like elections in Russia: the rulers decide who the candidates will be and the people get to vote yes and no.

More people are likely to become caught in such painful moral dilemmas as the Old Capitalism increasingly clashes with a growing concern for human welfare. We all want to maintain comfortable lives, yet modern Americans are assaulted daily by a rampant selfishness that violates their humanity. How does one accept the news that business is thriving while 10 million people go unemployed? Or the reduction of social programs for children, the aged, and other helpless citizens to increase the wealth of the powerful? What about the fact that half of the world is struggling to avoid starvation while most of us struggle to diet? Reporter Joseph Kraft noted how the problem has become more acute recently:[21]

> Greed at the top has been systematized, and even sanctified. . . . Institutions and leaders and doctrines rationalize mere hoggishness. The Reagan administration honors the rich as few administrations in our history . . . The press and television celebrate the throwing away of money in frivolous pursuits.

Now Things Get Serious—Capital Is Losing
Its Practical Value

Americans are pragmatists, above all, so morality always takes a back seat to what will work best. But now things are getting serious because profit is expending its practical value as it becomes a limited force in a far more complex economy. Management scientist Jay Forrester claims, "The productivity of capital peaked in the mid-1960s." Evidence is accumulating to challenge the conventional belief that a "hard" profit-centered stance is essential for robust economic growth. The data show that profit and social welfare are not only compatible, but that overall economic prosperity is strongest in nations like Austria, West Germany, Sweden, Switzerland, and Japan where social goals have been integrated into business to create the highest living standards and quality of life in the world.[22]

That is also the main lesson to be learned from the supply-side experiments in England and America. The 1980 tax cuts in the United States reduced corporate contributions to federal income from 27 percent to 6 percent, so business taxes have been virtually eliminated. Although these incentives were supposed to spur growth "immediately," capital spending actually declined for years and then rose only modestly, savings rates have declined, and the smokestack industries are still struggling for survival though they have abundant capital. When the economy did perk up in 1983 it was primarily because of a normal upturn in the business cycle and the massive consumer demand stimulated by $200 billion fiscal deficits. Journalist George Will noted, "Growth, unemployment, and investment are disappointing. Thatcher's recovery, such as it is, like Reagan's is driven by consumers, not investors, and that was not the plan."[23]

True believers will interpret the outcome differently, but the most significant conclusion seems to be that Reaganomics was a last ditch effort to reinvigorate the Old Capitalism. It had little effect in reviving the fading power of capital to drive economic growth, and all the hoopla over the supply-side boom only drowned out the deathknell that sounded for the profit motive as the dominant force in modern economies.

The reasons are simple. Economics is a social as well as a financial activity, and a huge range of more subtle factors have assumed increasing importance that now override the influence of capital: the adversarial labor-management relationship, poor products and service, and a host of other such "soft" considerations. C. Jackson Grayson, Chairman of the American Productivity Center, acknowledged this heresy:[24]

> *The almost single-minded preoccupation by members of the administration, economists, and managers with capital investment as the key to our economic recovery is a mistake ... concentration on capital investment has led to the relative neglect of 'other factors' important for growth—management, quality, technology, knowledge, employee involvement, process improvement, training, and labor-management cooperation.*

Financial realities will always be crucial, obviously, but capital alone cannot solve the more subtle, complex problems of an approaching era that is shifting the critical factors of production. Property ownership was prized in agrarian society because land was the most crucial resource of an agricultural economy, while in industrial society, profit was of paramount importance for the same reason: capital was badly needed to build a physical infrastructure, so profit became the supreme criterion of the public good. That's why we have focused on GNP as a measure of progress, and why our lives are suffused with the imperative of making money, commercials that seduce us to buy, adulation of extravagance, and other aspects of wealth.

But now the very nature of a post-industrial epoch is causing social, intellectual, and political resources to become the primary factors that determine business success, as the Japanese remind us to our peril. Thus, the power of capital that successfully guided the West through centuries of industrial progress has been waning slowly and without much notice for the past two decades, leaving only an empty shell of useless rituals that perpetuate the economic crisis. As we showed in Chapter 1, the emphasis on profit discourages productive collaboration, fosters the exploitation of scarce resources, exacerbates social costs, increases inflation, and obscures the more subtle concerns that are increasingly important to a mature society: human welfare, community, social justice, and other ideals that once founded the nation.

A Search for Corporate Identity

Because profit was the central principle of the Old Capitalism, its decline in power has thrown corporate executives into an identity crisis and caused wrenching new demands that exact a heavy toll on their time and energies. Most executives today devote more than half of their attention to quelling social issues. One study found that 60 percent of CEOs were fighting at least one lawsuit, many involving criminal charges, and the cost of defending against these threats is growing more rapidly than sales. The same conflict is seen in the excruciating ethical dilemmas that confront managers, and which they have such trouble resolving in spite of constant attention to ethical codes.[25]

However, this preoccupation with defending the virtue of business actually reveals more about the *lack* of a workable philosophy defining the corporate-society relationship. Mary Ann McGivern, a public interest group official, confronted a group of business managers with her frank opinion: "I believe there is no such thing as American business ethics." Daniel Bell summed up the historic significance of these changes:[26]

> The decisive social change taking place in our time . . . is the subordination of the economic function to the political order. . . . The autonomy of the economic order (and the power of the men who run it) is coming to an end.

With the very purpose of their profession questioned, managers have suffered great anxiety, loss of meaning, and low esteem. Studies of the personal concerns of executives, especially the reports of journalist Leonard Silk and professor David Vogel, reveal the following themes:[27]

Beseiged. Executives see themselves as beleaguered by the rapid social changes of the past two decades, and they are unable to understand why they have become villains. One said, "Business is being criticized and called a bum today for doing the same things that made it a hero just a few years ago."

Distrustful. Executives distrust government because it infringes on their freedom, they dislike politicians, they feel misunderstood because of the bias of the media, and they think the public is ignorant.

Impotent. They feel unable to deal with these attacks because the former source of their power is gone: "We are fighting for our lives . . . on the defensive . . . Formerly we had power—our goals and values were in the mainstream . . . We are seeing the lessening of the power of wealth."

Anguished. They suffer personally from feeling disliked. One man said: "Nobody gives a damn about us—the government, the consumers, our workers." And a CEO's wife lamented: "It makes me sick to watch the evening news night after night and see my husband and the efforts of his industry maligned."

Nostalgic. Business people have a hard time accepting the passing of the old "profit-centered" business ideology, and they feel the loss of their perogatives keenly. "Profit, the very foundation of our economic wealth, has become a dirty word," said one executive. Another lamented, "The incentives are less for the guy who scrambles to the top of the heap."

Needful. There is recognition of the need for a renewed sense of purpose, a grand strategy to develop a more legitimate new role in society. "We desperately need a massive, positive act of conscience and will—to search out, define, disseminate *and* practice a renewed set of moral principles."

Confused. But there is disagreement on how to do so: "Social responsibility has become a burden on productive America" versus "We should be able to foresee social problems better than government . . . Business will have to reexamine its social impacts to avoid getting into trouble."

Hopeful. Despite all these failures, however, there persists a strong underlying conviction in the unique abilities of business managers and the enterprise system: "Deep down in their hearts, most people trust us more than they do any other institution. We can still win their loyalty."

These comments help dispel common stereotypes that perpetuate the business-society conflict. For one thing, business executives are not as thick-skinned as often portrayed. They are usually quite pained by the criticism that has been heaped on them, especially because they feel unable to counter it with traditional beliefs that have been reduced to a confusing jumble of outmoded slogans. Vice versa, their critics fail to appreciate the difficulty of solving complex new social and political demands that most managers are unequipped to handle. The problem is made worse because executives are generally isolated from these very parties who create such havoc for them, and so they are unable to understand or address criticism in a useful way.

The result is an unfortunate misunderstanding as managers and the public self-righteously defend goals defined in black and white terms of profit versus social welfare. These extreme views cannot avoid producing a sense of impotent frustration because they are doomed to a grossly oversimplified battle in which both positions are perceived to be incompatible—whereas the richer reality is that the goals of any institution involve a subtle mix of financial and social factors. In the final analysis, the only real hope of avoiding these endless conflicts lies in developing a more appropriate role for business in a modern, highly complex society of sophisticated people who want difficult social problems addressed responsibly. Many scholars like Prakash Sethi have noted the urgent need for an ideology that reconciles the contradiction between profit and social welfare:[28]

> *The American corporation offers no ultimate vision of a just society ... The current challenge is for corporate managers to evolve an ideology that captures the notion of the public interest . . . that makes sense to large segments of the body politic.*

The Coming Metamorphosis of the Corporation

Regardless of where one stands on such issues, it is clear that a variety of diverse new claims have appeared which can no longer be resolved by the impersonal mechanism of the marketplace. The heart of the problem is an inability to achieve some form of unifying collaboration amongst this melee of competing interests. John Gardner, founder of Common Cause, summed it up this way:[29]

> *A high proportion of leaders in all segments of our society today— business, labor, the professions, etc.—are rewarded for singleminded pursuit of the interests of their group regardless of the damage it*

*may do the common good. . . . What is really undermining us—not
laziness or self-indulgence or spiritual exhaustion, but loss of trust
in one another and loss of a sense of common purpose.*

An effective way to view these changes is to see that they are
part of a process of social evolution in which business constantly
grows into a larger, more sophisticated institution.[30]

As we have seen, there was a remarkably stable consensus over
the rights of various economic parties during the golden years of
the Old Capitalism, and so the boundary between the firm and
society was precisely defined. The corporation was a closed, private
system, insulated from its environment by the impersonal mechanism
of the market and governed to serve its investors and managers,
while customers, labor unions, and the public were regarded as
outside interests. In the 1960s, however, the consumer revolt, employee participation, and government regulation created a great
new set of political intrusions that now override the market system
to force corporations toward serving social purposes.

Thus, just a decade or so ago business was a stable institution,
operating in a fairly smooth but distant symbiosis with its placid
environment, and governed by its internal financial values. Today
the corporation is surrounded by a turbulent and demanding society,
its boundaries are shifting and blurring, it is beset by political forces
seeking to control business decisions, and its central goal of profit-
making is being challenged.

Regarding such changes as "attacks on free enterprise," trivial
demands for "doing good," or other such simplistic explanations
merely obscures a very complex developmental process. The corporation can be best understood as a social organism with a vital
life of its own evolving to a higher, more complex form. The old
profit-centered model was well-adapted to an industrial past, but
now the constituencies of big business are rapidly springing to life
and expanding the system to serve broader needs. An empty niche
has developed in the ecology of modern economies, and since nature
abhors a vacuum, the emergence of a modern type of corporation
seems inevitable. One move in this direction was a series of conferences held by prominent business leaders on "Reinventing the
Corporation," which led to John Naisbitt's book by the same title.

From this organic view, the present conflict between business versus society can be thought of as representing traumatic birth pains as the old corporate structure is outgrown and replaced by a larger institutional form—much as some animals periodically shed their skins and shells as they grow. So too the corporation seems to be undergoing a metamorphosis from an insular, rather harsh institution primarily focused on profit into an outward looking, benign system that serves society more effectively.

THE EXTENDED CORPORATE COMMUNITY

All developed nations are struggling with this same problem of devising modern structures for large companies, although they are doing so by following unique paths in keeping with their own traditions. Europeans tend to be highly political people, so they have used the power of government to alter corporate behavior by requiring "industrial democracy," "social reporting," and the nationalization of industries. The Japanese have a cohesive culture, and they have drawn on this heritage to create a form of business based on collaborative decision-making among management, government, labor, and suppliers.

In the United States, the conflict between a once supreme profit goal versus the rising importance of social values is being resolved as progressive corporations integrate both needs into a powerful new corporate mission. Some firms have developed "social reports" to evaluate the impact of their operations on society, revealing the intrinsically political character of any institution created by the intersecting interests of employees, customers, investors, and other constituencies that comprise an "extended corporate community." Enlightened executives are developing roles as "economic statesmen" to form a "social contract" that welds these "stakeholders" into a political coalition. The result is that American business is inventing a "multipurpose" enterprise that creates not just financial wealth but "social wealth." Derek Bok, the President of Harvard University, described the challenge:[31]

> ... management arguably exists not simply to serve shareholders
> but to exercise leadership in reconciling the needs of stockholders,

customers, employees, and suppliers, along with members of the public and their representatives in government.

The Measurement of Social Performance

An old management axiom holds that one cannot manage what is not measured, and so a major obstacle to the development of this new corporate role has been the lack of useful information on the social impacts of business. Knowledge in this unexplored frontier was so poor that it was roughly comparable to the field of medicine when illness was attributed to various "humors," or to physics before Newton discovered gravity. In recent years, however, experimental studies by academia, government, and business have began to bear fruit.[32]

Chapter 3 showed how many companies now evaluate their performance vis-à-vis customers, and the impacts on other constituencies are being measured by firms in banking, life insurance, and other industries using an impressive variety of methods. I conducted a survey to assess the state-of-the-art and found that the dominant theme running through this new discipline is that the evaluation of social costs and benefits can be best understood as an extension of financial measurements—it is used to manage corporate *social* performance, just as financial data is needed to manage *economic* performance. The following brief examples illustrate some of these capabilities:[33]

Ernst & Ernst, an accounting firm, estimates that 90 percent of major companies now include an assessment of social performance in their annual stockholder reports.

Large Insurance Companies like Aetna have staffs of 100 or more social analysts who survey public attitudes toward the firm, business in general, and salient economic issues. The American Council of Life Insurance publishes periodic summaries of the social performance of the entire industry.

General Motors has published a *Public Interest Report* since 1970 that evaluates the firm's progress in improving auto exhausts, highway safety, minority employment, product quality, customer complaints, and the like.

Toyota distributes a brochure that highlights the benefits it contributes to the American economy, including the creation of 32,000 jobs, payment of $1.3 billion in taxes, capital investment in American plants, customer savings in maintenance, and so forth. The company claims that if all U.S. cars were as fuel efficient as Toyotas, Americans would not need to import oil!

The First National Bank of Minneapolis published a social report describing the number of housing loans issued, employee education, its safety record, employee promotions, health care, community assistance, business development, environmental protection, and other social impacts.

Atlantic Richfield published a report that grouped social costs it incurs versus the benefits it claims, thereby presenting a comprehensive assessment of its total impact on society.

Clark Abt and Associates, a consulting firm, has pioneered in developing a "social balance sheet" that includes all social costs, benefits, and assets in dollar equivalents, providing a more general counterpart to traditional financial statements. The system has been applied to several companies.

Robert Hay, an academic, developed a method for evaluating overall organizational performance using qualitative ratings obtained from employees, clients, the local community, and government officials.

100 Best Companies to Work For is a handbook published by Robert Levering, Milton Moskowitz, and Michael Katz that rates employers in terms of pay, benefits, job security, advancement, and other factors.

Social reporting has gone into a retrenchment phase recently because some critics claim that social reports are mere public relations imagery rather than useful measurements, and because support for social policy has declined during the economic crisis. Like most new fields, the early rush of enthusiasm and heady expectations has run its course, and now the serious work of developing practical systems lies ahead. Reporting all social impacts is impossible, so which should be selected for attention? Is it feasible to attempt rigorous cost-benefit analyses? How can the information be presented in a useful format? Should it be disclosed publicly or used only for internal management? Who should conduct these evaluations and how can the information assist decisions?

As these examples show, most social reports presently use the "process" or "activity" approach that simply presents key figures of concern, such as pollution levels, costs invested in remedial programs, results of attitude surveys, and the like, which are useful for comparing various firms or industries. GM, Toyota, and The

First National Bank present good cases. More rigorous methods, such as those of ARCO and Abt Associates, use cost/benefit figures to translate this data into dollar equivalents in order to reach "rational" decisions, but this approach is not used very widely because the "dollarizing" of social value is still considered a bit foreign. Still more sophisticated forms of analysis have been developed to evaluate the behavior of the entire firm as a holistic socioeconomic system, as illustrated by the Hay method and my study described in the next section.

Information gained from social measurements is useful in helping to forecast, analyze, and resolve complex social issues before they erupt into a crisis. But the benefits go beyond defending against outside forces and can create a more strategic posture that anticipates opportunities. Social reporting can help understand the needs of customers in order to create profitable new markets, improve organizational performance by surveying employee attitudes, and deal more effectively with investors, government, suppliers, and distributors. Gathering this information is time consuming, and its disclosure may provoke criticism—but these same drawbacks exist in financial reporting. Firms which have published social reports receive almost unanimous praise and favorable attention.

There is also a political counterpart that is unavoidable. To develop truly constructive working relations, the ultimate challenge is to share this information with credible representatives from various interests groups in order to jointly reach more enlightened policies. Without the support of outside interests, social measurement is likely to be perceived as simply "another Machiavellian plot of big business" to serve its own purposes, and outsiders will then monitor the firm using their own social reporting efforts, as labor, government, and consumer advocates have done for years.

Estimating such subtle factors within reasonable accuracy is difficult, but it must be remembered that what we think of as "hard" financial and economic measurements have much the same fuzzy quality. Profit has been called "an artifact of the accounting profession," and it is common for corporate CEOs to manipulate profit figures for appearances.[34] There is huge uncertainty in assessing the value of assets like real estate in a fluctuating market. Inventories can be valued under LIFO, FIFO, or other conventions to change financial reports dramatically. It is also important to put such innovations in historical perspective. GNP has only been measured since World War II. The evaluation of business products is so new that when *Consumer Reports* was first published a few decades ago, the magazine was branded as a "communist conspiracy"to discredit business.

Despite such obstacles, the evaluation of social impacts seems destined to become widely adopted in a modern technological society. The unavoidable fact is that all manufacturing processes, medical treatment, and even social programs produce costs as well as benefits. As social impacts escalate and resources become scarce, the critical need to balance these complex considerations is becoming unavoidable when making vital decisions. A report by the National Academy of Sciences stated:[35]

> *We are moving toward a position where quantitative assessment of both risks and benefits must be increasingly used. Since it is impossible to avoid all risk, society will have to decide in each case if the benefit . . . justifies the risk.*

If this new discipline can be developed using only a fraction of the resources devoted to financial measurement, it could become a powerful tool for managing the vast social domain of business activity that represents the frontier of modern economies. The conclusion was nicely stated by business professor George Steiner:[36]

> *If present trends continue, the measurement and forecast of such forces will stand beside the traditional economic and technical forecasts, with equal footing, in making decisions in corporations.*

The Return-on-Resources (ROR) Model

My associates and I have been investigating this broader perspective using an "open-system" model of business (Page 245) which views management as the hub of an extended corporate system involving various constituent subsystems: investors, employees, customers, the public, and associated suppliers and distributors. This view is becoming familiar to most managers now, although it has long prevailed among enlightened firms. The traditional IBM philosophy, for instance, is devoted to the following goals: "obligations to stock-holders," "respect for the individual [employee]," "service to the customer," "fair deal to our suppliers," and "corporate citizenship in community affairs."[37]

Table 6.1 illustrates specific features of these relationships in terms of a "Return-on-Resources" (ROR) model. For each constit-uency, three prominent exchanges are specified: resources the group invests in its dealings with the firm, the benefits it realizes, and the costs it incurs. These "social" transactions are just as real as financial figures, but we simply have not considered them in this light before. By quantifying such factors, we extend the traditional method used to evaluate the firm's **financial** performance, vis-à-vis stockholders, to include its **social** performance for other groups. Summing these factors for the entire system then, the traditional corporate goal, "Return-on-Investment," becomes a general equiv-alent, "Return-on-**Resources**."

Because the ROR model provides a complete account of all cor-porate transactions, it offers a means of rising above the endless squabbling over social responsibility versus economic gain. For instance, by including both the costs incurred by each constituency as well as the benefits it receives, the model clarifies the rights **and** responsibilities of these groups rather than simply regarding social issues in isolated moral or philanthropic terms. From this holistic view, the old profit-centered model can be seen to represent a special case in which the interest of only one group—stockholders—dom-inates the system. A larger role for business now becomes apparent whereby the firm's mission is to unite these diverse interests into a coalition that better serves all constituencies. As the U.S. Department of Commerce put it, "Large business corporations have become multipurpose institutions."[38]

Table 6.2 presents typical results from a computer simulation of corporate behavior translated into dollar equivalents using social accounting methods.[39] Naturally, there are technical difficulties in-volved in simulations of this type, and the accuracy of current social reporting estimates is still poor. Notwithstanding these limitations, we believe these figures are accurate within about a 10 to 30 percent range of error, which is good enough to permit general observations about the relative size of key factors. An important caveat must be

TABLE 6.1. THE RETURN-ON-RESOURCES MODEL

Constituent Group	(R) Resources Invested	(B) Benefits Provided	(C) Costs Incurred	(B – C)/R Return on Resources
Investors	Equity/Debt capital	Dividends/Interest Capital gains	Capital losses	Return on Investment
Employees	Upbringing Education Training Health	Wages & Fringe Training Job satisfaction	Disabilities Meals & Travel Job dissatisfaction	Return on Human Resources
Customers	Purchase price Search costs	Utility (consumer surplus)	Product damages Depreciation Maintenance	Return on Purchases
The Public	Public assets	Taxes Contributions	Government services Environmental damage	Return on Public Assets
Associated Firms	Assets of associated firms	Sales of associated firms	Expenses of associated firms	Return on Associated Assets
Total Corporation	Total Resources	Total Benefits	Total Costs	Overall Return on Resources

TABLE 6.2. XYZ CORPORATION
ANNUAL RETURN-ON-RESOURCES STATEMENT
($ THOUSANDS)

Constituent Group	(R) Resources Invested	(B) Benefits Provided	(C) Costs Incurred	(B − C) Net Return	(B − C)/R Return on Resources
Investors	$ 9,993	$ 583	$ 234	$ 349	3.5%
Employees	36,520	1,691	57	1,634	4.5
Customers	10,533	4,066	2,249	1,817	17.3
The Public	2,536	338	375	−37	−1.4
Associated Firms	507	314	312	2	.4
Total Corporation	$60,089	$6,992	$3,228	$3,765	6.3%

223

noted. We are not suggesting that firms should use the type of rigorous measurement used in these studies, which are primarily for research purposes, but the simpler, more practical versions described before. If these data are at all reasonable, however, the following three major conclusions become apparent:

1. The social impacts created by business activity far outweigh the financial impacts.
2. The corporation is inherently a political system in which the interests of other major constituencies are roughly equivalent to the financial interests of investors.
3. The successful integration of these various economic interests creates net gains in social as well as financial wealth.

The first conclusion starkly reveals the inadequacy of financial data alone. The figures at the bottom of Table 6.2 are greater than the financial performance reported for investors by about a factor of 10, so the social impacts that are usually disregarded as "externalities" are not inconsequential. In fact, they are so great that social concerns comprise the vast bulk of the firm's total impact on society.

These data suggest how the failure to consider this social dimension has seriously contributed to the decline of modern economies. The case of the auto industry illustrates the problem well. An average car now costs about $10,000, about $500 of which is profit. However, as we saw in Chapter 3, the total costs, including fuel, repairs, and so on, for operating an automobile over a 10 year product life amount to almost $50,000. The net effect is that all of the engineering skills, production facilities, management decisions, and other efforts of car makers are devoted to optimizing 1 percent of the resources used by their product ($500 profit/$50,000 costs). To believe that the other 99 percent in this complex array will successfully work itself out through the "invisible hand" of the market is akin to believing in the tooth fairy. Serious unnecessary costs persist because buyers and other groups simply do not have the information, skill, organization, or other resources needed to solve these problems.

The strong concern over social impacts, therefore, seems well justified. By failing to consider such soft factors, business grossly distorts its true value to society, and many companies with records of financial success may actually be creating serious net losses. The Manville Corporation, for instance, recently declared bankruptcy because it could not pay the huge claims for asbestos poisoning that it knowingly inflicted on thousands of employees over several decades. Yet the CEO declared, "This is not a financial failure," and now the firm portrays itself in ads and reports to stockholders as being in sound condition.[40]

This broader view of the ROR model helps us see the less visible reality that the corporation is far more than what goes on within the walls of its factories and offices. The real corporation—the actual economic microsystem that determines whether the business survives or fails—is out there in society; it is the "extended corporate community" composed of customers using the firm's products as intimate parts of their households, workers' lives revolving around their jobs, people living amidst the environment created by industrial plants, and countless other ties between the corporation and society that are an intrinsic part of the socioeconomic system they jointly form. One cannot be separated from the other. Daniel Bell noted the emergence of this broader role:[41]

> To think of the business corporation, then, simply as an economic instrument is to fail totally to understand the meaning of the social changes of the last half century.

The second major conclusion is that investors do not hold a unique position in the corporation. Other constituent groups also provide substantial resource investments, they receive comparable benefits, and they risk similar costs. In fact, as Table 6.2 shows, employees typically have far greater resources invested in their relationship with the firm than investors do. And although investors risk their capital, employees risk damage to their careers, their health, and occasionally they lose their lives in accidents. *The Wall Street Journal* noted: "On a dollars and cents basis, the people on the payroll have 10 times as much at stake in the corporation's affairs as those who receive the stock dividends." Because the role of all constituencies is roughly equivalent, there is no intrinsic or rational reason why the profit interests of stockholders should be paramount. Robert Dahl, a political scientist at Yale, challenged the old view:[42]

*I can discover absolutely no moral or philosophical basis for such
a special right. Why investors and not consumers, workers, or for
that matter the general public?*

This notion may run counter to prevailing beliefs, however, many
business leaders themselves acknowledge that profit is an essential
but highly limited goal:[43]

Fletcher Byrom,   former Chairman of Koppers Corporation, put it this
way: "Profits are to a corporation what breathing is to human life. We
cannot live without breathing, and a corporation cannot live in a private
enterprise system without profits. But breathing is not the sole purpose
of life, and profits are not the sole purpose of the adventure we call
business."

Irving Shapiro,   former Chairman of Du Pont, agrees: "Making money
is terribly important if you're going to be able to do the things you want
in running a business. But it's not the end that you're really reaching
for. . . . Running the Du Pont Company isn't worth a damn unless it
contributes to the nation, unless it provides jobs for people, unless it
does all those things that the nation has a right to expect from business."

James O'Toole,   a business professor, wrote: "It is the confusion of
means and ends that has gotten American industry in social and economic
hot water. [Profit] is socially unacceptable as a primary guide for managers
of large corporations. Society demands some higher, transcendent goals."

The confusion occurs because the traditional concepts of "profit"
and "ownership" impede understanding the changing role of business
in a more useful way. Entrepreneurs who found new ventures are
true owners in a meaningful sense, and so they have unquestioned
rights to control their property. This may be a valid claim for reasonably small firms that remain privately owned, but it is not true
for large quasi-public corporations whose "owners" can be anyone
who simply calls a broker to buy a few shares of stock. Modern
stockholders can't control the company in any real sense and haven't
the slightest interest in doing so. They simply expect a good return
on their investment or they will take their money elsewhere. Daniel
Bell noted:[44]

*The idea that the corporation's sole allegiance is to its stockholders
is a myth that is long out of date . . . The shareholder has a legitimate
claim to a share of the corporation's earnings, but nothing more . . .
True owners are involved directly and psychologically in the fate*

of the enterprise, and this description better fits the employees of the corporation, not its stockholders.

Yet a tenacious belief in special rights of ownership persists because it is a central tenet of the Old Capitalism that is deeply ingrained in our culture. The conviction that business should be operated primarily for profit is a relic of the past that has outlived its usefulness and now bears little relation to the needs of modern economies; however, such issues are matters of faith rather than reason, so they are not easily questioned even though the original purpose has been lost.

Another reason for the preferential claim accorded profit is that managers find it convenient to assert that they are primarily obligated to their investors in order to avoid claims by other parties. But investors actually make few demands other than at the annual stockholder meeting, so to whom are executives actually accountable? The myth of ownership serves to obscure the fact that executives are usually at liberty to do whatever the market and the laws will permit. It is certainly true that a Herculean challenge confronts managers once they admit that other parties have a claim on their performance; but it is quite another thing to avoid recognizing such rights in order to guard privileges that hold them accountable to no one but themselves.

It should be evident, therefore, that any enterprise is inherently political because the allocation of resources, power, and privilege depends on arbitrary choices among various constituencies. Although the traditional goal of business has been to maximize stockholder profit while minimizing the claims of other constituencies, in principle it would be just as feasible to limit profit and maximize the value customers receive or the welfare of employees. Theodore Levitt of the Harvard Business School asserts that the true role of business is to serve customers, while others would place employees foremost.[45]

Modern societies have become more cynical recently, and now this reality that was formerly hidden from view is rapidly emerging into public consciousness. During the present economic crisis, for instance, Americans often witness big companies lobbying for import quotas which raise costs to customers, and demanding that employees suffer wage cuts in order to become competitive—even as managers are rewarded with lucrative bonuses.

The unfortunate thing is that a far more constructive view is possible that strives to gain the support of these constituencies. For instance, the ROR model illustrates that all stakeholders must be satisfied by the benefits they receive if the firm wants to get the resources they contribute. Just as investors must receive an attractive financial return for providing capital, employees must receive equitable wages and good working conditions as an incentive for productive service, customers must obtain value from their purchases if they are to continue their patronage, and so on.

Moreover, the final conclusion of our studies shows that all these groups can win. The total benefits at the bottom of Table 6.2 greatly exceed the costs incurred, producing considerable "social profit" as a net gain for the entire system. Business does not simply redistribute resources as a zero-sum game. Instead, the legitimacy of the corporation lies in its ability to integrate the needs of these groups to create social value.

This evidence illustrates that the unremitting conflict between business and society is needless because economics is intrinsically a positive-sum game. Although some aspects of corporate performance may involve trade-offs over the short term, it is entirely feasible to produce larger gains for everyone over the long-term. The challenge of the New Capitalism is to unify these diverse groups into a political coalition that benefits all parties, an extended corporate community. As we shall see in the section that follows, progressive firms that expand their vision beyond the orthodox profit-centered view are more successful because they are able to integrate these multiple interests.

Ironically, then, executives do themselves a serious disservice by protecting their old role so fiercely since our data show that the total benefits they create exceed financial profit by about a factor of 10. As executives themselves are fond of boasting, business accomplishes far more than making money because it is the major engine driving economic progress. But to gain recognition for these accomplishments, managers must reorient their beliefs to see the bountiful reality before us: the very nature of economic activity is to create "social wealth" as well as financial wealth. If this can be done, major corporations could assume their rightful place as the most productive institutions in society.

Based on these findings, I suggest that the resolution of the economic crisis seems illusive because the prevailing "industrial" model of business systematically excludes the bulk of activities that actually make up modern economies. Once we understand that this more subtle realm of social functions is as important as the traditional financial functions, the way is then opened to a vast range of unforeseen possibilities that may strengthen corporations and invigorate the economy. And the heart of this broader vision is to unite the productive power of enterprise with the new frontier of social needs that now go largely unaddressed.

The Social Contract

This intimate relationship between the economic and social roles of enterprise reveals that big business is in trouble, not because it lacks sufficient capital or freedom to produce profits, but because of an inability to integrate social interests into corporate operations. As we saw in earlier chapters, most large corporations do not attract customers because product value and service are poor, and marketing is deceptive. Bureaucracy and adversarial labor relations prevent the employee support that is needed to improve productivity. Industrial pollution and other externalities have fueled the growth of a complex regulatory system. Many companies are well-managed, but large segments of the economy suffer from a myopic, outdated philosophy that regards profit as its main goal.[46]

The key to restoring economic vitality today is to recognize that social goals and profit are not only compatible, but so interdependent that the firm cannot succeed unless it unifies these two sets of concerns. If corporations can learn to create what many have called a "social contract" among their constituencies, business could fulfill its responsibilities to society while simultaneously improving its financial performance. The essence of this contract stipulates that the firm accept the welfare of employees, customers, the public, and other stakeholders as legitimate goals in addition to making profit for investors—and in return these groups would provide the resources that are essential to lasting business success: reliable

patronage of satisfied customers, productivity and quality work-
manship from committed employees, freedom from government
regulation and taxes, and so on. *BusinessWeek* noted in a special
issue on "The Reindustrialization of America":[47]

> *The most urgent piece of business facing the nation is to reverse the
> economic and social attitudes that have generated its industrial
> decline. It is a task that must involve all elements of society: business,
> labor, government, and public interest groups. It requires nothing
> less than a new social consensus.*

Like other business ideas, this concept goes back many decades.
At the turn of the last century, enlightened executives advocated
a similar role called the "American Business Creed" in which managers were to act as "stewards," or "trustees," responsible for balancing
diverse interests to promote the broader social welfare.[48] These
excellent intentions did not take root for the same reason that the
concept of social responsibility failed—they were perceived as philanthropic causes unrelated to economic success. What has really
changed?

The institutional role of business is rapidly evolving into a new
historic stage, just as Chapter 5 showed how the use of power has
changed. The profit-centered role dominated the industrial era, albeit
tempered by the philanthropic works of great "robber barons" like
Rockefeller, Carnegie, and Ford. Recently in a service society, the
concept of social responsibility represented a maturing of the economic system to the point where social welfare became obligatory—
but still unrelated to financial performance. Now as a knowledge
society approaches, however, the social contract has come of age
because it is **functional**. A crucial line in economic development
is being crossed as the onset of a complex frontier of smart growth
and the demands of a sophisticated public now make these vital
new interests essential to management success. Reginald Jones of
GE warned his fellow executives:[49]

> *. . . the main obstacles to achieving business objectives are external
> to the company. . . . Public policy and social issues are no longer
> adjuncts to business planning and management, they are in the
> mainstream of it.*

It is important to stress that there is a critical difference between the notion of "social **responsibility**" and the "social **contract**." Social responsibility failed because it was a one-sided, parternalistic relationship that only concerned the obligations of the firm. Jones points out that much has been said about corporate responsibility, but "almost nothing has been said about the responsibilities of society to its business corporations."[50] Now that a conservative revolt and an economic crisis have challenged this view, the resolution of these two sets of demands is emerging as a contractual model of enterprise—a **two-way contract** between the corporation and its constituent interest groups, as demonstrated in the ROR model and recent examples like the giveback bargaining with labor. Rather than some vague ethical sense of responsibility, the social contract is a pragmatic, "business-like" form of bargaining that unifies profit and social goals to create better corporate performance. William Andres, CEO of Dayton-Hudson Corporation, expressed it well: "We find no conflict in serving all our constituents because their interests are mutually intertwined . . . Profit is our reward for serving society . . . it is enlightened self-interest." This pragmatic new view is emerging from several quarters:[51]

Japanese Companies are so successful because they integrate the needs of their employees, the government, and their suppliers and dealers into a tightly knit management system. Akio Morita, founder of Sony, stated the typical philosophy: "My concept is that a company is a fate-sharing body, so to make a good business, we have to work together."

European Companies have been moving in this direction for years. A recent conference of business executives, labor leaders, politicians, and academicians agreed: "The growing awareness that society expects from business not only high economic performance but also an equally high responsibility in the social field is a keystone in the survival of our economic system."

Small Business Firms are typically close to their constituencies. Evan Sholl, founder of Sholl's Cafeterias stresses employee participation and bonuses, low prices, good food, and collaboration with suppliers. He noted: "There are three people you've got to be a servant to. Your employees, the people you buy from, and your customers. If you do that, they'll make you a king."

Public Institutions often advocate the same view. Robert McNamara, former U.S. Secretary of State and head of the World Bank, defined his role as "reconciling two things that most people think are irreconcilable—

hard headed management going for profit ... and advancing human welfare."

Intellectuals propose a concept of "stakeholder management." James Emshoff observed: "The central goal is to achieve maximum overall cooperation between the entire system of stakeholder groups and the objectives of the corporation ... The most significant problems corporations are facing today can be solved only if we are willing to consider such fundamental change."

Philanthropic Giving is even adopting the social contract. American Express told its clients it would contribute a penny to refurbish the Statue of Liberty for each use of its credit card. As a result, the company realized a 28 percent gain in credit card use while also donating almost $2 million to this charity. "The wave of the future isn't checkbook philanthropy," said Jerry Welsh, an AmEx marketing executive. "It's a marriage of corporate marketing and social responsibility."

These examples illustrate that the most powerful strategy executives could adopt today is to become "economic statesmen" who provide leadership to weld the interests of all their constituencies into a political coalition—not only to gain social legitimacy, but to make the firm more profitable.

Consider the decline of the auto industry. American buyers have turned to foreign cars because they offer better fuel efficiency, quality, and ease of maintenance; workers have been unproductive and overpaid to compensate for boring jobs, authoritarian foremen, and limited opportunities for advancement; auto makers have blanketed major cities with smog, promoted gas guzzling dinosaurs that led to an energy crisis, and permitted 50,000 highway deaths per year, which has predictably led to massive regulation. The key to success in Detroit now hinges on resolving these old conflicts to achieve both social and economic benefits: developing more useful car designs and better customer service to regain lost market share; improving working conditions in return for higher productivity and product quality; and working with government in remedying externalities like pollution and highway safety to restore business freedom.

The Europeans and Japanese are learning to master this art of economic statesmanship more effectively than Americans, although there are instances of brilliant leadership by some U.S. executives. Lee Iacocca is an outstanding example. His unusual success in rallying together Chrysler's management, employees, the government, investors, suppliers and dealers and enlisting the support of the buying public provided the crucial difference needed to survive a narrow brush with bankruptcy and catapulted him into becoming a national figure. This theme is emerging among the views of many forward-thinking American executives:[52]

3M Company attributes its success to a similar role defined by the CEO, Lewis Lehr: "The needs of business and the interests of society are **not** in opposition . . . For a company to be especially conscious of its responsibility to [customers, suppliers, employees, stockholders, and] the communities in which it operates is not altruism. It is good business."

Giant Food has led in developing the concept of consumer affairs because its former CEO, Joseph Danzhansky, believed: "Profits flow from the services you render. Profits are not the bottom line . . . to truly understand the motivations of the community [you] are trying to serve [you have] to be involved in their problems. Again, it's enlightened selfishness."

Aetna Corporation has been in the forefront of such changes because the CEO, John Filer, notes: "Experience has taught us that in addition to helping others, the pursuit of social goals can significantly strengthen a corporation's capacity to achieve its primary purpose of being profitable."

James Rouse developed the most acclaimed real estate projects in the nation on the premise that, "The most legitimate purpose of business is to find a need and seek to meet it, rather than find out how to make profit. If you do it in a way that's useful to society, it's likely to be more profitable."

Lotus Corporation is a highly successful software firm whose founder, Mitchell Kapor, represents the enlightened view of a younger breed of "neocapitalists" who advocate combining profit and social benefits: "It's possible to make money and at the same time have a company where people are proud to work."

Although earlier chapters showed how companies are forming contractual relations with customers and employees, little was said about associated firms. One reason the Japanese outperform Americans is that they develop close working ties with suppliers and distributors that result in coordinated deliveries, reduced inventories, lower material costs, and improved quality. U.S. companies are beginning to do the same. One manager said: "Our suppliers are becoming an extension of our business." Here are a few prominent examples:[53]

Ford Motor Company recently gave awards to 36 parts suppliers for their quality and service. A vice president said: "Our suppliers have moved from being mere vendors to acceptance as partners."

Sharp Company develops strong supplier relations. One supplier reported: "Sharp [is demanding] but at the same time, they helped us with our quality-control . . . We work it out together."

Caterpillar Tractor has formed family-like ties with dealerships that last for generations.

Relations with public communities tells the same story. Collaborative business-government relationships are revitalizing cities and states with healthy economic growth in Massachusetts, Indianapolis, Chicago, Norwalk (Connecticut), New Orleans, Baltimore, and Minneapolis. A number of national organizations are encouraging this movement for "Public-Private Sector Partnerships," including the American Association of Manufacturers, the Committee for Economic Development, and the Reagan Administration. Among the numerous examples:[54]

Lowell, Massachusetts had one of the nation's highest unemployment rates before working together with **Wang Laboratories** to locate the firm's headquarters in the city. Local banks and government agencies put together a development plan that included tax breaks, low cost investment capital, reduced government red tape, and refurbishing empty old textile mills into modern offices. The result was a rush of vital growth that has benefited all parties enormously. A vice president at Wang said: "Lowell didn't come back by accident. It had a group driving it . . . The city has helped us a lot," while the city manager beamed, "Lowell isn't a depressed old mill town any longer. It's a place to do business. It's a place to locate."

Indianapolis, Indiana fostered a renaissance when city officials worked with local businesses and the **Eli Lilly Foundation** to provide investment capital and tax breaks to develop a reputation as a center for medicine, the performing arts, and tourism. Now the city has flowered into shopping malls, restaurants, and hotels supporting international festivals. Mayor Richard Hudnutt noted: "We are blessed in Indianapolis with a business community that knows it has responsibilities to its city as well as to its stockholders . . . Our people have discovered that there is no conflict between private profit and social responsibility."

Community Development Corporations have been forming across the nation following congressional legislation in 1967. Massachusetts, for instance, has 40 CDCs that bring together local government, business, labor, universities, and other groups to form various projects that foster economic development.

But what about investors? Their financial interests were once considered the sole objective of business, so how can they accept the dethronement of the profit motive? Some may never agree, of course, but the social contract is actually in their interest as well because the support of other groups is the best way to lasting financial rewards. In fact, a sophisticated form of "social," or "ethical," investing is emerging that favors socially aware firms—not only for ethical reasons—but because they are more financially viable in the long-term. Dozens of investment funds, universities, religious institutions, communities, and untold individuals are now reshaping their portfolios along these lines. Social investing increased by 150 percent during 1981, and the amount of capital devoted to this purpose is growing at $1 billion per year.[55]

Some misconstrue this idea as compromising financial returns for moral purposes, and it is true that social responsibilities can be carried to the point of becoming sheer philanthropy. Studies show that economic performance is highest when social policy is at moderate levels, and the above evidence demonstrates that economic and social performance are indivisible if carried out on a contractual basis. Such questions will persist for years, even as the number of corporations that adopt the social contract grows. Rather than being fearful of this vision we should embrace it as a solution to the dilemma over financial gain versus social welfare that has drained modern economies of a unifying sense of purpose. John Gardner offered a bit of wisdom on this point:[56]

> The war of the parts against the whole is the central problem of pluralism today. [What we need is a] little less pluribus, a lot more unum.

Democratic Corporate Governance

But can this be done realistically without challenging the legal system of corporate governance based on shareholder ownership? After all, a logical corollary of the social contract is that the constituencies of the corporation should be represented within the board of directors. Actually, such changes are well underway. An authority on corporate governance, R. Joseph Monsen, observed that corporate "boards have been transformed, in a way, almost radically in recent years." Some trends in progress:[57]

Director Control.   Lawsuits holding directors liable for corporate abuses are forcing boards into an active role to the point of firing CEOs. Jeremy Bacon of the Conference Board observed, "The rubber stamp board is dead."

Outside Directors.   Largely because of pressure brought by the SEC, the number of outside directors has increased so that they outnumber insiders now on the average board. At GE, for instance, 15 of 20 directors are outsiders. Some argue that all directors should eventually become outsiders.

Wider Representation.   Many of these outsiders are not the traditional breed of bankers, attorneys, and other fiduciaries of financial interests but include women, minorities, college professors, and others representing divergent points of view.

Public Directors.   One new figure is the professional "public director" who works full time serving on the boards of only three to four firms in order to provide in-depth analysis and total attention to these responsibilities. In New Jersey, the state supreme court appoints six public directors to seats on the board of Prudential Insurance Company at the firm's behest.

Board Committees.   Various critical committees, such as the "audit," "social responsibility," and "public policy" committees, have become almost totally staffed by outsider directors and they often have their own staffs to provide independent sources of information and analytical work.

Employee Directors.   The representation of labor is gaining rapidly. Chrysler, Eastern, Pan Am, Western, and dozens of other major corporations now have at least one employee director, and the UAW is pressing to gain seats at GM and Ford. *BusinessWeek* noted, "Worker representation is spreading faster than anticipated . . . it has probably become a permanent part of industrial life."

Customer Representation.   There are estimated to be 3500 cooperative businesses in the United States directed successfully by their customers and the trend if growing. In Wisconsin, New York, Oregon, and California, "citizens' utility boards" are required by law, composed of customers or their representatives, to help guide policies of utility companies. The power utility in Virginia offers a stock-purchase plan to customers that is a model for the industry; to date, 24,000 customers have invested $12 million in stock, allowing the firm to raise capital and increase customer allegiance.

Europe. Almost all European nations use some form of corporate democracy, and more powerful new concepts are being proposed now in various countries. Norway is adopting a tripartite system in which shareholders, employees, and public directors appointed by the government would share equal control of the board, and the EEC is moving toward a system that would transfer a major share of ownership and control to employees.

Such trends may be gaining strength, but they are also meeting fierce resistance. Roger Smith, Chairman of GM, expressed the usual objections: "You can't have a dealer-director and an employee-director and a supplier-director. The shareholders pay directors to represent everyone." Here's how the Business Roundtable sees it:[58]

Other groups affected by corporate activities cannot be placed on a plane with owners. Many of these groups have conflicts of interest with owners . . . The viability of the system depends on the continued willingness of private persons and institutions to invest and this in turn requires permitting return on investment.

These objections reflect a legitimate fear of disruptive conflict, and it is technically true that only shareholders hold the legal right of governance. But the vigor of such reactions reveals a deeply rooted hostility because the very thought of stakeholder democracy is viewed as an invasion of private property. The corporation has been sort of an "exclusive business club" all these years, and so there is a natural sense of outrage that these "outsiders" should be able to "barge in" and "take over" the inner sanctum of the firm.

However, these views of the Old Capitalism are not very realistic. Rising demands for sharing corporate governance simply reflect the immutable fact that corporations have become political institutions, whether one likes it or not, so the success of modern enterprise hinges on gaining the support of stakeholders. The modern corporation *is* the creative synthesis of its constituents and has no meaning or purpose without them. The power of such groups is not created by systems of corporate governance—it exists now as a normal part of economic life, and the inability to resolve the conflicts that are inevitable is largely responsible for the economic crisis.

I've conducted a "role play" for years among managers and graduate business students which simulates a corporate "*stake*holder meeting." Persons representing the CEO and his/her staff are asked to convene a conference attended by others representing stockholders, financial analysts, labor leaders, employees, consumer representatives, public officials, suppliers and dealers. The purpose is simply to observe how this extended corporate system works. Invariably, the outcome convincingly demonstrates that the primary cause of the company's economic problems stems from conflict with its stakeholders, and, conversely, the key to future success lies in unifying these interests into a productive coalition.

The issue, then, is not whether corporations **should** have political systems of governance. Tacit political systems, controlled almost exclusively by financial interests, are already in place and the real question is who should participate in the systems that invariably exist. I suggest that the best way to minimize the business-society conflict that causes executives so much stress and corporations such poor performance is not to pretend that other interests are illegitimate, but to invite responsible, competent agents representing various constituencies into the policy-making process in order to address these matters as constructively as possible. For instance, the seating of Douglas Fraser on Chrysler's board met with dire warnings of disaster, while it turned out that he served a valuable role in a logical and reassuring manner:[59]

> If workers insights can save management from serious error—and I believe they can—that can benefit both workers and stockholders.

Some form of genuine corporate democracy is almost inevitable, one way or another, because it is becoming indispensable to the success of modern enterprise in a competitive international economy and because public values demand control over large corporations. Rather than procrastinate and provoke government to require it in the form of blunt regulations, it would be far better for business executives to voluntarily assume the leadership for this change themselves. A survey of CEOs conducted by the American Management Association concluded:[60]

> The corporation will either transform itself, or be transformed by the agents of the American public, into a unit that formally and continuously considers the desires, needs, and concerns of the in-

dividual (be he or she worker, customer, neighbor, or shareholder) and forms and executes its policies accordingly.

This transformation is going to pose a tough challenge because there are few guides on how to proceed, and the same solutions will not be best in all cases. Ideally, the concept may only be used in large quasi-public corporations rather than small firms that are actually governed by a competitive marketplace. It may be that companies will pass through a life cycle in which new ventures are accepted as profit-dominated young organizations—the brash but vigorous "youngsters" of business—and as they grow larger they would become more mature, responsible institutions—the "adults" of the economy.

The problem of instilling a social orientation into the firm requires serious commitment and the support of key figures or it will remain an ineffectual anachronism. Some suggest that "miniboards" representing diverse interests should be formed at the division level to implant democratic controls deeply throughout large corporations. McCormick & Co. has 15 "junior boards" comprised of elected employees, and Johnson & Johnson has organized boards for each subsidiary. Special staff units at the corporate level charged with advocating the interests of key constituencies may also be needed to counter a tendency for operating units to do what seems expedient. Offices of consumer affairs would monitor marketing, public affairs would work with public relations, and so on, just as quality control has always overseen manufacturing, thereby creating a dynamic system of checks and balances between operations and external functions. There is also a crucial need to reward managers for achieving social goals if they are to become more than lip service. Firms like Allied Chemical, Del Monte, and PPG base as much as 50 percent of management evaluations on social factors.[61]

Business Creates Social Wealth

Social reporting, the social contract, economic statesmanship, and democratic governance may seem foreign to us now. However, if present trends continue major firms should become institutions whose primary goal will still be to earn a handsome return for investors, but they will also serve the interests of their other constituencies, thereby fulfilling ideals articulated long ago by enlightened leaders that are now beginning to assume importance. Managers could then shed their image as enemies of the public interest and become recognized as creators, not only of financial wealth, but of social wealth as well. Some notable companies have been doing so for years:[62]

> **Hewlett-Packard** has used such a philosophy with great success: "The corporation's [goals are]: To serve as the customers' purchasing agent in fulfilling their needs and expectations for merchandise and services. To contribute to the personal and professional development of our employees. To provide an attractive financial return to our shareholders. To serve the community in which we operate."

> **Dayton-Hudson Corporation** is a fast growing chain of department stores because it stresses participative management and community service. Chairman William Andres attributes this success to the view that "business exists for one purpose only: to serve society—our customers, our employees, our shareholders, and the communities in which we do business . . . corporate responsibility is not only good for the bottom line, it *is* the bottom line."

> **Matshusita Electronics** follows the philosophy of its founder, Konoshuke Matshusita: "The real purpose of the enterprise is to benefit the nation . . . profit should not be the primary goal of business. The goal should be to contribute to society in return for using its resources. By producing products that please consumers in quality and price. By paying taxes to government and dividends to shareholders."

As Americans come to see social issues not as problems but opportunities, we should find that multipurpose organizations are better for all concerned, including investors and executives. The idea may be revolutionary, but I think Adam Smith and other founders of the Old Capitalism would approve heartily. After centuries of grappling with the conflict over profit versus society, the "invisible hand" of the market that was supposed to guide the public welfare has been found inadequate, and now a "visible" hand is materializing to serve human needs directly.

BEYOND THE PROFIT MOTIVE

Obviously, this broader concept of corporate behavior makes difficult technical demands in developing social reporting systems, and many executives are not prepared to manage political forms of governance. However, capabilities for social measurement are improving with advances in the social sciences and computerized information systems, and modern managers are beginning to learn the art of political collaboration.

It is also clear that the democratization of organizations is no panacea. It runs the risk of intransigent groups gaining control to create disruptive conflict or to freeze policy-making into a moribund deadlock—the perennial dangers of democracy. But if government requirements can be avoided, voluntary approaches may insure a balance of interests among reasonable spokespersons guided by strong chief executives.

We should also remember that the problem is not limited to business firms but cuts across all institutions. Government has yet to develop a role that permits freedom and avoids burdening taxpayers. Labor often resists its responsibility for aiding management. Business has become a more visible target largely because it plays a central role in modern society.

The Power of Multipurpose Enterprise: A Better Way to Make Money

Such obstacles seem likely to be overcome in time because a higher order of economic productivity should be released by this new form of enterprise that is becoming an imperative of the information age. The multipurpose model draws on a more subtle source of power that can be thought of as a vast unused reservoir of "social energy"— the productive energy that is released by integrating disparate power centers to create collaborative institutions. For instance, the most powerful Japanese and American corporations owe their strength to a rare ability for tapping this energy by forming a sense of "corporate family." Thus, the competitive race in business is no longer waged directly over new technologies, products, and markets, but in developing this stronger form of enterprise, which, in turn, can **produce** such innovations. A manager at Kollmorgen Corporation said it best:[63]

> Our way of operating is just so far superior in organizational and human terms to the way most companies work, others will have a

hard time competing. In a free society, this is the most potent force for change.

The benefits that could result seem likely to be so extensive that we cannot fully anticipate them. Inflation may be better controlled because a unified economic community is precisely what is needed to spur productivity and constrain unreasonable wage and price demands. Growth should be stimulated since customers' unfilled social needs would be more directly recognized and met. Brutal corporate takeovers could be minimized because the firm will no longer be simply a piece of chattel to be bought and sold, but a democratic system under the control of its constituents. The harshness of market competition would be ameliorated as business firms no longer gamble against the fickleness of labor, consumers, and the public but work with these groups to reduce the uncertainties they pose. Government regulation could be reduced since the corporation would become relatively self-regulating, thereby reducing the need for public controls.

It may be easier to envision this transformation in comparison to other great "revolutions," such as federal management of the economy, the labor movement, environmental controls, and the like. After the initial cultural shock subsides as these ideas are adopted over the next few decades, we should be pleased to discover that the multipurpose enterprise is simply a more reasonable form of business conduct and we will marvel at the primitive ideas that once prevailed.

Regardless of how enlightened and productive these concepts may be, many people will continue to view such notions as subversive threats to the free enterprise system. Even those who approve may be skeptical, and many will find it hard to believe that such a transformation could actually take place.

However, skeptics should see that the multipurpose model does not contradict the old profit-centered view but merely incorporates it into a more powerful synthesis. Einstein did not prove that Newton was wrong, he showed that Newton was right under limited conditions. Similarly, the new model does **not** contend that profit-making is bad or ineffective. From a traditional view, the concept of a social contract can simply be seen as a ***better way to make*** *money*. That is as it should be in a world of infinite meaning, and I, for one, would be content to see people act on this belief.

Liberating the Professional Manager

The multipurpose model should not only be more effective, it would also offer managers a truly professional role that is defensible, and that restores the dignity and social purpose business lacks today. As we saw earlier, many business people suffer from low esteem, loneliness, and other sources of stress because they are isolated from society. David Finn, who heads a large public relations firm, observed:[64]

> *A major cause of U.S. business' persistently low score in public opinion surveys, I believe, is the failure of corporate executives to convincingly present themselves as persons who truly care about the state of the world in which they live.*

The lack of a well-defined, honorable role is a great dilemma for a growing number of professional managers in large institutions today, especially the massive influx from the baby-boom, who are trying to sort out confusing role conflicts. To be a really professional manager, who is the client that is served? Only the investor by making money? The boss by following orders? How can managers hope to gain the allegiance of subordinates if employee welfare is secondary to profit? What happens when the interests of the customer and the public conflict with profit? These are tough problems, and the outdated notion that business is primarily intended to make money has made things worse by placing managers in an impossible situation where their duties are in opposition to the interests of their employees, customers, the public, and other groups on whom they are actually dependent.

Whereas the multipurpose model offers a role which is so well-defined and so justifiable that it provides managers a strong sense of professional identity and pride. From this view, managers are responsible for serving the collective welfare of the constituencies that comprise their institution. To that end, they bring their special knowledge to help this community resolve its internal conflicts and to collaborate together for their mutual benefit. They are accountable to these people, just as a physician or attorney should be accountable to his or her clients.

As this new role evolves, the time may come when corporate performance is judged, not by the amount of financial resources or profit a firm holds, but by the contributions it makes to the economic community it serves. Executives would then be evaluated and rewarded in proportion to the social welfare they produce. While in New York City a few years ago, I noticed a small sign in a Fifth Avenue shop window that quietly announced the secret of sound business we seem to have lost in a frantic race for money:

> *Business success is not for the greedy. On the contrary, lasting success results from giving more and charging less. The possibilities are infinite.*

The main conclusion which stands out is that a far more prosperous, harmonious world seems to await us beyond the profit-motive. Because the very essence of business productivity arises out of the synthesis of divergent interests, economics need no longer be a ruthless battle among conflicting needs in which the strong dominate the weak, if it ever was. With the onset of a new era, business has become a collaborative enterprise where diverse parties must be united into a political coalition to succeed. That, it seems to me, is a great innovation corporations should be eager to claim. In a world torn apart by conflict, managers could make a major step forward in human affairs by perfecting this institutional model of productive collaboration, especially because large corporations set the cultural tone for society. The philosopher Alfred North Whitehead noted, "The test of a great society is its ability to produce good roles for its businessmen."[65]

Societies that are able to create vital economic growth cannot be constructed on selfish, narrow goals of self-interested profit-seeking but require a more stirring vision based on community values that can inspire institutional and national purpose. Since the New Capitalism defines the firm as a symbiotic community formed of five main constituencies, the basic unit of economics is now seen as being inherently star-shaped (Figure 6.1). Without being overly dramatic, I want to suggest that this symbol of the multipurpose en-

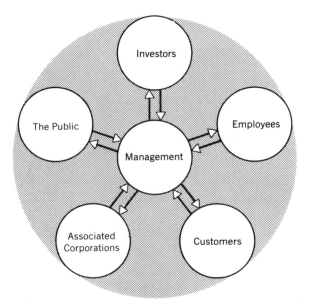

Figure 6-1.   Open-system model of the corporation.

terprise as a five-pointed star offers huge potential for capturing the democratic ethos of American culture.

The real "bottom line" then is that imaginative business leaders have an unusual opportunity to shed their old exploitative image and become heroes—the guys wearing the white hats. Americans seem eager to support leaders who can create this broader union of interests because there is a hungry craving for community today. Louis Harris finds that people "just yearn for leadership which will see a larger community of interests," and Daniel Yankelovich notes, "Americans often express a longing for connectedness . . . the 'Search for Community.' "[66]

If this is such a great opportunity for business executives, then why aren't they more willing to take on these challenges? And why aren't more of us urging them to assume this larger role?

Some people may misunderstand these possibilities because there is such a fog of nonsense spread by corporation haters on one hand and business sycophants on the other, so it is little wonder that we are all confused. And there is such a huge reservoir of distrust over the motives of business, based on decades of harsh experience, that it will take years to convince people otherwise, especially now that social concerns have been attacked once again by the neoconservative revolt.

But the biggest obstacle, it seems to me, is that business managers are prisoners of the old roles they have defined for themselves. Most of them are dedicated, bright professionals with families and relogous ideals like other Americans. Unfortunately, they have accepted the gospel of the bottom line at face value, and as a result they have trapped themselves in a limited posture as enemies of society. That is the tragic flaw in the Old Capitalism. Good men and women, when obligated to pursue profit alone, can do terrible things—not because they are bad—but because the present system discourages serving the public welfare. And the rest of us have added to the problem by being equally intent on our own self-interest.

Thus, I have come to the conclusion that business leaders may be the last group of individuals in need of liberation. Blacks, women, students, and others have been freed from the confining bounds of their old industrial roles, and now it is time to help executives gain their freedom as well. Herbert Stein, former Chairman of the Council of Economic Advisers, has called for a "Businessmen's Liberation Movement." If we could urge and cajole managers into shedding their masks as "Captains of Industry" to simply work with us as ordinary human beings, I think we would find that the old image of cold-blooded businessmen would quickly vanish and we could all engage one another in more productive and satisfying relations. So the key to getting this country moving again is to help business leaders free themselves of an outmoded notion of their role in society, which would then allow Americans to release them from the legal constraints that have hindered entrepreneurial growth. In what I hope may become the final liberation movement, then, I propose the following revolutionary slogan:

FREE THE FORTUNE 500!

7

Strategic Management:
CONVERTING THREATS INTO STRATEGY

Policy-makers are often stunned when their carefully laid plans fail badly. One reason is that institutions present fierce resistance to change, impervious even to the authority of presidents. When President Truman turned the reins of power over to President Eisenhower he worried that the general might be disappointed after giving a sharp military-like order to find later that nothing had been done. President Kennedy took office intent on overhauling the Department of State but had to yield after a fruitless struggle with this bureaucratic leviathan.

Even if plans are implemented, projects begun with great promise may easily go awry to become what have been called "great planning disasters."[1] The Concorde was expected to revolutionize air travel, but huge unexpected costs discouraged its adoption by nations other than the developers, France and England. Nuclear power was expected to provide energy "too cheap to meter," yet it has become economically and politically infeasible in the United States.

Sometimes strategies worsen the problems they were supposed to solve or produce the very opposite of what was intended—"fatal remedies."[2] The Vietnam war was fought to contain communism but instead spread it to other parts of Southeast Asia. Forced busing

---

Portions of this chapter are adapted from my studies, *Strategic Planning in Major U.S. Corporations* (A Report to General Motors Corporation, 1980); "Strategic Management: The State-of-the-Art & Beyond," *Technological Forecasting & Social Change* (May 1984); and "Beyond Strategic Planning: The Strategically Managed Corporation" (forthcoming).

often provokes parents to move or to send their children to private schools, adding to the segregation problem.

Such examples remind us to be a little humble in our plans. People are resistant, modern societies are complex, and human behavior is often surprising. But these failures also point out the truth about how change really works, rather than the way we want it to work. It has been traditionally believed that executives can control change, but, in reality, organizations are largely driven by forces beyond them. If we hope to adapt to a very difficult future looming ahead, it is necessary to begin by acknowledging that any institution is actually an inseparable part of a larger environment with a life of its own.

This intimate organization-environment relationship also helps explain what drives the New Capitalism. The last four chapters described major trends—smart growth, market networks, participative leadership, and multiple goals—which should dramatically alter institutions. However, these concepts have been adopted by only a minority of progressive corporations, while the bulk of business firms, government agencies, and other organizations are failing because they remain attached to values of the Old Capitalism that are deeply ingrained in our culture—growth, power, and profit. Why should anything change?

Because these chapters also showed that such obstacles are being overcome by great environmental forces: worldwide industrialization in an age of less-is-more demands a balanced form of growth; the exploding complexity of the information age is restructuring hierarchies into flexible networks; competition and new employee attitudes require participative decision-making; and political forces are expanding corporate governance to serve a broader range of goals. The key to successful change is understanding these inexorable forces and turning them to the organization's advantage.

This chapter describes a newly evolving perspective of change based on the concept of an organization-environment symbiosis. We first review the limitations of older approaches, focusing on strategic **planning**. Then I show how elements of the New Capitalism combine to form a more powerful framework of strategic **management** that is especially suited for introducing change because it unites the institution with the external forces that are the very source of change.

From this perspective, the New Capitalism can be thought of as comprising a "metastrategy" that goes beyond strategic planning to make the organization itself a flexible system for adapting to the discontinuities of a new era. Just as the oriental martial arts convert the strength of an aggressor to one's advantage, so should strategic management convert threats into useful strategies. The world moves on regardless of our puny efforts, so we face the choice of either being changed **by** it in ways we may not like, or changing **with** it to share in guiding the future.

THE CHALLENGE OF DISCONTINUOUS CHANGE

Earlier chapters showed that the need for strategic change is growing acute because the onset of a knowledge-based society is opening up a sharp, gaping discontinuity with the past. One of the newest things today is the very increase in newness—an accelerated rate of change feeding on itself such that the world changes ever faster as a result of earlier changes.[3] Peter Drucker effectively summed up the challenge of planning for this turbulent period that is buffeting institutions:[4]

> ... one certainty about the times ahead is that they will be turbulent times ... the most probable assumption in a period of turbulence is the unique event which changes the configuration—and unique events cannot, by definition, be "planned."

Even our very concepts for introducing change are proving inadequate. Not too long ago, large organizations developed "future studies," "organizational development," and "strategic planning" to bring about change. These approaches continue to be useful, but on the whole the hopeful enthusiasm they once captured has faded because of basic flaws.

Future Studies: Fascinating, but Divorced from the Present

When the economic transition began, a few pioneers responded by inventing a discipline for the formal study of the future. Max Ways, editor of *Fortune*, announced in a 1964 article that "The New Era of Radical Change" had arrived, and later Alvin Toffler popularized this theme with his best seller, *Future Shock*. Over the next few years the field grew dramatically. The World Future Society shot up to more than 50,000 members, 3000 courses on the future were introduced at colleges, and about 400 think tanks offered advice on the future to corporations and other institutions. In 1972 Toffler described how the study of the future had become an exciting new intellectual movement:[5]

> Until a few years ago, the word "futurist" was virtually unknown in American intellectual life. . . . Today the word has leapt into the language [denoting] a growing school of social critics, scientists, philosophers, planners, and others who concern themselves with the alternatives facing man as the human race collides with an onrushing future.

Despite this flood of spirited publications, courses, and studies that washed over the past two decades, interest in the future has had little impact on private or public policy. Many corporations and government agencies, such as GE and the U.S. Congress, started programs in "future research," but attention has wandered recently toward dealing with immediate issues. In my work as a consultant, I find that most executives do not take future studies seriously, and some are antagonistic to the very idea that a new era is imminent. Political debate, the media, and other aspects of public life had shown only mild curiosity about this historic transition until the energy crunch, the economic crisis, and the computer boom finally forced new realities onto public consciousness.

Why have Americans been so eager to immerse themselves in futurism as an intellectual field but so reluctant to put it to practical use before disaster strikes? Part of the problem is that forecasts of the future tend to use elaborate technical methods which are so complex as to discourage understanding, or they rely on sheer intuition which is so speculative that it is considered guesswork. And simple resistance to change has caused much apathy and reality denial.

But the greatest problem has been that the future remains divorced from the lives of people—which usually focus on concerns of the present. The future has been portrayed as a fascinating, rather science fiction type of distant world that lies "out there" waiting to happen, and so we can only predict it using ingenious computerized methods or the vision of gifted prophets. What is lacking is a more human concept of the future as largely emanating from choices made in the present by people. The future is not an immutable fate waiting to befall us, especially for powerful leaders who control major technical, economic, and political decisions that shape society. As Irving Kristol pointed out, for instance, the behavior of the "economy" is not preordained by some amorphous external force acting on a passive corporation but is to a great extent the result of collective actions taken by executives.[6] A new concept is evolving, as we shall see, that views the future as a product of human decisions, encouraging people to assume responsibility for shaping the future they want.

Organization Development: Dramatic but Fleeting Upheavals

The study of group process, the human potential movement, and other such influences coalesced in the 1960s into organization development (OD)—a method for creating change by altering "soft variables," such as personal values and working relationships, that were thought to cause all other aspects of organizational behavior. In a heady climate that focused on openly expressing feelings to clear the way for authentic working relationships, OD became, for a brief decade, one of the most powerful forces in management. Most big organizations in business and government undertook some form of OD program, and the results were often dramatic. At the height of interest in the late 1960s, an article in *Look* magazine titled "It's OK To Cry in the Office" captured the unusual mood that once prevailed:[7]

> Here we have a paradox: An American movement toward free emotionality and sensitivity—with implications running deep into family life, schools, and even politics—led not by flower children but by no-nonsense businessmen.

Great upheavals of change did occur but the effects were fleeting. Studies show that methods like sensitivity training often benefited individuals and entire organizations, but things typically returned to the status quo in a few weeks, sometimes overcorrecting with a vengeance as lowered emotional defenses exposed personal vulnerabilities.[8] Apparently, something else was lacking. It is now clear that an institution is far more than the good intentions of its members. The pressure of competing in a free market, the unavoidable complexity of large organizations, and other realities of work life impose exacting demands all their own. A well-known text stated:[9]

> The study and the accomplishment of organizational change has been handicapped by the tendency to disregard systemic properties of organizations and to confuse individual change with change in organizational variables.

The failure of OD warns us of the dangers of ignoring the **substance** of change by focusing on the **process** of change. OD was mostly process and little substance. Scant attention was given to technological systems, organizational form, the method of governance, or the other substantive areas we discussed in the past four chapters. OD practitioners made a lasting contribution by showing how to create deeply felt shifts in attitudes. The challenge now is to direct these powerful skills to issues that can bring about enduring structural changes.

Strategic Planning: The Maginot Line Falls

Strategic planning has always been conducted informally among entrepreneurs, but with the growth of large organizations and the unusual problems of a new era, formal planning systems seemed needed to coordinate the development of innovative strategies corporate-wide. It is estimated that by the mid-1960s three quarters of major firms were using strategic planning systems. When the economic crisis struck in 1980, strategic planning became fashionable, approaching the status of a management fad as the practice spread to government agencies, universities, and other institutions.[10]

I conducted a study of 25 corporations to survey the state-of-the-art in the mainstream of progressive business.[11] Table 7.1 outlines the dominant approach to strategic planning by highlighting key features of the systems used by these firms. Strategic planning has been developed over many years, the planning department has gained considerable importance, and the planning staff is fairly large. Planners perform nine common functions, which are typically organized about a planning cycle that is conducted annually to coordinate the efforts of individual strategic business units (SBUs). In their words, the cycle provides "a framework for managing the firm" and "a standard planning system." The planning cycle varies considerably but tends to consist of a few common steps. Broad goals are defined at the corporate level and translated into operating objectives for SBUs. The environment is scanned to forecast technological, economic, and social factors over a planning horizon that may extend from 5 to 25 years into the future. Problematic issues are identified and studied to suggest remedial strategies. Alternative strategies are formulated and tested until a feasible choice is decided upon, which is passed down to lower units for implementation.

It is generally agreed that strategic planning improves communication, creates a sensitivity to strategic thinking, allocates resources more effectively, and results in better financial performance. However, severe limitations are becoming widely recognized. After working with the strategic planning managers and executives of these companies for many months, it became clear that, although their planning systems were sound, they were seldom useful for solving difficult strategic problems. The conclusion we reached was that strategic planning has reached the limits of its influence because the major constraint facing large companies stems from the present nature of corporate management itself. Ironically, at the very time that strategic planning is becoming so popular, disenchantment has set in among leading firms like GE that are cutting back their planning efforts. Authorities describe the problem this way:[12]

> Strategic analysis has not been particularly successful. Unless you can implement plans, they have no value whatsoever . . . Corporate planning has been translated into an empty paper chase, which consumes management time, but which has next to no impact on real decisions . . . There is evidence that only 10 percent of all U.S. companies with strategic plans use them effectively.

My study shows that the basic causes of this failure are very deep, focusing on three main themes that correspond roughly with

TABLE 7.1. HIGHLIGHTS OF STRATEGIC PLANNING PRACTICES

Corporation	Years of Experience	Rank of Planning Officer	Reporting Position	Number of Planners	Planning Horizon (years)	Cycle Period (years)	Business Development	Mergers and Acquisitions	SBU Consultation	Management Training	Corporate Goals and Strategies	Issue Analysis	Critique SBU Plans	Resource Allocation	Environmental Scanning
Exxon	25	VP	Finance	40	2–10	1	*	*		*	*	*		*	*
General Motors	8	Director	Finance	20	10–25	1	*	*		*	*	*		*	*
Texaco	16	VP	President	12	5	1	*	*		*	*	*		*	*
IBM	19	VP	Chairman	60	5	17 months		*	*		*	*	*	*	*
General Electric	14	Senior VP	Vice Chairman	35	5–15	1		*	*	*	*	*	*	*	*
Atlantic Richfield	12	VP	Chairman	30	5, 20	1		*	*	*	*	*	*	*	*

Functions Performed

Company														
Dow Chemical	12	Director	Executive VP	40	7, 30	update	*	*	*	*	*	*	*	*
United Technologies	9	VP	Chairman	7	5	1	*	*	*	*	*	*	*	*
Boeing	14	VP	Finance	6	10	1	*	*	*	*	*	*	*	*
Xerox	7	VP	Chairman	40	7	1	*	*	*	*	*	*	*	*
TRW	10	VP	Finance	5	5–25	1	*	*	*	*	*	*	*	*
Texas Instruments	23	VP	R&D	4	10–15	1	*	*	*	*	*	*	*	*
Crown-Zellerbach	15	Assist. CEO	Chairman	6	5–25	1–2	*	*	*	*	*	*	*	*
Mead	12	V. Chairman	Chairman	4	5	1	*	*	*	*	*	*	*	*
Hewlett-Packard	19	Director	President	4	5	update	*	*	*	*	*	*	*	*
Digital Equipment	7	Director	Marketing	6	5	1			*	*	*	*	*	*
Clark Equipment	11	Director	Chairman	10	5	1	*	*			*	*	*	*
Rexnord	25	VP	Vice Chairman	6	5	1	*	*	*	*	*	*	*	*
BankAmerica	9	Senior VP	Chairman	5	5	1			*	*	*	*	*	*
Citicorp	15	Exec. VP	Chairman	8	10–15	none	*	*	*	*	*	*	*	*
Sears Roebuck	7	VP	Chairman	10	5	1	*	*	*			*		*
Mariott	9	VP	Chairman	3	5–10	1	*	*	*	*	*	*	*	*
Comsat	7	VP	Finance	6	5	1	*	*	*	*	*	*	*	*
Walt Disney	19	Director	Administration	12	5–10	none	*	*	*	*	*	*	*	*
Hoffman-LaRoche	17	Director	Public Affairs	6	5	1		*	*		*	*		
Averages:	13.6			15.2	Percent of Sample:		80	60	92	56	80	92	72	76	100%

the dilemmas of the Old Capitalism described in Chapter 1. Strategic planning tends to ignore critical new soft issues, it is conducted using an unwieldy bureaucratic process, and decisions are made in isolation from external parties.

The first limitation shows up in the way planning is usually restricted to "hard" business concerns like building facilities, setting up marketing programs, and balancing the portfolio of business units.[13] These are crucial matters, but there is a conspicuous lack of attention to the difficult new "soft" issues that have become so critical: the revolution in information technology, labor productivity, product quality, customer attitudes, government regulation, and a vast range of other social concerns. The crux of the matter is that these problems are so unusual and confusing that few people know how they should be handled, and they are often avoided because they involve sensitive sociopolitical controversies that can be personally disturbing. As we saw in Chapter 3, however, soft issues comprise the new frontier of smart growth, so they are unlikely to go away but seem almost certain to become even more severe. Kirk Hanson of the Stanford Business School urged:[14]

> In the 1980s, the principal task will be to integrate planning for social performance with corporate strategic planning.

The second problem involves difficulties in the working relations between executives, operating managers, and employees. Most companies advocate decentralized planning, but the reality is that the chain-of-command usually imposes decisions on lower units, thereby interfering with the autonomy that people need to do their jobs in an innovative way. One manager confided that the rule of corporate executives was so complete in his firm that it was surreptitiously called "socialism." Of course, this frustrating conflict is endemic because it simply represents the institutional equivalent of original sin. But the problem is made far more severe by a pervasive bureaucratic culture that prevents collaborative problem solving, as we saw in Chapters 4 and 5. A hierarchical, authoritarian organization is prone to create a planning system that is merely an appendage to its bureaucracy, transforming what should be a creative, entrepreneurial process into another useless chore. Business professor Richard Pascale observed:[15]

Procedures like the annual planning cycle haven't been terribly ef-fective. Strategy becomes a routine exercise. The process ends up having the perverse effect of desensitizing people to strategic issues.

The third limitation is that the planning process is isolated from the external groups that critically affect the company: labor leaders, consumer advocates, government officials, and the like. Large firms have staffs responsible for consumer affairs, public policy, and other such "boundary spanning" functions, but these units tend to focus on conducting studies rather than working with stakeholders. Chapter 6 showed that most companies are entangled in a hectic web of difficult external relationships, yet contacts with such groups are usually limited to accusatory exchanges which take place through the media and the courts. The participation of "outsiders" in strategic decisions is anathema to most managers, and it poses a realistic problem of consuming time and risking painful confrontations. The most severe obstacle, however, is a common belief that stakeholder collaboration is a moral luxury rather than a practical means of injecting a healthy dose of reality into the planning process. Donald Povejsil, a Westinghouse vice president, noted:[16]

The notion that an effective strategy can be constructed by someone in an ivory tower is totally bankrupt.

These limitations stem from serious misconceptions about the very nature of strategic change. The orderly, systematic approach of the typical planning cycle would lead one to believe that strategy formulation is a logical, quantifiable process of internal problem-solving undertaken to produce a written plan. However, the challenge of creating effective strategic change is so complex and far-ranging that it defies being captured in any set of procedures.[17]

Strategy formulation is not a simple linear problem-solving se-quence, but a cyclical process involving repeated passes through various phases of the problem over a period of years. If strategic change is thought of as analogous to operating a vehicle, it could be said that the executive's task is to steer the organization into the future. Further, the future terrain is unknown, there is no established road, and conditions are constantly changing. So the skillful executive is like an explorer who must continually sight ahead and make tentative, incremental changes to discover a route by trial and error that will avoid calamity and finally reach the destination.

The process may focus on financial figures, but this is merely a screen behind which lie a host of other critical problems that are more critical. Strategic change requires developing complex information systems to collect, analyze, and distribute huge amounts of information throughout the firm. It is also a social process of communication and education among hundreds of key managers who must understand the plan and carry it out. And it cannot ignore the political need to realign power centers of vested interests into a coalition that will support major reorganizations. Even after a strategy is agreed on, its successful implementation hinges on gaining the support of employees, distributors, and customers.

Moreover, strategic decisions are not simply "rational" or "objective" but embody a very personal, intuitive form of thinking. An effective strategy is based on abstract beliefs that executives use to interpret messy problems. A major decision requires an existential commitment that risks success or failure. It is also a symbolic act that reflects the basic ideals and values of the decision-makers. In short, strategy is derived from some poorly understood level of awareness that eludes formal planning.

As if this were not tough enough, the entire process takes place within a rapid swirl of technological, economic, and social change that causes the environment and the organization itself to be constantly in motion as they evolve to new forms that are not understood or predictable.

Thus, the challenge of creating strategic change is so poorly understood and hard to manage because this fluctuating, interwoven field of problematic technical and social patterns is almost incomprehensible. The "rational" approach of the planning cycle is quite blunt in comparison to this subtle complexity, allowing the mechanics of the process to interfere with the creative imagination needed to produce innovative strategies. There is "too great a fondness for numbers, research, and voluminous analysis," said one management consultant.[18]

Analytical methods and technical data are useful, however, good firms try to avoid undue paperwork so as to invite intuition and judgment as well. Planners claim, "Lots of creative insight is used rather than rigid models," and "We try to accept the organic, messy nature of strategic decisions." For the same reason, skillful executives do not rely primarily on systematic planning efforts, but are engaged in a more fluid, informal decision-making process.[19] As one manager told me, "The real strategic planning is what goes on in the CEO's head." Executives are pragmatically oriented to finding some course of action that will work, so they base their decisions on knowledge that is intuitively reasonable, rather than on complex studies that often seem esoteric and doubtful. Truly creative strategy formulation is a highly skilled problem-solving art whereby the decision-maker continually gathers opinions, bits of data, and new ideas from respected and influential persons, and the most useful of this information is integrated into a mental model, or "vision," that is constantly evolving until a solution emerges.

Progressive companies in my study are developing very different approaches now based on these realities, as we shall see, because it is becoming evident that the problem of creating effective change runs too deep to be solved by any form of planning as such; the very concept of strategic "planning" was merely grafted on to the Old Capitalism that is now outmoded.[20] The challenge facing corporations is not to formulate better strategic decisions, balance their portfolio of SBUs, forecast financial performance, or make other such improvements in the existing model of institutions—it is the model itself that is faulty, and strategic planning is simply part of that model.

Great hope was once placed in strategic planning as a powerful tool that would enable business to adapt to a new economic era, but now the sophisticated planning systems developed over the past two decades are taking on the implications of a "Maginot Line." The current loss of faith shows that this last line of defense against the threat of a turbulent environment has been overrun, and an increasing number of managers are being forced to see that fresh thinking is needed about the entire approach to management itself in order to handle the unusual, perplexing challenges just ahead. As one corporate executive put it: "The ruling sceptre is passing from those with the answers to those who ask the questions."

THE STRATEGICALLY MANAGED ORGANIZATION

The development of a new form of management that is good at creating strategic change represents an historic step in the evolution of business practice. Production engineering was most crucial earlier in the century when manufacturing systems were first developed, marketing dominated those halcyon post-World War II years of consumer demand stimulation, financial skills have reigned supreme in the recent period of corporate mergers, while today the problem of adapting to a radically different future is bringing the problem of strategic change to the fore. Thus, the focus of attention has moved from production management, to marketing management, to financial management, and now, as planning authority Igor Ansoff stated, "The new scope of post-industrial management should be called **strategic management**."[21] Strategic management represents a higher level capability evolving at a more mature stage in the life cycle of organizations that is needed to cope with the complexity of a post-industrial environment.

However, a great deal of controversy persists over what actually constitutes strategic management. One group of consultants noted, "Hardly anyone yet fully understands what strategic management is."[22] The concept remains vague and fraught with tough questions. Time and resources are limited, so which problematic issues should be addressed? How can planning be structured in large organizations to avoid the problems of bureaucracy? Who should be included in the planning process and how should it be conducted to create lasting change? In short, what really is there about strategic management that differs from what has always been thought of as just good management?

I present a framework here that draws on the concepts in earlier chapters—smart growth, market networks, participative leadership, and multiple goals—and integrates these principles into a coherent whole describing the new form of management now emerging. This view also employs more effective approaches that are evolving in future studies, organization development, and strategic planning, and it is organized about a new concept of "issue management" that offers a sharp focus on strategic action.

As these trends develop, the new ideal should be a "strategically managed organization" that is better able to foster change by moving beyond the old limitations of strategic planning. Organizations will direct attention not only to hard issues, but also to critical socio-political controversies that can be converted into opportunities for smart growth. Strategy formulation will take place not just in a planning cycle conducted within an authoritarian hierarchy, but in the ongoing decisions of an organic network of semi-autonomous ventures. The institution will interact with its environment not simply through forecasting by boundary spanning staffs, but by forming collaborative relations that integrate the organization with its external interest groups.

So strategic management is not simply "better" strategic planning, but a way to extend strategic change throughout the organization to become synonymous with management itself. George Steiner said strategic planning should become "intrinsically woven into the entire fabric of management."[23] The strategically managed corporation is best thought of as a **meta**strategy—it represents a higher level strategy that transcends strategic planning to create a more powerful type of organization that is especially adept at fostering entrepreneurial innovation, a system for creating strategies rather than a strategy itself. Hard technology, the planning cycle, authoritarian hierarchies, financial goals, and other such concepts continue to serve important functions. Strategic planning, for instance, is still used by progressive corporations, but it is done more selectively: existing plans may simply be updated, the planning cycle is conducted only when needed, and there is a focus on key units or issues. Now, however, these old practices are becoming simply a basic framework that supports a changing network of small, entrepreneurial units working intimately with elements in their environment to serve the purposes of the firm and its stakeholders. Thus, the main strategy becomes the transformation of the organization into an adaptive institution.

Figure 7.1 depicts the key steps in strategic management as a generic process for creating change. The model is generic because it represents the same basic idea used in the typical corporate planning cycle, concepts of learning developed by behavioral scientists, and the cybernetic principles of general systems theory describing how

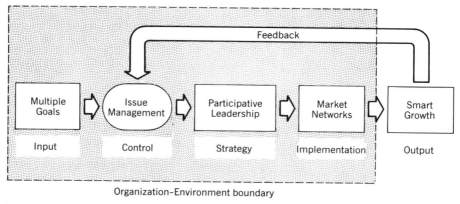

Organization-Environment boundary

Figure 7-1.   The strategic management process.

any system adjusts to its environment—in short, all forms of adaptive change. The following sections illustrate the logic underlying this process that makes strategic management a unique concept. For ease of exposition, these steps are discussed in an order that differs from Chapters 3 through 6; no particular significance is implied because this is an organic cycle of change, constantly shifting through these various phases as the organization evolves. I find that managers tend to think in such terms, but in a far more fluid, creative way as they continually wrestle with the problem of creating strategic change.[24]

Smart Growth Integrates the Organization Into Its Environment

The problem of anticipating unpredictable crises arising from a turbulent environment has typically been solved by using trend extrapolation, modeling, the Delphi method, and other techniques to scan and forecast the future: technological advances, the actions of competitors, performance of the economy, government legislation, and even social attitudes. As noted earlier, this approach assumes a passive view in which the environment is separable from the company. The objective is to provide information to decision-makers for constructing an effective strategic position that will withstand future threats.

This "detached" philosophy made sense when managers were primarily concerned with running internal operations efficiently, and so their posture was to shield the organization from external disturbances. But now a defensive stance is too weak to deal with labor conflict, a consumer revolt, and other threatening new problems. In the face of such mounting disorder, it is a bit luxurious to believe we can remain removed by simply "predicting" the future and then reacting. *BusinessWeek* observed that "a totally new type of strategic planning . . . is required in direct contrast to what worked in the halcyon days of the recent past."[25]

In previous chapters we saw that progressive managers are addressing these more complex external problems by integrating interest groups into the firm: client-driven marketing to bridge the customer gap; collaborative labor-management relations; joint business-community projects; and closer working ties with suppliers and distributors. The idea of absorbing strategic elements into the organization is not new. Firms have always reduced environmental uncertainty by vertical integration to control supply lines on the input end and distribution channels on the output end.[26] Now the need is to extend control over the social and political unrest that poses the greatest threat to a more desirable future. Futurist John Platt pointed out how these developments are leading to an active view of the future: "The problem is not to predict the future but to change it." Look at how some organizations are applying this powerful new perspective by collaborating with various parties in forecasting trends, identifying alternative scenarios, and forming plans to gain some measure of mutual control over their environment:[27]

Monitoring Teams.   The life insurance industry pioneered a "TEAM" (Trend Evaluation and Management) concept in which selected people throughout the organization monitor periodicals and report on crucial trends. Periodic meetings are held to synthesize individual reports, and the results are disseminated by the monitors back to their units. The process has been used successfully at many firms and government agencies, including Ford Motor Company and the U.S. Congress, as an early warning system that sensitizes the organization to the future and encourages proactive change.

Labor-Management Planning.   AT&T and the CWA have a contractual agreement to create "common interest forums" that meet periodically to examine common strategic problems and search for solutions.

External Liaisons.   Many organizations work with community groups, public officials, consumer advocates, labor leaders, and outside consultants to identify future issues and consider ways to resolve them.

Such programs have been used at GE, Shell Oil, Northern States Power Company, and many other institutions. The same idea underlies the research consortiums being used in various high-tech industries which have banded together to counter foreign competition.

Community Planning Conferences. Cities and states, including Hawaii, Georgia, Colorado, Minnesota, Washington, and recently San Francisco, have engaged large numbers of the citizenry in projecting future trends, developing alternative future scenarios, and determining strategic courses of action. Washington's effort involved 130,000 citizens. Mayor Feinstein of San Francisco said, "Other governments seem to be in crisis . . . We are planning ahead—not throwing up our hands."

Cross-Institutional Meetings. The American Association for the Advancement of Science is bringing together parties in the public and private sectors in order to jointly address critical technological problems. A series of seminars on biotechnology was organized for EPA officials, research scientists, and managers in pharmaceutical, chemical, and agricultural firms. Similar projects are underway for transportation and aging.

These examples illustrate some preliminary attempts to go beyond simply gathering "data" on the future in order to engage the parties that actually shape the future. The more subtle economic, social, and political issues that trouble both the institution and its constituencies may be better understood, leading to new possibilities for creating smart forms of growth, as shown in Chapter 3. Existing products or services may be modified, new projects can be defined to fill unmet needs, troublesome community impacts may be ameliorated, and so on. A far different frontier is opening up that focuses on the use of sophisticated technologies to improve the quality of life, and that can be best achieved through active participation by those involved.

Obviously, some environmental forces are far too large to be coopted, particularly by small organizations. The state of the economy, national politics, and many other factors are beyond the influence of national governments, much less ordinary business firms. So there will always remain powerful external influences that can only be dealt with using traditional passive approaches like forecasting. Still, any organization can extend its boundaries to include key elements that are critical to its success and thereby become better equipped to cope with other sources of turbulence which are beyond control.

Multiple Goals Establish Political Legitimacy

As external parties are brought within the organization's influence, they then become part of the extended institutional system rather than sources of environmental disorder. But the cost for this added control is that broader forms of governance are needed to create political legitimacy among competing interests. Thus, if management is to gain control over its constituencies, it must allow them to exert control on the institution as well. Whether invited or not, the fact is that effective strategy formulation in large firms is now unavoidably a political process to gain employee commitment, customer patronage, and other forms of support that are vital to successful enterprise. Academics Bower and Doz noted:[28]

> Managers of today's multinationals are not so much economic de-cision-makers as they are governors of a social and political strategic management process. . . . In large, complex organizations we cannot talk about the process of strategy formulation except in social and political terms.

Unifying these divergent interests is crucial because all else flows from developing some overarching social mission to create that essential sense of legitimate common purpose. Many excellent companies like IBM, Hewlett-Packard, and ARCO conduct an extensive dialogue throughout the organization to establish legitimate goals, but most large corporations tend to see themselves as simply an aggregated portfolio of business investments to be managed profitably. Impressive formal goal statements are common, but often these are issued without much involvement or conviction, so they are easily dismissed as a rhetorical exercise in empty platitudes. Generally speaking, poorly managed companies tend to lack inspiring values and a guiding vision that are needed to energize any organization.

We described in Chapter 6 how progressive companies are developing a social contract that unifies stakeholders into a coalition. Enlightened executives understand that the old technical approach to strategy is passé so they are cultivating the ability to form political liaisons. Consulting groups like the Human Resources Network in Philadelphia, Matrix in England, and the Wharton School at the University of Pennsylvania are developing "stakeholder management" as a form of strategic planning that focuses on forming collaborative relationships. Professor William Dill summed up the growing trend: "The move today is from stakeholder *influence* to stakeholder *participation*."[29]

The fact is that any enterprise is no more and no less than the sum of its intersecting interests, so organizations that learn to accept this reality should be better able to convert the sociopolitical turbulence besetting them into constructive forces for change. Even firms that resist are unwittingly moving in this direction, as seen in Campaign GM, because the information age urges business to fill a broader niche in society.

Issue Management Is the Heart of Strategic Change

Figure 7.1 shows that the heart of strategic management is issue management since issues are focal stresspoints that occur between the organization and its continually shifting environment. Change has become so great now that the social order represents a discontinuity with the past, creating a deep rift between most firms and their surroundings that allows the environment to bear against the organization like a drifting continental plate. Issues, then, can be thought of as strategic hot spots generated by the pressure at this interface, erupting unexpectedly into social volcanos that shower the corporation with operational brushfires. Because issues threaten to flare up into major conflagrations, they are the most central strategic problems facing any organization, and so managers know that resolving strategic issues is their main responsibility.

Issue management is intended to identify these potential stresspoints early enough to realign the organization's boundaries and relieve environmental pressure before it erupts into a crisis. Some analysts believe issues follow approximately a seven-year life cycle, so future disasters can be headed off if issues are caught at the early phase in this cycle when they are gathering strength.[30] When an organization fails to alert itself to a potential threat, it must later resort to "crisis management" to solve the problem, as exemplified by Johnson & Johnson's skillful handling of the Tylenol poisoning crises.

During the past decade or so the incidence and severity of issues has grown from about zero to the point where more than half of top management's time is devoted to quelling external disturbances. Issue management has become especially attractive because, unlike the bureaucratic systems involved in strategic planning, it goes directly to the heart of major problems with a minimum of fuss. As Table 7.1 shows, this overriding importance has caused almost all firms in my study to develop systems for issue identification, analysis, and resolution. Over 200 of the Fortune 500 companies have recently established issue management programs, and the field now has its own professional associations, publications, and meetings. A strategic planner at GE emphasized, "Our effort will be built more around specific issues, and less on specific businesses." Here's how a few corporations approach this task:[31]

ARCO has a committee represented by various organizational units to identify issues which are then assigned to teams for further study and recommendation. As many as 100 issues are tracked until they are resolved or disappear.

Digital Equipment's strategic planning department identified issues by interviewing corporate executives to determine their most serious concerns. Aggregating common themes then allowed key issues to emerge as clusters of problems described in the actual ideas and phrases of decision-makers.

TRW started an issue management function which is operated by a cross-disciplinary "Public Policy Council" of executives and is supported by an "Issues and Analysis Management Staff."

IBM has accorded such importance to the need that it reorganized into two major command chains starting from the board on down: one focusing on operations and the other on public policy.

Nabisco has extended the use of management principles to develop an issue management system which the CEO, Robert Schaerberle, credits for avoiding problems in food labeling, deregulation, and PCBs. He notes, "Proper resolution of these issues resulted in millions of dollars of savings."

Planning Research Corporation holds an annual meeting at which 100 or so top managers work in groups to identify key issues and propose solutions.

As these examples suggest, there are common guides for the way issue management works. Strategic planning typically focuses on hard technical matters, but issue management covers all areas including soft sociopolitical issues. The function is usually organized as an interdepartmental, high-level advisory group that may be called an "issue management team," "public policy committee," or an "environmental analysis unit."

Interviews, opinion surveys, economic trends, and other such feedback are obtained from the organization's managers, staff groups, and stakeholders to determine the most critical issues facing the firm over the next few years. Hundreds of potential issues can be identified, which have to be culled to select a manageable dozen or so for more complete study. Some firms maintain an extensive inventory of active issues that are monitored until they either drop from significance or appear to be entering a critical phase that requires action.

Once an issue is understood, strategic alternatives are explored to resolve it by redefining policies, changing operations, developing new ventures, or other courses of action. Unfortunately, most attention is directed to catastrophic crises that result from the failure to head off potential threats which exploded into live issues—but there are examples of sound foresight. IBM avoided being left out of the home computer field by anticipating the potential for microcomputers in time to introduce the PC (personal computer). GM responded to the growing energy crisis with studies on energy and auto design changes that finally led to the downsizing decision, albeit somewhat later than it could have done.

Although most organizations have a hard time confronting the sensitive, confusing issues that surround them, in a new era of unprecedented social change the need to do so is likely to grow even more acute. Issue management provides a sharply focused, nonbureaucratic means of dealing with this critically important heart of strategic change.

Participative Leadership Alters Awareness

As we saw earlier, strategy formulation cannot be a strictly rational process since creative solutions are intuitively derived from some vision of the future. As Igor Ansoff put it, "Strategic changes are by nature illogical deviations from the past."[32] Moreover, strategic issues are inherently subjective because people hold differing values that lead to incompatible strategies, so heated controversies are unavoidable. These differences must be resolved in a way that is suitable to major parties, either by brainstorming for new possibilities, altering values, bargaining, or some other means of changing the way an issue is viewed. Strategic solutions then are ultimately the result of a shift in awareness, an "altered state of consciousness," whereby opposing positions become united on some common course of action. It is only at that existential point when conflicting parties are prepared to commit themselves that a binding decision is made.

These problems are more severe now because a new era has produced nonauthoritarian personality types that think for themselves, and because the issues facing institutions are too complex for simple solutions. The messy problem of reaching agreement should grow even more difficult as labor leaders, consumer representatives, and other constituencies become part of the policy-making process. But Chapter 5 showed that a participative form of decision-making is evolving out of the growing awareness that real knowledge and commitment come, not from objective facts, but from the interaction of different persons to produce more insightful levels of understanding. We each have a piece of the truth and we shape how others see the truth when we confront one another with our views. Planners note that strategy formulation must be "inherently contentious" to "remove the barriers to change," so participation is necessary to explore differences and to thrash out a consensus for successful solutions. Some typical approaches:[33]

Opinion Polls. General Motors engaged corporate executives in a "strategy versus scenario matrix" study to rate alternative car design strategies against various future energy scenarios. The aggregated data represented the consensus of opinion on how well they believed various designs would work in different situations. Seeing the results of their collective judgment caused the executives to examine their beliefs about this critical issue, their differences of opinion, and to consider new possibilities, thereby creating a more sophisticated level of awareness.

Experiential Exercises. ComSat managers were deliberating the reorganization of the company into smaller profit centers, a sensitive move that would change the system of management control. The firm debated the possibility for many months until conducting a simulation helped reach a decision. After identifying tentative business units at a senior management conference, trial financial statements were generated to experience how this structure would look and work. Participating in this experiment convinced the executives that the drawbacks they feared were outweighed by the advantages, so they moved ahead on the reorganization.

Group Problem-Solving.   Burt Nanus at the Center for Futures Research of the University of Southern California uses a technique he calls "Quest" to engage a team of executives in a systematic problem-solving process that uses active participation to integrate diverse views into workable strategies. Volvo is involving 2500 blue-collar employees in its strategic planning process, and intends to expand this participation further.

Computerized Information Networks and Video Teleconferencing.   These increasingly powerful systems offer new methods for participative strategy formulation that facilitate collecting opinions and interacting at a distance. A good example is the Electronic Information Exchange System (EIES) being used for strategic planning among business executives. Another example is the Consensor, an electronic device for conducting polls at meetings, which is used by IBM, Xerox, and AT&T.

Organization Transformation (OT).   This vital new approach to organizational change is evolving now out of the old OD movement. OT recognizes that organizations are governed primarily by belief systems, so practitioners tend to focus on creating a "vision" of the intended future to release the "spirit" needed to initiate change. They then encourage participative forms of shared problem solving to channel these energies into constructive structural designs.

These examples reflect the heritage of the field of OD which laid the foundation for more effective group processes, although directed now to tough substantive issues that can bring about enduring change. Peter Vaill, an OD specialist working in strategic planning, notes that, "Strategic planning has brought process issues to the executive suite." Vaill proposes a new professional role that combines both OD and strategic planning, a "strategic planning process consultant."[34] In time the discipline may expand to fill this growing need by creating a broader form of "holistic OD." Just as holistic medicine moves beyond curing disease to encompass the entire patient in maintaining health, so would holistic OD extend its old focus on internal relations to encompass the entire extended organization composed of management and its stakeholders.

Such developments remind us that executives today must become skilled in the persuasive techniques of the statesman's art that are necessary to alter the views of others. Strategy formulation can no longer rely on "cool" rational authority, but requires "hot" human contact for gathering personal views, forming creative alternatives, testing possibilities, instilling attitudes, holding people accountable, reaching agreement, and engendering the entrepreneurial spirit to support successful strategic change. This is a task for charismatic leaders who can engage others in the give-and-take of mutual influence until the truth becomes evident for all to see.

Market Networks Provide Grassroots Implementation

Beyond the corporate level we have focused on thus far lies the hard reality of actually implementing strategic decisions into working operations. Not too long ago even the largest companies would have considered it sound practice to dictate commands to operational units deep within the bowels of the organization, but now this bureaucratic form of planning is being buried under an avalanche of complex problems and ineffective outcomes. As noted, much of today's planning is beautifully done, but it remains little more than a stack of impressive documents or good intentions that are never translated into practice.

The key to actually implementing strategy is to engage operating people as entrepreneurs, assisted by the corporate network they collectively form. We saw in Chapter 4 how a network structure of small, self-managed ventures is forming in sophisticated companies like TRW, GE, Dow Corning, Citicorp, and DEC to encourage organic change. "Some corporations are apparently coming to actually believe [that] an operating manager is his own best strategist," reported *Fortune* editor Walter Keichel.[35] The role of top executives then becomes, not to dictate strategies to lower units, but to provide leadership in fostering effective solutions. Progressive executives are giving up their traditional role as a boss to become more of a coach or consultant working with lower managers to solve the problems they share. One executive in my study described it this way: "Helping line managers look for ways to improve their own business."

So strategic management creates change by integrating the organization with its surroundings through political coalitions at the policy level, and it does the same at the operating level. Networks create vital links between top strategy formulation and its implementation at the grass roots where the reality of organizational life occurs: supervising workers on the shop floor, dealing with suppliers, providing sales and service to customers, representing the firm to the community, and so on.

Market structures are not only more effective because they implement strategy from the bottom up, but this interaction alters top-down views as well. One manager described it to me as "opening doors to the ivory towers to allow more input from the troops in the trenches." Perhaps the most debilitating problem in large institutions is that the traditional chain-of-command becomes a non-correcting system, impervious to signals of impending disaster from below. Authoritarian organizations unwittingly coerce loyalty from their members in the interest of maintaining order, thereby obstructing valuable strategic possibilities that local units usually understand more keenly than executives.

Whereas a network has the ability to create strategic change almost by itself, with only the encouragement and guidance of top management. Entrepreneurial units comprise the probing operational edge of the organization, adapting to the intricacies and uncertainties of a complex, changing environment, and feeding resources, information, and ideas to the brain of the system. The growth of market networks comprises one of the most powerful trends now forming this new model of strategic management.

YIELDING THE ILLUSION OF SELF-CONTROL

Organizations will emphasize different aspects of the New Capitalism because each must find its own way in adapting to a turbulent new era. Some focus on various approaches to forming working coalitions with their constituencies; others use programs in future studies, strategic planning, or issue management to handle external trends; still others adopt OD, OT, and participative management concepts to alter power structures; and many are creating entrepreneurial networks. Whatever path is chosen, however, the common destination all institutions are moving toward is a form of management suited for coping with complexity—a strategically managed organization that is especially good at creating change because it integrates the organization into its environment.[36]

This intimate organization-environment interface offers a strikingly different perspective from which individuals and institutions are no longer seen as isolated entities but as parts of a larger society that grants their ability to function. In this symbiotic conception of social reality, the world is not composed of discrete units, but is rather a seamless web of interconnected social systems that derive their very life from one another. The fact is that managers have limited power apart from the organization that supports them, and even major institutions derive their resources and their very identity from the larger social system. As John Donne observed long ago, "No man is an island, entire of itself." Fritjof Capra sees the same paradigm emerging in physical science:[37]

> The material world, according to contemporary physics, is not a mechanical system composed of separate objects, but instead appears as a complex web of relationships.

Thus, the power of strategic management relies on its ability to channel these environmental forces into constructive directions. Managers are seen less as the initiators of strategic change, and more as facilitators guiding far more powerful changes that flow **through** the institution from the social suprasystem. Today's conflict between business and society, from this view, actually represents a huge potential source of useful energy if the organization-environment schism can be bridged. The Peters and Waterman study of corporate excellence found that "Innovative companies are especially adroit at continually responding to changes of any sort in their environments."[38]

But there is a difficult paradox that must be confronted because this perspective requires giving up our cherished sense of "self." Planning authority Don Michael contends the disorders of society largely stem from the misplaced conviction that people can control events, that "we know what we are doing."[39] We can maintain this unrealistic belief, only to remain isolated from the environment and buffeted by its turbulence, or we can relinquish control and draw on the empowering energy flowing all about. This is a painful choice, however, since it involves nothing less than surrendering the illusion that we are in charge; it requires yielding the attempt to pursue our self-interest, entrusting a benign evolution to carry us along. Acknowledging these limits of our power may then allow us to see the true sources of change constantly at work and learn to influence them more skillfully.

The case of the auto industry offers an object lesson in which disaster struck mainly because oligopolistic car makers lost touch with enormous environmental forces for change: the energy crisis, international competition, customer demands for quality, and the like. In a true sense, it could be said that the crisis of the auto industry was the nation's way of forcing these firms back into touch with the changing world around them. They are recovering now only because they have been forced to yield a misplaced arrogance to the power of the larger social system that provides the vital resources which all institutions need.

This example illustrates that individuals and institutions are so intimately connected to other social systems that it is meaningless to speak of strategic change apart from the larger environment. Its dynamic life is the source of energy that fuels change, and we can only hope to become more sensitive receivers of this energy. Even the concepts that make up strategic management contain no special powers. Smart growth, market networks, participative decision-making, multiple goals, or any other ideas are only ways the institution may be integrated into the larger systems that surround it; they are focal points of attention that urge us to grapple with problems more effectively.

This does not mean that we are powerless and should passively accept whatever fate befalls. On the contrary, we can gain even greater power to shape our destinies—but by exerting control not **over** our environment but **with** it. The difficult challenge that cannot be avoided, it seems to me, is to really understand our surroundings in the hope of working out mutual solutions that move this web of life into new directions that are more beneficial. In short, to join with the very forces that seem threatening and by doing so to change both them and ourselves.

Because change flows from this living, unpredictable environment, it is hard to know how these forces will move to redefine the role of large organizations. Institutions are like people writ large. They resist change, they have a hard time understanding themselves, they don't know what they want, or what they should do. They often can't bring themselves to take actions they know are in their best interests, and so they await events to move them instead. In this sense, institutions are incapable of changing themselves and are being forced to do so by external forces: the threat of foreign competition, the advance of information technology, shifting cultural attitudes of a maturing baby-boom, women gaining power, the demands of disgruntled employees, political pressures, and other trends described throughout this book that are now relentlessly altering modern economies. It may be that economic catastrophes will destroy some institutions to leave fertile ground for the growth of new organizational forms.

As we saw in earlier chapters, however, the resilient nature of the free enterprise system is beginning to move organizations in these general directions out of the necessity to survive. Progressive companies have been leading the way for years, but we have simply lacked labels and concepts to recognize the new form of management they are creating. Now the need is to develop these embryo ideas into well-defined, workable models to replace the paradigm of the Old Capitalism that has become a barrier to economic vitality. The strategically managed corporation would then become a powerful stabilizing influence guiding modern economies through a dangerous, confusing period of intense competition and difficult readjustment that lies ahead.

If institutions can develop this New Capitalism that unites them more closely with their environment, they will be able to work more symbiotically with less risk, rather like islands of synergistic growth floating on a turbulent sea of change. I suspect we may find that the very issues which seem so problematic today—stagflation, technological change, resource limitations, big government, and the like—will then prove to be blessings in disguise. They will force us into tightly knit alliances that we resist so ferociously, but deep in our being we know they are badly needed to resolve the economic crisis, and, from a personal view they are even longed for.

8

Democratic Free Enterprise:

A SYSTEM OF BOTH COOPERATION
AND COMPETITION

Americans are beginning to face the harsh truth that neither the right nor the left wings of the nation really know how to restructure the economic system for a new era.

Despite all the furor over the "Reagan Revolution," the right wing's attempt to dismantle big government has run into solid opposition to reducing public services, so federal spending has actually increased and regulation has not abated significantly. "We're very disappointed in [Reagan's] legislative regulatory reform program," said an executive at the National Association of Manufacturers.[1] Inflation has declined and the climate for business has improved, which is a welcome change from the malaise of the 1970s. The cost, however, was a damaging recession, budget deficits that threaten future economic prospects, and social inequities that invite a sharp return to the left when the conservative mood runs out.[2] Reaganomics may have provided a needed jolt to get the country moving again, but there is a nagging fear that even the bitter medicine of supply-side economics will not restore lasting economic health.

The public also understands that there is no turning back to the old liberalism. Policies favoring big government were soundly discredited by the Reagan landslides of 1980 and 1984, and even the

---

Portions of this chapter are adapted from my article "Big Business versus Big Government—A New Social Contract?," *Long Range Planning* (August 1984).

"industrial" policies proposed by neoliberal Democrats carry the stigma of lavish spending and meddlesome intervention into the efficiency of the market. Big government is so out of favor that the socialist revolution in France is floundering. The French now believe "socialism doesn't work," and President François Mitterand himself acknowledged, "We were dreaming a bit, it is true."[3]

Thus, the simple choice between liberals promoting social welfare versus conservatives supporting free enterprise is not as clear-cut as it once seemed. Only true believers feel confident in the magic elixirs politicians tout for curing the ills of the economy, while most people are bewildered by a maze of alarming economic problems and ineffective remedies that seem unending. Economist Walter Heller recently observed:[4]

> Economic historians would be hard put to find in postwar annals any greater policy disarray in the face of recession and financial crisis than besets Washington today.

Such agonizing confusion stems from the wishful hope that one of these political persuasions holds the truth, thereby creating a polarity that drives nations to either the left or the right. Although the left wing now controls France, Sweden, Spain, Italy, and Greece, the right has gained power in the United States, England, and Germany. The strongest feature of the current debate over economic policy, therefore, is that thinking is stalled at two strongly held but diametrically opposed ideologies that hinge on the role of big government versus big business.

This chapter carries the ideas of the New Capitalism to a macroeconomic level by showing that the key to resolving this conflict is to encourage a crucial shift now underway in business-government relations. Corporations, entire industries, federal agencies, local governments, labor unions and other economic actors are forming working partnerships to restructure the economy into a system that fosters both cooperation and competition. This extraordinary union of democratic and free enterprise values is the most distinctive feature of the New Capitalism that gives it such great potential, and it also explains why I believe this emerging form of political economy should be called "Democratic Free Enterprise."

THE COMING SYNTHESIS OF LEFT AND RIGHT

If the present impasse between left and right is viewed from a long-range perspective, trends show a broader solution seems to be emerging that may synthesize both positions. Liberals could more effectively serve the public welfare—not through some type of national planning—but by providing collaborative government leadership that facilitates business-labor-community alliances to assist economic growth, thereby alleviating unemployment, poverty, and other social ills far better than the federal programs that led to the mushrooming growth of a welfare state. Likewise, conservatives could reduce the existing maze of government bureaucracy—not by trying to restore an obsolete laissez-faire past—but by creating a democratic form of socially responsible business to wean the nation from its dependence on government. The result would be a "decentralization strategy" that passes economic control from the public sector to a fairly benign, self-regulating private sector, fostering robust enterprise more closely attuned to the social welfare.

Liberal Big Government: Humane but Ineffective

One of the clearest trends in American history is the growth of government that began with antitrust laws against business monopolies, spurred when the Great Depression required federal programs to stabilize the economy, and peaked in the 1970s with social legislation to curb abuses to the environment, consumers, and workers. As a maturing nation developed more sophisticated needs, people have called for government protections over a broader range of economic activity, producing a spectacular increase in the public sector. Business historian Martin Schnitzer summed it up: "A massive shift from market to political decision making has occurred in American society."[5]

The federal budget alone now consumes 24 percent of GNP, and if state and local levels are included, total government spending takes about 40 percent of the nation's output—up from 10 percent in 1900. Regulations have mushroomed such that budgets for the 57 major regulatory agencies increased by 537 percent from 1970 to 1979 as the birth of new federal functions swamped business in a regulatory alphabet soup: EPA, OSHA, EEOC, NHTSA, CPSC, FDA, and so on. Economist Murray Weidenbaum points out the federal regulatory system now costs $100 billion per year and has led to "a 'shadow' organization of public officials matching the organizational structure of each private company," thereby constituting a "second managerial revolution." The first revolution occurred when control of business shifted from owners to professional managers; the second has now moved power from business executives to government officials.[6]

Environmental controls offer a good example. The new power of the EPA became manifest in 1976 when Allied Chemical was fined $13.3 million for dumping Kepone into the James River and when GE paid $4 million for discharging PCBs into the Hudson River. Total costs for pollution control in the United States increased from $400 million in 1957 to $7 *billion* in 1975. Why does the nation tolerate this economic burden? Because cost/benefit studies show that the savings in health care, building maintenance, and other damage caused by pollution more than offset these costs, and because polls consistently show that Americans are adamant about wanting a clean environment. As a result, business has been forced to yield control over decisions on manufacturing plant and equipment to politicians and government bureaucrats.[7]

Regulation of labor decisions shows the same trend. A landmark case occurred in 1973 when AT&T was fined $75 million for discriminatory practices. Recently the U.S. Supreme Court upheld regulations requiring protection against hazardous working conditions regardless of the cost because the health of workers "outweighs all other considerations."[8]

The problem may grow even more severe in Europe. The Vredling proposal would require major corporations in the EEC to disclose management information, consult with unions over plant closings, and increase liability for defective products. Sweden's Meidner plan could be enacted requiring business to pass financial control to labor unions over a 10-year period. Governments in France, Greece, and Spain have gained enormous power to nationalize industries and tax the wealthy.[9]

Lest we lull ourselves into believing such Draconian social controls would not be tolerated here, a possible foretaste of things to come may be seen in California. The Committee for Economic Democracy recently gained power in the cities of Santa Monica, Berkeley, and Oakland, imposing rent controls and requiring large buildings to provide public amenities such as child-care facilities. Proponents claim these moves are needed to prevent landlords from "exploiting" the community, while the building owners are outraged at the intrusion of "socialism" into their private affairs. And California is not just a "crazy state" but the leading edge of social change in the United States. A Hart survey shows that the majority of Americans favor seating representatives of labor, customers and other legitimate interests on the boards of major corporations.[10]

Corporate executives have fiercely resisted this growing encroachment on their prerogatives, but it was almost inevitable because modern societies badly need some form of control over critical areas of public interest. Fletcher Byrom told his business colleagues when he was chairman of Koppers Company: "You and I know that the market system would not give us environmental protection, worker safety, and health."[11] Behind the free enterprise rhetoric, even executives want import restrictions, financial aid, and other forms of government help for their companies. Charles Koch, a business executive and Director of the Council for a Competitive Economy, noted the contradiction:[12]

> Many businessmen advocating free enterprise are really working to eliminate any remaining free enterprise in their industry. They argue for subsidies, tariffs, regulations on their competitors, and any other interventions of government that may protect them from the rigors of competition.

Conservatives are correct, however, in that regulation is a terribly crude form of control that modern societies abhor as much as the abuses of business. Authorities point out that pollution, labor practices, and consumer protection are extremely complex, subtle issues that do not lend themselves to rules enforced by a central bureaucracy, and the volume of regulations is so vast that no corporation can faithfully comply with all of them. For example, worker accident rates have not improved substantially despite the huge costs in time, money, and lost freedom invested in developing OSHA regulations.[13] In some Scandinavian nations the government takes 70 percent of GNP, producing obvious disincentives on self-initiative, while the socialist government in France stifled economic growth to the point of angering even the "proletariat" as workers suffered from higher unemployment and lower wages. Peter Drucker warned:[14]

> The disenchantment with government cuts across national boundaries and ideological lines. It is as prevalent in communist as in democratic societies, as common in white as in nonwhite countries. The disenchantment may well be the most profound discontinuity in the world around us.

The underlying problem is that people have conflicting interests about government that are not easily reconciled. While Americans want the support and protection that government provides, they also want to be free from the intrusion of complex regulations and high taxes.[15] The Old Capitalism was built on a large base of federal services that have been indispensable: antitrust laws, insured savings, unemployment insurance, social security, labor legislation, pollution controls, consumer protection, and many other essential functions. But now the complexity of the information age has raised difficult new questions about the proper role of government. The search for answers leads to the other major institution that maintains a symbiotic relationship with big government—big business. As George Steiner put it, "Any serious exploration of business-government relations must be rooted in a deeper study of the proper role of corporations in society."[16]

Conservative Big Business: Enterprising but Irresponsible

Ronald Reagan's landslide victory in 1980 climaxed the coming to power of the neoconservative revolution that began with the election of Margaret Thatcher in England and the assault on property taxes led by Howard Jarvis in California. The significance of this event was summed up by that apostle of laissez-faire capitalism, Milton Friedman:[17]

> The confusion and uncertainty surrounding this election, the reversal of roles of the two major parties . . . are manifestations of a worldwide movement that has affected China and the Russian empire no less than the United States, Britain and the rest of the world.

It is now clear that the 1980 election marked the end of the type of government we associate with the industrial past. One objective of this revolt was to halt the indulgence of the welfare state that has encouraged an attitude of entitlement. In England, a banker noted, "The average person here feels he is owed health, education, housing, and a job," and Thatcher warned, "Many of our people have come to expect an automatic increase each year." In the United States, Reagan's former budget director David Stockman noted the same problem: "The federal budget has now become an automatic 'coast-to-coast soup line' that dispenses remedial aid with almost reckless abandon."[18]

This attempt to reinstill the virtue of self-reliance reflects a general imperative for insuring accountability, which we saw earlier, as the gravy train of industrial growth comes to a stop. The sacrifices are painful, so they are most severely borne by the powerless, producing what has been called "the revolt of the rich against the poor." Underlying the battle to limit demands on government, however, lies the bigger objective of rekindling economic progress. The industrial era seemed to offer unending expansion, so growth was driven by Keynesian philosophy to stimulate demand. When the limits to growth began pressing down, a supply-side approach seemed necessary to encourage new forms of enterprise.

As a consequence of this historic shift in sentiment, the focus of economic management has moved from dependence to self-reliance, from consumption to production, and from government to business. Journalist Edward Cody summed it up smartly: "America is returning, without embarrassment, to the original capitalism." Although many people are justly angered by what they stand to lose, many others are delighted by what they will gain. Enthusiastic proponents even include former radicals like Jerry Rubin who led the charge against the establishment in the 1960s. Now working on Wall Street, Rubin is as zealous today about making money as he was before about revolting against "the system":[19]

> *Politics and rebellion distinguished the '60s. The search for self characterized the spirit of the '70s. Money and financial interest will capture the passion of the '80s . . . the challenge for American Capitalism in the '80s is to bring the entrepreneurial spirit back to America.*

The stunning swiftness of this reversal reflects the powerful, widespread, and genuine need people feel to become free of government constraints, which is why President Reagan and Prime Minister Thatcher wield such awesome power. Both have strong political support among the majority of their citizens who clearly understand that the old habit of relying on others must end. One Britisher said of the Prime Minister, "A large number of people who dislike her and resent some of the things she does know in their hearts that she's on the right course."[20] Similarly, Reagan's great strength lies in being the right man in the right place at the right time; his adamant antigovernment bias uniquely qualified him to slay the dragon of big government, and his time came when the populace perceived its growing menace.

These reforms have produced substantial benefits. Taxes are down somewhat, regulations have eased a bit, and union obstructionism has declined. Lower inflation has been a particularly welcomed change, but at the cost of a severe recession, and it is doubtful that this chronic problem has been solved in a lasting way. The most significant effect has been a widespread change in mood as the gravity of the situation is impressed on people. "You have all kinds of criticism," said Walter Wriston, former chairman of Citicorp, "but the fact that the direction is changing is most important."[21]

Although the speed and conviction behind the conservative revolt are breathtaking, there is also a pervasive sense of unreality about it. Economist Paul Samuelson called it the "moonshine of 'supply-side economics'—that reducing tax rates across the board . . . will unleash a miracle of market growth," and even George Bush labeled it "voodoo economics" before becoming Vice President. When Friedman visited England he was cordially snubbed because his theories were viewed as "a religion" and "simplistic." John Kenneth Galbraith incisively summed up what many vaguely sense as an illogical and immoral philosophy: "I'm not persuaded," he said, "that the rich are not working because they are not getting enough income and that the poor are not working because they are getting too much."[22]

The fatal flaw in supply-side economics lies in its unquestioning faith in the benevolent creativity of big business. A recent survey of business executives is unusually revealing because these men and women were retired and felt they could be candid. Nearly three out of four agreed, "Government regulations are necessary to prevent unfair practices that affect workers, consumers, and competitors." They acknowledged that "competition and greed" of top management are responsible for emphasizing profit and thereby leading to unethical behavior.[23] Such limits of the Old Capitalism show that neoconservatives have only half of the answer to the ills of the economy. Changes in the public sector will fail unless the private sector can be restructured as well, so the other half of the answer lies in getting corporations to assume the responsibilities that federal agencies are asked to relinquish. In plain words, if we really hope to "get big government off our backs," big business has to get off its behind. Otherwise the conservative attack on government will continue to falter, it will prove unable to restore prosperity, and it seems likely to lead to a liberal backlash.

That's why public spending has not been reduced, although it has been shifted around. After California's Proposition 13 slashed state income, communities found that dropping social services simply raised other costs. The mayor of San Jose noted: "We've added 114 police officers . . . roughly since Proposition 13. At the same time we've cut about that number in parks and library staff." Likewise, the cutbacks at the national level have simply passed responsibilities on down, so taxes have increased by offsetting amounts in 40 states. And despite Reagan's image of heartless program reductions, the federal budget increased 30 percent during 1980 to 1984, although largely for defense, gaining from 22 to 24 percent of GNP. The fact is that it is almost impossible to reduce government support without providing some reasonable alternative. All industrial nations are struggling to limit taxes, but they can't simply abandon people who need help. A European politician summed up the problem: "[The welfare state] is a tottering edifice that can't be razed because of the millions of people clinging to it."[24]

Because of this inability to reduce spending, it is now clear that the main legacy of the 1980 tax cuts was unprecedented budget deficits. Even the President seemed a little sadder but wiser. Upon taking office in 1980, Reagan warned, "The federal budget is out of control, and we face runaway deficits of almost $80 billion." But after Reaganomics the deficits became, in the words of David Stockman, "stuck at $200 billion as far as the eye can see." Although publicly blaming profligate liberal spending, in a rare candid moment Reagan mused, "You can't really cut the budget enough to balance the budget." The deficits doubled the national debt during his first term of office, so the President has incurred more debt than all of his 39 predecessors combined, leaving the nation holding a financial time bomb; even if serious cuts are made the debt is likely to triple by the end of his second term. Economist Paul McCraken worried, "The deficit projections leave one with the feeling of standing on the edge of an abyss," while Alice Rivlin, former director of the Congressional Budget Office, simply called them "really dumb." Thatcher has run into the same massive resistance, so public spending in England increased from 40 to 44 percent of GNP, and taxes have gone from 35 to 39 percent of GNP.[25]

And the much vaunted attempt to reduce regulation has worked only marginally because the Reagan administration discovered that Americans may say they want less regulation but they will not permit lax controls on sensitive social matters. A recent survey showed a strong majority of Americans continue to want government to protect them from pollution, control working conditions, set food and drug standards, insure honesty in advertising, and safeguard against dangerous products. There has been a decrease in "economic" regulation of transportation, oil prices, and other sectors, which actually began under the Carter Administration, but the "social" regulations that guard against business abuses have not declined significantly. The attempt to dismantle the EPA, for instance, produced instead a backlash against all deregulation efforts. As early as 1982, journalist Caroline Mayer noted: "The [Reagan administration's] regulatory reform campaign appears to be grinding slowly to a halt." Some of these responsibilities have been shifted to the states, but this merely created a maze of local regulations to fill the gap. A corporate executive said the "New Federalism has resulted in a state regulatory nightmare." Joan Claybrook, former head of the National Highway Traffic and Safety Administration, pointed out the obstacle to deregulation:[26]

> It is not widely understood that health and safety regulation is a modern form of preventive medicine ... In its zeal to serve the Fortune 500 constituency, however, the Reagan crowd is subverting these achievements. The preeminent good is defined as business welfare, not the well-being of the American people.

What is more important, modern societies have changed so irrevocably with the onset of a new era that the Old Capitalism no longer works in terms of economic considerations. Earlier chapters showed that the supply-side tax cuts failed to revitalize the economy because the old power of capital is fading. The robust recovery of 1983 was achieved by permitting the most severe downturn since the Great Depression to turn the economy around, leaving a trail of unemployed workers, bankrupt companies, and hidden social damage. Growth has since declined to modest levels, inflation could easily be reignited, and the budget deficits spell future trouble. In England, the economy remains feeble after years of the same Draconian measures, so economists, business leaders, and politicians are worried. "The Thatcher experiment is in trouble," wrote *The Economist*. "It's a very painful way of increasing productivity, a very wasteful way of getting change."[27]

Further, the harshness of neoconservativism seems likely to invigorate a counter-revolution from the left:[28]

Class Conflict. A huge number of unemployed, liberals, bankrupt farmers, blacks, women, struggling businesspeople, the poor, and public interest groups feel strong resentment that can be seen in a sharp polarization on Reagan's performance along class lines: 68 percent of those with incomes above $30,000 approve while only 39 percent of those with lower incomes approve.

Media. Richard Munro, President of *Time*, fears a popular backlash: "Public support will vanish if the burdens of this program remain so uneven—if people think that the rich and big business get all the breaks."

Labor. Unions are hostile because they have suffered major setbacks which they attribute to the precedent set by breaking the PATCO strike. Glen Watts, former president of the Communications Workers of America, accused the Reagan Administration of "driving a wedge between labor and corporate America."

Politicians. Many legislators sense a growing bitterness. U.S. Congressman James Florio noted, "There is so much anger that it's painful to watch. With the cutbacks in Federal aid, people say they can't take it any more. I find myself trying to keep people I like from hitting each other . . . It's really gotten mean."

Political Analysts. Some political observers suspect the current "politics of selfishness" may spark a liberal revolt. Mark Haroff, a political consultant, believes, "If you look at the next election I think you will see hard left economics becoming just as popular as Reaganomics."

In the midst of all this controversy, pain, and doubt, Margaret Thatcher, Milton Friedman, Ronald Reagan, and others who initiated the conservative revolution remain implacable in their convictions. Prime Minister Thatcher scolds her English subjects, "We never promised you a rose garden," Professor Friedman patiently lectures, "I'm not surprised at the resistance right now,"[29] and President Reagan flashes his dazzling smile while cheerfully assuring us his program is working.

Revolt from the Center: The Decentralization Strategy

The main conclusion of this analysis is that the limits of the left and right wing philosophies have trapped the nation in an impasse between the smothering embrace of bureaucratic big government versus the corrupting power of profit-centered big business—a stalemate between two giants locked in battle, neither of them yielding nor winning.[30]

The liberal approach inherited from FDR has become outmoded because it is based on centralized government control to improve the social welfare, and that is the same tragic flaw that has discredited socialism in the Soviet Union, Cuba, and other planned economies. If liberalism is to revive from its resounding defeats in the 1980 and 1984 elections, it must recognize that the era of doing good *for* people is over, and that individuals can only be assisted in helping themselves.

The conservative revolt also seems likely to be short lived. President Reagan has mobilized the nation to the urgent need for reducing government, but his philosophy is a nostalgic throwback to the Old Capitalism rather than a workable vision for a more problematic future. The nation wants the free enterprise system rejuvenated, but people are not interested in returning to a crass form of business that flaunts the public welfare. A report of the U.S. Department of Commerce stated:[31]

> *If anything, public skepticism of government is likely to heighten expectations for the private sector. . . . It would be a mistake to assume that the public no longer cares about the issues which led to the erosion of confidence in business. . . . An important challenge for the 1980's will be to resist the temptation to assume that the new political climate heralds the end of public scrutiny of business performance.*

Conflict over these issues has led to a diversity of positions on changing the business-government relationship that span the political spectrum. The Libertarian Party and arch conservatives represent the extreme right wing that advocates almost complete laissez-faire freedom, while Reagan and most Republicans comprise the moderate right position of limited government. Senator Ted Kennedy, the neoliberals, and most Democrats represent the moderate left that advocates an industrial policy and corporate democracy, while on the far left the new Citizens Party urges the socialization of major industries.

This controversy is likely to continue escalating, especially as the limits of neoconservative policies become more evident during the late 1980s. This time, however, the focus may shift to the role of major corporations. With the attack on big government exhausted and the public's expectations of big business disappointed, the question of corporate governance may grow into a heated debate during the presidential elections in 1988 and beyond. As many authorities have noted, Americans intuitively sense that the future of the Republic hinges to a great extent on the power and purposes of the corporation.[32]

There is a long history of antibusiness sentiment that has erupted during the populist movement at the beginning of this century, the labor movement in the 1930s, and the student protests of the 1960s. Studies of sociopolitical trends show that such issues cycle through gestation periods lasting for decades until a critical point is reached. As increasing numbers of the public become involved, some stray event ignites widespread concern into a national issue that quickly seizes the forefront of attention and leads to rapid structural changes.[33]

The notion that Americans might challenge the autonomy of large corporations may seem remote, but it is no more remote than the attack on big government that erupted into one of the most powerful political issues in this century almost overnight. Just shortly before the 1980 election, almost no one believed that Ronald Reagan could win the presidency on an antigovernment platform, and most members of his own party were convinced he was "unelectable." Today the same type of unexpected change seems to be evolving as people like journalist David Broder sense "an upsurge in antibusiness sentiment." The following sources signal that the role of big business may become a major political issue over the next few years, particularly if Reaganomics fails:[34]

Public Opinion. A Hart Poll found, "The majority of the American public are calling for basic changes in our economic system that are as sweeping as the changes our founding fathers called for in our political system 200 years ago." The public favors consumer representation on corporate boards by 74 percent and employee ownership and control of corporations by 66 percent.

Liberal Democrats. Americans for Democratic Action President Patsy Mink stated: "The abuses of big business corporate power [are] tremendous. Large corporations control our resources and our jobs . . . it is urgent that Americans take back control of their own national resources." In 1980 Ted Kennedy, Tom Hayden, and others issued plans for a legislative program that would require corporate board directors representing various social interests, disclosure of critical information, and other forms of public control.

U.S. Congress. Committees in Congress are considering legislation such as HR 7010—The Corporate Democracy Act, sponsored by Congressman Benjamin Rosenthal. Said Rosenthal: "HR 7010 would encourage directors 'to balance corporate goals against a variety of social and political objectives.'"

Federal Officials. Some public administrators support corporate democracy. Harold Williams, former chairman of the SEC, predicted: "The issue of the 1980s . . . will be the power of [business] ownership and how it might be used and by whom . . . to discharge social and business responsibility."

Public Interest Groups.   Ralph Nader claims federal laws requiring responsible corporate behavior are coming: "While the political agenda of the 1970s focused extensively on the size and abuse of *big government*, the political agenda of the 1980s should focus on the size and abuse of *big business*." And Philip Moore, one of the former leaders of Campaign GM, forecasts: "The 1980s are going to see more use of shareholder democracy and union representation on boards . . . getting a piece of the decision-making process."

Political Consultants.   The public relations firm of Hill & Knowlton identified corporate governance as a potentially explosive issue: "Socioeconomic pressures may well be pushing for new forms of corporate accountability and corporate governance," they told their clients.

Coalitions of Labor, Consumer, and Other Groups.   The UAW, the CIO, the Machinists Union, the Newspaper Guild, the United Food and Commercial Workers Union, the Coalition of Public Employees, and various consumer and religious groups have organized to campaign on the need to control big corporations.

Intellectuals.   Many academicians and intellectuals support various approaches to corporate democracy, including John Kenneth Galbraith, Robert Leckachman, Christopher Stone, Michael Walzer, and many others. Courtney Brown, Dean of the Columbia University Business School, said: "What is required is a fresh examination of the complete system of corporate governance."

It is impossible to predict when this issue will gain prominence and how it will be resolved, of course. What is clear is that there are great opportunities for centrist politicians who are able to work both sides of the present fruitless conflict. The key is to recognize that the right and left wing positions are ***not*** incompatible, but that a far superior solution is possible by drawing on the unique strength of each perspective while overcoming its drawbacks. Conservatives can succeed in freeing the economy from government constraints, but only if business assumes responsibility for its social impacts. Likewise, liberals could regain power to foster the social welfare, but they must develop a different role for government that encourages local forms of economic collaboration.

Thus a "political bargain" is needed in which politicians would provide business the freedom it needs (supply-side economics) *if* corporate executives adopt some form of democratic system (the social contract). Management of the economy would thereby be distributed from a centralized government bureaucracy to a dispersed private sector—a "decentralization strategy." All modern nations exert some form of social control over large corporations, and the only question is whether they will be controlled by government regulation or by responsible self-governance.

This union between supply-side economics and the social contract is illustrated by the results of a survey I conducted.[35] Table 8.1 provides opinion data estimating how these two strategies and the decentralization strategy combining both of them would fare under three different scenarios of the future. The sample is not large enough to be conclusive, but it does show that people tend to consider either approach alone to be lacking under all scenarios, while the combination of the two is rated higher in all cases. This demonstrates that the "hard" philosophy of conservatives can be united with the "soft" philosophy of liberals to form a "strong" political alliance.

Such a synthesis represents the type of solution that seems needed to restore economic vitality in a new era. If the large quasi-public corporations that comprise the primary actors in modern economies were to adopt this broader role, they would be converted into institutions that are politically legitimate and vastly more productive. The mission of business would thereby be expanded into a benign posture that formally serves the interests of society at large, while retaining the flexible, voluntary nature of the free enterprise system. In place of their old adversarial relationship, the goals of big business and big government would then become compatible, leading to various forms of badly needed collaboration, as we will see in the next section. One attractive outcome is that business could become fairly self-regulating and it would alleviate the bulk of social costs, thereby permitting government to relinquish much of its burden for maintaining the welfare state.

The decentralization strategy can be best understood as a national equivalent of the decentralized organizations discussed in Chapter 4. Executives in progressive corporations are creating market networks that hold operating units accountable for performance, which then permits wide-ranging freedom to gain the advantages of enterprise. The present centralized government controls are roughly comparable to a bureaucratic organization, so, as Professor William Ouchi has pointed out, the same concepts apply to the entire nation.[36] By holding corporations accountable for their "national" performance,

TABLE 8.1. THE DECENTRALIZATION STRATEGY

Alternative Strategies	Future Environmental Scenarios[a] (year 2000)			Weighted Sum (expected value)
	Worst Case (economic breakdown) $p = .27$	Average Case (muddling through) $p = .58$	Best Case (economic revitalization) $p = .15$	
1. Maintain the status quo	.4	3.5	5.4	2.9
2. Supply-side economics: business de-regulation, tax relief, and so on.	1.1	4.2	5.8	3.7
3. Social contract: corporate democracy, social reporting, and so on.	1.4	4.5	6.1	3.9
4. Decentralization strategy: (both 2 and 3 above)	3.1	6.1	8.4	5.6

Source: William E. Halal, "Big Business vs. Big Government—A New Social Contract?," Long-Range Planning (August 1984).
[a] Entries indicate estimates of overall corporate performance rated on a scale of 0–10. Data is from management training conferences and graduate seminars. Sample = 105.

big business could be permitted the freedom it needs to foster entrepreneurial innovation, while the role of government would be to provide leadership in redefining the economic system and making it work.

This illustrates that the compelling need in post-industrial societies is to decentralize all forms of economic control in order to handle higher levels of complexity and to gain the autonomy that is indispensable for committed workers, responsive managers, and involved citizens. The problems facing institutions and the economy as a whole are identical conceptually and so the solutions are also identical; they simply take place at different levels in the economic hierarchy. The New Capitalism is a general paradigm for managing the information age because it resolves the major contradiction that has plagued industrial societies—the ageless conflict between private gain and public welfare is converted into a constructive force that unifies the creative productivity of free enterprise with the political legitimacy of democracy.

So widespread is the need for decentralization that the concept is shared by staunch ideological adversaries like Mitterand and Reagan. One of Mitterand's fond desires is to decentralize the government of France into numerous small communities, or "arrondissements," governed in a self-managing form of participative democracy. Behind the labels of "socialism" and "capitalism" that isolate them, these men share a striking similarity in political ideals. Reagan expressed his vision in terms almost identical to that of Mitterand:[37]

> If the dead hand of government can be lifted—or ignored—groups of citizens can come together to deal effectively with problems facing them. The key is in devising a system in which power and responsibility are dispersed at the grassroots, instead of being concentrated in a hierarchy of bureaucrats and institutions.

Although the need for economic decentralization is gaining currency, many troublesome questions remain. Can corporate democracy be implemented to avoid the type of "socialism" that is unacceptable to Americans? What political force can unify the economic goals of conservatives with the social goals of liberals? Where will leaders be found to chart such a difficult course, and how can the resistance of business be overcome?

These are tough questions that are likely to persist for many years, but there are signs that such changes are taking place. As we saw in Chapter 6, democratic corporate governance is emerging now as large firms find it productive to work with their constituencies. Many other studies and authoritative opinions show this trend should grow to encompass all economic levels of industrialized nations:[38]

John Naisbitt's study of megatrends concludes, "We are reformulating corporate structures to permit workers, shareholders, consumers, and community leaders a larger say in determining how corporations will be run."

James Robertson, a former English government official, notes these changes are well underway in Europe and predicts, "We may expect to see the interests of all the main stakeholders (employees, investors, customers, and the public) represented in decision making at national, regional, and local levels."

Alvin Toffler foresees this approach becoming common: "In Third Wave societies, corporations will ... no longer be responsible simply for making a profit or for producing goods but for simultaneously contributing to the solution of extremely complex ecological, political, and social problems.

Proposals for implementing this strategy usually focus on various forms of corporate democracy, specifying critical information to be publicly disclosed, restraints to be observed, and responsibilities to be shared. But there has been a serious flaw in earlier approaches. They usually reflected the underlying assumption that controls have to be forced down the throat of big business, and so such ideas are invariably regarded as socialist attacks on private property and the rights of corporate executives that must be fought off.

Some degree of pressure may be necessary, and this may be the final outcome, but it seems unlikely that either business or society would be served by this punitive approach. People are enormously inventive, so there is little doubt that simply passing legislation requiring responsible behavior would soon create many subtle and ingenious schemes to circumvent the law. Prohibition did not stop people from drinking.

What is more important, the main objective is to foster more effective enterprise by unifying capital investment, labor productivity, consumer purchasing power, government support, and other economic factors into a ***voluntary*** political coalition. Legislation may be needed to require minimal compliance, but the spirit of corporate democracy must be a willing, freely given commitment. The most useful government action would be to pass enabling legislation that enlarges the legal definition of the board so that directors may represent these other constituencies in addition to shareholders who are still quaintly regarded as the "owners." Antitrust laws should also be modified to allow firms, unions, and other parties to work together. In the final analysis, the social contract must grow or die on its merits as a more productive form of enterprise and a civilized form of economic behavior. So ultimately, the notable success of pioneering efforts to adopt these ideas should provide the greatest impetus for widespread implementation.

As we also saw in earlier chapters, a variety of creative ventures are being initiated at the grassroots that seem to be moving toward this collaborative business-society relationship. Firms like Control Data and IBM are solving social problems while earning handsome profits. Numerous cities and states are forming alliances among business, local government, and other groups to foster economic growth. Research consortiums are appearing among competitors to share the results of technological advances. Stanley Karson, Director of the Center for Corporate Public Involvement for the life insurance industry, noted the significance:[39]

> . . . something exciting has been happening at the local level while most politicians have been looking the other way . . . both parties must begin to acknowledge and encourage the reality of our evolving [social] fabric: the emergence of community coalitions of business, government, community groups and non-profit institutions to address common needs.

Further, there are encouraging signs that new political forces are beginning to provide the leadership needed to move in this direction. Large portions of the American public are disenchanted with both major parties because they represent extreme positions, leaving great opportunities for "progressive moderates" to fill the vacant center. The electric appeal of Gary Hart in the 1984 presidential campaign was a good example. A group of 500 Democratic and Republican leaders recently called for unified action to halt the budget deficits, and Ted Sorenson, a former assistant to President

Kennedy, proposes the two political parties share in leading the nation. These incidents suggest that a centrist political force may be emerging in the United States—a "radical center" similar to Denmark's "Revolt from the Center," the Social Democrats in England, and the Greens in West Germany. David Broder believes a younger breed of politician is waiting to take over from the old men who lack the vision for this task:[40]

> The next generation [of] politicians, the men and women between 30 and 50 years old . . . has been raised in affluence, not deprivation. It has been shaped by television more than the written word. Its military experiences have ended in frustration, not victory. But it has been the source of sweeping social change at home. . . . Their bands are rehearsing a variety of tunes—from the free market economics of the new right to the corporate responsibility plans of the new left. . . . They are impatient for power and . . . the public is probably eager for them.

A simple illustration of what may result can be seen in California's recent example of passing a "work-for-welfare" program that combines welfare with job training, which may become a national model because it should save $100 million in its first year. The state's Secretary of Health and Welfare, David Swoap, claimed, "We've done something that never has been done, and that is to bring the liberals and conservatives together."

Pork-barrel projects, logrolling, and other attempts to serve special interests at great cost to the nation are passing due to the tight margins of economic crisis, so politicians—like everyone else—will have to fill a more productive purpose if they hope to survive. Today, power is shifting from those who control large institutions or wealth to political statesmen who are able to integrate diverse economic actors into coalitions that benefit all groups. This concept could solve the current identity crisis that liberals are suffering because it would extend traditional Democratic values into a more productive economic role that focuses on improving the well-being of all interests comprising the public welfare.

However, it would be a mistake for business to wait for politicians to resolve these issues because the outcome may not be to their liking. Regardless of what the public sector may do, corporate executives could take advantage of the unusual opportunities that abound during such times of change. As we showed in Chapter 6, many enlightened executives advocate the social contract because it is in their interests; it offers a powerful corporate strategy for creating a more productive form of enterprise that avoids the need for government control. If the executives who head our major corporations were to take on this responsibility and consolidate their collective influence through associations like the Business Roundtable, they could play a major role in shaping the new business-government relationship that is now evolving. Thornton Bradshaw, Chairman of RCA, described the challenge:[41]

> *Those who believe, as I do, in the intrinsic value of the decentralized market system must act now to develop a more humanistic, responsible, and innovative form of capitalism to meet society's demands as well as satisfying its needs. Accomplishing that difficult but necessary objective will be central to any intelligent discussion of American business for the foreseeable future.*

REDEFINING THE ECONOMIC INFRASTRUCTURE

The decentralization strategy helps make sense of an imaginative but bewildering array of solutions proposed for revitalizing the economy: President Carter initiated tripartite (labor-business-government) planning groups for major industries; Paul Craig Roberts, Arthur Laffer, and other economists shaped the supply-side concepts underlying the policies of neoconservatives; reindustrialization was proposed by sociologist Amitai Etzioni and California Governor Jerry Brown as a "semi-targeted" approach for providing assistance to industry; and economists like Lester Thurow and Robert Reich have advised neoliberal politicians Gary Hart, Paul Tsongas, Bill Bradley, and Timothy Wirth who advocate industrial policy. Senator Gary Hart described their approach this way:[42]

> *What the new generation of Democrats is trying to do is figure out how to get the economic pie growing again . . . structural reforms that will enable us to come up with a comprehensive successor to the New Deal.*

Debate on these ideas continues to heat up because great confusion persists over the Herculean challenge of redefining the economic system for a new era. The supply-side approach has been effective in alerting the nation to the need for change, but it violates American humanitarian values and it is ineffective because it is based on the Old Capitalism. Industrial policy has not been taken very seriously because it lacks a sharp, convincing focus. The concept left historian Arthur Schlesinger, Jr. wondering: "[The neoliberals are] in favor of—what?" The main theme that comes through is targeting investment capital and other forms of federal assistance to promising industries, which allows Democrats to hold on to their traditional belief in an active big government. But government intervention is anathema to many Americans because it smacks of political interference with the efficiency of a free market. Some typical objections:[43]

> Federal government is not capable of making investment decisions ... money will go where the political power is ... anyone who thinks government funds will be allocated to firms according to merit has not lived or served in Washington ... industrial policy usually means, sooner or later, government subsidies to protect jobs in stagnant or failing industries.

These ideas are like fertile intellectual seeds falling in the rich soil of an economic crisis. The work ahead involves weeding out extremes from the right and the left to allow a unified conceptual framework to flower and bear fruit. Americans long ago rejected the conservative ideal of a laissez-faire economy dominated by a brutal struggle for survival as well as the liberal vision of centralized national planning. The decentralization strategy solves this impasse by unifying the strong points of both views: voluntary business-government collaboration to create more "perfect" market competition that fosters productivity and social welfare. In short, by redefining capitalism as a system of political economy that combines **both** cooperation and competition. Sinichiro Asao, U.S. consul from Japan, attributed his country's success to a similar strategy:[44]

> Competition and cooperation are ... both essential to healthy economic development ... government advisory councils formulate long-range "visions" ... as a result of careful deliberation by the government with all interested parties: business, banking, labor, con-

sumers, academic experts, etc. . . . to foster a climate in which the mechanisms of a free and competitive market operate most vigorously.

The next section presents examples illustrating how this more sophisticated infrastructure is beginning to emerge as corporate executives, labor leaders, government officials, consumer representatives, and trade association managers collaborate to redefine the way the economy should work, the "rules of the game." The old conflict between democracy and free enterprise is passing, and we are about to learn that markets behave best when they are guided by people working together.

Participative Policy Bodies, Facilitated by Government Leadership

There is wide agreement on the need to form national policy bodies that would bring together respected leaders from various key interest groups to resolve critical macroeconomic issues such as productivity and trade policy. Federal officials would play a leadership role as "facilitators" to assist these parties by overcoming political obstacles, encouraging constructive solutions, providing tax incentives, and other forms of support. Government might also strike bargains in which an industry would agree to modernize plants, retrain workers for new jobs, or other remedial actions in return for help with loans and import protection.

Although this "democratic" approach to economic policy is unusual in the United States, it is recognized as essential now to compete abroad. Almost all Americans know that the strength of the Japanese, Germans, and others who are able to outperform U.S. business is largely a result of collaborative working relationships that increase productivity, hold down inflation, spur technological innovation, and generally provide a favorable climate for private enterprise to thrive.[45] Economist Howard Samuels advised, "Generous tax breaks to business alone will not stimulate investment . . . for Reagan, that means thinking about the unthinkable: a major effort to involve labor and business in a new social compact coordinated by an activist government." Consider the wide range of support for this central concept:[46]

Democrats. Congressman Timothy Wirth said after a study of the economic crisis, "About the clearest message we heard from the hundreds of Americans with whom we conferred . . . was that the politics of confrontation among business, government, and labor must give way to the politics of cooperation." Democrats have advanced proposals for tripartite bodies that would "gather the right information and improve our ability to make long-term economic decisions—not as a centralized monolithic planning agency, but as a national arena to clarify complex choices and build broad support for national initiatives."

The President's Commission for a National Agenda called for an "American Economic Council" that "would provide a mechanism for a group of people who have a major influence on the economic direction of the nation to move toward more understanding, and perhaps consensus, on national economic issues."

The Public. Polls show a majority of Americans like the idea of "committees composed of government, business, and labor leaders to encourage collaboration on economic policies." What they reject are "interventionist" concepts, such as the "investment bank" proposed by liberal industrial policies.

Business Leaders A *BusinessWeek* poll showed 61 percent of executives favor a tripartite board to foster collaborative economic relations. Robert Price, President of Control Data, said the most important difference between the United States and Japan is the "development of a Japanese tradition of cooperation."

The President's Commission on Industrial Competitiveness was formed to "generate a national dialogue on how to make the United States more competitive" using policies in R&D, education, and training.

The U.S. Department of Commerce has proposed merging the U.S. Trade Representative into the Commerce Department to create a new Department of International Trade and Industry (DITI) to match Japan's Ministry of International Trade and Industry (MITI).

Below the national level, some states, cities, and industries are presently reaping the benefits of a similar form of collaboration at the grassroots:[47]

Michigan is recovering from a deep recession because of alliances among state government, industry, and labor; $400 million has been invested in 16 new companies that provided $100 million of their own capital. "We're trying to be a positive catalyst in encouraging our economic structure to adjust," said Governor James Blanchard.

Massachusetts has founded "The Massachusetts Technology Development Corporation," which has invested $7 million in 33 companies and 20 industries.

State Enterprise Zones have sprung up in 23 states offering tax relief, training assistance, and other help to encourage new business formation, prompting $2 billion of private capital investment in 400 communities. Connecticut, for example, started six zones in which firms have invested $97 million and created 6000 new jobs. "We are flabbergasted at how much difference they have made in revitalizing areas," exclaimed a state official.

State Small Business Administrations exist now in all 50 states to help small firms get started. Montana has $30 million available to fund new ventures.

Communities are forming collaborative economic relations. Chapter 6 showed how American cities like Indianapolis, Minneapolis, and New Orleans are helping business firms, banks, labor groups, and ordinary citizens work together on local economic problems. In France, local town governments act as mediators to bring together community interests to manage growth and reduce unemployment.

We saw earlier that large corporations are becoming democratically governed institutions, and government agencies may also handle troublesome issues more effectively through participation by concerned interest groups. When Michael Pertschuk was chairman of the FTC he invited business and consumers to testify in order to get a balanced view from differing interests. "As an individual commissioner, I know that I have benefited enormously from this clash of advocacy," he said.[48] Two examples:

Nuclear Power. The U.S. Supreme Court has permitted states the discretion to accept or reject nuclear power plants, so active community participation is essential on sensitive political issues. Many communities will not consider having a nuclear plant nearby, while others are delighted to have the energy and the economic growth they produce. Authors Susan and Martin Tolchin have shown that public involvement in regulation of nuclear plants has an effective record of spotting safety hazards without holding up construction.

Environmental Pollution. Eugene Bardach and Robert Kagan point out that pollution control could be more effective if focused on the few major sources that contribute most pollutants rather than treating all cases by the same strictly legal standards. But this use of discretion requires a political body of diverse interests empowered to exercise judgment on behalf of the community to make complex, sensitive decisions.

Collaborative economic policy is also appearing to guide the development of critical industries:[49]

Auto-Making. Individual manufacturers would be better able to address their common problems using a concerted effort of auto firms, labor groups, consumer representatives, suppliers and dealers, led by government agencies. Before President Carter left office, he formed a tripartite advisory group to assist the auto makers in working with the Federal Government on a joint research project to "reinvent the car." Adviser Stuart Eizenstadt saw the prospects as a "model for industrial policy-making in the 1980s." When Carter visited Detroit in 1980, he urged, "We're all in this together," while Lee Iacocca of Chrysler chimed in, "We've got to cooperate," and Philip Caldwell of Ford proclaimed, "The greatest lesson from the Japanese is to have government, industry and labor all working together." Estes of GM noted "a tremendous change in attitude."

Air Travel. Because deregulation has caused chaos for airlines and passengers, some representative body is needed to restore a semblance of order without returning to inflexible government controls. U.S. Senator Andrews proposed to "establish a presidential commission—made up of former airline presidents, past CAB officials, airline employees, academicians, and travel agents." Even now airline executives are working together in alleviating problems like crowded flight schedules that lead to delays.

These efforts have their limits, however, because they may intrude on market efficiency and personal freedoms. An example is the failure of a proposal in Rhode Island. State voters disapproved a highly promoted plan to create a commission that would supervise four "greenhouse" research centers backed with $40 million in venture capital to promote high-technology industries. "Most people saw this as just another government program," lamented one of the backers, business consultant Ira C. Magaziner.[50]

An even better approach is to focus on **structural** solutions that enhance the functioning of the free enterprise system. Economists agree that sound markets require accurate information for buyers and sellers, the freedom to enter and withdraw from the market, a large number of small competing enterprises, the inclusion of all social costs and benefits in transactions, and abundant supplies of capital, labor, and technology. As we saw earlier, however, a major cause of the economic crisis is that the Old Capitalism led to a complex regulatory bureaucracy, numerous economic externalities, distorted market information, oligopolies, restrictions on the movement of labor, barriers to trade, and other such market defects.

Economist F. A. Hayek claims the free market system has not really been tried yet.

The following sections outline structural innovations being developed to overcome such limitations: market supplements to internalize social costs and benefits in lieu of regulation, contracts to privatize government functions, indicative planning systems to provide better market information, assistance in obtaining investment capital, collaborative R&D projects that advance science and technology, policies that facilitate full employment, and self-regulating institutions. As we will see, the key to such change requires participation by affected parties to resolve political issues that are unavoidably involved.

Although participative policy-making is perfectly acceptable to most people because it is badly needed, some regard these possibilities as "socialism" because they restrict unfettered economic freedom. But socialism involves a state dominated economy, so this is not socialism but a mild form of **democracy** that only requires voluntary participation by parties seeking to further their self-interest. In fact, the decentralization strategy is an alternative to socialism; it offers a way to replace the maze of regulations and public services that led to a growing welfare state—**that** is the direction of socialism.

There are serious doubts as to how these ideas can be worked out, of course, and nobody can foresee the precise form of the economic system that will result. That is precisely the point. There is no single "right" way to restructure the economy for the future, but myriad possibilities that have to be discussed and resolved among Americans to get the type of system they want. The best guide is to draw on the principles of democracy and free enterprise that served so well in the past.

Market Supplements: Internalizing the Externalities

One badly needed structural improvement is to internalize social costs and benefits in lieu of detailed regulations that are inefficient and that have created a storm of protest from business. The growing complexity of an information age makes the old command and control form of regulation unrealistic in an economy of rapidly changing technology, varying plant sizes, different geographical regions, and a wide range of communities standards.

The ideal solution is to use "market supplements" that levy taxes on parties inflicting social costs and pay rewards to those producing social benefits, thereby achieving the same regulatory objectives less expensively while preserving the freedom of the marketplace. Economists like Charles Schultze have shown the effectiveness of this approach in solving complex externalities. For example, the problems of traffic congestion, pollution, and gas shortages caused by the automobile persist because drivers do not pay the full social costs of driving. In localities like Singapore where autos are taxed, the problem solves itself.[51]

One of the most useful applications is pollution control. The EPA has developed a variety of new concepts, like the "bubble" and selling pollution "rights," that control pollution by internalizing the social costs it creates. These systems have allowed Armco Steel, 3M, Du Pont, and other firms discretion in changing the production process, using different raw materials, shifting production to other sites, installing pollution control equipment, or other changes that are most efficient for each situation but which cannot be foreseen by regulators. The result is to maintain environmental standards at lower costs that can be passed on as savings to customers and taxpayers. In some cases, costs have been reduced by half. The EPA estimates that savings in 1982 exceeded $1 billion.[52]

There is resistance to the concept because some people are disturbed at the prospect that business can pollute if it simply buys the right to do so—a sort of privilege extended to corporations and the rich. These valid objections underline the need for participation in reaching acceptable political solutions. Most people understand the deeper logic that absolute control of these sensitive matters is not possible, so the best we can do is to create a system whereby the damage to society is paid for by the responsible party. Where a social harm is prohibitively injurious, of course, it would simply be taxed very highly or outlawed entirely. A Harris survey shows that a strong majority of Americans endorse the idea of taxing corporations that create pollution, waste energy, and cause employee accidents, and a study finds that businesspersons and academics foresee the use of market supplements becoming widespread.[53]

The beauty of the concept is its elegant simplicity and its effectiveness in dealing with almost the full range of regulatory problems: controlling litter by taxing containers, limiting excessive airport noise by having airlines pay residents disturbed by flight operations, reducing unemployment by paying employers the costs saved by the community when hiring disadvantaged job seekers, and many other situations.

Privatization: Creating Private Markets for Public Services

Another major structural change underway is the "privatization" of functions normally performed by the public sector. *Newsweek* noted the trend:[54]

> *In cities across the country public services are going private. Faced with shrinking revenues and rising prices, local governments are increasingly turning to businessmen to provide fire and police protection, collect garbage, run airports, and operate libraries.*

This "creeping capitalism" has been advocated by a variety of groups, including the American Enterprise Institute, as an alternative to the problems of bureaucracy that are endemic in a monopolistic government. Here are a few interesting examples of the hundreds of cities and states now using competing firms to provide public services more effectively at lower cost:[55]

The U.S. Government has contracted claims processing to firms like Electronic Data Systems, and allows local communities to contract out airport management services. Said one government official, "It's the wave of the future."

California has led the way. Los Angeles is saving $21 million per year and has eliminated 1447 government jobs with 434 contracts worth $108 million. Pasadena is saving $250,000 a year using a private janitorial service, and Ventura hired Xerox to process bills at lower cost and with faster collection.

Rural Grants Pass, Oregon, lets two private fire departments compete to protect its citizens at a flat annual fee per home or office. "It gives people freedom of choice," said one member of the community.

Phoenix, Arizona, encouraged city departments to compete along with business firms in bidding for work. The jobs went to outside contractors for years, until city managers improved their operations and won back the contracts.

Chandler, Arizona, hired Parsons Corporation to build and operate a water treatment plant.

Louisville, Kentucky, asked Humana Corporation to take over its general hospital, after which the company treated all indigent patients, is subsidizing the hospital's medical school, and turning over 20 percent of all profits.

Newark, New Jersey, is saving $5 million over three years by contracting with a private garbage collecting firm.

Newton, Massachusetts, has turned over ambulance service to a private firm, improving operations and saving the community $500,000.

Other possibilities include the use of vouchers for training, health care, and other government benefits in order to permit users to choose among competing suppliers, thereby gaining the advantages that only free markets can provide. Some even believe the private sector can operate sensitive public functions like prisons better. RCA Corporation has run a profitable prison for juveniles for seven years, and Behavioral Systems Corporation has a minimum security prison in Pomona, California. Corrections Corporation of America has started a full prison in Texas and foresees a "huge market" for their services. Authorities predict a dozen private prison facilities will be operating by 1990.[56]

The English are moving in this same direction by ending the government monopoly on mail, setting up a voucher system for education, and encouraging greater use of private health care.[57]

As privatization grows, difficult questions will be raised because a zealous pursuit of profit may interfere with the public interest. At Twinsburg, Ohio, the chief of police said of the attempt to use private firms for police protection: "One guy is trying to make a profit and the village is trying to get the most amount of service. Quite simply, those two goals clash."[58] If business is to successfully manage public functions, government must work with contractors to insure they adopt a broader institutional role that serves the public welfare. So once again, we see great possibilities for creating a more efficient economic system, but collaborative policy making is needed to handle the political aspects that are unavoidable.

National Indicative Planning: Making Markets Work Better

Business has done itself a disservice by opposing attempts to introduce some form of national indicative planning. Because of traditional opposition to any form of government intrusion, corporations have prevented gaining better planning data, whereas knowledgeable advocates of free enterprise know that the system can only work if accurate information is available to guide market choices.

The cry that national planning would intrude on business freedom is a red herring. Responsible parties do not advocate the type of planning used in "planned economies," but merely having some research group at the national level examine the performance of various industrial sectors, provide forecasts of the future, and highlight threats and opportunities. No targets, guidelines, or other forms of control are intended other than the guidance provided by the sheer data.[59] By blocking proposals to establish this type of system, business has shielded itself from economic realities that must be faced to achieve success, as though ignorance were preferable to knowledge.

This intense opposition reflects a fear of being dictated to by government and having business performance scrutinized—a belief that the federal government intends planning to be done *to* business rather than *for* business. These fears may be dispelled by involving corporations in the planning process in order to draw on their expertise and to give the process political legitimacy. Ideally, one could envision a body composed of representatives from business, labor, government, and other institutions working together to gather information, analyze it, and disseminate results to private and public policy-makers. The effect would be to have concerned economic actors hold a systematic, ongoing debate on critical business issues.

To conduct this process effectively, there is an important need for social data as well as the financial data that now dominate attention. As we saw in Chapter 6, a new discipline of social reporting is rapidly providing the capability to evaluate various social costs and benefits that can be larger and more critical than financial impacts, and economists have pointed out the need for a broader equivalent of GNP to measure not simply dollars spent but the actual degree of social welfare.[60] The quality of life has become as important as money today, yet we are generally ignorant of why it varies and how to improve it.

For instance, studies show that car accidents are a result not only of physical problems like car design but driver negligence, so driver education programs can reduce accidents by half. As another example, European products are associated with high quality because their governments distribute consumer evaluation data that encourages manufacturers to improve their wares by rewarding excellence. June Kronholtz, a journalist, notes that this information is more useful than government regulations:[61]

> Consumer groups in all nine EEC countries agree that the Common Market's most important contribution to consumer safety would be to act as a clearinghouse for information on defective or dangerous products, a far simpler and perhaps more effective undertaking that [establishing] complex rules.

Chapter 6 suggested how such data may be organized conceptually. The ROR model, for instance, logically reflects the interlocking structure of business in which the outputs of suppliers and distributors become inputs to their client companies. Major corporations thereby aggregate the social resources, benefits, and costs generated by smaller firms to form a hierarchy of national *social* accounts, similar to the manner in which financial accounts are now aggregated to estimate macroeconomic factors such as GNP. As social reporting improves in large corporations, therefore, it may form a system for evaluating social welfare from the bottom up, in addition to top-down social indicators, just as financial performance is measured from both micro- and macroeconomic perspectives. The need was anticipated by sociologist Daniel Bell:[62]

> What we need, in effect, is a System of Social Accounts which would broaden our concept of costs and benefits, and put economic accounting into a broader framework. The eventual purpose would be to create a "balance sheet" that would be useful in clarifying policy choices.

Fostering Investment Capital: The Politics of Money

Enhancing economic growth through targeting government funds is probably the most widely discussed concept, probably because of the central role that money plays in American society. The range of clever schemes for directing the flow of capital truly boggles the mind: deductions for investments, lower corporate taxes, accelerated depreciation, loans to promising industries, and consumption taxes that encourage savings, to name a few. Proponents of industrial policy propose various national banking systems to perform such functions. Financier Felix Rohatyn advocates a "Finance Reconstruction Board" reminiscent of the New Deal, Harvard's Robert Reich a "National Industrial Board," and the House LaFalce bill proposes $8.5 billion to fund a "Bank for Industrial Competitiveness." Criticism hinges on the wisdom of letting Uncle Sam gamble with the taxpayers' money to back losers, and polls show the public does not favor the concept.[63]

However, this view of the issue is unnecessarily framed in black and white terms that are not very productive. Since a sound investment capital sector already exists in the United States, perhaps the most useful role for government is to act as a facilitating agent rather than an investor, bringing investment bankers together with promising enterprises to help them work out solutions for finding sources of funds, lowering interest rates, and resolving problems in the capital investment system. As fellow entrepreneurs, venture capitalists are more likely than politicians or government bureaucrats to appreciate the prospects for success, and their job is to take on risks.

Like all proposals for restructuring the economy, this problem presents many feasible options, but the central issues involve difficult political choices. Who should provide risk capital to back important ventures? How can the misuse of funds by powerful interests be avoided? Should they be used to bail out failing firms? So once again, the need is to develop policy bodies that provide constructive dialogue to resolve sensitive matters involving the politics of money.

Technological Innovation: The Power of Sharing Knowledge

One cause of the economic success of the Japanese and Germans is their ability to create and apply technical knowledge. The United States seems to be developing a unique approach using collaborative R&D consortiums sponsored by corporations, government, and universities to advance the state-of-the-art in computer science, steel, aerospace, bioengineering, and even in the clothing and textile field. The rapid growth of these projects reflects the powerful advantages that result from sharing knowledge to the benefit of all parties. Some examples:[64]

Computer Technology. The Microelectronics and Computer Technology Corporation (MCC) is a collaborative R&D venture of 20 firms founded by Control Data, and the Semiconductor Research Corporation is a similar project sponsored by IBM. Although there is skepticism, proponents are enthusiastic over the prospects: "The industry is increasingly recognizing that we all need each other," said one executive, while MCC President Robert Inman believes, "The advent of cooperative R&D is the most significant step forward [in the computer industry] since large scale integration."

University of Texas. The location of the MCC consortium at the University of Texas has expanded into an effort to propel the state into becoming a major center in high-technology. Business leaders working with state officials have donated funds to endow 32 chairs at the university, so it may rival Harvard and Berkeley in years to come for national excellence.

Rensselaer Polytechnic Institute has created an unusual "incubator" program in which scores of fledgling high-technology companies are located on the campus actively working with students and faculty to advance the state-of-the-art in electronics, robotics, energy, and other fields.

Pennsylvania. The Governor has formed a "Ben Franklin Program" in which collaboration between business, government, and academia is used to stimulate the development of high-tech industries. The program has $100 million in venture capital available, and has set up centers in state universities.

Employment Policy: Collaboration to Create Jobs

As rapid technological change creates structural unemployment among those unprepared for the more sophisticated jobs of the future, there is a growing need for retraining and relocating large numbers of workers, as Sweden, Germany, and Japan have done for years. Government is too removed from the marketplace, so programs are being developed in which universities, corporations, and government work together:[65]

Government Supported Corporate Training. Private Industry Councils (PICs) are spending almost $2 billion per year for training 1.3 million unemployed people by potential employers, rather than government, in order to make the training relevant to future job prospects. The Department of Labor reports that a "phenomenal" 70 percent of the participants have gained jobs.

Job Creation.   States are using tax benefits and outright subsidies to encourage business to create jobs, leading to a "market for jobs" concept. The approach has been used in North Carolina, Louisiana, and New York.

Self-Regulating Institutions: Freeing Up Enterprise

The profound implication of these changes is to transform major corporations and other institutions into self-regulating systems. As the above examples show, various elements of the decentralization strategy are now falling into place to make this transformation possible. Here are a few other ideas:[66]

Voluntary Pollution Control.   A consortium of chemical companies working with environmental leaders has started "Clean Sites, Inc." to clean up the nation's 17,000 to 22,000 toxic dumps. One of the environmentalists, William K. Reilly, claimed the project represented "a new kind of consensus-building institution [that could] set a new pattern of cooperation."

Insurance Replaces Regulation.   There are interesting trends toward requiring insurance in lieu of government inspections now performed to protect against employee accidents, unsafe building construction, product related damages, and other dangers. The result is a system of incentives that serves everyone better. In its attempt to reduce liabilities the insurance company is keen on inspecting the firm carefully and instructing managers to take preventive measures, the firm is freed of liability and government regulations, victims of accidents are guaranteed compensation, and the burden on taxpayers is reduced. All parties must assume their responsibilities to make the system work, so many firms are creating joint labor-management safety committees to work together in reducing accidents and insurance fees.

Joint Business-Government Consumer Protection.   "Mixed systems" combining business-government collaboration are being successfully developed in advertising, chemicals, electronics, and other fields to provide minimum standards of safety and quality, disclosure of product information, policing of deceptive practices, grading of products, and codes of conduct.

This possibility is still in its infancy, so it will be years before the outcome becomes clear. The trends in this book all suggest that this would be a logical outcome, however, and the advantages seem to be vast. As the former antagonism between business, labor, government, and the public is converted into working alliances, more sophisticated multipurpose institutions should emerge that allow economic snags to be untangled far more effectively where they originate, freeing enterprise from the debilitating costs and loss of autonomy that centralized government controls impose.

BEYOND CAPITALISM

These are simply some of the more prominent concepts being proposed for restructuring the economy, but they demonstrate that the choice facing Americans is not between interfering big government versus untrammeled big business. These are simplistic extremes that obscure far more preferable possibilities. Clearly, government cannot be so confining as to shackle innovation, yet laissez-faire economics is not really freedom but more like the anarchy of a jungle that is outmoded in modern nations. True freedom results from developing self-discipline and a sense of community to foster productive collaboration.

There will always be opposition to these ideas, but Americans seem to be moving toward the use of participatory policy-making in corporations, public agencies, industries, communities, states, and the nation to shape a system of political economy that better serves the needs of all parties. Drawing on the type of structural concepts outlined above would then create the conditions for economic revitalization: entrepreneurial freedom, lower taxes, new growth opportunities, accurate information, abundant capital, rapid technological innovation, close working relations, and an educated work force. The result would be a modern equivalent of the infrastructure that successfully fostered physical growth during the industrial past, the Old Capitalism. Now we are simply adding a different infrastructure for a new era, a New Capitalism. George Steiner noted, "We are now, in this nation, redefining capitalism."[67]

Of course, nobody knows what this system will look like because almost any type of economy could be constructed. A rich diversity is certain to flourish as various corporations and local governments evolve into different economic subcultures that serve their unique needs. Notwithstanding these differences, however, the common denominator should be a form of political economy that exemplifies both the liberal ideals of democracy and the conservative values of free enterprise. There seems to be no good reason for ideological conflict because these principles are not incompatible, and, as we have shown, collaboration is needed to create an economic system that will permit healthy competition. This distinguishing spirit of the New Capitalism is captured in the concept of Democratic Free Enterprise—a central theme running through this book which represents the synthesis of two dominant forces that have long formed an antagonistic polarity at all levels of economic activity.

At the level of employee relations, I referred to this conflict as a "conspiracy of dependence" between the superior's demands for job performance versus the subordinate's rights and rewards. At the level of operating units, it was a clash between the organization's need for control versus a new venture's freedom. Likewise, the entire institution is caught in a bind between the need for financial gain versus demands for social responsibility. For the larger macroeconomy, Daniel Bell described this polarity as the "cultural contradictions of capitalism": the technological, financial necessities of the market powered by free enterprise values versus the interest in human welfare and cooperation that comprise democratic ideals. This same dichotomy corresponds with what Robert Reich called the "business" versus "civic" cultures.[68]

Most of us are partial to one of these two polar orientations, but objectively both are evolving through a historic process that corresponds roughly with the dialectic pattern proposed by the German philosopher Hegel. In his terms, the free enterprise pole represents the "thesis" originating from the status quo of the Old Capitalism which seeks to perpetuate itself, as in the neoconservative revolution. Democratic values form the "antithesis" that arose during the revolts of the 1960s to challenge the Old Capitalism. Thus, both of these ideologies seem to be advancing to higher stages, although in cyclical swings that sharpen the emphasis on one and then the other.

The significance of our time is that the information age is providing a creative spark to unify the "thesis" and "antithesis" into a "synthesis." The inexorable explosion of information technology is driving social change in an unusual new direction that unites free enterprise and democratic values. John Naisbitt put it this way: "hi-tech/hi-touch."

Previous chapters showed how these two principles are being integrated at all economic levels to create the type of tacit contractual agreements that have always formed the basis for advances in the social order.[69] At the employee level it is emerging in the form of an "employment contract" that holds subordinates accountable for performance but offers them autonomy in doing their work. For internal ventures a "business contract" is being used to insure organizational control while permitting freedom for intrapreneurs. The equivalent at the corporate level is the "social contract" that unites profit with the public welfare. For the entire macroeconomy a "political contract" between the left and the right should form a system of political economy that fosters both cooperation and competition.

This extraordinary union of opposing forces that locked economies in an impasse holds the key to creating an especially powerful form of business for the information age. As we learned so painfully in the industrial past, either free enterprise or democracy alone pervert business into harsh, exploitive conflict on one extreme or soft, indulgent fantasy on the other. Whereas the successful integration of these two principles provides a healthy balance: free enterprise holding corporations accountable to the realities of the market, while democracy insures that the firm is guided by the interests of its constituencies. Today this unusual synthesis is releasing vast unused energies that are now carrying both ideals to higher levels of development.

As we have seen, the New Capitalism is powered by a fresh growth of vital enterprise. Competition is burgeoning, smart growth is opening up an unlimited frontier, industries are being deregulated, accountability is tightening, entrepreneurial ventures are booming, organic networks are forming internal markets, intrapreneurs are revitalizing big organizations, stakeholders are working together, strategic management is adapting firms to the future, and the economic infrastructure is being redesigned to create near-perfect competition. In sum, a flowering of free enterprise is now restructuring the former bureaucratic economy into a dynamic system that exemplifies the creative responsiveness of markets.

The New Capitalism is also propelling business toward a remarkably different focus on democracy and human values. A mature populace seeks self-fulfillment, smart growth is improving the quality of life, companies are striving to serve their clients, networks are enhancing individual freedom, participative leadership is granting people power, the social contract is instilling corporate democracy, strategic management fosters a symbiosis with society, collaboration is growing among entire institutions, and tripartite policy-making is beginning at the city, state, and national levels. Warren Bennis foresaw how high-technology exerts an imperative for democracy:[70]

> . . . democracy in industry is not an idealistic conception but a hard necessity in those areas in which change is ever present and in which creative scientific enterprise must be nourished.

This realization of our traditional principles through a creative union with one another represents a critical maturing of modern economies that forms the central difference between the Old Capitalism and the New Capitalism. Progress is no longer driven by big business to reap financial gains, but by myriad small enterprises that serve the public welfare. In the past, oligopolies banished free enterprise from major industries, and their profit-centered behavior was hardly democratic, in spite of the claim of those who called the old system "democratic capitalism."[71] Only the political system was democratic, creating a conflict with big business that would more accurately be described as "democracy *versus* capitalism." The Old Capitalism was beneficial, but this was a fortunate by-product rather than the aim of most businessmen intent on using employees, customers, and the public to serve the interests of those owning property—"capitalists." The words of William H. Vanderbilt echo down through the ages: "The public be damned."

So we come to an interesting contradiction in terms: the New Capitalism is really no longer capitalism at all if it is governed democratically to serve a full range of human goals rather than profit alone—yet it is still free enterprise. In fact, it raises the principles of free enterprise to a far greater degree of freedom and entrepreneurial vigor. It is certainly not the central state planning of socialism in Russia or Cuba; nor is it the dictatorship we see in Chile, North Korea, or other authoritarian capitalist nations.

The Old Capitalism designed by capitalists to serve capitalists seems to be slowly but surely passing. It is being transformed into a cooperative system that serves all interests, and that fosters near-perfect competition among large numbers of small, innovative ventures. Although I've called it the "New Capitalism" as a relative concept to contrast it with the "Old Capitalism," the most useful thing Americans could do is to stop thinking of our economy as "capitalism" of any form. In a decade or two, it should become clear that the new economic system emerging now is a ***democratic*** type of ***free enterprise*** that goes beyond capitalism altogether. Democratic Free Enterprise exemplifies the two central ideals of Western nations which were poorly realized in the past, much less unified, but which now offer the potential for creating almost unlimited prosperity, for the people and by the people.

9

Hybrid Economies:

A WORLD ORDER BRIDGING CAPITALISM AND SOCIALISM

One of the most telling aspects of the antagonistic relationship between the two superpowers is a striking similarity in their views of each other. In 1983, President Reagan issued a famous condemnation of the Soviet Union: "The Soviets have not slowed the pace of their enormous military buildup . . . they are the focus of evil in the modern world." But his counterpart at that time, President Yuri Andropov, had precisely the same harsh view of America: "[the United States is] the root of evil perpetuated in the world, the evil which threatens the very existence of mankind."[1]

This obdurate hostility is largely the result of an ideological clash between the two major systems of political economy—capitalism and socialism—that have polarized the earth into warring camps. Unfortunately, most of us are unable to see this conflict for what it is because of a fierce self-righteousness pervading both nations, which is exactly why it continues. But lately a growing number of people are beginning to realize this is a senseless struggle that can only lead to world disaster, and that a different type of outlook is needed to free us from this morbid state of mind. Political analyst Richard Barnet described the problem this way:[2]

Neither "communism" nor "capitalism" remains a credible philosophical system for organizing society in the contemporary world. . . .

Portions of this chapter are adapted from my paper, "Beyond Left vs Right," *Futures* (June 1985).

> There is no way out of the national security dilemma as it is now
> being defined. Unless we change the conceptual framework, we are
> doomed to a series of military moves and countermoves that cannot
> be kept under control.

If this sensitive issue is examined free of prejudice, however, a
far richer perspective emerges in which the two ideologies are seen
as part of a larger world system. The USA and the USSR share
strong underlying similarities because both are great industrial powers
that govern empires covering half the globe. Their forms of political
economy may be vastly different, but each is a polar opposite of
the same basic industrial paradigm, so they complement one another
to create a remarkable symmetry. Many years ago Alexis de Tocque-
ville cogently anticipated the symbiotic nature of this relationship:[3]

> There are, at the present time, two great nations in the world which
> seem to tend toward the same end, although they started from different
> points. I allude to the Russians and the Americans. . . . Their starting
> point is different, and their courses are not the same. Yet each of
> them seems to be marked out by the will of Heaven to sway the
> destinies of half of the globe.

In this chapter, we explore how capitalism and socialism are
logically related as bipolar subsystems of the industrial order. Then
we see how the Third World is emerging as an intervening new
force in this conflict. Third World nations need help to speed their
industrial development, while industrialized nations need new
frontiers to rejuvenate their stagnating economies. In their enlightened
self-interest, global corporations are defining a new role that integrates
both needs, thereby accelerating the growth of a global economy
for the information age. Moreover, the cultural diversity among all
these nations is encouraging the proliferation of a variety of economic
systems that form hybrid combinations of capitalism and socialism.
And the model described in the last chapter—Democratic Free Enterprise—is emerging as the center of this rich economic spectrum.
The new world order that results should comprise a diverse network
of political-economic relationships that unifies the Earth into a
coherent whole, bridging the explosive gap between the two superpowers.

THE USA AND THE USSR AS POLES
OF INDUSTRIAL SOCIETY

Former President Nixon expressed the attitude that prevails among most Americans about the Soviet Union:[4]

> The US-Soviet contest is a struggle between two opposite poles of human experience—between those represented by the sword and by the spirit, by fear and by hope. Their system is ruled by the sword; ours is governed by the spirit. Their influence has spread by conquest; ours has spread by example.

Obviously there is a lot of truth to this view. Few of us are interested in living in the Soviet Union, whereas the flow of Russian defectors to the West is considerable. The Berlin Wall, the way life in Russia is dictated by the state, the heavy heel of Soviet troops marching around the world, and the recent downing of a Korean civilian jetliner continually reinforce this impression of a brutal regime. But there is another reality that we fail to see by concentrating on this negative image. Roughly half of all nations have turned socialist, and it is too self-serving to contend they have been forced into "totalitarian oppression." The fact is that most of these people have chosen socialism, with all its faults, because they think it is a better alternative to the serious flaws they perceive in capitalism.

Table 9.1 provides a simple outline of these two systems to highlight their differences, similarities, unique strengths, and characteristic weaknesses. This comparison shows that the USA and the USSR are subsets of the same basic industrial paradigm in which each offers a different solution to the problems of industrial development. Capitalism permits an efficient form of economic freedom that has produced a high standard of living, but at the cost of harsh competition, great social inequities, wasteful overconsumption, and a precarious existence. Socialism uses centralized state control to provide personal security, better welfare benefits, and more uniform social equity, but it is cumbersome, inefficient, and dictatorial. The two systems are polar opposites, so they have different advantages and drawbacks. In fact, from a larger "systems" view this bipolar division of the world has been functional. The mutual antagonism of the superpowers served to drive both nations to develop their

TABLE 9.1. COMPARISON BETWEEN CAPITALIST VERSUS
SOCIALIST SYSTEMS

	Capitalism (USA)	Socialism (USSR)
Major strengths	Freedom Productivity Innovation	Security Social welfare Equity
Major weaknesses	Harsh competition Social inequity Excessive consumption	Bureaucracy Loss of freedom Low productivity
Political system	Two-party	One-party
Economic institutions	Profit-centered big business	State-managed enterprise
Stage of development	Services	Manufacturing

technological skills quickly, to draw together into cohesive societies united against their enemy, and other such purposes.

Socialism Does Have Its Strengths

The drawbacks of socialism are dwelled on at great length, but consider the advantages Soviet citizens see in their system. True, their freedom to start a business, buy a home, and travel abroad is limited, and they suffer shortages of many consumer goods. However, they do not have 10 million unemployed people who have been thrown out of their jobs with little concern for the fearful struggle they face over the future of their families, nor do they endure the merciless contempt of those who withhold badly needed resources from the helpless and pontificate about waste and industriousness while indulging in orgiastic splendor. Russians envy our higher standard of living, but in spite of the horror stories we hear, objective evaluations by knowledgeable Americans indicate they are generally satisfied with the way their system assures them of basic needs like education, employment, housing, food, health care, and pensions, which are increasingly precarious in the United States.[5]

These benefits of Russian life are due to an impressive record of economic progress. Americans ridicule the backward state of planned economies, however the Russians have made enormous gains from a feudal society of impoverished, illiterate peasants just a few decades ago. Between 1950 and 1980, Soviet GNP quadrupled and per capita consumption tripled. Yes, their economy has been stagnating lately, but this is largely due to the general economic crisis affecting all industrialized nations, as we have seen in our own country.[6]

Further, this progress is the result of a high degree of technical skill. Most Americans believe that Russians are technologically inferior, especially because they try to steal American scientific secrets. But the fact is that we emulate much Russian technology because they lead in many fields. Soviet scientists and engineers launched the first space satellite, they developed titanium submarines that are faster than ours, and they perfected key concepts now used in nuclear reactors. American companies like Bristol Myers, Du Pont, 3M, Kaiser, Olin, Varian, and General Dynamics have imported Russian products and used their ideas because they are superior to those of the West. The main reason we do not use more Soviet technology is that most American scientists cannot understand Russian, and, in the words of international consultant John Kiser, because of "widespread U.S. arrogance and parochialism."[7]

The aspect of socialist life most difficult for Americans to comprehend is their one-party political system that we fondly call a "totalitarian police state." Russian politics are certainly different, and few Americans would choose their system over ours. However, that does not mean it is a brutal form of repression without a legitimacy of its own. A one-party system is not the same thing as a dictatorship; it is a form of government that channels conflicting political opinion **within** the party to arrive at a consensus needed to establish legitimate rule. One-party systems may tend to concentrate power, yet they do make needed reforms, as in the recent election of a man like Mikhail Gorbachev with precisely the right blend of affability and pragmatism needed to rejuvenate their nation. Instead of the political conflict and change that Americans seem to prefer, a one-party system has other advantages that tend to emphasize unanimity and stability—rather like the governance of large U.S. corporations. These features are attractive to some Western nations, which is why Italy, Mexico, and other countries with multiple party systems actually have been dominated by a single party for decades. There are enormous differences between the political systems of the USA and USSR, but they reflect cultural preferences. Pat Derian, Assistant Secretary of State for the Carter Administration, noted: "Our diversity seems mad to them and their intolerance of diversity seems mad to us."[8]

In short, life in the Soviet Union may be less exciting and comfortable, but it is more secure and orderly. Many Russians who have immigrated to the United States say we have "too much freedom" while "the Russian is secure." A Russian novelist living in New York claims the anonymity and stress of competitive American life is "in many ways . . . even worse than the Soviet World." Another said, "My possibilities are as limited here as in Russia." Journalist Michael Kernan's studies led him to conclude:[9]

> *The price we [Americans] pay for our freedom from authority [is] the fact that nobody is responsible for you, that the state doesn't care for you in the all-embracing way the Soviet state takes care of its own . . . Emigres [in the United States] speak of the indifference, the coldness of people absorbed in getting ahead, the status based on money.*

Capitalism Does Have Its Weaknesses

If the Soviets are content with their system, why are they such goldbricks on the job, and why is drunkenness so epidemic? The fact is that Americans consume more alcohol per capita than Russians. Drinking is such a major problem in many American homes and businesses that it costs our nation $120 billion each year. The need for relief from the grinding anxiety of our competitive society has also created a major scandal in the use of drugs that costs at least another $26 billion per year. Further, the problem is not just young kids, blue collar workers, and athletes, but includes successful professionals and executives. Corporate officials see the problem in these terms: "Today drug use at the workplace is as common as the coffee break . . . I think it's the biggest problem in industry today . . . the root of drug abuse [is that] many jobs are simply too boring or stressful." This similarity in the two systems was highlighted when the Pope issued an encyclical, "On Human Work," criticizing both socialist and capitalist nations as equally guilty of failing to provide social justice for workers.[10]

We all prize our high standard of living, of course, whereas only a small privileged elite in Russia can afford the material comfort most of us take for granted, despite their claim to a classless society. But reflect on the far greater social inequities created by capitalism. Average families in America earn an annual income of about $26,000, which may be luxurious by some standards. Yet this only provides a marginal existence in today's economy and about one-fifth of the nation lives in poverty—while all about us the economic system glorifies the million dollar incomes of paper entrepreneurs, mediocre rock musicians, television announcers, athletes, and B-rate movie stars. The big winners in the capitalist sweepstakes earn so much beyond their most extravagant possible needs that money ceases to have any meaning, and one can only wonder what purpose such gross wealth may serve. Marlon Brando earned $6 million for a 15 minute role in the film, *Apocalypse Now*, and Johnny Carson makes $1.5 million per **month**—about a **thousand** times the average! Some people applaud these differences as proof that capitalism offers opportunity, but much of the world regards them as simply decadent. Polls show that the vast majority of Americans feel such high incomes are excessive and unjust. One person put it this way:[11]

> *Now let me see if I have my values straight . . . An executive in an industry that was broken down for several years is suddenly worth over $7 million a year. A baseball player is worth $2 million a year. . . . But a teacher for our children is worth about $18,000 a year. . . . It certainly makes one proud to be a part of such an intelligent species.*

Another major fault that is often claimed to discredit the Russians is the savage way they use their secret police to spy, assassinate heads of state, and topple governments. I don't want to imply that this is excusable, but we often ignore the fact that our nation does the same thing. The CIA engineered coups that assassinated Diem in Vietnam, Allende in Chile, and hired the Mafia to kill Castro. Yes, the Russians have invaded Poland, Hungary, Afghanistan, and other countries to expand their empire, but our early history is, once again, not too different. The United States took Puerto Rico, Cuba, and the Philippines by force during its period of expansion. It overthrew the government of Iran in 1953, and launched the Bay of Pigs invasion against Cuba. Even now the Reagan Administration is using rebel forces to topple the government in Nicaragua while flouting the authority of the World Court. One American acknowledged: "I fail to see any substantial difference between [the terrorism of Iran, Russia, etc.] and the CIA-financed and directed terrorism against Nicaragua."[12]

Another aspect of this similar use of violence is that the USA, the USSR, and South Africa are the only modern nations that still put criminals to death. The Soviets may have a "gulag archipelago" that suppresses political freedom brutally, but Americans put roughly the same proportion of people in prison—criminal deviancy in our society just takes different forms.

Modern nations like the United States and the European states have worked hard to ameliorate the oppressive features of the Old Capitalism, but it still persists in many capitalist nations that are our allies: South Africa's repression of blacks, the dictatorships in Taiwan, South Korea, and so on. The cause for most of the revolutionary unrest in South America is unjust economic systems, like those of Chile, Bolivia, Guatemala, and El Salvador, in which a small oligarchy of rich capitalists own the bulk of land and business, subjugating the rest of the population to a life of endless squalor.[13]

No dictatorship can last forever, so such injustices eventually force people to revolt, as we have seen in Cuba, Iran, Nicaragua, and the USA and USSR themselves. Most recent revolutions lead to socialist systems because, rather than being feared as "totalitarian," socialism seems attractive precisely because the authority of the state is needed to eliminate the inequities created under such "free" enterprise. The tragedy is that revolution usually solves nothing but simply swings political control to the other extreme, leaving the United States identified as the force behind the overthrown enemy. "Revolutions have never lightened the burden of tyranny," said George Bernard Shaw, "They have only shifted it to another shoulder." In his farewell speech before stepping down as head of the Episcopal Church, Bishop John Allin warned how our international role has grown more stridently self-serving in recent years:[14]

The American image of a great democratic republic and generous good neighbor has become overshadowed in the sight of many . . . by the image of a bully, preoccupied with profits.

It is ironic that conservative Americans attack communism with such single-minded ferocity because these excesses of our own system are the major cause for its continuing vigor. Socialism has spread over much of the world as a reaction to the limitations of capitalism. As that great American philosopher Pogo once said, "We have met the enemy and he is us."

Variations of Economic Enterprise

Beyond these antagonistic but complementary differences, however, the USA and the USSR share strong similarities. Both are great industrial powers that dominate huge portions of the world to serve their own needs using authoritarian, bureaucratic institutions. The major institution in Russia may be a dictatorial state controlled factory, but how different is this really from the typical large American business corporation run by dominating, highly paid executives in the interest of making money? As we've noted before, many employees and middle-managers themselves view their firms somewhat like a capitalist equivalent of "totalitarianism." Max Weber saw capitalism and socialism not as contradictory systems, but as two faces of a common system of bureaucracy. The similarities are far stronger if it is recalled that the Soviet Union is not an advanced "service" economy like ours. Because of its late start and the cumbersome inefficiency of central planning, Russia is still at the "manufacturing" level of development that existed in America before World War II, so its institutions are roughly similar to the brutal conditions that prevailed in the United States at that time. Alvin Toffler noted:[15]

While each side [capitalism and socialism] promoted a different ideology, both were essentially hawking the same superideology . . . the superiority of industrialism . . . the society of big organizations, big cities, centralized bureaucracies.

The explanation for these similarities is more apparent by examining the structure of both systems from a general perspective.

Figure 9.1 shows the open-system model we saw in Chapter 6, now portrayed as a generic form of enterprise with different ideologies representing variations on this basic model. All economic systems are intrinsically composed of these same key constituencies that of necessity make up any enterprise: investors, the public, employees, customers, and so on. The main difference between capitalism, socialism, worker democracy, and other possible variations is that different political interests control what is fundamentally the same system.[16]

The central idea that Americans and Russians should see is that the differences between us are simply variations on the same realities of economic and political life. Each nation has found a unique

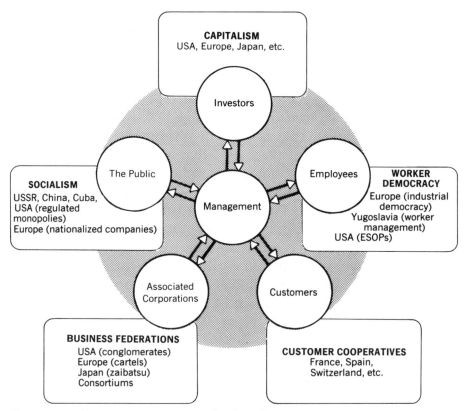

Figure 9-1.   Variations on systems of political economy.

Note: Each form of political economy is shown as a variation on the same generic model of enterprise in which one particular interest group controls the system. For instance, socialism is controlled to serve the public, capitalism is controlled to serve investors, and so on.

solution to the common problems of industrialization, with its characteristic strengths and weaknesses. Although I join the vast majority of Americans in strongly preferring our own system because we do not find socialism "morally equivalent," who can claim the right to judge that one is superior to the other?

These underlying commonalities make the conflict between the two superpowers seem exaggerated and unnecessary, but it persists because of such mutual hostility that neither side is able to see themselves or their adversary accurately. Social psychologists who study conflict identify a few symptoms that are vividly apparent in both nations: a withdrawal from communication and contact, followed by fabricating reasons that justify one's righteousness and the other party's blame. In spite of the crucial importance of the two superpowers learning how to get along together, only about 20 percent of their leaders have ever visited each other's country. In the U.S. Senate, the most avid hawks are senators who have never seen Russia.[17]

What is most striking is the strong symmetry between the positions of both nations. Americans claim the Russians cannot be trusted, yet interviews with Soviets show they feel precisely the same way. One study concluded: "Wherever they turn, Soviets . . . see the hand of the United States, restraining their actions, hindering their plans, and working against their interests." Polls show that 76 percent of Americans believe we share the blame for bad relations with the Soviet Union. Many observers have pointed out how the superpowers are locked in this fruitless conflict perpetuated by self-serving stereotypes:[18]

Reporter Michael Dobbs noted: "The visitor to both Moscow and Washington is struck by a kind of symmetry of attitudes. . . . Each superpower sees the other as inherently aggressive and depicts its own posture as primarily defensive. Each believes that the other is out to secure world domination through military superiority. And each is convinced that the other country is governed by men who are scheming, conspiratorial and diabolically clever."

Journalist Lewis Lapham observed: "Both sets of caricatures serve the purpose of instilling in their respective audiences the salutary emotions of fear and loathing. . . . The Soviets portray the U.S. as a lawless frontier where, except for the ruling elite, nobody is happy and nobody is safe. The Americans portray the Soviet Union as a monolithic prison, a dull and confined place where nobody is safe and nobody is free."

Historian Arthur Schlesinger, Jr. concluded: "The hardliners in both countries reinforce each other, strengthen each other's case, increase each other's budget, enlarge each other's influence."

In a sense, the downing of the Korean jetliner was not so much the result of an "evil Soviet empire," although they are certainly harsh people. This unfortunate and stupid tragedy was largely due to the intense hatred and penetrating fear that grips both superpowers, especially the Russians, causing them to be so utterly distrustful that they resort to such barbaric acts.

Those intent on hating communism will not be swayed by this brief analysis, but I believe it demonstrates the symmetry in this intimate, symbiotic relationship between the two dominant ideologies. Each system dwells on the sins of its opponent as proof of its evil intent, but the opponent also embodies great strengths that build on one's own weakness. Socialism owes its attraction to the flaws of capitalism, and vice versa. Because the superpowers do not have the moral strength to acknowledge their own failings, however, they both remain blind to this self-inflicted cause of their conflict, while the very existence of their opponent implies a self-condemnation that each nation senses subconsciously but very deeply.

Thus, the underlying source of the animosity that divides the world is not the evil of either superpower. It is their inability to see the truth about their own system—the self-righteous insistence of people like Ronald Reagan and Yuri Andropov that they are moral and others are not.

RISE OF THE THIRD WORLD

Although the West has usually ignored the Third World or viewed it as a problem, this forgotten dark part of the globe may now hold the key to resolving the conflict between the superpowers as it becomes a major new force in world affairs. Industrialization has been spreading rapidly to underdeveloped nations during the last decade, so their slumbering giant populations are springing to life and promising massive disruptions. The Iranian revolution is just a single example hinting at the conflicts that may lie ahead. A study by the Population Reference Bureau shows that the population growth rate of the less developed countries (LDCs) is over 2 percent per year, compared with 0.6 percent in the developed countries (DCs), so 80 percent of the world's population will soon be concentrated in the Third World.[19] To put it a little more sharply, the predominantly white, affluent people who make up the bulk of the United States and Europe may soon become as conspicuously out of place as the Dutch settlers are now in black South Africa.

From Aid to Trade

Further, these nations are no longer ignorant peasants pleading for "economic justice" because their relationship with the West has switched fundamentally from "aid to trade." LDCs bought 40 percent of all American exports in 1980, which is more than the United States sells to Europe and Japan combined. Oriental nations in particular have huge numbers of low-paid workers who have been trained by their culture to be cooperative and industrious, and so they are rapidly forming one of the biggest economic powers in the world. The most successful of the LDCs—South Korea, Taiwan, Hong Kong, Singapore, Thailand, Malaysia, Indonesia, Brazil, Saudi Arabia, and Red China—have annual economic growth rates that average twice that of the DCs, while their inflation rates tend to remain below 5 percent. By the year 2000, these nations should manufacture about one third of the world's goods, presenting a far greater threat to the West than Japan did when it wiped out Swiss watch-making, took over the market for English motorcycles, captured the bulk of American consumer electronics and television sales, and then became the largest producer of cars in the world. Economist Paul McCraken noted:[20]

> By the end of the next decade, the complex represented by [the Third World] will be an aggregation of industrial power and dynamism exceeding that of Western Europe or the United States.

Nations like Japan and France are assisting the LDCs in using the revolutionary power of information technology, photovoltaic cells, and other new hi-tech advances to solve endemic problems that have hindered economic progress, such as obtaining modern medical care, energy, education, and communication systems. As a result, some claim the LDCs may simply leapfrog over the "industrial" stage of development and go directly to the information age.[21]

This may seem a fanciful prospect, but it would be wise to remember that just a decade or two ago the label "Made in Japan" signified cheap goods. Who would have believed the Japanese would soon become the greatest industrial force in the world because of their sophisticated manufacturing skills, and that they would threaten to take the lead in the next generation of computers? The upshot is, where just a few years ago the fate of the Third World was a moral concern that could barely stifle the yawns of the prosperous West, now this dimly understood part of the globe may become a pivotol force in the evolving global economy.

The World Problematique

Another aspect of this critical role of the Third World is the international debt crisis. Because the LDCs cannot pay the interest on their huge debts, much less the principle, they threaten to bring the lending banks of the rich nations down with them if they are unable to stave off bankruptcy. A. W. Clausen, President of the World Bank, claims "The economic distress of the poorest nations is a time bomb ticking away," and Belisario Betancur, President of Columbia, warned, "The deluge, if not avoided by all of us together, will be worldwide."[22]

The debt crisis reflects the fact that the LDCs and the DCs are at different stages of development, so, in the words of Germany's Willy Brandt, "The fate of the rich and the poor countries . . . is inextricably linked." The LDCs are trying to coax their fledgling economies past the take-off point, so they are in need of the capital, technical know-how, and management skills that the DCs have in abundance. Conversely, the economies of the DCs are maturing, hence they must find a new use for these idle resources to revive economic growth and take 30 million unemployed workers off their welfare rolls. This complementary nature of both problems stems from a structural imbalance in the world economy that joins the DCs and the LDCs together, whether they like it or not, and so they need each other badly. Henry Kissinger summed it up:[23]

The debt problem is the symptom, not the cause, of a structural crisis. It reflects the fact that severe inequalities in the distribution of wealth producing capacity persist among the world's nations . . . I feel we are at a watershed. We are at a period which is either going to be of extraordinary creativity or a period when the international order came apart . . . there now exists an extraordinary opportunity to form, for the first time in history, a truly global society. . . . Only American can lead the world to rapid economic recovery, and we cannot fulfill this role without a long-term strategy. The free market is the most successful mechanism of producing prosperity and freedom. But the free market alone will not overcome the present economic crisis. [The debt crisis] signals the need for collaboration.

Furthermore, the future of both sets of nations is also intertwined because the growth of the LDCs may bring the larger crisis of the entire industrial order to an urgent focus. As we saw in Chapter 1, the drive for economic development in the exploding populations of the Third World should relentlessly increase the shortage of scarce resources, environmental decay, and competition for consumer markets by about a factor of 10 over the next few decades—creating a constellation of interrelated disorders that forms a massive, systemic global crisis which has been called the "world problematique." As this threat grows to such catastrophic proportions that it can no longer be ignored, procrastination must finally yield to some form of action.[24]

The World Crisis Is a World Opportunity

The significance of this critical linkage between the developed and undeveloped sectors of the world is that a profound transformation seems required in the entire global order. The Pope summed up the challenge in an encyclical:[25]

So widespread is the [gap between the rich and the poor nations] that it brings into question the financial, monetary, production, and commercial mechanisms that, resting on various political pressures, support the world economy. . . . [the] indispensable transformation of the structures of economic life [will require] a true conversion of mind, will and heart.

Americans like to think in pragmatic terms of furthering their self-interest, and the LDCs offer a vast frontier for the stifled economic power of nations like the United States. For instance, they may provide an outlet for the saturated consumer markets of the West. Like other troublesome issues, then, the global crisis forces us to see that the Third World is more than a great problem but a great opportunity. President Carter observed, "The greatest potential for growth is in the developing world," and the Organization for Economic Cooperation and Development noted:[26]

> Nothing would be more dangerous than to forget the potential market for industrial products represented by the ill-satisfied demands of an enormous segment of mankind. Developed and Third World countries do not have to divide up fixed global demand. They have to build a new industry to the scale of billions of men and women.

Not only would closer economic alliances between the DCs and LDCs serve both sets of interests, they may also create the type of international economic order needed to defuse the world crisis. A variety of global modelling studies has been conducted by different groups following the original limits-to-growth study, all pointing to three main conclusions:[27]

1. The main obstacles to worldwide prosperity are sociological and political because there is no technical reason why the needs of all nations cannot be satisfied in the near future.
2. Present policies cannot continue much longer without catastrophic consequences, so a transition to some form of different world order seems inevitable.
3. Cooperative approaches to resolving these problems will be most effective.

THE EMERGING GLOBAL SYSTEM

Obviously, it is hard to envision how these enormous obstacles may be overcome, and even under the most favorable outcomes there is sure to be a painful amount of international disorder and conflict. But the long progress of the world since ancient times has always struggled along this same difficult path. There seems to be an historic trend toward ever larger social aggregations —from cave-dwellers, to tribes, to cities, to nation states, to superpowers— inexorably leading to the next logical step of some form of global order, although by way of unforeseen events that we cannot possibly anticipate.

If major disasters like nuclear holocaust can be avoided, the coming information age should somehow integrate the planet into a single coherent, but highly diverse, economic-political system, possibly around the end of this century. International trade is growing twice as fast as domestic commerce, and the rise of the Third World should produce an additional burst of growth to accelerate this transition over the next few decades. The result would be a shift to a predominantly international mode of economics as global corporations produce and sell goods and services throughout the world:[28]

> **Global Markets.**   Theodore Leavitt of the Harvard Business School notes: "A powerful force drives the world toward a converging commonality . . . the emergence of global markets for standardized products on a previously unimagined scale of magnitude . . . The globalization of markets is at hand."
>
> **World Products.**   Laurel Cutler, vice president of a New York ad agency, claims: "By the 1990s, we'll have world-class brands throughout the world."
>
> **International Services.**   Henry Freeman, a senior vice president at American Express, notes that the 1983 General Agreement on Tariffs and Trade (GATT) conference created "an invisible revolution . . . toward international services such as banking, insurance, data processing . . . [It is] a major milestone in the history of international trading."

Further, the Third World should become a major force in this global economy. The LDCs possess the bulk of the population, land mass, natural resources, inexpensive labor, untapped consumer markets, and other economic assets in the entire world. Since their late start can allow them to avoid the problems that took the DCs so long to resolve, they could industrialize as quickly as the Japanese have done. In addition to the sheer size of this impact, their role is likely to be critical because it represents the intervention of a neutral "third" party which may serve as a bridge to unite the capitalist and socialist superpowers.

The Social Contract Abroad

The main barrier to this transformation, however, is the international equivalent of the same conflict over the role of large corporations that hinders the economies of the DCs. Whatever one calls them—multinational corporations (MNCs), transnational corporations (TNCs), or global corporations (GCs)—big business suffers from a lack of political legitimacy that prevents taking advantage of the opportunities for forming collaborative relations with the LDCs. "Multinational is still a dirty word in the developing countries," noted Peter Drucker.[29]

There is a host of reasons why many people in the LDCs, and even the DCs, believe the power of MNCs is misused. Jobs are often exported to the Third World to take advantage of cheap labor while serious unemployment prevails in the DCs. Tax revenue is lost to both DCs and host LDCs by juggling books to take advantage of low tax havens. Many foreign facilities are staffed with personnel from the DCs rather than local workers, and inappropriate high technology often prevents employing their unskilled labor forces. Monopoly power is used to extract scarce raw materials at low prices. A vivid example occurred when the U.S. government, acting on behalf of American business, was alone out of 157 nations to vote against the U.N. code for protecting children in LDCs from the misuse of infant formula.[30]

In short, there persists abroad the same conflict between social responsibility versus financial gain. However, in the international sphere the conflict takes on larger proportions because the massive size of MNCs affects the entire planet. It is estimated that 200 to 300 MNCs will soon control 80 percent of all the productive assets of the noncommunist world. Authors Richard Barnet and Ronald Muller concluded:[31]

> The men who run the global corporations are the first in history with the organization, technology, money, and ideology to make a credible try at managing the world as an integrated unit.

This prospect of having the world economy controlled by a relative handful of anonymous business executives answerable to no one does not exactly have a calming effect. The World Council of Churches believes MNCs constitute the largest concentration of power in history, and so the time has come to question their purposes and system of governance. The United Nations is beginning to address this issue. It has formed a committee to study the impact of TNCs; set up international arrangements that control their operations; and is helping nations deal with them.[32]

Despite their bad reputation, the fact is that MNCs often play a very productive role. Studies by former Secretary of Agriculture Orville Freeman show that the more successful firms create far more domestic jobs than they export, they contribute substantially to the United States balance of trade, provide greater employment at higher wages in host countries than local firms, conduct more R&D, and pay higher taxes.[33] As we showed in Chapter 6, large corporations may be the most productive generators of wealth in society, but their avowed focus on profit prevents recognition of the social benefits they create and instead fans antagonism, so a new approach is needed. Even CIA Director William Casey acknowledged: "We must find a way to mobilize our greatest asset in the Third World—private business."[34]

The heart of the problem is the same whether at home or abroad. If the firm sets profit as its main goal, it unavoidably alienates itself from the social interests it must serve to gain political legitimacy. Likewise, the solution is also the same, although involving different actors. A social contract is needed between the MNC and its foreign constituencies: local host governments, workers, consumers, and other stakeholders. The goal would be to have the MNC meet the needs of these groups, and in return to claim their help in gaining political support, labor productivity, patronage of the firm's products, and so on.

In fact, this type of role is evolving slowly out of political pressures and enlightened action. Foreign governments will rarely tolerate MNCs to establish subsidiaries without negotiating favorable conditions on workers to be employed, tax rates, limits on the repatriation of profits, plans to turn control over to local business, and other such arrangements that insure the firm serves the national interest. A study at Harvard University estimates there are more than 1000 MNCs with operations abroad, and many of them are forming collaborative relations that serve both the host nation and their own needs:[35]

> **IBM**'s overseas subsidiaries offer a model. IBM-Japan, for instance, is essentially an indigenous company staffed by loyal Japanese managers and employees who work closely with local suppliers, distributors, customers, and the government to produce the same social contract IBM uses so successfully in the United States. The result is that IBM-Japan has become a major threat to its Japanese competitors on their own home ground.
>
> **Phillips Corporation** has developed a reputation as an enlightened MNC by creating 560 semi-autonomous ventures in LDCs like India; these units provide thousands of skilled jobs, serve local needs, and add to the host nation's capital base, while also being profitable to the parent firm and local entrepreneurs.
>
> **Gulf & Western** has a successful sugar plantation in the Dominican Republic that serves as a prototype for joining the managerial expertise of big business with the industriousness of local farmers. The company has organized farmers into quasi-independent entrepreneurs, financed by the firm to grow and sell sugar cane or other crops for a profit. Recently a cooperative has been formed among 1000 farmers, providing social services, the creation of 10,000 jobs for women, construction of 2700 houses, 128 schools, and 7 health clinics.
>
> **Gulf Oil** proposes a social contract for large projects. One executive described the idea as, "A trilateral relationship between the developing host country, one or more [MNCs], and an international financial consortium."
>
> **Sears World Trade** is one of several American companies to extend their domestic business into international trade by linking together a network of local interests around the globe. A corporate executive said, "When we go to Mexico, the Philippines, Indonesia, Malaysia, China, we are welcomed with open arms because the hallmark of what we are trying to do is to add value to their country."
>
> **Castle & Cooke** has successful operations in Honduras and the Philippines based on contracts in which the firm provides financial and technical support to farmers and agrees to purchase their output.
>
> **Matsushita Corporation** built a plant in Singapore that employs skilled local personnel to make state-of-the-art compressors for export to Asian and U.S. markets, upgrading the talents of the indigenous labor force while creating profitable business for itself and the local economy.

Hybrids of Capitalism and Socialism

Naturally, there are formidable obstacles to the growth of this collaborative type of international business. Severe political risks abound in some nations because of unstable governments. Many countries lack an educated work force, adequate communication systems, and other basic aspects of economic infrastructure. There are also decades of mistrust to overcome.

But the biggest challenge is that nations need to develop more effective systems of political economy that go beyond the present rigid ideologies of the Old Capitalism and the "Old Socialism." Being forced to search for solutions to the growing world crisis, various new systems are evolving that do not adhere neatly to either ideology, especially in Third World countries which tend to be politically neutral. The unique needs of this potpourri of cultures cannot be met by simply grafting on ideas that have been used in other parts of the world at other stages of development, and so a rich panoply of hybrid political-economic experiments is flowering as each nation struggles to find its way through the adolescence of industrialization.[36]

Many nations with free-market traditions remain firmly committed to pure capitalism, of course, like South Korea, Brazil, and Taiwan. However, many others are deviating from the capitalist model, such as Japan's form of "people's capitalism," the many variations on "economic democracy" practiced in Europe, and countries like France, Italy, and Spain that have moved toward socialist economies. A few recent examples:[37]

Greece is trying to develop a form of "competitive socialism" that uses the participation of workers, consumers, and government to guide companies competing against one another in free markets, in contrast to the bureaucratic type of centralized state socialism practiced by the Soviet Union.

Egypt seems intent on creating its own unique system that is a blend of both capitalist and socialist features, with major industrial sectors owned and operated by the state. One Egyptian politician said to his American friends, "We reject your capitalist definition of efficiency."

Hong Kong is scheduled to be taken over by Red China in 1997, so this fiercely capitalist colony is now anticipating the shift to a novel form of "red capitalism" that should be a blend of free enterprise traditions and new socialist values. A Hong Kong shipping entrepreneur notes the traditional way of greeting fellow businesspersons is changing from, "May you get rich," to, "What good are you doing for society?"

Even more astonishing is the widespread experimentation of many socialist nations that are adopting some desirable aspects of capitalism to rejuvenate growth. These moves toward "market socialism" typically permit small business ownership, incentive systems for workers, prices set by the market, and greater freedom for managers of state enterprises:[38]

> **Red China** is undergoing an economic revolution because, as Premier Zhao Ziyang put it: "If we do not remove the obstacles to the effective management of socialism we cannot advance . . . we must encourage competition." Small entrepreneurs can now own their business; one shop owner in Canton said: "It's pressure all day, but I like the idea of being able to earn more if I work more." Factories accounting for half of the nation's output are being turned loose to operate as profit centers, which has instilled a healthy new mood of worker accountability for performance and responsiveness to consumer markets. The Chongqing Iron and Steel Works, for instance, now uses financial incentives to motivate workers and urges: "The more you work, the more you get." State companies are forming joint ventures with other nations, and 14 special zones have been designated to offer low taxes, cheap land, and other incentives to foreign business development. A U.S. business executive dealing with the Chinese noted: "The difference now is like night and day. They are really talking concrete deals, they have a business-like approach."
>
> **Vietnam** is adopting many of the same free enterprise concepts, such as allowing small business ownership, creating incentive systems for workers, and granting managers greater freedom.
>
> **Hungary** has enjoyed a mixed economy for decades and is now moving even closer to free enterprise in order to create "a new economic mechanism"—small independent businesses, profit incentives for workers and managers, breaking up big state monopolies, shutting down enterprises that do not show a profit, and the state is even considering—a stock market! Janos Hoos, an official in the Central Planning Commission, said the goal is to "give everyone a chance to earn well if he works well . . . That doesn't do any harm to socialism." An interesting development is a democratic form of social control in which company decisions are jointly made by councils composed of management, workers, trade union leaders, and party officials.

East Germany is adopting a "modified Japanese economic model" that would permit more managerial discretion to be used by various industrial sectors experiencing strong market demand.

Bulgaria is using a new economic plan that emphasizes cost-effectiveness rather than arbitrary quotas.

Yugoslavia long ago found a margin of freedom to develop its own socialist form of "workers democracy," which is now recognized as an inventive model for meeting the needs of both social welfare and productive enterprise.

The Soviet Union is permitting this "creeping capitalism" in its satellites because there is a growing realization that the old approach of a planned economy has reached its limits and must yield to a more decentralized system. Soviet officials describe their thinking this way: "[The Soviet economy] has long passed the point where it was possible to regulate it effectively from a single center. . . . But we cannot simply copy the methods of capitalism; we are trying to develop means natural to our own system." Russian plant managers are being allowed to do more local planning, retain profits, and use other free-market principles. A "law on labor collectives" has been initiated that grants worker organizations a measure of participation in planning decisions, financial incentives, and accountability for performance. Changes of this type began in 1984 and now cover 15 percent of the economy.

It is especially revealing to note how closely these changes in communist states parallel the trends of earlier chapters describing the transformation of capitalist economies. Just as in the West, such reforms are being driven by the need for competition to revive stifled economic growth, and for participation to gain the support of more sophisticated younger people who want interesting work, financial rewards, and control over their jobs. Shortly before passing away, President Yuri Andropov visited plants to talk with workers because he saw the new breed of Russians in terms reminiscent of the way older Americans speak of their own youngsters: "The young generation is not foreign to ours; it is just different." Now his successor, General Secretary Mikhail Gorbachev, seems intent on forcing the tired old Soviet bureaucracy to yield control to a more entrepreneurial cadre of Russian managers, not too unlike Reaganomics:[39]

Life demands a profound restructuring of the management of the entire economy to get this country moving forward again . . . We are facing a major restructuring of attitude too . . . everybody must change,

from the worker to the minister to the Secretary of the Central Com-
mittee . . . Those who do not intend to will have to be moved from
the road.

Divergence and Convergence

Some of these experiments, like those of Greece and Yugoslavia,
are not doing well, so the outcome is not clear, and the consequences
of such unusual moves are so enormous that they cannot be fully
understood. Still, if the general trends noted in these examples
continue, one key conclusion stands out. A proliferation of hybrid
economies seems to be moving both sets of nations along a common
path toward free enterprise and democracy, leading to a form of
economy roughly similar to that discussed in the last chapter—
Democratic Free Enterprise. The result could synthesize both capitalist and socialist ideologies into a more powerful single framework,
along with wide differences among various nations, producing the
type of convergence that H. G. Wells, John Kenneth Galbraith, George
Cabot Lodge, Clark Kerr, and many others anticipated long ago.[40]

As shown, both capitalist and socialist nations are infusing their
economies with market principles to renew growth. Earlier chapters
noted how the United States and other Western nations are deregulating industries and breaking up big corporate bureaucracies
into networks of small ventures to improve the productive creativity
of enterprise that has often been a distant ideal in capitalism. Similarly, these examples show that China, Vietnam, and the entire
Soviet bloc are doing the same to overcome the bureaucratic inefficiencies that have plagued planned economies, albeit without
relinquishing some form of social control. Thus, both systems are
moving toward a common ground that takes advantage of the attractive features of free enterprise to avoid the drawbacks of oligopolistic capitalism on one hand and centralized state socialism
on the other.

The same convergence is also moving both systems toward democratic forms of economic governance. Europe, Japan, and more
recently the United States are all incorporating some form of participation in business management, which represents a move toward
the social welfare goals advocated by socialism—although they are

doing so using democratic principles rather than through the centralized control of the state. Likewise, some socialist nations are broadening and decentralizing their old form of state control to move toward democratic plant governance, as in Hungary, Yugoslavia, Russia, and Red China. For instance, the Central Committee of the Communist Party in China announced, "We must resolutely ensure the workers and their elected representatives the right to participate in democratic management of the enterprise." The crisis over the Solidarity Union in Poland indicates the fierce strength behind the interest in worker participation, which is likely to persist unless reforms are made. Franz Loeser, a former official in the East German Communist Party, believes the change is inevitable:[41]

> The communist countries are losing the economic race with the West. People in the communist countries feel it and the party membership know it. . . . What we are likely to witness is the painful dying out of an outmoded model of socialism and a fierce struggle for new, diversified and more democratic forms . . . neither the Western capitalist world nor the communist countries have a clear vision of how to resolve their antagonisms peacefully . . . The best hope is for both socialism and capitalism to become more democratic.

These trends may be converging, but they present sensitive political obstacles because they disturb fundamental beliefs in both ideologies—with each pulling in opposite directions. In capitalist nations, corporate executives tend to be fearful that social control will infringe on business freedom and efficiency; while in socialist states, government officials are reluctant to yield control over economic decisions in order to maintain their power, and because of a general belief that free markets produce chaotic inequities. Thus, both systems are struggling to develop useful applications of foreign ideas, but they must also change their "mythology" to make such radical changes palatable.

To resolve these "symbolic" issues, nations like the United States are beginning to accept the idea that "capitalist profit-making" should be "broadened" or "modernized" by incorporating Western principles fostering "democratic human values" and "entrepreneurial freedom" to make business "more productive." For communist nations, these same changes are coming to be regarded as an extension of "socialist principles" whereby workers, local communities, and other "citizen groups" share directly in controlling the "means of production" to serve the "common welfare" using "decentralized planning" in order to complete the "revolution of the proletariat." So both ideologies are in the process of moving toward a single philosophy, although it may be seen differently in terms of each set of values.

However, it would be misleading to believe that some single "ideal" system may become universal because the opposite tendency toward *divergence* can also be seen in the above examples. The world is growing far too complex for any monolithic approach, so it seems more likely that hybrid economies will "fill in the gap" that now separates capitalism and socialism, turning the barren no man's land lying between these two extremes into a rich field of fertile alternatives. Thus, a full spectrum of diverse models of political economy should spring up over the next few decades to suit the unique cultural backgrounds of various nations. The "generic model" forming the center of this economic spectrum—Democratic Free Enterprise—may be most popular in Europe, Japan, and other "moderate" nations. Countries like the South American and Oriental dictatorships that prefer laissez-faire economies will tend toward the "capitalist" end, while Russia, China, Cuba, and other nations favoring collectivist values will lean toward the "socialist" end. Some nations like the United States swing between both poles occasionally, as we saw in Chapter 8, going from a conservative emphasis on "capitalist big business" to a liberal focus on "socialist big government."

Individual nations may be able to develop a single variation that suits their needs, but the role of global corporations seems destined to be far more complex. They face the challenge of developing sophisticated networks of information systems and economic partnerships now emerging to form the sociotechnical infrastructure of the planet, thereby becoming the central institutions uniting this enormous global diversity. So GCs will have to use a wide range of institutional styles to accommodate different cultures. They may have to allow for greater state control in the more "socialist" countries, while enjoying greater laissez-faire freedom in more "capitalist" nations.

Notwithstanding all these variations, I suggest that the Democratic Free Enterprise model is likely to be the central focus of the emerging global order because there is an unyielding imperative created by two major forces that are moving on inexorably as a revolution in information technology spreads around the globe. As earlier chapters showed, the information age seems to inevitably drive the development of free enterprise to manage an exploding level of diversity, while also fostering democracy to integrate these differences into a coherent whole.

We saw in Chapters 3 and 4 how the new economic order is evolving into an extremely complex mix of diverse cultures and subcultures that are modernizing rapidly to create a huge increase in consumption, placing far more difficult demands on resource allocation, ecological controls, and other such problems as the planet's population grows to roughly 10 billion people living at an industrial level of development. Such massive levels of complexity can only be handled with economic systems that permit innovation, flexibility, and local control, moving the modern world relentlessly toward the "free enterprise" feature that forms one component of Democratic Free Enterprise.

The other major force underway is the creation of democratic institutions that integrate communities, corporations, nations, and the entire world into unified individual networks, all organized into some loose form of huge hierarchical system. A rich diversity may be inevitable, but collaboration is also essential to create productive synergy out of these disparate parts. As we saw in Chapters 5 and 6, one of the most powerful new ideas today is that cooperation outperforms adversarial relationships because the dynamics of a knowledge-based society favor it. This unyielding imperative drives the second principle of "democracy" in the model of Democratic Free Enterprise.

So it seems that the transformation to a new world order will be characterized by both divergence and convergence. This conclusion agrees with studies showing an increase in both trends, and it is also in keeping with the same tendencies at the institutional level that show identical trends toward what is often called "differentiation" and "integration."[42] Where growing complexity encourages entrepreneurial freedom to accommodate diversity, there is an equally great need for democratic collaboration to hold these explosive differences together.

The Race for World Leadership

It should be clear that such momentous changes are not inevitable, they are certain to meet fierce resistance, and they will occur in a highly unpredictable manner because nobody really understands this historic transition very well. However, amidst all this doubt it is also clear that an international race is underway to discover the principles of economic success for a very different era now evolving. The United States, Europe, Japan, the Third World, and the socialist bloc are all experimenting with various modifications of their traditional economic systems—as if the planet had become a great social laboratory working frantically to unlock the secrets of the future before disaster strikes.

Although each nation will position itself at a point on this continuum between capitalism and socialism to suit its own needs, my guess is that the first nation to successfully develop the center position will gain world leadership simply because it will have the most effective economy. That's why progressive American and Japanese corporations that have developed prototypes of business combining democracy and free enterprise are in the lead thus far. Because Democratic Free Enterprise is based on a social contract that "collapses" both ends of this spectrum into the middle, it should prove to be an especially powerful combination of both economic productivity and political legitimacy. After all, there has to be something between the jungle of laissez-faire capitalism and the dictatorship of state-controlled socialism. Economist Clark Kerr expressed the need best:[43]

> . . . the people [in capitalist nations] never had it so good in terms of GNP per capita, yet the growth of material welfare has not been matched by an increase in satisfaction with life . . . [the people in socialist nations] want more control over their unions and over political leaders, and better quality and quantity of goods and services . . . Some new visions of the future beyond either socialism or capitalism will be required: visions of reasonable adjustments between efficiency and equality, between individual freedom and stability.

The unavoidable challenge posed by the global crisis is to synthesize the ideologies of capitalism and socialism into a common conceptual framework upon which to construct an integrated world economy. So when some system like Democratic Free Enterprise does emerge, it will not only be the New Capitalism—it should also be the "New Socialism." All of the energies we now waste in a fruitless conflict between the superpowers could then be redirected into more constructive directions. The United States and the Soviet Union may never get along very well, but the best way Americans could beat the Russians is to develop this more powerful form of political economy needed to lead the coming transformation toward a global order.

Part 3

Toward a New Economy

10

Cases:

WHAT TO DO UPON RETURNING
TO THE OFFICE

Conceptual discussions can be inspiring, but they often fail to give us much guidance when we go to work on Monday. The most exciting ideas are of little use if they cannot be translated into concrete actions that improve our lives. For instance, authorities point out that supply-side economics and industrial policy are too "abstract" and "glib." The test of sound economic policy today is its power to address those severe problems that plague troubled industries: adversarial labor relations, poor product quality, low productivity, and the like. But supply-side economics and industrial policy only advocate various forms of capital investment to support some broad industrial sector rather than specific remedies, so many feel they are "trivial" in resolving these critical causes of the economic crisis.[1]

This chapter moves to a more pragmatic focus on how the New Capitalism can be implemented to actually solve such specific problems. The plan is to circle back in order to show how the strategic concepts presented in Part II can remedy the disorders of economic institutions identified in Chapter 1. First we analyze major corporations, but now with a focus on the dominant firms in two key sectors: GM, the giant of the smokestack industries, and IBM, the king of the sunrise industries. Then we examine how the Communications Workers of America (CWA) is defining a productive role for labor unions. Finally, we consider new possibilities for the

Federal Aviation Administration's (FAA) management of the air travel industry to explore the changing role of government.

My goal is not to predict what these institutions will do, nor to claim that these are the best courses of action. I have simply drawn on my experience working with organizations to provide case studies illustrating how the ideas of the New Capitalism could help improve typical situations.

These cases show that change is well underway, and they suggest the far greater potential lying ahead if Americans could restructure the institutional foundations of their economy. Unlike concepts like supply-side economics and industrial policy, the New Capitalism can help executives, politicians, managers, workers, customers, citizens, labor leaders, professionals, and other economic actors understand what they could do upon returning to the office on Monday.

GM: GIANT OF THE SMOKESTACK INDUSTRIES

In spite of the decline of the auto industry, GM continues to stand today as the prototype of big business, especially in the struggling smokestack industries. Ever since Alfred Sloan established the foundations of modern business practice at the start of this century by shaping GM into the first systematically managed corporation, the company has been the most successful, widely emulated corporation in the world.[2]

In an industry that has seen about 1000 car manufacturers fail, GM grew into a corporate giant that headed the Fortune 500 list, employed 600,000 employees, had total assets of about $30 billion, and annual sales of about $60 billion. It's impact on the entire economy was so massive that it dominated over 60 percent of the car market, which accounted for a quarter of all retail sales in the United States, used one-fifth of all the steel, and employed one-sixth of the total labor force. The size of the GM empire exceeded the entire economy of most large nations.[3]

This golden era of the automobile ended in the 1970s with the advent of the "post-industrial revolution." The energy crisis raised gas prices from 20 cents per gallon to almost $2. Foreign competition captured a third of the domestic market. Stagflation killed buying power. High interest rates curtailed installment sales. Government regulations for exhaust emissions, fuel efficiency, and safety added about $600 to the cost of a car. These changes cut sales almost in half, producing such a deep plunge in jobs and profits that American car makers lost $5 billion in 1980 alone. The decline was dramatized when Exxon edged GM off the top of the Fortune 500 list. Lee Iacocca mused, "We will look back on that era as a rather baroque period in our lives."[4]

Like a great ocean liner, GM may be slow to react but when it finally moves it carries enormous momentum with it. Strategic changes it initiated in response to these threats served as a new model for American business. The famous "downsizing decision" redefined the entire GM product line to introduce an era of limits in manufacturing. GM also revised its production systems to stress product quality, pressured the UAW to reduce labor costs, and closed inefficient plants to reduce overhead. It then took on the Japanese using their own weapons by forming a joint venture with Japan's leading robot maker to build 20,000 robots, and it forged another compact with Toyota to produce small cars in the United States. When Reagan was elected President, the company urged deregulation of the auto industry.

There were many other such bold, creative responses, as we shall see, which placed the firm on a profitable basis again. However, the old confidence seems shaky now because the company remains mired in habits of the past that continue to plague its efforts to put the economic crisis behind it. The public is still disenchanted with American cars, so Japanese competition remains a serious threat. Productivity has not improved because of hostile labor-management incidents. And poor relations with the public have kept the industry regulated.

This combination of success and failure reveals the same crosscurrents described in Chapter 1 being experienced by other firms as they struggle through a difficult economic crisis. Such stubborn problems persist because firms like GM must make sweeping changes to restructure the entire industry. Studies show the U.S. auto market has matured, so domestic car sales are unlikely to rise much above the peak levels of the 1970s, and world sales should grow less than 3 percent per year. In addition to the 30 percent loss of jobs that recently occurred, employment in auto-making is expected to drop another 40 percent by the year 2000.[5] Philip Caldwell, CEO of Ford, summed up the significance:

> It is no exaggeration to say that the automobile industry as a whole [is] engaged in the most massive and profound revolution in peacetime history.

Thus, GM serves as a fitting example of the difficult challenges facing business because it is at the center of a storm of change that is now transforming the entire economy. Just as GM was a paragon of sound management in the past, today it is an exemplar of the problematic issues caused by the onset of a new era. The following analysis focuses on the way GM has dealt with key dilemmas presented by the shift from an Old Capitalism to a New Capitalism: the need to initiate strategic change, manage a new frontier of growth, reform bureaucratic structures, and expand the goals of the enterprise.

Strategic Planning Begins—but Decision-Making Is Unchanged

Despite many alarming threats that first appeared decades ago, GM had no formal system for strategic planning. As a result, the company was forced to deal with the gas shortage, pollution controls, labor conflict, and other issues in a crisis management mode that dissipated energy needlessly and produced too little too late. Peter Drucker charged that the company "has been dead from the neck up," since the 1950s.[6]

GM set up a strategic planning function in 1977, which I was involved with as a consultant. Later the planning group started a strategic planning cycle for operating divisions, and the company formed an issue management group to focus on critical strategic issues. Recently an effort has been made to decentralize planning by moving this responsibility to operating units.[7]

Because of the limits to planning noted in Chapter 7, however, these efforts had little impact but usually met with passive resistance in many forms. Executives couldn't find more than a few hours each year to meet with the planning staff. The planning function was often regarded as an elitist "brain-trust" that would usurp management prerogatives. There was a burden to "prove that strategic planning would work." Today the company remains controlled almost exclusively by the CEO, Roger Smith, and a few executives who are altering the firm's entire strategic posture.

Some of these moves may succeed brilliantly, but it seems risky to entrust the biggest corporation in the world to the personal judgment of a few men. As we also showed in Chapter 7, progressive firms are engaging employees and managers in confronting difficult strategic issues together, and outside interests are being brought into the planning process to shake companies out of their rut. The most powerful force for change comes from the environment, so the key challenge facing the auto industry is to collaborate with labor in improving productivity, to understand customers needs better, and to work with government on alternatives to regulation. As we will soon see, some effective contracts are being made with interest groups, however the most striking aspect of GM today is that decision-making remains perilously isolated from external realities.

Cars are Smaller—but Hardware Still Prevails

Although it was late in coming, GM's downsizing decision was a brilliant move that recognized the limits to growth had arrived. The new fleet of compact yet roomy X-cars introduced in 1980 appealed to American buyers who still wanted large cars without their fuel inefficiencies; however disenchantment soon set in as the much vaunted X-cars suffered 15 recalls, and the newer models are rated well below average. Meanwhile, the recent designs of Toyota, Honda, and Mazda have such advanced engineering that *The Wall Street Journal* reported, "The Japanese are pulling further ahead of U.S. car makers, despite the billions American companies have invested in recent years to catch up." Even GM's stronghold of luxury cars in under attack. "Since 1975, foreign makes have doubled their share of the U.S. luxury-car market to 35 percent," the *Journal* noted. Studies at Harvard University estimate that imports will cause U.S. auto makers to be operating at about 60 to 65 percent of manufacturing capacity by 1990.[8] An American business manager illustrated the cause of the problem:

> *Our company leases one-year-old Buick Skylarks for three executives. All three cars have spent substantial time in the shop. Meanwhile, my 100,000-mile Subaru wagon rolls on with only periodic check-ups. . . . Why should I replace my Skylarks next year with American cars?*

This problem persists because GM remains preoccupied with horsepower, accessories, and other "hard" factors that no longer impress buyers. A good example is GM's purchase of Electronic Data Systems, Hughes Aircraft, and other high-tech firms. This may be a sound way to acquire capabilities of the information age, but the new emphasis on computer-laden cars suggests that hardware will simply be replaced with equally unnecessary electronics. The firm is now working on "auto guidance" systems based on "satellite communications" to convert the car into what the CEO called "a computer on wheels."[9] How many people want a costly, complex, electronic marvel that will make today's repair nightmares look like kid stuff— when their main need is to get to the office and the supermarket?

A more useful approach would be to apply the concept of smart growth in order to address the real problems that concern car owners. As we saw in Chapter 3, the "soft" factors in auto ownership are many times as great as the price of the "machine" itself. The average automobile now costs about $10,000, but fuel, repairs, maintenance, and insurance amount to almost $40,000 over a 10-year vehicle life. The failure of auto makers to consider these "externalities" is the chief reason that buyers are sour on American cars. Studies of the U.S. Office of Consumer Affairs and the Department of Transportation show that people complain about autos far more than any other product group. For instance, the money spent on repairs exceeds the total purchases of new cars, yet despite the appealing GM ads showing cars being lovingly attended to by "Mr. Goodwrench," more than half of these expenses are wasted on unneeded or improper work. Corporate CEOs consider autos the most overpriced, lowest quality, poorly repaired products on the American market. The problem is so bad that states have passed "lemon laws" requiring auto makers to replace cars with serious defects.[10]

In a new era of limited resources and growing interest in quality of life, most people increasingly want safe, efficient transportation rather than large flamboyant autos that fulfill childhood fantasies. "America's romance with the automobile seems to be over," observed one business consultant. It is in these critical areas where huge new gains lie for inventive auto makers who can solve the costly, time-consuming, dangerous problems that plague car owners. Entrepreneurs like Takashi Ishihara, CEO of Nissan Motors, are leading the way:[11]

> Our strategy will be to produce even more fuel-efficient, small, low-priced, high-quality cars . . . a trouble-free car that will require infrequent maintenance. That is the direction to compete in and win.

To realize these opportunities, a new "total transportation system" concept is emerging that should bring together design engineers, market research analysts, customer affairs staff, and others to collaborate in optimizing the overall performance of the automobile. Imagine GM advertising "total system designs" by showing breakdowns of all costs over a 10-year life cycle in comparison to their competition. The following chart lists approximate but hypothetical figures that illustrate how this approach focuses on maximizing the product value delivered to the car owner:

	GM	Ford	Toyota
Price	$11,100	$10,600	$10,300
Fuel	9,500	11,500	11,100
Repairs	7,000	8,200	8,400
Maintenance	7,700	8,800	8,500
Insurance	6,200	7,300	9,100
Total life cycle costs	$41,500	$46,400	$47,400

If such data is not provided by the firm, consumer advocates and other car makers will soon do so to clobber companies that still believe they are selling a piece of machinery alone. Car makers are moving in this direction because they see the handwriting on the wall. For instance, Ford is developing a Lifetime Service Guarantee. A Ford vice president said:[12]

Quality is the approach on how you do everything—the design, the engineering, the delivery, and service of a vehicle. . . . The company that first adopts the total approach is the one that gets additional sales.

With this smarter overall transportation system concept serving as a new "bottom line" for car performance, a host of new possibilities could be evaluated in meaningful terms.[13]

Auto Design. Various combinations of new auto technologies are expected to increase fuel efficiency to the range of 60 to 100 mpg, improve safety, and reduce maintenance. Small electric cars using powerful batteries are going to be feasible soon. Flywheel systems are being developed to store energy. Lighter materials like plastics and spun glass construction should reduce weight. Improved design of bumpers and bodies using space-age honeycomb construction could reduce the risk and cost of accidents. New fuels like hydrogen and alcohol are being produced from biomass. Computer systems may prove useful to increase operating efficiency and simplify maintenance.

Solar Car. Future development of a "solar car" could revolutionize short-haul travel. Solar panels mounted on the top, hood, or trunk of a car are technically feasible and have been demonstrated in trial runs. They would be used to augment the normal power source used to charge electric cars, possibly contributing the bulk of energy used to drive the typical short distances to and from work, shopping and the like, thereby producing a vehicle that operates almost free of fuel costs, it would be so simple that maintenance would be minimal, and it would be almost totally nonpolluting. Rapidly dropping costs of photovoltaic cells suggest that the idea may soon be economically feasible.

World Car. Ford and other firms are planning an integrated global system for the manufacture and sales of a standardized auto. The central idea is to design a basic *system* employing modular parts that can be interchanged to maximize commonality and thereby minimize costs, while offering a wide range of configurations to serve diverse needs around the world. A "solar module" might be especially useful in Third World nations because they tend to be located in equatorial regions with high solar density. Considering the ecomonies of scale that would result from selling such cars around the world and the enormous potential for low cost transportation, the opportunities for creative entrepreneurs are vast.

Alternative Transportation. There is growing acceptability of using buses, trains, jitneys, and other group modes of transport, as well as rental plans for those who want private transportation without the hassle of ownership. Such approaches are common in Europe, while a firm called "STAR" (Short-Term Auto Rental) has been formed in San Francisco to provide convenient auto rental on a hourly or daily basis. John Crain, the founder claims, "The concept works—it's economically viable [and] creates social benefits." Members of the plan exclaim, "I sold my car just so I could use STAR [to live] a carless and careless existence. It has been very, very economical."

Successful development of such concepts involves complex problems in engineering, and new forms of marketing are needed. But over the next decade or two as the Third World becomes more mobil, oil becomes more expensive, pollution more severe, and customers more discriminating, auto makers that can respond to these changes by offering intelligent forms of transportation will be among the firms that survive intense competition in the global auto market. *BusinessWeek* warned, "The challenges ahead [make] the downsizing decision seem like child's play."[14]

Labor Made Concessions—but Management Took Bonuses

These changes are not going to be accomplished with hierarchically structured organizations operated by blue collar workers performing menial tasks under authoritarian supervision. That is the system of the past. The need to create flexible, participative organizations that are productive enough to compete with Japanese car makers is going to test GM sorely.

Its massive, cumbersome size and complex, hierarchical structure causes the GM organization to behave more like a government bureaucracy than an entrepreneurial business. As in most big firms, GM has passed power from "car-men" who understand the nitty-gritty of making autos to "finance-men" who are more concerned with financial controls. The result is that Sloan's original strategy of "coordinated decentralization" has been turned into such a highly centralized system that some GM managers call it "communism." This loss of self-initiative has occurred at a time when most employees want greater autonomy and when large organizations must nurture entrepreneurial freedom to survive. John DeLorean, the maverick former GM executive who headed Chevrolet, described how the system stifled operating divisions:[15]

They were being hassled to death by a cumbersome management structure. . . . No one in Chevrolet could take a meaningful step in a profitable direction. . . . In place of sound policymaking, much of the time of upper GM management is being occupied with the day-to-day business. . . . The divisions are more under the operational control of corporate management than at any time in the peacetime history of the corporation. . . . The system is so rigid now that . . . an innovative thinker like Alfred P. Sloan, Jr. could not qualify for a job in the upper ranks of General Motors.

As the production line becomes automated, the logical outcome would be that auto makers should develop more sophisticated organizations whose different functions—R&D, product divisions, manufacturing plants, and regional sales outlets—would act as semi-autonomous profit centers operating within a market network. Lately, GM claims it is beginning to decentralize into "150 self-contained units." However, the most prominent change has been to combine its six car divisions into two major groups—one for small cars and another for big cars—which implies even greater centralized control. One can only wonder how long this giant monolith can withstand the forces that are now breaking up other big firms into fluid systems.

At the bottom of the hierarchy, the bureaucratic management of assembly line jobs costs GM $1 billion each year in absenteeism and results in productivity that is roughly half that of Japanese firms. To make these jobs palatable, pay and benefits rose to more than $22 per hour, which is about 70 percent higher than the pay of both Japanese auto workers and the average American. This combination of high labor costs and low productivity is responsible for a Japanese cost advantage of about $1500 per car *after* shipping and tariff charges. Journalist David Jenkins put the problem in perspective:[16]

There is scarcely an activity more engrossing and attractive to young men than tinkering with automobiles; yet the designers of auto plants have performed the considerable achievement of transforming this fascinating activity into the world's most hated work place.

In addition, the way executives rule this organization in a tradition of loyal deference to authority has led to other serious problems.

DeLorean acutely described how the obeisance required by superiors created an organizational underground to circumvent the chain-of-command:[17]

> *This system quickly shut top management off from the real world because it surrounded itself in many cases with "yes" men. . . . Original ideas were often sacrificed in deference to what the boss wanted . . . [there was] a secret network in the corporation to find out the likes, dislikes, and ideosyncracies of the boss.*

GM management is so distant from workers that Roger Smith made the revealing mistake of announcing an improved bonus plan for his fellow executives on the very day the UAW signed its 1982 contract yielding huge wage and benefit concessions to preserve their jobs. "I've never seen [workers] so upset," said UAW President Douglas Fraser, "They felt they were doublecrossed."[18]

This is unfortunate because GM has been a leader in American experiments to improve job satisfaction and productivity. Lately these programs have started moving out of the laboratory and onto the shop floor. The Saturn project, for instance, may set a new American standard in employee relations by replacing the assembly line with semi-autonomous work teams sharing management responsibilities.

However, even the most inventive techniques will not overcome a persistant distrust between management and labor that is the fundamental barrier to organizational effectiveness. The auto industry's crisis was averted largely because of the above UAW givebacks that totaled $6 billion; but in 1984 GM and the other car makers stunned the nation once again by announcing what William Brock, Secretary of Labor, decried as "unbelievable management bonuses" averaging $31,000 for almost 6000 managers. UAW officials bitterly pointed out how such "obscene" and "outrageous" sums were more than the **total** pay of workers. These bonuses were justified as rewarding managers for creating the lucrative profits auto makers enjoyed in 1984, but the real cause of success was that government import quotas protected Detroit from competition, forcing car prices up by about $2000. Naturally, a resulting sense of injustice pressured the UAW to become more militant. At a time when GM badly needed to simplify work rules, increase productivity, improve quality, reduce labor costs, and gain other critical concessions from labor, the outcome could not be more detrimental:[19]

> *A local UAW official exploded, "Hell, the membership reads the papers and they know its not fair when Roger Smith takes a $1.5 million bonus after we gave up what we did." A worker complained: "We feel like we were lied to. The companies begged for concessions, took away pay raises and holidays. Then they raised the price of their cars and split the profits between their top executives and their stockholders."*

After all the accusations, tough bargaining, automation, and clever work plans are tried, the only real solution to the labor problem in Detroit is to form a constructive social contract. The focus should be on adopting a serious profit sharing plan that would grant management lower wages and higher productivity in return for giving labor some control and a piece of the action. The sooner all parties accept this reality, the sooner GM, other auto makers, the UAW, and the nation will be better off.

A Focus on Serving the Public—but Without Giving Up Power

These issues reveal the damage caused by an insular focus on profit and management self-interest that form the central values guiding GM, like most other firms. Profit-seeking urges selling large expensive cars rather than providing genuine product value; excessive financial controls destroy entrepreneurial initiative; employees are viewed as simply a costly factor of production, polarizing the labor-management relationship.

An acute example is the irresponsible stand GM took on auto safety. Automobile accidents kill 50,000 people annually in the United States, more than the Vietnam war, and millions more are maimed. The cost runs about $45 billion per year—as much as total car sales. Studies show that air bags or automatic seat belts could save 12,000 lives, that 70 percent of drivers want them, and that the cost could be offset by lower insurance premiums. Yet, in 1981 GM reneged on an earlier agreement to install air bags and pressured the Reagan administration to drop the requirement. The courts later declared the Reagan decision void, so they may soon be required as once planned. Now, however, they will be provided only after a divisive, drawn out conflict that has cost tens of thousands of needless deaths, highlighted the disregard of auto companies for the public welfare, and allowed foreign makers to gain the lead in solving the problem. Mercedes Benz has introduced air bags in its 1985 cars.[20]

There are many other examples of the conflicts created when institutions serve private interests to the exclusion of their public, such as the long battles over pollution controls, fuel efficiency, working conditions, and product quality. Just recently, the U.S. Government fined GM $4 million for starting production of its X-cars while knowing of brake defects. The firm has been so successful financially that for decades it earned as much as 50 percent per year on stockholder equity, which was spent on stockholder dividends, executive bonuses, annual model changes, and styling. Why was some portion of these funds not used to remedy the above problems before they came to haunt the firm later? Peter Drucker pinpointed the cause of GM's troubles when it first appeared many years ago:[21]

> GM is in trouble because it is seen increasingly by more and more people as deeply at odds with basic needs and basic values of society and community. . . . GM's present predicament is, above all, the failure of the "technocrat" approach to the management of institutions. [the failure to see] business in the community; business as a life rather than a livelihood; business as a neighbor; and business as a power center.

The real source of the decline in the auto industry goes beyond auto design, labor productivity, and other technical matters that can be addressed by engineers and managers, but involves more subtle concerns about the role institutions play in society. Because the traditional role of large firms like GM ignores the needs of stakeholders, many Americans have simply become angry at their car companies for showing little concern for their welfare, and so they are withholding their support because it is the only way they have of exercising some control: customers switch to foreign cars, employees refuse to provide loyal commitment, the public forces politicians to regulate business, and so on. Here's what one typical American said:[22]

> Why should American consumers have any sympathy? For decades auto makers offered us cosmetics instead of engineering ... When did any auto executive ever make a public statement of concern about the consumer of his product? ... The solution is easy: Get design and quality up and prices down, and there will be no problem. Are you listening?

These deeply rooted problems will only be overcome when quasi-public institutions like GM are able to redefine their role to emphasize the well-being of all interest groups making up the bigger corporate community. GM has been moving slowly in this direction since Campaign GM, as acknowledged by the previous chairman, Tom Murphy: "The objective of business, no less than that of government, must be the public's interest."[23]

This view is demonstrated by management attempts to work more closely with labor leaders on the Saturn project. GM has started a "Third Party Arbitration Program" operated by the Better Business Bureau to resolve customer disputes. To understand the needs of car buyers better, the firm has opened an "Advanced Concepts Center" in California to get closer to new trends in the car market. GM has used an automotive "Dealer's Council" for years in which representatives from its dealerships meet with corporate executives to discuss common problems. It has started to collaborate with suppliers to reduce inventories and improve quality. The GM *Public Interest Report*, now a 13-year-old institution, showed an awareness of this new imperative that is replacing the old profit-oriented concept:[24]

> ... as a result of changing societal demands and preferences, a corporation finds that, in addition to its stockholders, it also must be responsive and publicly accountable to many other constituencies—employees, consumers, dealers, suppliers, governmental groups, and the public at large.

However, GM remains reluctant to make this concept a hard reality by representing such groups on the board of directors, and without some measure of real power the ideal of providing genuine public service is not taken very seriously. GM's customer arbitration program, for instance, has been neglected to the point that long, infuriating delays are common. Roger Kirkpatrick, a staff attorney at the FTC, noted, "The steady flow of complaints we receive are most disturbing . . . they indicate violations of the commission's orders against General Motors." The typical GM reasoning goes something like this:[25]

> In view of the multiple constituencies with which business must be concerned, it has been suggested that individual board members should represent specific constituencies that reflect the major elements of society. General Motors does not agree with such an approach as it could lead to factionalism and divisiveness.

There is some justification for these objections, but the fact is that the present insular system of governance has caused precisely the divisiveness that executives fear. Representative policy making does not create conflict; it simply offers a way to deal with the conflict that already exists. In a society based on principles of democracy, the old focus on profit and self-interest runs counter to a basic American belief that the interacting interests of diverse groups will in the long-run produce the wisest decisions and a common sense of commitment. Without this support, no institution—public or private—can long stand.

GM's hesitancy on this issue shows a lack of imagination about the changing role of enterprise. Today, the great opportunities lie with creative executives like Lee Iacocca who understand that business success requires building political coalitions. Consider the power that could accrue to an influential, quasi-public corporation like GM if its management were to show great leadership in a time of economic crisis by adopting a broader institutional role. Through developing working relationships with a few responsible spokespersons from various key constituencies—say, Douglas Fraser for labor, Esther Peterson for customers, and Coleman Young, the mayor of Detroit, to represent the local community—the company could have access to unusually well-informed advice, and it would gain considerable public support. It is hard to see how such a strategy could injure the firm, and the potential for leading the way to a more productive form of business is unprecedented.

At the national level, there is a great need to form collaborative labor-management-government partnerships to revitalize the auto industry. Government and consumers might accept temporary import restrictions, the unions could restrain wage demands and increase productivity in exchange for generous profit sharing, and management could pledge to reinvest all gains and hold down prices to recapture the market for American cars. This same type of collaboration could be used to redefine the industry's infrastructure. The major auto makers, working in conjunction with the Federal Government, the UAW, and possibly public interest groups, could form R&D consortiums to develop new car technology, a national system for evaluating car performance, retraining programs for unemployed workers, some form of self-regulation, and so on. Many authorities now advocate such steps, which Alfred Sloan himself envisioned decades ago:[26]

> Industrial management must expand its horizons of responsibility. It must recognize that it can no longer confine its activities to the mere production of goods and services. It must consider the impact of its operation on the economy as a whole in relation to the social and economic welfare of the entire community. Those charged with great industrial responsibility must become industrial statesmen.

Looking back over all the change that has taken place since the economic crisis hit large corporations like GM, it's clear that an important start has been made but major challenges remain. Roger Smith showed strong leadership by acknowledging the task realistically: "Not long ago, many of us felt that the hard work would be over [by this point]. But in my view, we have as far to go as we've already come."[27] Time will tell if he appreciates the even more disturbing changes that seem needed before the transition to a new era can be successfully completed.

IBM: KING OF THE SUNRISE INDUSTRIES

If GM exemplifies the struggles facing the smokestack industries, IBM represents the leadership guiding the sunrise industries toward a creative new form of business that is now powering a boom in hi-tech fields.

"Big Blue" has its shortcomings, of course. The 13-year-old antitrust action that was recently dropped suggests the predatory power IBM exercises using questionable marketing practices to maintain a near monopoly over the computer industry. The company also has a paternalistic culture that cares for its employees, but at the price of exacting standards of behavior that often require a confining conformity. The private joke that IBM means "I've been moved" hints at the resentment some feel.

However, these criticisms mainly reflect the great power the firm has gained through its enormous success. One hundred shares of IBM stock purchased at its founding in 1914 for less than $3000 would today be worth many millions. IBM has risen up the Fortune 500 list to the number six position, and future prospects look so bright it may reach the top in a decade or two. Despite its late entry into the microcomputer field, the firm gained the lead among 170 competitors within two years. The IBM personal computer (PC) has set a new standard in machine design and software that now dominates the industry.

Why has IBM succeeded so brilliantly where GM has not? The problem is not size because large firms like IBM are thriving, but is instead a response to the imperatives of technology. Auto making is an "industrial" sector of large scale, routine production, so GM had to develop a "mechanistic" organization that could handle this technology efficiently but was thereby unresponsive to change. Information technology, though, is a "post-industrial" frontier still in its infancy, which encourages IBM to retain a youthful vitality. The company's genius lies in its ability to develop high-quality, sophisticated products and bring them to market on a massive scale, while maintaining a flexible organization that can produce dynamic new ventures and gain the commitment of its employees and customers. In short, IBM is an early prototype of the New Capitalism.

As Chapter 7 showed, IBM has been one of the pioneers in creating planned strategic change. The company developed its own version of strategic planning almost two decades ago, which uses a blend of product planning and a periodic planning cycle. Business units perform their own strategic planning, while the corporate level provides central guidance, sets performance goals, and integrates individual plans into a coordinated whole.

This powerful approach to strategic change was needed to manage the revolutionary upheavals of its field. In the mid-1970s the personal computer was just a gleam in the eye of Apple Computer Company. By 1979 it had so changed the entire industry that the National Academy of Sciences claimed, "Within a decade most homes will contain at least one computer." Electronic financial transactions have also progressed so rapidly in the last few years that banks, stock brokers, insurance firms, and related institutions are being restructured into a single automated network. With the break up of AT&T, the entire communications industry is being transformed as a host of new competitors struggle to redefine the market for telecommunications systems.[28]

The complexity of this task and intense competition has forced IBM to lead the way in developing a flexible, decentralized matrix structure of semi-autonomous divisions to provide the freedom needed to respond quickly and creatively to market opportunities. For tough new projects, it uses an "independent business unit" (IBU) concept that successfully developed the PC. The IBU contains its own R&D, manufacturing, marketing, and other support services, operating free of normal hierarchical controls in order to get a small, highly spirited project moving quickly. The PC project, for instance, rallied around the goal, "Let's beat Apple." The company is using IBUs now for robotics, analytical instruments, a fifth generation computer, and a score of other hi-tech ventures.[29]

The foundation of IBM's strategy that has sustained it through decades of change was established by its founder, Thomas Watson, and later promulgated by his son, Thomas Watson, Jr. This view centers about the conviction that business success requires collaboration among employees, customers, shareholders, suppliers, the public, and other constituencies.[30]

For instance, IBM realizes that the exploding frontier of information technology is too enormous to handle alone, so it is in the firm's interest to share the wealth by forming collaborative ventures with its competitors. The operating system for the PC was developed by Microsoft, microprocessor chips are provided by Motorola and Intel, joint ventures have been set up with Japanese firms and the Artificial

Intelligence Corporation, and equity interests were bought in Rolm and Intel. Rather than develop its own software and accessories, IBM encouraged small firms to design and sell their own PC compatible packages. It also asked Sears and Computerland to distribute the PC through their retail outlets. IBM formed an R&D consortium with other computer makers, as well as a joint R&D project with Carnegie Mellon University to develop a campus computer network that may become a "prototype for every major university in the country."[31]

IBM's well-known strength in employee relations hinges on the principle that management must provide "respect for the individual." All employees are on salary status, there have been no layoffs in the firm's history, joint participation in problem-solving is stressed, the firm has become a leader in protecting employee rights, and management maintains a "small company atmosphere" in a company that employs 400,000 people. This approach is motivated not simply out of altruism but by seeing that the welfare of employees and the firm is mutual. "We respect our people and help them to respect themselves [because] the company would make the most profit," said Watson.[32]

The same social contract is stressed with clients. The company proclaims, "We want to give the best customer service of any company in the world." Engineers and managers work so closely with the buyer's representatives that the client firm becomes virtually an integral part of the IBM organization. This type of customer-driven system is going to be especially valuable in years to come as chips, computers, and other information technology products become customized, requiring tight working liaisons between suppliers and users.[33]

By integrating the interests of suppliers, employees, customers, and shareholders, IBM has produced the system of multiple goals described in Chapter 6. Watson explains why this concept works better than the profit-centered view that has caused such poor performance for other large corporations:[34]

Undoubtedly, the principal reason these beliefs have worked so well is that they fit together and support one another. If you hire good people and treat them well, they will try to do a good job. They will stimulate one another by their vigor and example. They will set a fast pace for themselves. Then, if they are well led and occasionally inspired, if they understand what the company is trying to do and know they will share in its success, they will contribute in a major way. The customer will get the service he is looking for. The result is profit to customers, employees, and stockholders.

Despite all this success Big Blue will continue to face huge challenges. Future prospects in its field look so bright that IBM's markets will be under continual attack from competitors like AT&T and the Japanese. There is a need to provide employees with even greater freedom as intrapreneurs if this mammoth organization is to cope with the difficulties ahead. Large firms like IBM will come under increasing scrutiny as their power in modern society grows, so a formal social contract that empowers employees, customers, suppliers, and the public in policy-making will be needed to retain political legitimacy.

At the national level, business-government-labor collaboration is needed to provide the economic infrastructure that will enable the information industry to compete abroad. Antitrust laws are being modified to permit joint ventures like the R&D consortiums. Industry standards must be set in areas like information networks before serious progress is possible.

There may be a long way to go before the information age becomes a reality, but companies like IBM are developing the New Capitalism that will get us there.

THE CWA: DEFINING A NEW ROLE FOR LABOR

The Communications Workers of America (CWA) offers a model for the transition all labor unions will have to face in the information age. Its members work in communications and electronics with firms like AT&T—the heart of the new information system fields that are the forefront of technological advances. And as the automation of old "manual" jobs like the traditional telephone operator restructures the industry, new labor-management practices are inevitable.

To respond to these challenges, the CWA has been the first labor union to use strategic planning. It held a national conference in 1979 called "Today and Tomorrow" in which 50 outside authorities like Alvin Toffler worked with union members in anticipating critical future trends and forming strategies to adapt to them. The conference was so useful that the union formed a "Committee on the Future," which sponsored a second conference in 1983, somewhat like a periodic planning cycle. The union is also developing "strategy centers" to focus on key issues, similar to the issue management concept developed in business.[35]

The resulting changes reflect other features of the New Capitalism. For instance, the union is stressing a new concept of **employment** security to replace the old *job* security. As AT&T's 1985 layoff of 24,000 workers shows, it is futile to fight for jobs that will inevitably be automated, so the union's strategy is to retrain employees and insure that benefits are portable in order to move people to new jobs. The concept fits well into the idea of smart growth and flexible organizational structures employing intrapreneurs.[36]

The CWA is almost alone in advocating a collaborative role with its various constituencies. A woman vice president has been elected to office. The union has also redefined its relationship with management; it's 1983 contract initiated a series of "Common Interest Forums" in which the union and management meet periodically to discuss critical issues in a cooperative spirit. And rather than simply demanding higher wages and benefits, the CWA is assuming responsibility for improving labor productivity. Glen Watts described it this way when he was union president:[37]

We've got to impress them with the fact that we can do the job over the long run much more cheaply, more efficiently, and better.

By facing squarely the central challenges that most unions have avoided, the CWA could gain huge bargaining power by being able to deliver one of the most important elements of sound business — a well-trained, committed, productive work force. If the CWA can make this vision a reality, it will define a new union role in which labor and management become partners whose common goal is the success of the enterprise. Even now, bricklayers, postal workers, and other unions are adopting some of these innovations that the CWA pioneered. Douglas Fraser noted the reason:[38]

> *If the automobile industry had demonstrated 10 years ago the kind of foresight and long range thinking that CWA has shown, we would not be seeing auto workers on the unemployment lines.*

THE FAA: ENTERPRISE IN THE PUBLIC SECTOR

Not long ago, the Federal Aviation Administration (FAA) was considered a model agency because it operated a safe, orderly air traffic system. But deregulation allowed airlines to compete freely on prices and to choose their routes and flight schedules, while the 1980 strike of the Professional Air Traffic Controllers Organization (PATCO) reduced staffing by 25 percent. The result was to throw the system into an upheaval that is characteristic of the turbulence government agencies face in adapting to a new era. Air travel is suffering from congestion and flight delays; airlines are struggling for survival; passengers are bewildered by a maze of flights and prices; public safety is being jeopardized by stress on the system; air traffic controllers suffer from information overload; and labor-management relations are locked in a bitter conflict.[39]

Part of the problem was that flight monitoring equipment was inadequate, but the FAA is rapidly upgrading to computerized radar systems so the technical difficulties should be solved soon. The major problem was FAA management. Numerous studies found that an "autocratic" management style and "heavy-handed supervision" failed to address air traffic controllers' repeatedly expressed concerns for job burnout and safety. One study concluded that FAA officials "[have] little sense of the rigors of the controller's job," and another warned of "bitter resentment and antagonism between management and its employees . . . the FAA risks future rebellions from its employees." Compounding the problem was a workforce of young controllers who do not automatically respect authority. They would "think nothing of confronting their supervisors," said a union official.[40]

Given this explosive mix of crowded airlanes, the challenging attitude of young employees, and unresponsive FAA management, it is not surprising that a confrontation flared up. Polls showed most Americans believed the air controllers had strong cause for grievance but that PATCO should not have led them into an illegal strike. However, a major share of the responsibility lies with the Reagan administration for failing to remedy the conditions that led to the strike and then using excessive force to quash it. Reagan applauded the Polish Solidarity union for standing up to communism, but the actions of the Polish Government are not too different from his destruction of PATCO and the careers of its 11,000 members. Glenn Watts said, "Using the full force of the Presidency in an attempt to crush PATCO is the moral equivalent of sending in the tanks."[41]

The costs of this unnecessary confrontation have been huge. Most big airlines like Eastern, United, and American lost millions of dollars each day for years as flights were restricted by a lack of controllers. One airline spokesperson said, "It's really kind of tragic. I don't know if you ever recover from anything like this." The Air Transport Association estimated the industry as a whole lost $35 million per day, while the total costs of the entire strike were estimated at $12 billion. Including the cost of training new controllers at $175,000 apiece, inconvenience to the public, and employment lost by the strikers, the true cost to the nation must be on the order of $20 billion.[42]

The real tragedy is that little purpose was served except to bolster a false sense of power, which simply prevented seeing the true problem. Shortly after the strike, the National Transportation Safety Board (NTSB) cautioned that unless the FAA improved its relations with air controllers, "we'll be faced with another labor dispute downstream." Two committees of the U.S. Congress criticized the Administration's handling of the strike and warned that the problems in the system would soon reappear. A consultant stated: "Eight or 10 years down the road, they'll have [another strike] because no one will attend to these long-running problems. There's a real cancer there."[43]

The FAA was impressed by all this criticism, so a "human relations" program was created to remedy the situation. However, an

FAA task force reported later that the program was "viewed as inconsequential . . . slogans and superficial window dressing"; the conditions which led to the strike are "resurfacing" and are now "as bad, or perhaps a bit worse" than before the strike, so "the FAA seems headed toward more people-related problems." The NTSB found that safety conditions were poor due to heavy workloads and controller stress. Claims by the FAA that the system would soon resume 100 percent flight levels led one controller to question, "It makes us wonder if top management knows what's happening."[44] *The Wall Street Journal* reported:

> *Post-strike cooperation is crumbling under the persistent strain of heavy workloads . . . many controllers complain of a return of uncaring, autocratic attitudes. "With union protection gone," contends one controller, "Things are worse than ever."*

Sure enough, in 1984 controllers at the Washington, D.C., and New York City centers petitioned to create a new union, and interest seems to be spreading. "It's just taken off. The wave has gone across the country," said David Kushner, an organizer of the American Federation of Government Employees. The cause was explained by Anthony Skirlick, one of the "loyal" controllers who stayed on the job during the 1980 strike: "The FAA has beaten up, kicked around, and overworked controllers," he charged. "We can't work in this environment." While Larry Philips, the head of PATCO's successor union, observed, "It's history repeating itself. The FAA creates the conditions under which unions are necessary." U.S. Congressman Guy Molinari agreed: "The FAA has no one to blame but itself. If it had addressed the problems of controllers, there would be no need to unionize."[45]

If this costly cycle of labor-management conflict is to end, federal administrators must acknowledge that the pabulum of human relations is inadequate and peace will only come with genuine participation in management decisions. This might result in forming autonomous work teams, allowing controllers wider freedom in choosing assignments, and permitting flexibility in workloads. The lesson that has been learned, however, is that the management of government agencies, like most other organizations today, now requires the active involvement of employees.[46]

Other causes of the chaotic air traffic problem stem from larger flaws in the way the industry is managed. As I showed in Chapter 1, present thinking focuses on two equally poor choices. The old regulation of ticket prices and air routes prevented competition, reducing airlines to bureaucracies that could lure passengers only with fancy meals and in-flight movies. Now a complete reversal has occurred to a laissez-faire system that has eliminated any semblance of order. The chairman of Pan American Airlines was bitter: "The air traffic control problem has gone from bad—to worse—to horrible—to intolerable."[47]

The unavoidable fact is that these are intricate, political concerns that can only be addressed adequately by some form of collaboration among the various constituencies involved: employees and their unions, airline executives, the flying public, and the FAA. Disorder persists because there is no such forum in which these various parties can formulate sound, acceptable policies. Congressional oversight is much too circuitious, unwieldy, and politicized by other goals. To remedy the problem, representative bodies could be formed at the national level, for each FAA region, and at each facility. The role of FAA administrators would be—not to "run" the system as they have done in the past—but to provide leadership in creating these forums and facilitating their operation. The result would be a much more defensible, more powerful approach to government.

In fact, such a system is evolving out of necessity. In 1984 the FAA and airline executives worked together to reshuffle 1000 flight schedules to alleviate congestion. There were complaints that free market access was restricted, yet most parties seem pleased that a return to FAA regulation of schedules was avoided and the public outcry over flight delays was eased. FAA Administrator Donald Engen noted the welcomed result: "We greatly appreciate the cooperative spirit shown in these meetings."[48]

This approach could also be used, as we suggested in Chapter 8, to mold a more effective infrastructure that fosters a balanced form of smart growth. Peak loads could be alleviated by increasing airport fees or inviting competitive bids for a fixed number of slots during crowded times. The airport noise problem could be resolved by assessing fees on airlines to internalize costs suffered by nearby residents; the added cost to passengers would then compensate for the intrusion on the community. Air traffic services could be contracted out to private businesses, providing savings to tax payers and better service to the public.

There is a special need to restore order to airfares and flight schedules. With the demise of regulations, about 800,000 different fares are now listed covering 2200 routes with 55,000 changes being made monthly. Rates can vary by as much as 70 percent. This jumble is so incomprehensible that *Money* magazine reported, "Air fares today are as complicated as the legal code and change even faster."[49] Further, airline reservation systems often distort flight information by not listing promotional flights, and they systematically list their flights before those of competing lines. One obvious solution is to have the FAA take on the responsibility for insuring that comprehensive, accurate information is provided to the public in order to permit the market to work efficiently. Another possibility is have airlines set uniform rates, while maintaining competition by allowing airlines to choose which routes they service.[49]

Although there are many other options, none are best in some objective sense because a workable solution to restructuring the air travel industry can only be developed by the various parties that are involved. That is the main point of this analysis. The key to success lies in providing strong government leadership to unify the collaborative efforts of FAA employees, air passengers, the public, and the airlines in order to create a system that serves all these diverse needs. Government agencies, just like any other form of enterprise, must create social wealth to justify their existence, albeit in the public sector.

These parties should be consulted, not only out of a sense of justice, but because the motivation to bring about this type of difficult change can only arise out of appeals to their enlightened self-interest. For instance, the best way the airlines can thrive economically while preserving their entrepreneurial freedom is to assume greater responsibility for finding solutions to the problems of peak loads, airport noise, disorderly fares, and chaotic route schedules. If government hopes to surmount the stigma of bureaucracy that has led to a citizen's revolt, therefore, it will have to share its management of the economy with those who must make the system work.

REVITALIZING AMERICA

These are isolated cases and they are more complex than this brief analysis, of course, but they show that major institutions are starting to move in new directions. Corporations like GM in the smokestack industries are struggling through the economic crisis, while others like IBM in sunrise industries are leading the way into the future. Progressive unions such as the CWA are defining a more constructive role for organized labor. Government is slowly being transformed by powerful new economic and political forces. A few themes run through all this change to show how the New Capitalism offers useful concepts for coping with the difficult challenges that still lie ahead.

Strategic capabilities play an important role in the way these diverse organizations adjust to a turbulent environment. Inadequate change mechanisms prevented GM from adapting to the crises it faced, while the strength of IBM's planning contributes to its long pattern of success. The CWA's outstanding progress hinges on its unique strategic orientation. The FAA has not developed methods for change, which largely explains the cause of its difficulty.

Almost without exception, computerized information systems are driving a more sophisticated form of smart growth. The introduction of robots and smart products in manufacturing firms like GM, the relentless pace of technological advance in computer firms like IBM, the impetus that a communications revolution presents to the CWA—all represent different aspects of the power of information technology to transform institutions into more useful roles for an information age.

We've also seen that network structures composed of participatively managed, entrepreneurial units are evolving to handle these complex new tasks. IBM serves as a model, while GM and the FAA suffer because they have been slow to adopt such concepts. The CWA illustrates how unions are fostering flexible, collaborative labor-management relations.

The central importance of broader forms of governance is also vividly illustrated, although more is needed in this sensitive political area. GM's adherence to a traditional profit-centered model is a major cause of its weakness, in contrast to the strength IBM has derived from a philosophy that serves customers, employees, and investors. The FAA illustrates how the complex problems facing government require working with various stakeholders to manage industrial sectors better.

At the national level, we are reminded that the New Capitalism offers specific, constructive solutions that overcome the unproductive debate over vague ideas like supply-side economics and industrial policy. The concepts of Democratic Free Enterprise can guide the development of new policies in the automobile industry, high-technology sectors, and services like air travel in order to build the more sophisticated infrastructure needed for a complex new era. Because large corporations are the linchpin of this megaeconomic system, big business has a unique opportunity to lead in this task, as these cases also show. Firms like GM, IBM, and AT&T are helping to defuse the adversarial role of unions. Collaboration between major airlines and government is beginning to transform air travel. The challenge was well-stated by Professor Malcolm Salter of the Harvard Business School:[50]

> Management, labor and government must be willing to create and use policy-sharing forums at various levels in the industrial hierarchy ... to end the stale and irrelevant debate over industrial policy versus laissez-faire economics.

Although there is enormous resistance and a prevailing cynicism that doubts big business might move in such enlightened directions, earlier chapters showed that scores of other progressive companies like TRW, GE, 3M, Eastern, Chrysler, Hewlett-Packard, People Express, MCI, Delta, Dow Corning, Digital Equipment, Control Data, Dayton-Hudson, Kollmorgan, and Wang are doing so. These well-managed firms are planning strategic change, developing smart forms of growth, designing flexible structures, and starting entrepreneurial ventures. They are also developing strong organizations that integrate the interests of their stakeholders into a broader coalition. Quietly, without much fanfare, such companies are inventing a powerful new type of economics that raises the principles of democracy and free enterprise to a higher level of sophistication, thereby instilling a spirit of creative competition and a productive sense of community that is needed to revitalize the nation.

11

Extensions:

THE NEW CAPITALISM
AND THE SOCIAL ORDER

A young man playing Santa Claus at a department store was struck by the insatiable greed of many children, and he later saw that slick television ads and indulgent parents had led them to believe that an endless stream of toys was their rightful due. "Slowly I began to suspect that Santa is a rite of passage for the children of a consumer society," he concluded. This common reminder of the way material values and profit have taken over Christmas emphasizes that economic matters are not limited to business but depend on all social institutions for support—public media, the family, and even sacred figures like Santa Claus. The evolution of a New Capitalism, therefore, cannot be fully understood without examining its extensions into the social order.

As we noted many times, business generally serves as an archetype for the management of all organizations, so these other "quasi-economic" institutions contribute to the economic crisis because they share the same faults of the Old Capitalism. And because they are also undergoing the same transition to a new era, although in a variety of forms, the concepts of the New Capitalism being pioneered by progressive companies can be usefully extended to guide strategic change in schools, hospitals, and other large organizations. Michael Blumenthal, former Secretary of the Treasury and now CEO of Burroughs Corporation, noted how business is the central focus of modern society:[1]

The large corporation continues to provide the essential framework in which we spend our lives . . . it is the terrain on which we met, interact with each other, work out our ambitions, achieve or fail to achieve our purposes.

As a result of this vast influence, big corporations not only dominate the economy, they also fix the character of the larger institutional infrastructure, and they set the cultural tone for the entire nation. No one would argue, for instance, that the values of the Old Capitalism—growth, power, and profit—have not left their strong mark on the general flavor of life in the United States. So in a broad sense, the New Capitalism defines the type of society that seems to be evolving now in Western nations; it *is* the coming social order.

This chapter provides an analysis of the transformation now under way in higher education, medicine, the legal system, the military, public media, and organized religion. We first examine the major problems confronting these institutions that led to the decline of confidence noted in Table 1.1 of Chapter 1, focusing on how they all suffer similar dilemmas of the Old Capitalism: the limits of hard growth, the ineffectiveness of bureaucracy, and the corrosive results of self-interest. Then we highlight major trends that are forcing strategic change: the way information technology, intense competition, and new values are relentlessly driving the development of smart growth, market networks, participative leadership, democratic governance, and other innovations that are now revitalizing modern institutions.

Obviously, these complex arenas of life cannot be addressed adequately here, so I've only touched on a few central issues in each case, leaving it to the reader's experience and imagination to build on the sketches that follow. Although these analyses are brief, they are sufficient to show that a central theme runs through all this institutional change. The economic renaissance is being extended to society at large, led by the same ideals now powering a New Capitalism in business—the legitimacy of democratic collaboration and the productivity of free enterprise.

HIGHER EDUCATION

Chapter 1 showed that higher education is one of the most respected institutions, but structural faults persist which were first identified during the student protests of the 1960s. A major cause championed by dissident students was the "rationalization" of the university into a mechanistic system of little relevance to personal life or the pursuit of knowledge.

Rise of the Knowledge Factory

In place of their traditional role of providing a liberal education for a small national elite, after World War II colleges began to serve a new role as gatekeepers for industrial employers who developed a great need for trained professionals. Universities became "knowledge factories" patterned after the model of manufacturing firms: new students were "raw material" to be "processed" by "worker" professors, through a "production line" of courses, from which the "output" of degree holders was "marketed" by the college placement center. Thus, the student was no longer the client of this system, but a passive object to be molded into a finished product; the true clients became the corporations who hired, or "bought," college graduates.[2]

It is astonishing to note how precisely this model has been fulfilled today. Instead of havens for exploring new ideas, large universities have become bureaucracies ensnarled in their own red tape. They typically employ between one to three staff personnel for every faculty member in order to operate the complex machinery of higher education: admitting new students, evaluating credits for prior work, registration into courses, recording grades, ensuring completion of degree requirements, issuing transcripts, and so on. Most of this has little to do with learning, but simply runs an educational production line that cranks out about 1000 different programs of study nation-wide.

University governance also reflects the same industrial model. An administrative hierarchy runs this elaborate system, alongside staff experts in public relations, finance, and law—just like business. Despite a perfunctory bow to democratic rituals, higher education is usually managed in a firm authoritarian manner, although it is subtle. In some ways universities are worse than other institutions because they self-righteously profess lofty ideals like a "community of scholars," and "academic freedom," yet these treasured concepts usually yield to vested interests of deans, department chairpersons, and faculty committees who ferociously maintain control over their turf and resources. One professor expressed a typical view: "The university is run . . . like a medieval fiefdom."[3]

Where has all this left students? Pressure, loneliness, and lack of purpose have fostered what one study called an "epidemic of despair" within some of America's most prestigious colleges. Studies also show that grades and other measures of academic performance bear little relationship to actual career success, but seem more related to **unhappiness**. Even future prospects for getting a good job seem uncertain. It is estimated that about one third of graduates finally find work in fields not requiring a college degree.[4]

As always, these problems result from the good intentions of competent people working with an outmoded model of education. In an age of interdependence that demands understanding whole systems, the fragmentation of knowledge is so complete that most scholars cannot converse with each other intelligibly, on the rare chance when they do meet. A revolution in information technology rages outside academe, yet courses are usually taught by lecturing to a class, unchanged from the middle ages. Universities have perfected an ability to mass produce degrees, while a social upheaval is creating such intellectual havoc that most people are struggling through widespread confusion. A recent study of American education concluded, "Our very future as a nation is threatened by a rising tide of mediocrity."[5]

The Wired University Cometh

This archaic "industrial" model seems doomed to fade away as the revolutionary power of information technology sweeps today's old bureaucratic teaching factories into the dustbin of history. "The biggest thing in American education these days is the computer," reported journalist James Lardner, "On campus after campus, in department after department, the drive is on to gear up for the computer revolution."[6]

This "wired university" is being invented at Carnegie Mellon, the University of Chicago, Rensselaer Polytechnic Institute, the University of Iowa, Dartmouth, Drexel, and scores of other institutions. Students and faculty are being provided personal computers tied into a campus-wide network. Video systems are becoming available that provide lifelike, moving images of textbook concepts. Libraries of data, text, and software are stored electronically for remote access. When these capabilities are perfected, students should be able to register for classes, review written course material, view a lecture, access information from data banks, write term papers, study programmed instruction, or solve a scientific problem—directly from their home or dormitory. Individual campuses are also being linked together by telecommunications systems that unite universities and other institutions into networks covering the nation and possibly the world.[7]

The implications are so vast that we cannot grasp the full impact, but one result should be to eliminate the routine drudgery that now occupies so much of learning. Machines are good at conveying knowledge that can be codified in textbooks (math, languages, etc.), so computerized instruction should automate most elementary courses, offering a boon to the "back to basics" movement now trying to remedy the crisis in education. The computer should also help scholars survey the knowledge available on some topic, rather than laboriously digging through stacks in the library.

Obviously, a computerized mode of study will not appeal to all people, and even those who enjoy working with such systems are not likely to use them exclusively. The volume of available data is expanding geometrically, however, so it is almost impossible for anyone to really know what is available on most subjects. What is truly humbling is that the present situation should pale before the explosion in knowledge that is imminent with an approaching information age, making computers indispensable for understanding any field.

As with office automation, the biggest effect will be to redirect attention from these "hard" mechanical tasks to the "smarter" aspects of education. Less time should be spent on well-defined topics, leaving students and faculty free to attend the complex, subjective matters that demand personal interaction—counseling students, locating educational materials, discussing controversial issues, and the like. In short, the computer will shift emphasis from "teaching" to "learning."

This freedom should also allow a closer relationship with the "real world." One of the greatest criticisms of modern education is that it is often divorced from practical experience, especially in professional fields. Schools of medicine, law, and business, for example, are now the largest departments on campus, but many practitioners are dismayed at how unrelated they are to the realities of the discipline. Andrew Hacker wrote:[8]

> ... *professional schools have ascended to such heights that they are out of touch with the ordinary conditions that comprise our national life. [They] have little if anything to do with reality.*

This urgent need to link ideas with reality is spawning various forms of collaboration between universities and society. Corporations, government agencies, and other institutions have a growing interest in keeping abreast of a rapidly changing world, while universities lack the healthy discipline of practical applications. These complementary needs are encouraging innovative managers and scholars to cultivate alliances for developing training programs, research projects, and other forms of consultation. There are about 1000 universities in the United States that grant credit for relevant work experience, corporate training, cooperative education, and internships. Dozens of business-college consortiums are forming to conduct joint research efforts.[9] Thus, the old ivory tower is becoming more of an open forum for gathering information from society, shaping it to create new knowledge, and testing the result in the crucible of reality. Some may fear the noble goals of academe will be corrupted, but this dynamic tension between the world of thought and the world of action seems essential to sound scholarship, even in the humanities and liberal arts.

The net effect of the information age on education, therefore, seems to involve a general movement toward synthesizing knowledge: within some field of study, across fields, between the student's personal aspirations and a career, from theory to practice, and covering various institutions. Here's how some university presidents view it:[10]

> *The new role of the university will be to build bridges between and among disciplines, to develop ways of coordinating and helping the learner to synthesize the knowledge which comes from many different sources. ... The creation of conceptual linkages among various fields of study, among graduate divisions, and among arts and sciences*

*and the professional schools . . . career workshops and internships
so that multiple career options are clear to students . . . multidis-
ciplinary programs which can best help toward resolving the tough
problems facing government, business, labor, or other segments of
society.*

In order to manage the unusual complexity of this new role,
progressive universities are developing organizational structures
along three different "dimensions." The most basic is the "academic"
structure of departments that focus on faculty development, research
and publication, and creating new curriculum within their discipline.
The second is the "program" structure composed of administrative
offices that draw on the expertise of departments to develop and
manage degree programs. The third dimension is the "professional"
structure of institutes that also draw on academic departments to
provide consultation, hold conferences, and other forms of aid to
external groups.

As noted in Chapter 4, this type of market network facilitates
both accountability and innovative freedom. All of these units —
academic departments, degree programs, and professional institutes — can be held accountable for covering their use of resources,
and then allowed to operate as self-managed entrepreneurial ventures.
Programs and institutes obtain their revenue directly from their
students and other clients, but academic departments are a little
more complex because their source of revenue is obtained indirectly
by charging such units for their service.

Nonfinancial aspects of performance are important, of course,
but the place to begin is by establishing financial independence to
break up universities into small, self-managed units able to define
their mission as they themselves feel is best. Professors would then
think of themselves, not simply as teaching in some department,
but as "intellectual intrapreneurs" free to contract for a variety of
courses, research efforts, or any other assignments that comprise
their professional "practice." Some of this is done now, but if these
concepts can be clarified and formalized, the result would be to
translate into reality the ideals of an "intellectual marketplace" that
academicians have always aspired to but rarely achieved. It should
be noted that this internal market structure parallels the strong
interest in using vouchers to introduce free markets in lower ed-

ucation in place of the present monopoly of public school bureaucracies.

From the student's view, a similar issue involves the way grades
and degrees subvert the educational process and restrict the student's
freedom. Rather than focus on truly educating people by increasing
their grasp of enduring knowledge, their ability to think, to critically
examine the world about them, most university education focuses
on certifying them for jobs. Certification in academia is somewhat
like monopoly in business; once enrolled, it serves the institution
rather than the client by using various requirements to maintain
control over students. Some type of certification may be needed,
but it should be job related and conducted working with students
and employers; the result would be to place education in its proper
role as a service rather than an end in itself, and to free students
to use the system with discretion. Listen to the way one person
described his experience in obtaining bachelor's and master's degrees:[11]

> ... this artificial credentialing system consumes two things [students]
> don't have a limitless supply of: precious time and money ... going
> to lectures three times a week, sitting passively while a lecturer
> parrots some textbook is the worst way to learn and is terrific at
> producing boredom.

The biggest obstacle to this more enlightened approach is that
professors are reluctant to acknowledge such matters because they
involve highly sensitive issues of responsibility, authority, and rewards. The almost hysterical opposition in lower education to merit
pay, for instance, reveals how the ferocious resistance to dealing
with these provocative concerns borders on making them almost
taboo for open discussion.

There are strong forces at work, however, that seem to be moving
universities in new directions. The declining number of young
people left in the wake of the baby-boom, the difficulty of degree
holders getting jobs, and other such trends are forcing competition
among colleges, and hence demands for improved performance and
innovation. Employers are also questioning the value of degrees
and setting up their own educational programs. There are now
about 400 "corporate campuses" operating in the United States,
taking $40 billion per year of lost college revenues.[12]

These forces should eventually encourage change in higher education, and the most urgent focus would be to redesign the outmoded
form of governance that continues on most campuses. Despite a
public image as democratic institutions, faculty members dominate
academic decisions that concern students, administrators preempt
organizational matters that affect the entire academic community,
and employers are almost totally excluded. Attempts by students
and faculty to gain seats on boards of trustees, for instance, are
invariably met with the same rationale about "a conflict of interests"
that corporations use to defend the board of directors from democracy.
One university president offered a typical explanation:[13]

> Trustees who are removed from the institution and certainly not
> direct beneficiaries of the actions of its governing board are potentially
> in the best position to make decisions which are in the best interests
> of the institution [on an] objective, unattached basis.

But here's how some students see it:

> The struggle has been going on for years and still students have no
> voice. . . . There's no consultation, no explanation. Students must
> passively accept [decisions]. . . . If it is a "conflict of interest" for
> students to take an active role in the decisions which determine
> their own future, then what has happened to the democratic principles
> this country was founded upon?

The traditional system of trustee governance may have made
sense in a simpler past, but now it has become a paternalistic
anchronism in a more difficult world that requires collaboration;
the system has little bearing on the complex problems of modern
universities in an information age, it ignores the needs of today's
sophisticated adult students, and clashes with the reality that faculty
usually feel they **are** the university. Effective policy-making cannot
be "objective" or "unattached," but must address the personal and
political issues that are always involved in any institution, much
less one that professes to be a community of scholars.

Participative policy-making is no panacea and it can be a messy,
unsettling affair, however, it should allow these various stakeholders
to seriously address the troublesome issues they all struggle with.
Professors should be confronted by their students, colleagues, and
administrators with the need to introduce new teaching methods,

to allow students and employers to share in course designs, and to be paid in accordance with their work load. Conversely, students must be told to accept the primary responsibility for their education. Learning is an active process, rather than having knowledge pumped into a passive receptacle, so ownership of the process should be transferred to the student where it belongs, with professors serving as "advisers" rather than "instructors." Employers also have their responsibility of playing an active role to insure that education is relevant to the external world. And administrators face the most difficult challenge of providing the leadership to integrate the interests of all these groups into a workable whole.

A new era is now before us in which the social order is being transformed so completely by the computer that a revolution in the nature of knowledge itself is under way. Rather than fuss over grades, degrees, and turf, universities should be leading the way into this future, and the place to begin is by redefining their own institution. Peter Drucker predicted:[14]

> Within the next 15 years . . . we will surely see the most profound changes in the way we teach and learn since the printed book was introduced 500 years ago.

MEDICINE

Medicine has always been one of the most respected institutions, but, as Chapter 1 shows, confidence declined from 73 percent in 1966 to 43 percent in 1984 because medical care is expensive and often ineffective in the United States. Medical costs have increased three times faster than inflation, so now 60 percent of Americans favor controls on physician and hospital fees. In contrast, other nations like Canada have superb medical systems that cost far less while ranking well above us in longevity, infant mortality, and other indicators of health.[15]

The Medical-Industrial Complex

The pervasive influence of business is seen again in the way medicine is organized along the "industrial" model. A few decades ago the typical doctor was self-employed and looked after the health of his neighbors by visiting their homes. Now the average physician works for a large medical corporation interested in profit. Joseph Califano observed, when he was Secretary of Health, Education and Welfare, "Health care in the U.S. is big business." Revenues presently total about 11 percent of GNP, making health care the third largest industry, and there are about 1000 for-profit hospitals mostly controlled by five corporations. *Newsweek* described the emerging "Medical-Industrial Complex" this way:[16]

> *Health care is evolving into a network of corporations running every-thing from hospitals and home-care services to retirement homes and health spas.*

A major problem caused by this "industrialization" of medicine is an emphasis on hard technology that slights the personal care patients badly require. Modern medical technology is essential, of course, but there is a strong need to move away from an undue reliance on its use to treat disease and toward maintaining health— a subtle but crucial distinction so rarely accepted by the profession that the term "holistic" has become a dirty word to many physicians. This need for a broader view arises because the nature of serious illness has changed dramatically over the past few decades. Most people once died of infections like pneumonia, influenza, tuber-culosis, and other "physiological" factors that have since been rem-edied, which is why we live longer now. Instead, the prime causes of death today are heart failure, cancer, and the like, which are matters of diet, stress, and other subtle, poorly understood "social" factors.[17]

A continuing absorption with mechanical solutions, however, as well as the public's eagerness for quick fixes, is largely responsible for the fact that modern medicine itself creates much of the poor health it claims to treat. Congressional studies found that 2 million unneeded operations were performed yearly at a cost of $10 billion and 10,000 deaths. It is estimated that about 30 percent of hospital patients suffer health problems afflicted by medical interventions, and one third of hospital deaths are caused by preventable errors.[18]

Because medicine is organized about the imperatives of tech-nology, it invariably creates complex, authoritarian bureaucracies that exacerbate these problems further. Even some physicians are critical. Dr. Irving Page acknowledged that medical staff have become "increasingly indifferent and isolated from personal responsibilities for patient care." But attitudes are changing. The old view that once regarded doctors as akin to God is being challenged as nurses and patients rebell against being ordered about. Nursing is in a state of crisis because nurses are no longer willing to serve as handmaidens to physicians, but are demanding increases in pay and authority. And the underlying cause of skyrocketing malpractice suits is that a sophisticated populace now recognizes that physicians are fallible. As one patient put it, there is an unwillingness to "passively accept whatever the doctor orders."[19]

Modern medicine also emulates business in that it is a self-serving system. Despite the profession's claims that it embodies free enterprise ideals, the medical establishment constitutes one of the best managed monopolies in the nation. Organized medicine controls the supply of physicians through admissions into medical school, and it discourages dissemination of information needed to make the market system work, such as fees, performance of physicians and hospitals, and the like. The AMA has one of the strongest political action committees in the country, which lobbied fiercely to exclude physicians from federal antitrust regulations. The cost of most health care is paid by insurance and public plans like Medicare, so there is little incentive to economize. Pharmaceutical companies prevent the use of inexpensive generic drugs by patent protection. A study in the *New England Journal of Medicine* reports the growing number of for-profit hospitals increased medical costs by 15 to 25 percent.[20]

These problems all stem from an industrial model of medicine that discourages innovative, caring, cost-effective approaches to health care. Medicine today is analogous to dining in an extravagant restaurant, in which the waiter orders for you, from a menu that contains only rich indigestible foods, without telling you what the prices are, and gets paid directly by your bank. A patient mourned the loss of trust: "I used to think the purpose of a hospital was to benefit the patient." While today, as Dr. William Rassman admitted, "The health care system is designed to capture the consumer dollar."[21]

High-Tech Systems and Soft Health Care

Recently, however, medicine began experiencing the same changes affecting other institutions that are entering the frontier of smart growth. A revolution in medical science is underway as powerful advances continue in genetic engineering, medical instrumentation, organ transplants, and other sophisticated new high-tech fields. Meanwhile, various new developments are also shifting attention to a "soft" approach that offers great promise in preventative methods for improving health and reducing costs.

A major force driving all this change is the use of information technologies to monitor vital signs, diagnose illness, prescribe treatment, and assess the outcome. For instance, with the development of powerful computer systems, it will not be long before each person should have a complete medical history stored electronically to create a living model of the unique way their body behaves. Rather than rely on our faulty memories and sketchy files, such records could permit far better understanding of individual health problems, including psychological factors. Further, they would collectively form an unprecedented national data bank for scientific study, instead of conducting *ad hoc*, expensive medical experiments. This information would also guide clients toward more effective health care providers, making the free enterprise model of medicine a reality. Prototypes of such systems are in use now, and the impressive results suggest revolutionary potential for cheap, convenient, and more powerful understanding of illness and its remedy. For example, computerized diagnosis is **more** accurate than the unaided knowledge of physicians, although their intuitive judgment is invaluable for interpreting the results.[22]

With much of the routine work that now occupies physicians automated, medical care should move toward the soft aspects that have become more important as the major cause of serious illness shifts from physical infections to socially induced disorders. Thus, having conquered the problems that hard technology can solve, the challenge today is to address questions of lifestyle, dietary habits, exercise, working conditions, environmental pollution, stress, emotional states, and other subtle factors that are increasingly critical.

This fundamental move from a disease-centered emphasis to a preventive, health-centered focus lies behind the strong interest now
flowering in "holistic medicine," "wellness," and "soft health care."
A broader approach of this type is far more complex and personal,
and so it requires active involvement between clients, physicians,
medical staff, and public health authorities, leading to a participative
form of treatment that some call the "active patient" model.[23]

Why will the profession accept these changes? Because the medical
monopoly is splintering into a very competitive field. A more health
conscious population strives to avoid being dependent on physicians,
which has caused a sharp drop in the demand for medical services,
while a glut of 185,000 unneeded young MDs is expected by 1990.
Now discriminating patients are aggressively shopping for lower
fees and better treatment, and governments and employers are increasing the pressure to hold down costs. Many consumer groups
like the People's Medical Society publish evaluations of physicians
and hospitals, and they provide useful medical advice. Corporations
have formed 130 coalitions to share information on fees and to
identify the best providers for their employees, while cities like
Minneapolis and Columbus are publishing price lists on their hospitals.[24]

The result has been a flurry of innovation in health care as a
variety of special treatment programs emerge to meet these diverse
needs. There are estimated to be about 3000 walk-in medical centers
in the United States now ("Docs in a box") and the number should
increase to 4000 units by 1990. Prepaid Health Maintenance Organizations (HMOs) are growing dramatically, presently numbering
300 plans covering 17 million people. One administrator noted,
"National HMO networks are the wave of the future." Additionally,
a variety of creative hybrid systems are emerging, such as Independent
Practice Associations (IPAs) that are loosely organized prepaid systems, and Preferred Provider Organizations (PPOs) that have working
agreements with institutional clients. Thus, the medical bureaucracies
of the past are rapidly becoming free enterprises competing to serve
clients better. The Wall Street Journal noted:[25]

> In an increasingly competitive market, hospitals are scrambling for
> patients through vigorous marketing, special programs, and new
> clinics. Doctors are fighting back with clinics of their own.

Over the next few decades medicine is likely to mature into a far more sophisticated institution. It will address the whole person in order to enhance health in addition to curing illness, and it will do so using powerful high-technologies and flexible organizations. Medical care has come a long way from its humble origins in the small town family doctor, and now it is undergoing another transformation to a new era. Dr. Paul Ellwood, president of a health care research firm, summed up the change:[26]

> *Doctors and hospitals sense the jig is up. . . . We're watching the start of an economic transformation in the health care system.*

THE LEGAL SYSTEM

The legal profession is suffering from a low confidence level of 23 percent because of—as Ernest Gellhorn, Dean of the Case Western Law School, expressed it so nicely—"Too much law, too many lawyers, and not enough justice."[27]

Swelling Legal Niceties, While Crime Runs Rampant

The structure of American law has reached such a state of complexity that the United States employs 20 times more attorneys per capita than Japan, 10 times more than France, and 5 times more than Germany. It costs 100 times as much to probate an estate in the United States than in England. Yet with all this high-priced legal help, the delays in justice meted out by overcrowded courts are so great that Chief Justice Warren Burger warns the court system could "literally break down before the end of this century."[28]

Just as in business, the problem occurs because the law has been organized by lawyers to serve their own interests. Unduly complex legal proceedings form a convenient esoteric maze that only lawyers can maneuver through, little useful information is provided to help the public, and artificial demands are created for legal services, as in attempts to block no-fault auto insurance. Chief Justice Burger noted: "The legal profession exercises a monopoly." Moreover, most lawyers are not interested in the public's welfare, but in working for wealthy individuals and corporations. The American Bar Association itself acknowledged, "The middle 70 percent of the population is not being served adequately by the profession." Even some lawyers are becoming disaffected, as a recent survey showed:[29]

> *After a while you begin to ask a lot of questions about what you're doing. Does it really make a difference to society who wins or loses— or even to your client? . . . litigation is so destructive, such a waste of people's energies. It's not doing anything productive . . . I find it embarrassing how much I make.*

As attorneys have been elaborating on this unmanageable system for their own benefit, however, the public has grown outraged over legal niceties that permit criminals to remain free while failing to recognize the rights of law-abiding citizens. And the unrealistic, moralizing stance of laws against victimless offenses causes an avalanche of crime to terrorize society.

A good example of the latter problem can be seen in the enormous success of organized crime. For instance, the Mafia has grown into one of America's biggest industries. Their net worth totals roughly $150 billion, annual sales run about $50 billion, and annual profit is about $10 billion—comparable to the largest U.S. corporations.[30] What permits this vast organization to prosper in spite of the continued war against crime waged periodically by reforming politicians?

Because drugs, prostitution, gambling, and other private, moral vices are outlawed to become a lucrative market served with great skill by "realists" like the Mafia. Marijuana is now America's largest cash crop, grown in all 50 states and sold for $14 billion per year. The expensive black market for this cheap weed exists only because it is illegal, yet alcohol is acknowledged to be the nation's "number 1 drug problem." Cocaine sales run about $30 billion per year, well ahead of tobacco and alcohol, for the same reason. We may regard all this as immoral, but the refusal to face such realities by declaring drugs illegal simply drives the market underground where it cannot be controlled, and the police, politicians, and others responsible for rooting out these victimless crimes become corrupted. Frank Serpico, the New York City cop who was almost destroyed for trying to expose the pay-offs that pervade "New York's finest," despaired, "The American dream has become a nightmare." Lately, even conservatives like William Buckley now admit the only solution is to decriminalize drug use.[31]

From Hired Guns to Peacemakers

As with other institutions, change is underway. One driving force is that the complex paperwork which abounds in law is being automated as information technology computerizes the typing of documents, researching precedents, and managing cases. "The computer . . . has transformed the tradition-bound practice of law, and more changes are ahead," wrote *The Wall Street Journal*.[32] Pressure to simplify proceedings is also building because of intense competition caused by the increase of attorneys. The number of new legal graduates has risen from 250,000 in 1960 to 650,000 now and is expected to reach 1 million by the 1990s, thereby encouraging innovative approaches like the use of low cost legal clinics, prepaid arrangements, and other alternatives to traditional practice.[33]

As in other institutions, easing such routine work should shift attention to the "softer" aspects of law that are more critical: reducing the flood of litigation that now crowds the courts, thereby freeing the legal system to find ways of alleviating the rampant crime that imprisons us all.

A serious disenchantment is setting in over traditional adversarial proceedings in which attorneys serve as "hired guns." This role is sustained by an outdated belief that conflicts are unavoidable, and a pernicious myth that the law is a rational process for discovering objective truth. Whereas, it is precisely this conflict-oriented, impersonal logic that has produced endless delays in resolving disputes and an inability to rehabilitate criminals. True justice is for most people a matter of personal and community standards of equity, yet this "inner" aspect of the law is considered "prejudicial" by the present system. There is something fundamentally lacking when the victim of a serious crime is not permitted to condemn the accused in a direct confrontation, to demand apology, receive some form of compensation, and then to extend forgiveness—all of which are necessary to absolve guilt and allow genuine rehabilitation.

Now, however, a preference for mediated settlements is slowly spreading as it becomes clear that a complex society cannot function effectively without some form of collaboration, along with the use of intuition, personal values, and other messy realities that pervade all other aspects of life. Judge Patricia Wald of the U.S. Court of Appeals acknowledged:[34]

> *We delude ourselves if we believe that decisions are made solely on the basis of clear judicial precedents and legislative intentions . . . intuition, instinct, and life experiences come into play in fashioning arguments.*

Some adversarial trials will remain unavoidable, of course, but a variety of experimental moves are in progress that may evolve into a "smart" form of justice in which the law serves more as "peacemaker." Creative attorneys are using arbitration and conciliation for divorces and other proceedings to avoid the expense and emotional damage of drawn-out legal battles. Private trials are being held on a voluntary basis to resolve disputes constructively. No-fault divorce and auto insurance are moves in this same direction. Various alternatives to prison are being tried, such as having criminals pay restitution to their victims. Chief Justice Burger summed up the new direction:[35]

> *We need to consider moving some cases away from the adversary system, from the trial by battle in the courtroom, to administrative processes or to mediation, conciliation, and especially arbitration.*

THE MILITARY

While support for the military has rebounded strongly following the United States' decline in international strength during the failures of Vietnam and Iran, no amount of firepower can overcome the deep fear Americans live with under the prevailing strategy of "mutual assured destruction" (MAD).

Hardware Has Become the New Maginot Line

Once again, the problem stems from an obsession with hard technology—in this case, the belief that more military hardware produces security. A single B-1 Bomber costs $230 million, triple the price of silver, pound per pound. Total world expenditures on arms now run around $1 trillion per year—more than is earned by the entire poor half of the world. There are now about 50,000 nuclear warheads in existence, each equal to all the destructive energy unleashed during World War II. The power of this arsenal amounts to the equivalent of 6000 pounds of TNT for every man, woman, and child on the planet.[36]

A specific example of the "MADness" resulting from this hardware approach to defense may be seen in the contradictions abounding in the MX missile. Although President Reagan claims the system's role is to insure peace, its technical purpose is to deliver a strike force of 1000 nuclear warheads to Russian cities. At a time of federal deficits and mounting deprivation, billions would be spent on a weapon that will only heighten tensions. And there is something basically illogical about the idea of building up defenses in order to have "bargaining chips" for disarming. Republican Senator Jack Edwards worried at a congressional hearing:[37]

> I am supposed to be one of the hawks on the committee, I guess, but I swear the more I sit here and listen to this, the more I wonder what in the world we are up to.

This focus on technology also causes the familiar "industrial" form of organization that has converted the modern soldier into a bureaucrat in uniform. Critics claim the United States lost the Vietnam war because our rigid military machine was no match for the fluid, organic North Vietnamese guerrilla army. The same bureaucratic ineptness was apparent in the failure to rescue our hostages in Iran, although a private business corporation was able to free two imprisoned executives. In Beirut, the American chain-of-command ran through nine levels before reaching the field.[38]

Although this emphasis on the technology of war is perpetuated by a fear of the Russians, it is also encouraged by the handsome profits that military spending provides the defense industry, and by our combative culture. Many Americans even believe an occasional war is actually good because it stimulates the economy, drives technological progress, and forces social cohesion. However, non-defense spending produces more jobs, it is certainly more constructive, and there is no lack of stimulating challenge with the future of humanity itself in doubt.

Some people still yearn to fight wars, and we should be grateful to have them available when they are needed. However, the heroic adventure of armed conflict no longer has wide appeal to a mature nation that is increasingly repulsed by unnecessary violence, and younger people are reluctant to sacrifice their precious lives needlessly after a me-decade has convinced them of their self-worth. Americans are likely to defend themselves if really threatened, but they no longer accept the necessity of war, much less glorifying it. The late English Admiral, Lord Mountbatten, expressed this change of attitude:[39]

> War today is useless, horrible, degrading. It hasn't got the heroism and the comradeship of past wars to redeem it. There's no honor or glory in war now.

Advocates of a traditional "hardware" solution to the problem now claim the "star wars" concept could use defensive missiles launched from space satellites to intercept nuclear attacks, thereby moving from the old strategy of "Mutual Assured Destruction" to "Assured Survival." This is a brilliant idea that may work despite all the doubts, but the absence of nuclear war does not constitute peace if intense hostility continues between the superpowers. Frequent outbreaks of violence seem almost certain to persist, and there always remains the fear that star wars weapons could be used offensively, thereby simply reigniting the arms race at a higher level.

The fact is that sheer armed might is now outmoded from a strictly military view. Modern weapons have been rendered impotent precisely because they are so destructive that they cannot be used to resolve conflicts, as demonstrated in Vietnam, the Beirut war, uprisings in Central America, and terrorism anywhere. In a world threatened by nuclear holocaust, weapons have become the new Maginot Line—they represent superb culminations of defense systems that worked well in the past but are now dangerous because they provide a false sense of security. The military faces an enormous task of redefining its role in a fragile new epoch that has made conflict unwinnable and cooperation mandatory. President Eisenhower noted:[40]

We have come to the point where safety cannot be assured by arms alone . . . both sides know that in any outbreak of general hostilities . . . destruction will be both reciprocal and complete. The human race must conform its actions to this truth or die.

Beyond MAD to PeaceSats

After all the think tanks have studied the problem, all the brilliant strategies simulated in war games, and all the powerful systems deployed, the unavoidable realization must ultimately dawn that any strategy relying on weapons eventually leads to more conflict. The search for mechanical solutions through superior hardware in order to "win the struggle against the enemy" is endless and doomed to fail because it reflects a mentality that only made sense in an industrial past. It is now abundantly clear that the conflict between the superpowers cannot continue for long without triggering a nuclear exchange, so the solution does not lie in more weapons but requires an entirely different, more constructive perspective. One American expressed it perfectly: "The weapons are just symptoms of the disease. The real problem is our relationship with the Soviet Union."[41]

As more people have recently become aware of the perverse way we have come to accept the idea of nuclear holocaust, that old passive attitude has ended with a growing debate over the arms race. Obviously, some form of defense may always be necessary. However, the "peace movement" is of great significance, not because it has a feasible solution, but because it represents a switch to a set of more benign, intelligent attitudes about war itself. Demand for relief from the threat of holocaust is so great that the nuclear freeze concept has drawn mass demonstrations in the United States and Europe, been advocated by most religions, and was approved by 10 out of 11 state referendums in 1982. The peace movement may be quiescent now, but it is still supported by a solid majority of Americans and is almost certain to resurface again. Even former CIA director William Colby urged:[42]

I think it's time people take this matter away from the priesthood that has gotten us into this mess, and simply insist that we stop building these things. Just stop.

Interesting new possibilities are also emerging through the same force that is transforming all other institutions—information technology. The success of any disarmament scheme hinges on the ability to provide accurate surveillance in order to remain protected against attack, and studies show that conflict diminishes if secrecy is eliminated by making information available to the opponents. Arthur C. Clarke, "inventor" of the space satellite, testified before the U.S. Congress on the potential of "PeaceSats" to prevent war by providing worldwide knowledge of all military actions. They could also offer information on weather, pollution, resources, and other such data to form a Global Information Cooperative that fosters collaboration among nations.[43]

These embryo ideas suggest the profound impact that seems likely on international conflict as the information age becomes a reality. As always, there are no panaceas, and nobody can guess how all this will work out. However, the inexorable growth of information technology has a special power that reveals the futility of conflict and creates an imperative for collaboration, as we noted throughout this book, thereby urging parties to seek alternatives. The really interesting thing about the concept of a global information system is that agreement is not needed for its use. Unlike disarmament, PeaceSats could be used unilaterally and without risk in order to foster cooperation among nations.

Finally, as Chapter 9 on the changing relationship between capitalism and socialism showed, there is a realistic prospect of strengthening the economic, cultural, and political bonds needed to form a civilized world order, which is ultimately the only real hope for lasting peace. The emerging information age seems likely to provide solutions that transcend physical technology and focus on smarter, more powerful high-technologies: forming economic relationships that join nations in productive ventures, extending information and communication channels to build understanding, and creating a spirit of collaboration.

The history of conflict reveals a fairly steady trend. From the continual wars among city states in the middle ages, to the brutal violence of the wild west in the American frontier, to the U.S. Civil War, conflict persisted until a larger social order evolved to unify parties into a common system that could handle disputes in a more civilized way. So will the conflict between the superpowers persist until some form of coherent world system evolves that is able to create international order. Among the last words he wrote, FDR warned:

> *We are faced with the preeminent fact that, if civilization is to survive, we must cultivate the science of human relationships.*

PUBLIC MEDIA

Most newspapers and television networks earnestly try to fulfill their role as the fourth branch of government entrusted with the responsibility of maintaining an informed public, but a low confidence rating of 23 percent suggests that the nation's expectations for this difficult function are not being met.

Television and the Press Become Big Media

As long as the treatment of violence, sex, politics, and other sensitive issues is decided upon by news editors and television executives who believe they have a right to publish virtually anything they alone decide is useful, large segments of society will continue to feel exposed and manipulated. For example, the press was outraged that being barred from the invasion of Grenada violated the First Amendment, but the public supported the government blackout because it felt reporters could not be trusted with such sensitive knowledge.

Another problem is that the financial interests of the media often interfere with their public trust. The obvious reason is that some journalists are less motivated by being informative than in reporting sensational gossip that will sell in order to reach the rarified status of media stars. Top television anchor people, for instance, are commonly paid about $1 million per year. The more subtle cause, however, is that the public would appear to be the legitimate clients of television networks and newspapers, but, in fact, the true clients are the corporations that buy advertising. Just as in business, government, and other institutions, the intended client has been reduced to merely a resource for making money.

The concentrated nature of the media also creates typical problems of unresponsive oligopoly that harm customers in any tightly controlled industry. Three out of five newspapers now belong to chains. Most big cities have only one or two papers. The three major networks dominate national television.[44]

Thus, where once the media were regarded as defenders of the public against the establishment, now they *are* the establishment. Journalist Daniel Schorr claims that "Big Media" is replacing Big Government and Big Business as a metaphor for irresponsible self-interest, and Charles Kuralt of CBS said, "There has arisen a breed of [television] managers which feels a greater responsibility to the bottom line than to the public good."[45]

Citizen's Journalism

With the revolution of telecommunication technology, however, a different role is evolving as the media struggle to effectively use the powerful new communication systems that are becoming the lifeblood of any nation. The information age is creating such limitless communication channels that an enormous diversity of news is becoming available as people with widely differing values interact in infinite ways, altering the very sense of community awareness that makes society work.

One can only speculate on the ultimate effects of these unprecedented changes, but one impact is to move journalism from a "hard" preoccupation with "reporting" the news to a "smart" role for managing the increasingly complex "meaning" of the news. The average citizen participates in society today primarily through the media. Television in particular provides our common understanding of public events, it shapes values, and forms our general view of life. Thus, journalists are beginning to help us find our way through this avalanche of information and to make sense of it all, becoming the gatekeepers to reality in a world of exploding confusion. This softer role of the media as a "facilitator of social awareness" is especially important because it helps resolve critical issues that affect the nation. Watergate was a good example in which continual, live television reports were instrumental in removing Nixon from office by allowing countless Americans to judge his guilt directly— which would not have been possible before the information age.

That is why any attempt to interpret the news by journalists themselves is bound to be seen as biased by somebody, and so the media now act primarily as traffic cops directing the flow of this information and its interpretation by others representing the range of public opinion. The great interest in television talk shows (the Phil Donahue Show), guest shows (Johnny Carson), authorities explaining news events (the medical expert on television networks), consumer hotlines, call-in radio stations, letters to the editor, and the like merely hint at many other possibilities for this "participative" type of "citizen's journalism." A study commissioned by the American Society of Newspaper Editors recommended developing a role as a "populist" institution that would serve as a "people's advocate," encouraging readers to think of the news as coming from "my paper."[46]

Other strategies might include inviting people representing various social interests to advise a television station or newspaper on its policies for sensitive coverage, like children's shows, sex, and violence, in the same way corporations use consumer panels. Polls are also needed to learn what the public wants since Nielsen ratings only cover about half of the population that now watches television. Whatever techniques are used, journalism must adopt some form of "democratic" process that reflects the needs of the public more directly. Otherwise, major newspapers and television networks have little hope of retaining their autonomy as this storm of controversy grows even more turbulent. Tom Goldstein, author of a critical book on journalism, noted:[47]

> If the media behave just like any other business, they will be treated like any business, and soon they will be regulated.

ORGANIZED RELIGION

Table 11.1 shows that even organized religion suffers from a low confidence rating of only 22 percent because of an imbalance between the traditional church and a spiritual revolution now under way. George Gallup claims the United States "may be in an early stage of a profound religious revival."[48]

Pray, Pay, and Obey

Religion has been around for a long time, to understate things a bit, but Americans have matured spiritually as well as in other respects. Today, a far more "personal," sophisticated form of religiousity is emerging that emphasizes genuine spiritual growth, an existential sense of awareness, and service to others. The old-time religion of paying faithful obeisance to dimly understood dogma handed down by lordly priests no longer seems adequate, and so many people have turned to countless forms of quasi-religious groups in what is loosely called the "human potential movement."

Yet, most members of the clergy remain committed to the former authoritarian view—what has been called the "pray, pay, and obey" school of thought—creating a serious loss in legitimacy. Modern people have a strong new sense of their own identity and personal strength, so they are not amenable to being dictated to even by their church. For instance, a majority of Catholics violate the church's rules on birth control, abortion, and other matters of personal conscience, and they disagree with its opposition to the ordination of women and marriage for priests. Americans also resent a paternalistic attitude that has caused notorious conflicts between stern pastors intent on guiding their flock with a firm hand and parishioners who want to share in the control of their churches. One member of a church that was assigned a dominating pastor expressed the outrage that results: "He considers the parish to be his alone, and the laity's role is to accept his unilateral decisions."[49]

This conflict between an authoritarian church hierarchy and independent new attitudes has also created serious problems in attracting young people to religious life. For example, the Catholic church has experienced a mass exodus of priests and nuns, while the enrollment of students in seminaries and convents has dropped precipitously. As a result, the number of clergy is expected to decrease from 60,000 to 25,000, at the very time when church membership is growing. A vivid example of this incompatibility is the way nuns are questioning the harsh manner they have traditionally been ordered about. Sister Donna Quinn, President of the National Conference of Catholic Nuns, asked:[50]

> *Are we being asked to obey as people in a totalitarian state? Are we being asked to obey blindly, without dialogue, without due process, without the proper representation to officials?*

Most religions, and especially Protestant churches, have tried earnestly to respond to these cultural changes. The Second Vatican Council of the Catholic church, for instance, liberalized the ritual of the mass, included the laity in most religious services, and advanced the principle of "shared responsibility" to include parishioners in church governance. But these are minor moves that only allow people to participate at the fringes of their faith: administrative matters, performing auxiliary roles at services, and the like. The fact remains that religion is something people continue to observe passively in our society, and it is almost totally removed from the hard realities of life at home, in the community, and at work. These difficult problems seem likely to persist until more fundamental reforms are made, because the crisis stemming from the transition to a new era is so widespread that even religion is not exempt.

Carrying the Sacred Outside of Church

As always, however, crisis is the other side of opportunity. Growing demands on a diminishing clergy coupled with the interest of parishioners for a more active role may dramatically alter the way churches behave.

This may sound a bit unusual, but I do not believe religion can become the profound spiritual experience Americans increasingly want unless the clergy yield exclusive control over performing religious rituals, and instead assist worshipers in conducting "personalized" services for themselves—in effect, to give the power of their calling to the people. Like business and other institutions, the old form of religiosity may have been best for our parents, but today a more sophisticated form of "participative" religion is needed to recover the sacred meaning that is frequently lost in old religious routines. Reverend Thomas Moore at Georgetown University notes that a "do-it-yourself Catholicism" is emerging.

The power to perform spiritual functions would then be passed on to ordinary members of society in order to carry a personal, intrinsic sense of spirituality into everyday life. One member of a "participative church" found a broader meaning in religion: "Now when I go out I carry the church with me." This ability to impart a higher level of awareness to ordinary events is precisely what is so badly needed to alter the entrenched modes of adversarial behavior from which the disorders of our time all flow. Consider how decisions in government, business, or law, for instance, could be improved if those involved were to engage in some form of meaningful spiritual act together—like reflective meditation or simply a moment of silence.

We are all aware of the realistic dangers that careless or excessively fervent religiousity presents, but the fears seem exaggerated. Journalist William Raspberry asks, "What is the danger in a moment of silence?" There is an enormous amount of inventive thought and practice being devoted to these questions, including the application of spiritual values in business. Some firms like Mary Kay Cosmetics owe their unusual success to the energizing force of religious ideals that permeate the corporation. Consider this simple example of a woman who introduced the use of brief periods of contemplative silence to facilitate meetings of her organization:[51]

> We were able to move prayerfully through decisions, feeling less pressure, more patience, and more willingness to attentively hear one another out . . . It has totally stunned a few people, but generally the value was quite overwhelming.

The consensus that seems to be emerging from countless such people is that a transformation in consciousness is necessary, it is morally desirable, and it is occurring today. Like other aspects of the transition to an information age, the spiritual revolution now underway is unlikely to be halted because there seems to be an inevitability about it that is spreading to encompass the entire social order. Theologian Harvey Cox observed:[52]

> There is a dramatic resurgence of religion as a potent political force today . . . a "post-modern" theology that recognizes religion's role as a legitimate force in shaping political thought and public policy.

12

Choices:

ALTERNATIVE SCENARIOS OF THE FUTURE

Americans are often accused of being less politically intense than Europeans, but during the Presidential election of 1984 Democrats and Republicans gloried in their strongly held differences.

The Democratic platform was appropriately represented by the site of their convention—San Francisco is one of the great melting pots of the nation, bringing together the rich gentry of Nob Hill, immigrants in Chinatown, labor leaders from local industries, black communities across the Bay in Oakland, and the women who dominate that city's government. Integrating this diversity has been the party's major strategy since the 1930s when FDR formed a grand coalition based on America's democratic principles. The Declaration of Independence states that "All men are created equal," and the Constitution claims the purpose of the Union is to "promote the general Welfare." Today, such bedrock values have evolved into a democratic philosophy in which government unifies members of the "American family" for the common good. As the Democratic presidential candidate, Walter Mondale, put it, "America is one indivisible community."

In contrast, the Republican convention took place in a city that reflects a different set of values—Dallas embraces the spirit of rugged individualism, self reliance, and property rights that tamed the Wild West. Now its thriving economy based on oil, agriculture, and electronics offers great opportunities for lavish wealth through hard work and entrepreneurship. Republicans have supported this growth of enterprise by developing a philosophy that draws on other American traditions. The Declaration of Independence proclaims "certain unalienable Rights" including "Liberty and the pursuit of Happiness," while our national songs glorify "the land of the free" and "sweet land of liberty." The incumbent, President Reagan, promised to broaden this freedom through further tax cuts and reductions in government. He joked, "You ain't seen nothing yet."

What is most intriguing, however, is that spanning across this apparent political chasm—democratic government to foster the public welfare versus free enterprise to promote individual opportunity—both parties professed to be serving the same patriotic goals. The nation has seldom witnessed on its television screens such a sea of flag-waving and heartfelt allegiance to insuring a strong economy and national defense.

Conservatives were kept in power because economic conditions looked so rosy at the time of the election that Republicans claimed to have started a "new era" of prosperity. GNP was growing at a robust pace, inflation was down, and capital investment and productivity were rising nicely. Many attributed this revitalization of a sagging economy to President Reagan's personal charisma, which instilled an infectious mood of optimism to dispel the dark malaise hanging over the 1970s.

There is a fine line between charisma and fantasy, however, and Reaganomics may have passed over that line. Colorado Governor Richard Lamm questions the "mindless optimism" of the Reagan era. As Chapter 1 showed, the recovery that began in 1983 was caused by a complex mix of factors, mostly unrelated to supply-side policies: the deregulation of markets that began under the Carter Administration; the recession of 1980 to 1983 that triggered an economic turnaround; and the stimulus of deficit spending. Herbert Stein, Chairman of the Council of Economic Advisers under Presidents Nixon and Ford, claimed, "I don't think the Reagan Administration deserves primary responsibility for the recovery."[1]

The real test should come during the late 1980s when the budget deficits begin to bite. Regardless of whatever Congress or the President may do to legislate a solution, unless Americans are able to find unusual courage, wisdom, or luck, massive debt seems likely to persist as the distaste for raising taxes clashes with the resistance to giving up federal support, locking the nation in a stalemate over the budget problem. The unavoidable reality is that, without some heroic combination of booming growth, painful spending cuts, and major tax increases, the national debt will soon approach $3 trillion, interest payments will grow to $200 billion, and the deficit may possibly swell to $300 billion.[2]

This unprecedented level of indebtedness is ample cause for alarm, but it could become catastrophic during the next decline. Unless Reaganomics has repealed the business cycles that have been occurring with regularity for centuries, the likely outcome is that the conservative spell gripping the nation in a frenzy of self-interest may be finally broken as economic disaster forcefully reminds us that there is no free lunch. Alan Greenspan, former chairman of the Council of Economic Advisers, called the problem "A Greek tragedy, where we seem to be drifting in a direction that is dangerous . . . and we don't seem to have the ability to divert it." Almost anything could happen in such uncharted territory, but the present direction seems headed toward a major recession as all this debt raises interest rates, chokes off growth, reignites inflation, drives up unemployment, and possibly causes an especially dangerous plunge if confidence collapses. Financier Felix Rohatyn warned, "We are entering financial outer space," and Henry Kaufman, another banker, warned that the nation is "lurching toward a national economic emergency."[3]

Even if the economy stays healthy, a political backlash may produce a sharp swing back to the left. Americans want prosperity, but the materialism, inequality, and greed now in vogue cannot last for long because it violates deeply held traditions of social justice and human welfare, thereby quietly fanning great resentment. There is a lavish oppulence about the Reagan Administration, for instance, that is more similar to the type of monarchy this nation once rebelled against than the democracy Americans cherish. Poverty has increased so that the lower fifth of the population receives 6 percent of the income while the upper fifth receives 43 percent, and one quarter of all American children are born poor. Yet the Reagans spent $207,000 for china and $10 million to redecorate the White House. The public pays $5 million each time the Reagan entourage goes on a trip. This regal spirit was highlighted at a White House ball during which maids filled toilet bowls with carnations after each flushing, not too unlike the style of Louis XIV. Ronald Reagan may be a fine man, but his deepest hopes reveal a limited view of the public weal: "What I want to see above all else is that this country remains a country where someone can always get rich." However, one American expressed the concern many others share:[4]

> Moral and spiritual values are being overwhelmed by selfishness, materialism, and sensory stimulation. We are pushing needless products on each other to make money, and polluting and consuming limited resources in the process. As a result, our quality of life and our quality as people are declining. This is not what God gave us life for or what our forefathers fought and died for.

This vignette of contemporary American politics portrays a major theme running through this book—the transition to a new economic era is marked by a sharp polarity between right and left wing views. Such conflicts remind us that the future is not preordained so it cannot be forecast except in broad terms. The future is inherently political because it involves critical decisions that all people make to shape their lives, and these choices are based on deeply held values stemming from a personal vision of what is good. Presently, the nation seems to be poised at a crossroads branching in three very different, unexplored directions. Where is America headed if it continues to follow the neoconservative revolution to the right? Is it possible to return to the old liberal reliance on big government? Can a path midway between the left and the right be pioneered?

The following sections clarify these crucial choices Americans face in deciding the type of economy they want. Three scenarios are presented that differ primarily in their political orientations. The first, "Corporate America," shows the type of future that seems likely if the neoconservative movement were to dismantle government in order to free big business for revitalizing the economy. The second scenario, "Regulated America," outlines a liberal counterrevolution in which the federal government resumes control to create an equitable society, as advocated by some prominent people.[5] The third describes what would happen if a centrist movement could combine the principles of both free enterprise and democracy to create a "Democratic Free Enterprise America."

I've tried to explore where these different paths would take us by following the logic of each vision to a fully developed, plausible conclusion. Whether the results are accurate or not is hard to say, and, obviously, these are not dispassionate, equally desirable outcomes. Both the "Corporate" and "Regulated" versions are feasible, and they each offer some advantages as well as problems; however, this book has obviously argued that the third solution would be best. So rather than being studies in the objective sense, these scenarios are more like exercises of the imagination that allow us to gain a more realistic, tangible glimpse of the unique way each alternative would actually work, to feel the texture and taste the flavor of their competing visions, to probe the boundaries of what is possible in order to decide what is preferable. Some will think my biases have colored the outcome, but I believe these sketches help us see that the first two paths represent extreme limits to what most Americans want, while the third offers a more desirable future.

To understand these scenarios, it should be noted that each presents a different "historical" perspective from the vantage point of an observer looking back from the year 2000 to explain what has occurred since the present time in 1985.

CORPORATE AMERICA

During the late 1980s when I was in college, the neoconservative revolution proceeded to roll on until the major political "realignment" that many once doubted became an obvious reality. The eventual success of supply-side policies combined with the irresistible charm and cunning skill of President Reagan encouraged the American people to fully restore laissez-faire ideals, giving big business almost completely free reign to revitalize the economy. Thus, the "neo-capitalist" period that was launched in 1980 lasted up to the present time in A.D. 2000.

Yes, we still have problems, such as continued high unemployment, periodic bouts of inflation, and rising hostility among different social elements—especially since most welfare programs were abandoned. But those of us in the middle-class enjoy a prosperous life, so we continue to support the Republicans, and the Democrats remain unable to challenge them. The mood of the nation is to avoid disturbing changes that might prove risky, entrusting itself to the leadership of major corporations. Even with its flaws, business is thought of as the most capable institution for running the country, while government is still discredited. One of my neighbors said it best: "I know capitalism has its faults, but it works."

Herman Kahn's vision of a "Super-Industrial Society" was implemented during the early 1990s as technological fixes were developed to treat problems like energy shortages and pollution. A consortium of oil companies led by Exxon produced a working synfuel program that now mines the Western states to produce fuel selling for $9 per gallon, while nuclear plants have proliferated because fossil fuels are running out. Industry is booming because autos are used fairly heavily and due to a growing demand for goods. There has been a decline in air and water quality because of this high level of consumption, especially since the dismantling of regulations, but we adapt in a variety of ways. Huge plastic enclosures patterned after the Astrodome now cover downtown business centers, suburban shopping malls, and private communities. Many of us drink bottled water, avoid going outdoors during pollution alerts, and use air conditioning. Some advocate ways to reduce these problems, but they're regarded as Utopian do-gooders. "Those demanding environmental purity are simply unrealistic," said an executive at my firm.

Fierce competition prevailed for a while to create a flurry of efficient innovations, but, as the economic transition matured, mergers and acquisitions consolidated most industries into a few large corporations. With government more aware of the need for growth, trade restrictions were enacted during the late 1980s to protect American companies from unfair foreign competition. Large numbers of small competitors constantly appear to challenge big business or to open new fields, but most are willingly bought out at huge profits by large corporations.

During the late 1990s, big firms expanded so much that even the world economy is managed now by a few dozen megacorporations. One example was the merger in 1996 between three companies— General Motors, General Electric, and General Telephone and Electronics—which is today called "General Technology" (GT). Global corporations like GT control several major industries so they are virtually recession proof. And as they grew to dominate their fields worldwide, they were able to overcome political constraints of most nations and remain fairly unaffected by wars or revolts. In short, they transcend ordinary economic and political problems because they are truly global in their size, scope, and power. The GT advertising campaigns, for instance, proclaim: "General Technology for the global welfare."

Obviously, large organizational structures have been needed to operate these megacorporations. GT, for example, has nine divisions, each employing about 800,000 people who are organized in a hierarchy of about 22 to 25 levels, working all over the world as supervisors, technicians, and administrators. The great complexity of these systems couldn't be managed without the powerful ninth generation computers that permit detailed reports to be entered by roughly 180,000 offices in each division, processed into centralized files, and analyzed by top level staff groups, with new instructions issued back down the chain-of-command.

Superior-subordinate relations are rather formal because of this complexity, but people are treated in a polite manner to compensate for the loss of personal autonomy. For instance, as a class T-43 manager I have the authority to demote employees and transfer them, however, they may always file a complaint through the corporation's internal judicial system. Employees with good records are rewarded with vacations to one of the company's resorts around the world and many other leisure activities. Overall, work may be a bit dull, but it is more than offset by the exciting rewards of recreational drugs, sexual escapades, violent sports, and other pleasures that are now even more common than during the 1960s I've heard so much about. "Sure, my job is a little meaningless," said one of my computer technicians, "but we really have a ball after work."

At the policy-making level corporations are typically governed by an "Office of the Chairman," which consists of a team of three executives. Performance of divisions is evaluated on the basis of "resource usage efficiency" (RUE)—a sophisticated form of profitability that accounts for the effects of inflation, theft, political disturbances, and other factors to provide a more rational form of control than the old method, ROI.

Since these megacorporations operate across national borders, many have "Offices of Political Relations" staffed by former diplomats who work with local politicians to arrange favorable laws in return for attractive tax payments. When differences occur between individual corporations or with some nation, the "Federation of Global Corporations" (FGC) is asked to intervene, and it can usually strike an agreement. If necessary, it can impose an economic blockade on nations or even on corporations to gain their support.

Life goes on much as before, but with somewhat more of a businesslike quality. People have become even more attracted to the strength of big business since the election in 1992 of Lee Iacocca to the U.S. Presidency. Big corporations now manage schools and universities because education has become increasingly critical for running a complex technological economy. Medicine became almost totally managed as a business after the move to private for-profit hospitals in the 1980s, and even religion uses business practices since the "electronic church" grew in strength. The head of World Religious Enterprises advertised, "Our business is the saving of souls, and we use all the resources at our command efficiently for this noble purpose."

Some resistance persists, of course, from former consumer advocates, labor leaders, environmentalists, and other liberal groups who despaired and went underground to attack corporate facilities with bombs, kidnap executives, and commit other acts of sabotage reminiscent of the 1960s. Ralph Nader organized a coalition of interest groups who identified themselves as "Americans Against Capitalism," which still campaigns for reform. But the system serves most of us fairly well, so we think of these dissidents as radicals limited to the fringes of society.

People have come to accept the fact that modern life cannot avoid pollution, psychic disorders, crime, and violence, but more sophisticated technology is being developed to keep these problems under control. Brief market crashes occasionally sweep through the world economy, and although the cause of these instabilities is not yet understood, economists are confident they will be worked out soon. Another source of some concern is that the two superpowers continue to threaten one another, and there have been a few local outbreaks of nuclear war among Third World nations. I must admit this destruction causes most of us great anguish, however there are compensating benefits because it does provide a major source of economic growth, especially now that the arms race has been extended into space.

REGULATED AMERICA

Many typical Americans like myself were becoming disillusioned with the harshness of neocapitalism, and when workers, farmers, the aged, ethnic groups, the poor, women, and the baby-boom began feeling their interests were ignored, a counter-revolution swept through the nation during the election of 1988. Under the leadership of Democrats and the influence of liberal media figures like television producer Norman Lear, a resurgence of political support was mustered for new government programs to curb business excesses and to form an equitable social order. The winning campaign theme was: "Return to an America that Cares."

Memories of the old welfare state provoked a lot of opposition, but it was overcome by claims that we had learned to manage government effectively now. Decentralized policies were proposed to control the economy without seriously hampering growth, and computerized information systems were to monitor social programs more efficiently. We enjoy a more secure and fairly well-administered society, but somehow the promised gains remain a bit illusive. Reforms have improved the public welfare, but only by replacing business megacorporations with federal bureaucracies. Isolated from the market and protected from criticism out of fear of returning to corporate abuse, big government has come back stronger than ever.

For instance, to direct the use of technology more carefully, social forecasting and assessment studies of major industrial projects by "Technological Effectiveness Centers" (TECs) were required beginning in 1990. These controls have prevented the use of nuclear power plants, questionable computerized information systems that may invade privacy, the more dangerous biogenetic research studies, and expensive medical techniques that are not cost-effective. They have also alleviated energy shortages and pollution, although some believe it is only because they have slowed economic growth.

Federal and state regulatory efforts were intensified; some industries were taken over in public interest areas like the utilities, banks, and transportation; and wage and price controls were enacted to reduce inflation. All this required large government agencies employing hundreds of thousands of people. The Kennedy Corporate Control Act of 1992 was passed requiring the boards of the Fortune 1000 to include labor leaders and public directors approved by the government. Some people are unhappy over these restrictions, but most seem satisfied that the system is more orderly and it serves the common good. A traveler I met in my new job managing flight schedules told me, "Well, the low fares before made it easy to visit my children, but to tell you the truth I got tired of figuring out all those different prices and flight times and worrying about a crash."

Business goes on fairly normally even though a few quirks have appeared. A lot of talent has been diverted into the underground economy in which outlawed items like hand guns, toxic pesticides, unapproved medical drugs, and so on sell for many times their cost on the black market. Shortages occur when the government makes a major mistake in allocations, causing lines to form for ordinary products unexpectedly, like toilet paper and camera film. People feel differently about this, but a friend summed it up pretty well: "I don't know which is worse, the shortages or the price-gouging we had before."

Congress responds to complaints by producing needed adjustments—a welcome change from the chaos and privilege of the old neocapitalist period. Unfortunately, the passage of legislation and its translation into programs is divisive and drains the nation's energy, leaving little time for much else. I've lost interest in politics, and most people don't bother voting much. Because the nation remains committed to avoiding the risks of trusting big business, however, these political changes are usually absorbed by the bureaucracy which rolls on as before.

On the global level, America's leadership, combined with a similar anticapitalist mood in Europe, led to a long-awaited solution to international conflict by uniting the governments of major powers into a single quasi-administrative system. Since the idea closely paralleled what the Russians had advocated all along, in 1995 the Soviet bloc joined the move to develop a successor to the United Nations that has legislative, judicial, and enforcement powers which span the entire world—the United Socialist and Capitalist Nations (USCN). "Now that you Americans appreciate the principles of Socialist Democracy," said Misha Rupinski, the President of the Soviet Union, "At last we can learn to live together." Thus, world government has been ushered in to regulate the economies of all nations and to avoid the outbreak of hostilities. Local wars still occur, but they are quelled by the Academy of World Peace, a para-police unit.

Some freedoms are limited now by requirements that a license be obtained to start a business, move to other parts of the world, and have more than one child. Science and technology advance a bit slowly along state guidelines but there is steady progress. And the standard of living has been raised for most people, albeit modestly. So life is relatively calm and secure, but somehow I feel uneasy. The world will probably not go out with a bang, but it may slow to near death with a whimper.

DEMOCRATIC FREE ENTERPRISE AMERICA

I wouldn't have believed the upheaval of the late 1980s was possible if I had not seen it myself. When it became clear that the budget deficits couldn't be controlled, a crisis of confidence hit the financial markets. The public felt this added threat and chaos was the last straw to the ordeal they had suffered during the past two decades, and so a populist movement was ignited that roared through the country. This time the target was big business. As the role of major corporations suddenly exploded into the biggest political issue of the 1988 election, the media focused on the need to redefine the "invisible government of big business" that ran the economy.

After much finger pointing, a leading group of centrist politicians and business executives saw this wave of change as an opportunity to rejuvenate the nation by working together as a coalition. Initially, only a few visionary leaders were prepared to make a commitment to this movement because most people regarded it as so idealistic as to be hopelessly romantic. But the logic of the concept caught widening attention as there seemed to be a yearning for human values. One politician put it well: "This nation doesn't belong to big business or big government—it belongs to the people."

Not only was there receptivity at the top, the movement coincided with similar initiatives taking place at the grassroots. Some business firms, labor unions, communities, and public interest groups were collaborating to revitalize cities, retrain the unemployed, recycle waste, and other joint ventures to form a sort of "People's Capitalism." It took many months of agonizing discussions among a growing range of influential Americans, but eventually the politicians who started the idea brought together moderate leaders from the Business Roundtable, the AFL-CIO, the Consumer Federation of America, the U. S. Chamber of Commerce, former presidents, and movie stars to announce a plan for restoring democratic values in a revitalized economy—the Campaign for Democratic Free Enterprise was launched, with the slogan "A United America is a Strong America." I was dubious, but now I have to admit it has helped.

The basic platform simply called for new political structures to address our economic problems in a systematic and equitable manner. Democratic policy-making bodies were to be formed at the national level in a Council for Economic Policy composed of representatives appointed by the President and approved by congress from business, labor, consumers, and other constituent groups. Similar bodies were intended for each major industry, state, city, and major corporation that wanted to participate. Opposition was intense, but the program was voluntary so you could hardly stop these parties from pursuing their mutual self-interest together.

Long, heated debates took place to allay the doubts of various interest groups, but many never did believe the idea was possible because it was too much to think people could work together. Powerful individuals from the far right and far left denounced the idea with ferocious attacks, the right branding it "socialism" while the left called it "fascism." However, most of the policy bodies were formed despite all these objections, and enthusiasm started to spread

as energy and fresh ideas began to produce workable solutions. For
the first time in my memory, the notion of the common good pre-
vailedover individual interests. "I've never felt so hopeful about
the future," said a friend.

After a few years of intense debate and tough bargaining, the
movement led to various changes that redefined much of the economic
system. In the auto, steel, and other smokestack industries, agreements
were reached to automate roughly 60 percent of blue-collar production jobs and 40 percent of white-collar office work over the
next 10 years combined with a plan to retrain workers for new
technologies. Some plans lagged for a while, but when South Korea,
China, and other developing nations began to move into our markets,
it became clear that the economy must be restructured to compete
internationally.

As these old jobs became largely eliminated during the mid-
1990s, attention shifted to external problems like pollution that
were reaching dangerous levels. This growing threat forced the
formation of joint business-government programs to guide industries
in managing their impacts on the community. Exxon and a few
other energy companies, public power utilities, and materials producers like Alcoa developed programs for working with cities to
provide "natural resource management" (NRM) services that use
the region's energy assets most effectively, control environmental
pollution, and recycle trash into useful products. Such projects
were undertaken voluntarily, as simply attractive ventures, with
politicians helping the parties work together. An Exxon executive
was pleased: "We may have found a way to control our escalating
costs while also helping communities avoid disaster."

While these basic problems were being contained, a wave of new
ventures was spreading to improve transportation, create powerful
information systems, provide better education, foster health care,
and serve other "quality of life markets," usually working closely
with the clients. Car makers, for instance, now use consumer advisory
panels and complaint monitoring systems to better understand the
customer's needs, which has led to more successfully designed cars
and new modes of transportation. The biggest marketing idea of
the 1990s was the "car club" concept launched by GM in which
families pay about $75 per month to use cars maintained by their

local service station for occasional trips to the grocery store, vacations, and going to the office two to three times a week. Neighborhood information centers operated by IBM and AT&T are within walking distance, although most people have their own equipment at home.

Big corporations have broken up their old hierarchies to handle this complexity at the grassroots level. They now find it more effective to attract competent professionals and then simply contract with them to start and manage new ventures. "We can't possibly control all these projects, and shouldn't be trying to," said one hospital administrator, "Let the program directors have the freedom they need to produce results." As this contractual mode of work grew, a constant flux of people, programs, and organizations began merging into a messy but flexible web of relationships that now ties cities and nations into a single institutional network.

The result has been to create a surge of interest in free enterprise. My son, for instance, attends a high school that offers entrepreneurship courses. Most of our friends feel free to start a new venture and then move on to something else, and the majority of people are self-employed professionals who work on several projects simultaneously, usually for three to four organizations. However, it is unfortunate but true that some people find it hard to handle this responsibility, which has created an increase in personal crises and business failures.

These ventures are pretty diverse affairs. Some are run in a very formal manner, others have a family-like atmosphere, and many are self-managed with a fiercely democratic, egalitarian flavor. A lot of people still prefer working for a strong leader, so authoritarian management methods continue to thrive, but most of us believe that sharing responsibility is useful and people generally want to be treated like adults. One of my workers in an autonomous work team said, "It's as if we're in business for ourselves." Executives monitor the group's performance, reward them in accordance with their output, and are available to offer help when it is needed. "A more civilized and more effective way to run a big company," as one woman manager put it.

A model of democratic governance has evolved for big corporations out of the realization that political alliances are needed to compete in world markets. Most auto firms, airlines, and hi-tech companies, for instance, have appointed labor leaders, consumer advocates, government officials, and executives from their suppliers and deal-erships to the board. Many business firms remain unmoved, and some shareholders are outraged, but the success of the concept is slowly quieting the opposition. "We may have some heated argu-ments," said a long-time Chrysler director, "but the give and take among these different views is useful." GM announced the company's new slogan, "Serving People is Good Business," while a manager saw the advantages this way: "The key to good planning is to work closely with our employees, customers, and communities."

Surprisingly, these moves are forming a business ethic in which corporations focus on the social benefits they create as well as profits. The result has allowed executives to discover a role that not only defuses the painful criticism they suffered for years, but even accords them prestigious status as civic leaders. Most have been stunned at the approval they've received, which they relish, and they are still amazed by the commitment elicited from their constituent groups who work as a somewhat fractious but effective political coalition. "It's nice to feel like a good guy for a change," said the CEO of Dow Chemical.

At the macro level, government is shedding its old role of regulation and enforcement, and now focuses on working with various economic interests in a decentralized economy that is largely self-controlled. Many of the social programs that had been such a burden were curtailed because their responsibilities have been assumed by firms working with communities, labor unions, and other groups. As a result, the Campaign for Democratic Free Enterprise produced the first reduction in federal and state budgets in history, although it was rather modest. The President of the United States ran for re-election in 1996 on the promise, "More responsible big business means more effective big government."

But there have also been troubling failures. Some people and corporations find ways to take advantage of the system, and many political elements are still convinced this is ruining the nation. A few firms and entire industries have become so politicized that they can't seem to budge. On the whole, however, the mainstream seems to be thriving in spite of all this complexity and doubt.

In world affairs, at the end of the twentieth century the United States and Europe have been credited for creating a more benign form of free enterprise, although in some nations, most notably in

South America, capitalism still retains its old image of exploitation. Americans are accepted more warmly around most of the world now, and they feel restless with the lack of challenges at home, so many are seeking adventurous opportunities working abroad. The resulting exodus has fueled the movement of global corporations into Third World countries, forming partnerships with nations in Africa and the Orient to foster their development. It came as a surprise to find that these ties are proving a boon to economies in the West. Variations of capitalism and socialism are common now, which seems to be uniting most countries in a loose alliance. The Soviets are still pretty isolated, but it was heartening recently when consortiums of American corporations and Russian enterprises started working together to build production facilities in each other's country.

There remain very difficult challenges to be overcome, of course. Complex global information networks now conduct world-wide business transactions, measure social impacts, operate a complex array of incentives and taxes, and exchange scientific knowledge, which has made information overload endemic as people struggle to find their way through masses of data. And most common problems persist to some degree, such as spotty unemployment, regions of low growth, periodic inflation, and occasional outbreaks of violence.

So life has improved, but it is hardly Utopian. In fact, it is more difficult in some ways because we are all aware of the challenges that have to be faced. But on the whole, it seems to me there is wide agreement that these human dilemmas are being addressed about as effectively as possible, and a new golden age in science, art, and religion seems to be opening up that should eclipse anything in the past.

Epilogue

Future Prospects:

OBSTACLES AND PROMISES FOR A
SECOND AMERICAN REVOLUTION

Obviously, there are huge obstacles that block the development of a New Capitalism—but there are also powerful forces at work that hold the promise of overcoming these obstacles. This epilogue draws together earlier themes along with some final thoughts to sum up the prospects for a Second American Revolution that may create this system of political economy.

Out of the Crucible of Crisis ...

One of the most characteristic features of our time is a sense of turbulent disorder created by the barrage of perplexing, contradictory events blaring from the media to constantly remind us what a difficult place the world has become. Consider the following jarring incongruities I noted recently while watching some well-groomed television announcer cheerfully reporting an endless stream of bizarre stories on the evening news:

Poverty vs. Wealth. The government announced a distribution of old cheese to the poor from its overflowing warehouses, inviting comparisons with the unemployed during the Great Depression—punctuated by commercials hawking "designer chocolates," somewhat like the way Louis XIV played parlor games in the Chateau of Versailles as mobs of the French Revolution raged outside.

Low-Tech vs. High-Tech. Computer ads keep us dizzy trying to keep up with the new wonders of science flowing into our homes and offices—

but the aging smokestack industries seem so unredeemable that many feel they should be allowed to die or transferred to less developing nations.

Space vs. Earth.   Pioneer 10 spacecraft left the solar system, gliding silently through endless time to convey a message from our planet to the outer edges of the galaxy—while a medieval culture of squalor, ignorance, and hostility prevails in Lebanon, Iran, and other major sections of the Earth.

Logic vs. Spirit.   Suave, urbane people appear on the screen, speaking authoritatively in rational tones—although drug use is epidemic among such groups because we are all desperate to flee the straightjacket of orderly logic imprisoning our minds in order to experience the transcendent.

Life vs. Death.   A ray of hope appears in the rise of women to power, a revolution in spiritual values, and even a movement to protect the rights of animals—yet the world is gripped by the terror of nuclear holocaust as the superpowers wage a macabre battle of nerves that threatens to destroy us all.

I don't profess to be able to explain all this chaos, and I'm not even sure it will pass sometime. However, I do find some comfort in knowing that these are more than stray, random events without meaning, but profound patterns of change that are altering our world in a highly significant way. Such confusing, wrenching conflicts remind us that the coming era may not be "rational," "peaceful," or otherwise "superior." The essential difference is that the new epoch is producing unusually challenging problems along with equally powerful new capabilities to create a more intense level of "awareness" or "existence." In short, the future may be more satisfying in some ways, but it also seems destined to be far more difficult, especially during the present crucial period of transition. The German author Hermann Hesse described this painful disorientation that occurs when we lose our social bearings during times of great change:[1]

> *Human life is reduced to real suffering, to hell, only when . . . a whole generation is caught between two ages, two modes of life . . . it loses all power to understand itself and has no standard, no security, no simple acquiescence.*

Although modern nations are starting to form more sophisticated economic systems to cope with all this disorder, most people find it hard to shake a belief that life in the marketplace must unavoidably remain a brutal, dog-eat-dog affair. Unfortunately, the force of old habits and past experiences often seem to make the central tenets of freedom and cooperation which underlie the New Capitalism seem like unrealistic indulgences.

But the New Capitalism does not promise some Utopian future. On the contrary, it is precisely because prospects look exquisitely grim in the years ahead that such ideas are going to be badly needed. Modern economies are engulfed in exploding complexity and deeply felt political conflicts that are sure to grow even more disruptive, so progressive corporations are creating the New Capitalism because it is the best strategy for survival. Not only is this paradigm emerging because it is offers a practical way to manage disorder, but, in fact, it is the threat of disorder that drives such adaptive change. As we have seen throughout the book, institutions, like people, tend to avoid action until it is forced upon them, and the unrelenting crises of our time comprise the major force powering the development of a new economic system.

Futurists warned of the need to curb excessive consumption for decades, but it was only the stark necessity of crisis that finally brought about the beginning of a wiser form of growth: long gas lines drove car owners to favor small cars, pollution alerts produced demands for environmental controls, heart attacks created a taste for simple diets, and so forth. Likewise, many people had long urged flexible, participative forms of organization, but the harsh impetus of Japan's invasion into American markets was required to make these ideas a reality. And the concept of democratic governance remained a lofty ideal until potential bankruptcy forced Chrysler, Eastern, and other firms to begin extending control of big firms to employees.

It would be nice if people could behave in a more rational, anticipatory fashion, but that does not seem to be the way the world works. For the present at least, necessity remains the mother of invention. Severe crises are likely to continue threatening us for years, and it is in the crucible of such trials that a hard, enduring, new economic system is being forged to withstand the challenges of a disorderly future.

Even the solutions that are evolving will be difficult. More robust free enterprise will encourage innovation, but it will also mean failure for those unable to survive in a demanding world of intense competition. Likewise, democratic cooperation may foster more legitimate policy decisions, but at the cost of facing painful disagreements and hectic conflict. The New Capitalism is not evolving out of the hope for a benign world, therefore, but out of a struggle to meet the test of reality that an indifferent universe poses to challenge our development as individuals, organizations, and societies.

... the Meek Shall Inherit the Earth ...

The most difficult challenge is to overcome a conflict between left and right that polarizes the country. So severe is the problem that most people seem unable to listen to one another but are more intent on insisting their view is right. As a result, the doublespeak of 1984 that we feared has quietly crept into American life—not from Big Brother—but from our own distortion of the truth. A powerful missile escalating the threat of nuclear holocaust is called the "Peacemaker," tax increases are called "revenue enhancements," and dictatorships "moderately repressive regimes." A tragic example of this polarization is how the abortion of a living being has been called "pro-choice" by proponents—while "pro-life" advocates would outlaw abortion and thereby force women to undergo illegal operations in primitive conditions that threaten their lives.

These conflicts will persist as long as we maintain a conviction in the self-righteousness of our views, rather than admit to the doubt, uncertainty, and complexity that pervades today's world of half truths and compromise. When thinking about this problem, I find myself led to traditional old sayings and realizing how little we really understand the subtle meaning they hold for us today. For instance, the biblical prophecy that "The meek shall inherit the Earth" is usually considered ludicrous in today's high-stakes power games. The real message, however, is not that "weakness" will become widespread, but that a gentle humility is more honest and realistic than arrogant self-pride in a world far too mysterious to comprehend, much less control. Rather than being a sign of weakness, true humility is a virtue of strong people who do not feel the need to prove their might by dominating others. Thus, the meek shall inherit the Earth because they have the ability to grasp complexity, to integrate opposing views, to reconcile conflict, and other qualities that are becoming the essence of effective action in a difficult new era.

Today, the "meek" who are gaining influence are centrists who recognize that both the left and right wing dogmas represent complementary aspects of our common heritage. Whether the focus is on democratic or free enterprise values, the middle ground that unites us all is an overriding concern for improving the lives of people. So ultimately we are led to the conclusion that the goal of post-industrial economies should be—not wiser growth, flexible social structures, sharing power, or any of the other concerns discussed before—but to maximize human welfare. I know this sounds idealistic, especially because it is so easy to be cynical about such things in the hard world of commerce, but the many trends described in this book suggest that a basic reorientation of this type is well underway. As always, these commendable changes are occurring—not out of dedication to human values, although that may be one reason—but mainly because of the urgent need to tame a disorderly future.

A global crisis of resource scarcity, ecological decay, and international competition caused by the industrialization of a planet teeming with people is forcing the automation of factories and offices, an acceleration of science, careful management of natural resources, and client-driven institutions—producing a new form of smart growth that focuses on improving the quality of life and human well-being.

Survival in this complex era now demands decentralized organizations, self-managed ventures, entrapreneurship, profit sharing, participative management, and employee rights—thereby restructuring institutions to offer freedom and opportunities for developing the creative potential of their members.

Growing political conflict among differing economic actors is forcing institutions to pursue multiple goals that integrate the investor's profit, the worker's job benefits, the consumer's product value, and other economic interests—which are all human goals that make up the broader social welfare.

Such trends show that the idea of human-centered institutions is not as unlikely as it may first appear, and, in fact, many authorities have noted a surge of interest in "humanistic capitalism," "people's capitalism," and related concepts. Business author Milton Moskowitz claims, "Capitalism and Humanism are converging." The same theme is emerging in the media. Advertisers are no fools, so now commercials play up serving people because the concept has become a central cultural norm that sells: IBM—"Helping put information to work for people;" Giant Food—"The people who care;" and even ITT, the former archetype of "bad business," now proclaims—"The best ideas are the ideas that help people."[2]

Human values are as old as civilization, and the reason we are in such trouble these days is that we have been cut adrift from our moorings to this great heritage. Blake put it simply but perfectly long ago: "Put man at the center of all things." The major weakness of the Old Capitalism was that it lost its former social purpose, while today the power of human values is driving a paradigm shift in economics. Tom Peters, co-author of *In Search of Excellence*, claims, "The No. 1 managerial problem in America is, quite simply, managers who are out of touch with their people and out of touch with their customers," while social scientist Irving Kristol noted, "The common sense of the American people has been outraged . . . by the persistent un-wisdom of their elected officials." Kristol summed up the change:[3]

> *There is a powerful moral impulse behind the new [humanistic] economics, and an equally powerful moral revulsion against contemporary capitalist society.*

The transformation to a truly humane society based on institutions oriented to serve the needs of people is so profound that it would be revolutionary. It would constitute what John D. Rockefeller III called a "Second American Revolution" that fully implements the original intentions of the First American Revolution. The first revolution transferred power from the English monarchy to form the beginnings of a democracy, although society was still controlled by aristocrats and property owners. Later, scholars like James Burnham observed that a "Managerial Revolution" had moved power lower still to the professional managers of big organizations that dominate society. Now a Second American Revolution may complete this historic trend by transferring power once again, although this time from the "ruling class" of today—the business executives, politicians, labor leaders, professors, physicians, judges, generals, media stars, and priests who control major institutions in a quasi-dictatorial manner. Journalist J. F. ter Horst noted:[4]

> There is a radicalism abroad in America these days that is reminiscent of the spirit that gave birth to the Declaration of Independence . . . Everywhere we look, our venerated institutions are under attack for lack of performance. . . . The goal is nothing less than to recapture the country from big government, big business, and big brother.

Something new seems to be happening since the information age dawned a few years ago. All of the contemporary upheavals in science, economics, and values indicate that the power latent in the human potential is coming to life, activated by the electrifying force of information speeding through the world at an increasing rate. One significant sign occurred in 1984 when the Catholic Bishops of the United States issued a controversial pastoral letter that took a position on economics for the first time:[5]

> The experiment in political democracy carried out by America's founders [provided] civic and political rights in our nation. The time has come for a similar experiment in economic democracy . . . America needs a new experiment in cooperation and collaboration to renew a sense of solidarity, enhance participation, and broaden the sharing of responsibility in economic society.

If this revolution succeeds, the results could be so great that we can only speculate on what may occur, but a major change should be to make human character "complete" or "whole." The economic system of today typically produces child-like adults because it fosters dependence on higher authorities: submissive employees, indulgent overconsumers hypnotized by extravagant advertising, helpless poor served by a welfare state, and other limited social beings that populate an immature society. In place of this crippling dependency, a human-centered economic system should produce more rounded person-alities as people are required to take responsibility for their lives under the free enterprise ethic, and as they are provided the support needed to do so through the democratic ethic—balance.

In fact, such changes seem to be beginning as a "New Populism" emerges combining both left and right wing ideals: community, freedom, equality, individuality, social welfare, and other humanistic values now spreading through both the conservative and liberal camps. Slowly but surely, power is being taken by the meek whom institutions should serve. Employees are sharing management decisions, customers are insisting on value and service, citizens are demanding accountability of their government, patients are assuming responsibility for their health care, and many other humble, formerly powerless groups are moving to gain control over their lives. The spirit of this movement is best captured by the popular phrase, "People should not work for the system, the system should work for people."[6]

As we've noted before, rather than harming those in power the effect should be to "liberate" the ruling managerial class as well. Most executives today suffer from stress, loneliness, anxiety, and other maladies resulting from the way power isolates them from people. Human-centered institutions would place authorities in a far more reasonable role in which they assist their employees, clients, and the community in helping *themselves*—becoming what Robert Greenleaf called "servant leaders"—and thereby rejoin the mainstream of humanity.[7]

This reoriented economic order may solve some of the most towering problems of our time that seem so impossible because they stem from deep structural faults in the present system. The economic crisis should pass as automation eliminates routine jobs to produce a socially oriented economy that greatly increases productivity, improves the standard of living, and ameliorates pollution and other troublesome impacts. Capital, hi-tech capabilities, and the vast unused talent of our dynamic, inventive culture would then be freed to create robust growth serving higher needs and providing a fulfilling work life.

A people-based economy may also resolve the budget deficits that haunt government. The problem does not seem amenable to tinkering with tax rates or spending cuts because it reflects a structural imbalance in which the demand for public services exceeds the resources people are willing to provide the government sector. However, the shift to a human-centered economy may provide a solution over the long-term because it encourages individuals to look after their own interests instead of being dependent on government. For instance, we showed that a socially responsive form of business is more productive and it would alleviate the social costs that burden society, such as unemployment, poverty, and the like, thereby providing a feasible alternative to the welfare state.

It is even possible that the legitimacy of a human form of capitalism may in time resolve the global conflict with socialism, as we saw, diminishing the enormous cost and threat of all this hostility.

... Sometime, Somewhere, Somehow.

All these gains are possible, but the main barrier between the problems of today and the promises of the future is our prevailing beliefs. The underlying premise of this book is that the most difficult challenge Americans face is not to alter the tax system, improve technology, revise organizational structures, and other such moves, although these are essential, but to change the way we view the world. I am constantly astonished at how ferociously people will defend concepts of the Old Capitalism, even though they may be clearly inadequate, which reminds us of the intrinsic resistance to paradigm shifts. Shedding these old myths in favor of something like the New Capitalism is roughly comparable to the intellectual trauma people once faced in accepting the reality that the earth is round, that it revolves about the sun, that humans evolved from lower species, that there exists an inner world of the subconscious, that manned flight is possible, and other new ideas that challenged old beliefs.

Today, Americans are being forced to make a similar leap in logic and faith to see the almost obvious but extremely well-disguised reality that business is not powered by money but by **people**. This inward shift in awareness would then lead to the outward political changes needed to bring about the Second American Revolution, and thereby convert the economic crisis from a difficult problem into a fortunate opportunity. We couldn't take this unusual step earlier because the transition to an information age had not yet begun, values hadn't changed, and there was no pressing urgency. But now the conditions are ripe, so procrastination must yield to necessity by striking new paths into dimly lit regions of the American experience. In a passage on his memorial, Thomas Jefferson long ago envisioned the need:

> *I am not an advocate of frequent changes . . . but laws and institutions must go hand in hand with the progress of the human mind. As that becomes more developed, more enlightened, as new discoveries are made . . . and manners and opinions change . . . institutions must advance also to keep pace with the times.*

What is most remarkable about our time is the enormous difference between this imminent transformation into a knowledge-based society versus our origins in medieval Europe, and the even more stunning contrast to the beginnings of civilization in ancient times. After untold millennia of widespread deprivation, brutality, and ignorance, humans are poised to step into a world of unprecedented beneficence, although it will be far more challenging and there will be occasional moments of terror as well. Toffler believes it will be "the first truly humane civilization in recorded history."[8] During all the confusion, doubt, conflict, and other obstacles that will block this passage into the future, Americans should feel fortunate to have inherited the most powerful instruments yet devised to guide societies through such change, the principles of democracy and free enterprise that founded the nation.

The great irony is that, behind all the fierce resistance, the everyday actions needed to create this new social order are not very heroic but involve little more than encouraging people to work toward their enlightened self-interest. If investors, customers, employees, citizens, managers, executives, politicians and others simply pursued their concerns together in a spirit of mutual understanding, then all of the future developments described in this book would likely become a widespread reality.

Beyond all these logical arguments, however, the transition to this more sophisticated economy will occur only when people are prepared to undertake such an existential step. Despite the present forces of change urging us to a new stage in history, despite the fact that an information age requires this type of economic system, despite its power for containing the disorder that will arise, despite a popular movement to channel political energy in this direction—

despite all such valid reasons—there remains a serious possibility that these difficult changes will not be taken seriously, or possibly they will be adopted in some marginal, distorted fashion. Might Americans pass up this unusual opportunity to realize the potential of their ideals?

Obviously, nobody really can know when, where, or how the move to a new economic system will occur because the future flows from a mysterious juncture of human actions and unpredictable events, so it is likely to take some surprising turns ahead. But we've seen how broad patterns stand out in the long trend of social evolution. In fact, I am amazed at how accurately and rapidly all this has unfolded as predicted. Only a few years ago people reacted with strong disbelief at the prospect of "home computers," "intrapreneurs," and "participative democracy," yet now these "outlandish" ideas are becoming commonplace.

From a strictly objective, scientific view, it seems fairly certain that technological change is leading roughly along the path outlined here, and so something resembling the New Capitalism should appear within a decade or so. Mendelev's understanding of the Periodic Table of Elements accurately predicted the discovery of physical elements that occupied feasible niches in atomic structure, and Arthur C. Clarke forcasted the development of earth satellites to fill an open niche in spaceflight. Likewise, there exists an empty niche for this more productive, more civilized form of political economy, and the main question is which corporations and nations will be first to develop it—sometime, somewhere, somehow.

However, I hope this book has convincingly shown that the transition to a New Capitalism is already well underway— spreading right now in the late 1980s as an economic renaissance grows, led right here by progressive corporations in the United States, and inspired right out of our heritage to perfect a unique new blend of cooperation and competition. While the outcome may be uncertain, I think America is about to make another major contribution to the world by creating a prototype of the political economy needed to manage the information age, a system of Democratic Free Enterprise.

References

CHAPTER 1

1. *Statistical Abstract of the United States* (U.S. Government Printing Office, 1985).

2. Kenneth Clark, *Civilization* (New York: Harper & Row, 1970). Max Weber, *The Protestant Ethic and the Spirit of Capitalism* (New York: Scribner's, 1958). For authoritative histories, see Reinhard Bendix, *Work and Authority in Industry* (New York: Harper & Row, 1956), and Ralph Henry Gabriel, *The Course of American Democratic Thought* (New York: Ronald, 1956).

3. Rockefeller is quoted in Ralph Henry Gabriel, *American Democratic Thought*. The Coolidge speech was delivered to the Society of American Newspaper Editors, *The New York Times* (January 18, 1925).

4. Schlesinger, "American Politics on a Darkling Plain," *The Wall Street Journal* (March 16, 1982). *Time* (April 21, 1980).

5. "The Reindustrialization of America," *BusinessWeek* (June 30, 1980).

6. "Shifting Strategies," *The Wall Street Journal* (August 12, 1985).

7. Alfred L. Malabre Jr., "Tracking a Trend," *The Wall Street Journal* (May 13, 1981).

8. See Fred C. Allvine and Fred A. Tarpley, *The New State of the Economy* (Cambridge, MA: Winthrop, 1977). Quotes are from: "Consumers are Still Playing it Safe," *BusinessWeek* (April 25, 1983); "Balky Customers Sap Japan's Economic Growth," *The Wall Street Journal* (April 29, 1982); Art Pine, "Continental Gloom," *The Wall Street Journal* (May 10, 1982).

9. "America's High-Tech Crisis," *BusinessWeek* (March 11, 1985).

10. Robert Dunn, "Bye-Bye, Supply-Side," *The Washington Post* (July 30, 1985).

11. Ward Morehouse and David Dembo, *The Underbelly of the U.S. Economy* (Special Report # 3, Council on International and Public Affairs, May 1985).

12. Eckstein is quoted from "Economists See Votes in Reaganomics," *The Wall Street Journal* (October 10, 1983). The Urban Institute study is reported by John L. Palmer and Isable V. Sawhill, *The Reagan Record* (Boston: Ballinger, 1984). Harvey Brenner, *Estimating the Effects of Economic Change on National Health and Social Well-Being* (U.S. Government Printing Office).

13. Edward Dennison, *Accounting for Slower Economic Growth in the 1970's* (Washington, DC: Brookings Institution, 1979).

14. See Arthur M. Okun, *Prices and Quantities* (Washington, DC: Brookings Institution, 1981), John Kenneth Galbraith, *Money* (Boston: Houghton Mifflin, 1975), and John Case, *Understanding Inflation* (New York: Morrow, 1981). Lasch, *The Culture of Narcissism* (New York: Warner, 1979). Kraft, "Two Kinds of Greed," *The Washington Post* (March 11, 1984).

15. Stockman is quoted by Hobart Rowen, "Stockman: Records and Epitaph," *The Washington Post* (July 11, 1985).

16. Stein, *Presidential Economics* (New York: Simon & Schuster, 1984). The views of business executives are reported by Mike Connelly, "Executives Say Size of U.S. Deficit Is Most Serious Economic Problem," *The Wall Street Journal* (January 12, 1984). Charles Mathias, "We're Ignoring the Outside World," *The Washington Post* (January 22, 1984). "What the Supply-Siders Are Recommending Now," *Fortune* (April 2, 1984).

17. "America," *The Washington Post* (October 27, 1982).

18. Lee E. Preston, "Meso-Economics: Analysis and Policy," (Presented at the AFEE meeting in San Francisco, December 1983).

19. Daniel Bell, *The Coming of Post-Industrial Society* (New York: Basic, 1973), p. 162. Joseph Kraft, "The Polish Season," *The Washington Post* (December 25, 1980).

20. "The Harris Survey" (December 17, 1984). Other studies have been conducted by George Gallup, Opinion Research Corporation, Seymour Lipset and William Schneider, *The Confidence Gap* (New York: Free, 1983), and Anthony Sampson, *The Changing Anatomy of Britain* (New York: Random, 1983). These polls all show similar results, although some data tend to be higher because of scaling differences, averaging in the range of 30 to 40 percent for all institutions. Results of the Harris poll are presented here because only Harris has been collecting such data longer than 1973 and for all major institutions.

21. Byrom's quote appeared in "A New Era For Management," *BusinessWeek*, (April 25, 1983), p. 82. Reich, *The Next American Frontier* (New York: Times, 1983), p. 119.

22. Daniel Yankelovich and Bernard Lefkowitz, "The New American Dream," *The Futurist* (August 1980) Vol. XIV, No. 4. Also see Murray Weidenbaum, *Business, Government, and the Public Interest* (Englewood Cliffs, NJ: Prentice-Hall, 1981).

23. Kristol, "Some Doubts About 'De-Regulation'," *The Wall Street Journal* (October 20, 1975).

24. Martin C. Schnitzer, *Contemporary Government and Business Relations* (Chicago: Rand McNally, 1978).

25. Ewing, "The Corporation as Public Enemy No. 1," *Saturday Review* (January 21, 1978).

26. Stuart Auerbach, "Steel Industry Pushes for Quotas," *The Washington Post*. Young, "Global Competition," *California Management Review* (Spring 1985). On the profits of U.S. business, see Peter Drucker, *Managing in Turbulent Times* (New York: AMACOM, 1980). Douglas Sease, "New Inroads," *The Wall Street Journal* (March 29, 1985). "The Reindustrialization of America," p. 58.

27. The businessman is quoted in Leonard Silk and David Vogel, *Ethics and Profits* (New York: Simon & Schuster, 1976), p. 34. Jones' comment was reported by Laura Landro, "Electric Switch," *The Wall Street Journal* (July 12, 1982).

28. See "Who's Excellent Now?" *BusinessWeek* (November 5, 1984) documenting the decline of many companies that were in the famous Peters and Waterman best seller, *In Search of Excellence*.

29. Norman C. Miller, "Union Decline," *The Wall Street Journal* (February 22, 1979). Martha M. Hamilton, "Corporate Accountability," *The Washington Post* (March 8, 1981).

30. Geneen is quoted from William F. Mueller, "The Social Control of Economic Power," in Frank J. Bonnello and Thomas R. Swartz (eds.), *Alternative Directions in Economic Policy* (Notre Dame, IN: University of Notre Dame Press, 1978), p. 132.

31. Mancur Olsen, *The Rise and Decline of Nations* (New Haven, CT: Yale, 1983); Hazel Henderson, "The Entropy State," *Planning Review*, Vol. 2, No. 3 (April/ May 1974). Also see John Lukacs, *Outgrowing Democracy* (New York: Doubleday, 1984).

32. Caddell was quoted in "The Tranquillity Trap," *Newsweek* (April 2, 1984). The other quotes are from Alan L. Otten, "Opinion Analysts View Americans as Troubled and Looking Inward," *The Wall Street Journal* (August 4, 1978).

33. Bell and Kristol, *The Crisis in Economic Theory* (New York: Basic, 1981). Robert J. Samuelson, "Outmoded Ideas Add to Political Problems," *The Washington Post* (November 2, 1982).

34. See George Steiner, *Business and Society* (New York: Random, 1971). Edward R. Tufte, *Political Control of the Economy* (Princeton, NJ: Princeton University Press, 1980).

35. Donella H. Meadows et al., *The Limits to Growth* (Washington, DC: Potomac Associates, 1972). See Herman Kahn and Julian Simon, *The Resourceful Earth* (New York: Basil Blackwell, 1984); Herman Daly, *Steady-State Economics* (San Francisco: Freeman, 1977); and Kenneth D. Wilson, *Changing Prospects for Growth* (New York: Praeger, 1977).

36. The World Bank, *Poverty and Human Development* (Washington, DC: Oxford University Press, 1980) p. 63.

37. Estimates of a 10-fold increase in growth have been made by Herbert Robinson, "Can the World Stand Higher Productivity and Incomes?" *The Futurist* (October 1977), and Jay Forrester, "Counterintuitive Behavior of Social Systems," *Technology Review* (January 1971). Future levels of pollution and energy use are from *Energy Productivity* (Worldwatch Institute, 1985).

38. Daniel Yankelovich, "The New American Dream," *The Futurist* (August 1980). Patrick Sullivan, "John Paul Lashes Out at American Way of Greed," *New York Post* (October 3, 1979).

39. See Daniel Wren, *The Evolution of Management Thought* (New York: Ronald, 1972).

40. See Michel Crozier, *The Bureaucratic Phenomenon* (Chicago: University of Chicago, 1964), or more recently, Henry Tosi et al., *Management* (New York: Wiley, 1982). Robert Greenberger, "How Burnout Affects Corporate Managers," *The Wall Street Journal* (April 23, 1981). For a candid account, see J. Patrick Wright, *On A Clear Day You Can See General Motors* (Gross Pointe, MI: Wright, 1979).

41. Herbert Kaufman, *Are Government Organizations Immortal?* (The Brookings Institution, 1976). Eliot Richardson, "The Maze of Social Programs," *The Washington Post* (January 21, 1973). Pete Earley, "Grace Report On Efficiency Hits Congress," *The Washington Post* (November 10, 1983).

42. Thurow, "Why Productivity Fails," *Newsweek* (August 24, 1982).

43. See Clark Kerr and Jerome M. Rosow, *Work in America: The Decade Ahead* (New York: Van Nostrand Reinhold, 1979).

44. See Charles Lindblom, *Politics and Markets* (New York: Basic, 1980). Arthur S. Miller, *The Modern Corporate State* (Westcourt, CT: Greenwood, 1976).

45. An interesting analogy can be made comparing the role of the entrepreneur to that of a farmer in an earlier age. Whereas the farmer raises crops, the businessperson "grows" capital. The higher the "yield" of profit, the faster the growth of capital. Nixon is quoted in William G. Capitman, *Panic in the Boardroom* (Garden City, NY: Anchor/Doubleday, 1975), p. 245.

46. Merrill Brown, "Pertschuk: White House Tilts Toward Big Business," *The Washington Post* (January 8, 1981).

47. See Joseph Schumpeter, *Capitalism, Socialism, and Democracy* (New York: Harper & Row, 1950). Martin C. Schnitzer, *Contemporary Government and Business Relations* (Chicago: Rand McNally, 1978).

48. Steven N. Brenner and Earl A. Mollander, *Harvard Business Review* (January–February, 1977).

49. See William Simon, *A Time for Truth* (New York: McGraw-Hill, 1978), and Milton Friedman, *Free to Choose* (New York: Avon, 1981). Import protections are reported by Tom Wasinger, "Fashioning An Industrial Relief Act," *The Wall Street Journal* (June 21, 1984).

50. Morgan is quoted in Edward H. Carr, *The New Society* (Boston: Beacon, 1957), p. 25.

51. Comments are reported by Hobart Rowen, "Airline Deregulation Comes Back to Haunt," *The Washington Post* (March 14, 1982); Albert R. Karr, "Airline Deregulation After Braniff's Fall," *The Wall Street Journal* (June 14, 1982); Hobart Rowen, "Deregulation: A Bankrupt Policy," *The Washington Post* (September 29, 1983).

52. See "Deregulating America," *BusinessWeek* (November 28, 1983), and "Did It Make Sense to Break-Up AT&T?," *BusinessWeek* (December 3, 1984).

53. Best is quoted in *The Wall Street Journal* (September 26, 1985).

54. Comments of Jones are reported by Art Pine, "An Era Ends at GE Company," *The Washington Post* (March 29, 1981).

55. See J. Peter Grace, "The Disincentivization of America," *The Wall Street Journal* (June 26, 1978), and James Lorrie, "The Second Great Crash," *The Wall Street Journal* (June 2, 1980).

56. Akio Morita is quoted by Hobart Rowen, "Economic Impact," *The Washington Post* (April 12, 1981).

57. Nicholas Von Hoffman, "Carter and the Client Syndrome," *The Washington Post* (February 2, 1977).

58. "No Sign of a Recession in Pay at the Top," *BusinessWeek* (May 10, 1982); "Executive Pay," *BusinessWeek* (May 7, 1984).

59. Professor Kotter's work is unpublished, but preliminary results were reported by Larry Kramer, "Harvard Checks on Class of '74," *The Washington Post* (June 10, 1979). Larsen and Rogers, *Silicon Valley Fever* (New York: Basic, 1984).

60. See Peter J. Frost et al., *Organizational Reality* (Glenview, IL: Scott Foresman, 1982).

61. DeLorean's comments are from Wright, *On A Clear Day*, p. 19.

62. "The Underground Economy's Hidden Force," *BusinessWeek* (April 5, 1982).

63. Drucker, *Toward the Next Economics* (New York: Harper & Row, 1981).

64. Anderson's comments are reported by Michael Schrage, "Blue Ribbon Panel Says U.S. Losing Ability to Compete," *The Washington Post* (May 16, 1983).

CHAPTER 2

1. Gilder, "Reagan Can Finish What JFK Started," *The Washington Post* (October 28, 1984).

2. Lodge, *The New American Ideology* (New York: Knopf, 1975).

3. Ward, *Progress for a Small Planet* (New York: Norton, 1979), pp. 1, 13.

4. Halal, "The Life Cycle of Evolution," *Technological Forecasting & Social Change* (forthcoming).

5. Bronowski, *The Ascent of Man* (New York: Little, Brown, 1973).

6. Bell, *The Coming of Post-Industrial Society*, (New York: Basic, 1973).

7. Thurow, "Why Productivity Fails," *Newsweek* (August 24, 1981).

8. A summary of estimates is provided by Lionel Fernandez, *Projections of Information Technology Employment to the Year 2000* (Doctoral Dissertation, American University, Washington, DC, 1977).

9. For a visionary forecast of these implications, see Teilhard de Chardin, *The Phenomenon of Man* (London: Collins/Fontana, 1955).

10. McLuhan, "Automation: Learning a Living," in Toffler (ed.), *The Futurists* (New York: Random, 1972), p. 66.

11. Servan-Schreiber, *The World Challenge* (New York: Simon & Schuster, 1980), p. 197. The figures on growth of the computer industry are from Ulric Weil, *Information Systems in the '80s* (Englewood Cliffs, NJ: Prentice-Hall, 1982); William Buckley, "Microcomputers Gaining Primacy," *The Wall Street Journal* (January 13, 1983); Bob Davis, "Computer Makers are Trying to Build All-in-One Machine," *The Wall Street Journal* (January 21, 1983); "Software," *BusinessWeek* (February 27, 1984).

12. Bernard Nossiter, "Economists Have Run Out of Ideas," *The Washington Post* (June 30, 1977).

13. "The New Corporate Elite," *BusinessWeek* (January 21, 1985).

14. See "Suddenly U.S. Companies are Teaming Up," *BusinessWeek* (July 11, 1983); "Cooperation, Not Conflict," *BusinessWeek* (April 29, 1982).

15. Drucker, *Toward the Next Economics* (New York: Harper & Row, 1981).

16. Kenneth Schwartz, "What Opinion Leaders Think," *The Wall Street Journal* (July 28, 1983).

17. Capra, *The Turning Point* (New York: Simon & Schuster, 1982).

18. Toffler, *The Third Wave* (New York: Bantam, 1980).

CHAPTER 3

1. James M. Perry, "Down and Out," *The Wall Street Journal* (January 20, 1983).

2. See Barry Bluestone and Bennett Harrison, *The Deindustrialization of America* (New York: Basic, 1982).

3. Quoted in Lewis Benton, *Management for the Future* (New York: McGraw-Hill, 1978), p. 239.

4. See Gary Gappert, *Post-Affluent America* (New York: New Viewpoints, 1979), p. xi; William Ophuls, "The Scarcity Society," *Harpers* (April 1974). The two executives are quoted in Joseph Kraft, "The Downsizing Decision," *The New Yorker* (May 5, 1980).

5. These changes are documented in Don Fabun, *Children of Change* (Beverly Hills, CA: Glencoe, 1969).

6. See Theodore Roszak, *The Making of a Counter-Culture* (Garden City, NY: Anchor, 1969); Charles Reich, *The Greening of America* (New York: Bantam, 1969); Jean François Revel, *Without Marx or Jesus: The New American Revolution Has Begun* (New York: Doubleday, 1971); John D. Rockefeller, III, *The Second American Revolution* (New York: Perennial/Harper, 1973).

7. Daniel Yankelovich, *The New Morality: A Profile of American Youth in the '70s* (New York: McGraw-Hill, 1974).

8. Louis Harris, "Many Americans Feel Quality of Life is Worsening," *The Washington Post* (November 21, 1977); "Deep Skepticism is Expressed About Un-

limited Economic Growth," *The Washington Post* (May 23, 1977); and "Youth Lifestyle of the 1960s Swimming Into Mainstream," *The Washington Post* (August 7, 1977).

9. Margot Hornblower et al., "Cathy Wilkerson: The Evolution of the Revolution," *The Washington Post* (July 15, 1980).

10. Tom Wolfe, *In Our Time* (New York: Farrar Straus Giroux, 1980).

11. See Daniel Bell, *The Cultural Contradictions of Capitalism* (New York: Basic, 1976), and Saul Bellow's acceptance speech for the Nobel Prize in Literature (1976).

12. Daniel Yankelovich and Bernard Lefkowitz, "The New American Dream," *The Futurist* (August 1980). Daniel Yankelovich, *New Rules* (New York: Random, 1981). Harris, "Deep Skepticism."

13. Harris, "Deep Skepticism."

14. Bill Abrams, "Pepsi Sociologists Detect New Mood," *The Wall Street Journal* (February 8, 1980).

15. Elgin, *Voluntary Simplicity* (New York: Morrow, 1981).

16. Nelson Foote, "From More to Better to Different to Less," *California Management Review* (Fall, 1978), Vol. 21, No. 1.

17. See "A Capital Crunch that Could Change an Industry," *BusinessWeek* (March 23, 1981).

18. Blaine Harden, "High-Tech Revolution in Robotics Under Way," *The Washington Post* (December 19, 1982). "The SpeedUp in Automation," *BusinessWeek* (August 3, 1981). Robert Ayres and Stephen Miller, *The Impact of Industrial Robots* (Pittsburg: Carnegie-Mellon University, 1981).

19. These examples are reported in William Chapman, "Japanese Open Offensive For Technological Gains With Robot Development," *The Washington Post* (October 30, 1980); Laura Landro, "GE Promotes Factory Automation," *The Wall Street Journal* (October 21, 1982); John Holusha, "The New Allure of Manufacturing," *The New York Times* (December 18, 1983).

20. David Barcomb, *Office Automation* (Bedford, ME: Digital Press, 1981); "A Productivity Revolution in the Service Sector," *BusinessWeek* (September 5, 1983); "The SpeedUp in Automation;" p. 58.

21. Joann S. Lublin, "Steel Collar Jobs," *The Wall Street Journal* (October 26, 1981); "The SpeedUp in Automation"; Sar A. Levitan and Clifford N. Johnson, "The Future of Work: Does It Belong to the Robots?," *Monthly Labor Review* (September 1982).

22. Alvin Toffler, *The Third Wave* (New York: Bantam, 1980), pp. 183, 185; Thomas Hout and George Stalk, "The Big Revolution on the Factory Floor," *The Wall Street Journal* (July 12, 1982).

23. Paul Ingrassia, "High-Tech Track," *The Wall Street Journal* (April 7, 1983).

24. Irving Canton, "Learning to Love the Service Economy," *Harvard Business Review* (May-June 1984).

25. Examples are drawn from: "New Forces Will Fuel Consumer Spending in the 1980s," *Business Tomorrow* (October 1980); "Computerized Training May

Finally Be About to Take Off," *BusinessWeek* (March 28, 1983); "For Profit Day-Care Chains Have Grown Into Big Business," *The Washington Post* (July 6, 1983); "The Robust New Business in Home Health Care," *BusinessWeek* (June 13, 1983); Jerry Knight, "Quality Inns Plans Mod Motel Suites," *The Washington Post* (June 15, 1983); "A Wizard's Plan for an Electronic University," *BusinessWeek* (March 19, 1984); Peter Drucker, "Our Entrepreneurial Economy," *Harvard Business Review* (January-February 1984).

26. John Young, "Global Competition," *California Management Review* (Spring, 1985). "A Computer Industry Pearl Harbor," *Technology Transfer News* (1983).

27. "America Rushes to High Technology for Growth," *BusinessWeek* (March 28, 1983).

28. As reported by Alvin Toffler, *The Third Wave*, p. 140.

29. Yoneji Masuda, *The Information Society* (Washington, DC: The World Future Society, 1981). Starr Roxanne Hiltz and Murray Turoff, *The Network Nation* (Reading, MA: Addison-Wesley, 1978).

30. "Computers that Speed the News of Science," *BusinessWeek* (January 25, 1982).

31. John Naisbitt, *Megatrends* (New York: Warner, 1982) p. 24. The effects of knowledge are described by Robert M. Solow, "Technical Change and the Aggregate Production Function," *Review of Economics and Statistics* (August 1957), Vol 39, and Peter Drucker, *The Age of Discontinuity*, (New York: Harper, 1968).

32. Information on scientific trends is from The National Research Council, *Science and Technology: A Five Year Outlook* (San Francisco: Freeman, 1979).

33. Jack Rothman, *Planning and Organizing for Social Change* (New York: Columbia University, 1974); Helmer, "Prospects of Technological Progress," in Alvin Toffler (ed.), *The Futurists* (New York: Random, 1972), p. 157; Walter Berns, "Congress is Saying, Give Peace a Grant," *The Wall Street Journal* (August 2, 1982).

34. "Superchips," *BusinessWeek* (June 10, 1985); "Chip Wars," *BusinessWeek* (May 23, 1983), p. 208; Jon Roland, "The Microelectronic Revolution," *The Futurist* (April 1979), p. 83; Edward Feigenbaum, *The Fifth Generation* (Reading, MA: Addison-Wesley, 1983); "Will Japan Leapfrog America on Superfast Computers?," *The Economist* (March 6, 1982); "The Wiring of Britain," *The Economist* (March 6, 1982).

35. Teilhard de Chardin, *The Phenomenon of Man* (London: Collins, 1955).

36. Peter F. Drucker, "The Innovative Company," *The Wall Street Journal* (February 26, 1982).

37. Barbara Ward, *Progress for a Small Planet* (New York: Norton, 1979), p. 36.

38. Daniel Yergin and Robert Stobaugh, *Energy Future* (New York: Ballantine, 1980); "Energy Guzzling: Most Consumers are Cured," *BusinessWeek* (April 4, 1983).

39. Christopher Flavin, "Photovoltaics," *The Futurist* (June 1983). David F. Salisbury, "Americans' First Choice: Solar Power," *The Washington Post* (April 25, 1981).

40. Murray, "The Impending Energy Crisis," *Newsweek* (June 10, 1985). *World Energy Outlook* (The International Energy Agency, 1982).

41. See Naisbitt, *Megatrends*, pp. 118–20; "Are Renewable, Solar-Based Energy Sources Surviving," *Energy* (1983); *Inform: The First Decade* (1983); and John Sawhill, "Transformed Utilities," *Harvard Business Review* (July-August, 1985).

42. See "Hazardous and Toxic Wastes," *Inform* (March-April 1983).

43. Marlin, "Corporate Social Performance," in Bradshaw and Vogel (eds.), *Corporations and Their Critics* (New York: McGraw-Hill, 1981), p. 167.

44. These examples are from Michael G. Royston, "Making Pollution Prevention Pay," *Harvard Business Review* (November-December, 1981); "The Coming Industrial Miracle," *U.S. News & World Report* (November 30, 1981); Barbara Ward, *Progress*; William Chandler, "Converting Garbage to Gold," *The Futurist* (February 1984).

45. Train is quoted in John H. Jennrich, "Keeping the Good Earth Clean," *Nation's Business* (December 1979).

46. The National Research Council, *Science and Technology.*

47. Eugene Carlson, "Some High-Tech Firms Have Made Inner-City Plants Work," *The Wall Street Journal* (April 27, 1982); "Jim Rouse's Revolution in Housing for the Poor," *BusinessWeek* (March 28, 1983).

48. William C. Norris, "Business Opportunities in Addressing Societal Problems," in Bradshaw and Vogel, *Corporations*, p. 105.

49. Philip Kotler, "What Consumerism Means for Retailers," *Harvard Business Review* (May-June 1972).

50. Louis Harris, "Quality of Life."

51. Martin C. Schnitzer, *Contemporary Government and Business Relations* (Chicago: Rand McNally, 1978), Ch. 13; Arthur Elkins and Dennis Callaghan, *A Managerial Odyssey: Problems in Business and its Environment* (Reading, MA: Addison-Wesley, 1981).

52. Stephen A. Greyser, "Americans' Attitudes Toward Consumerism," *Marketing Science Institute Special Report # 77-113* (Cambridge, MA: Marketing Science Institute, 1977); Louis Harris Associates, *Consumerism at the Crossroads* (Sentry Insurance Company, 1977); James J. Kilpatrick, "No Cheers for American Business," *The Washington Star* (June 17, 1979); Molly Sinclair, "Consumer Unhappiness Growing," *The Washington Post* (February 17, 1983).

53. Bill Abrams, "Research Suggests Consumers Will Increasingly Seek Quality," *The Wall Street Journal* (October 15, 1981); E. F. Schumacher, *Small Is Beautiful* (New York: Harper & Row, 1973).

54. David Garvin, "Quality On the Line," *Harvard Business Review* (September-October 1983).

55. Esther Peterson, "Consumerism as a Retailer's Asset," *Harvard Business Review* (May-June 1974); Richard T. Hise et al., "The Corporate Consumer Affairs Effect," *MSU Business Topics* (Summer, 1978); "Disgruntled Customers Finally Get a Hearing," *BusinessWeek* (April 21, 1975).

56. Caroline E. Mayer, "FTC's Role In Ad Cases Stirs Debate," *The Washington Post* (March 28, 1982); Alan R. Andreasen and Arthur Best, "Consumers Complain—Does Business Respond?" *Harvard Business Review* (July-August, 1977).

57. Elizabeth Gatewood and Archie B. Carroll, "The Anatomy of Corporate Social Response," *Business Horizons*, Vol. 24, No. 5 (September/October 1981).

58. "Making Service a Potent Marketing Tool," *BusinessWeek* (June 11, 1984).

59. Examples are from Thomas Peters and Robert Waterman, *In Search of Excellence: Lessons from America's Best Run Companies* (New York; Harper & Row, 1982); "Marketing: The New Priority," *BusinessWeek* (November 21, 1983); "Making Service a Potent Marketing Tool," *BusinessWeek* (June 11, 1984).

60. "Making Service" *BusinessWeek* (June 11, 1984).

61. Salvatore F. Divita, "Marketing Quality Control," *California Management Review* (Summer, 1978), p. 75; Ronald Kessler, "Insurance: Costly Enigma," *The Washington Post* (March 20, 1983).

62. Data on car costs can be found in Charles G. Burck, "A Comeback Decade for the American Car," *Fortune* (June 2, 1980). The executive is quoted from "Why Detroit is Not Selling Cars," *BusinessWeek* (August 30, 1982).

63. James T. Yenkel, "Wheels," *The Washington Post* (February 5, 1982).

64. Douglas B. Feaver, "Car Book Is to Have Short Run," *The Washington Post* (August 2, 1981).

65. Hirotaka Takeuchi and J. A. Quelch, "Quality is More than Making a Good Product, *Harvard Business Review* (July-August 1983).

66. Mary Gardiner Jones, "The Consumer Affairs Office," *California Management Review* (Summer, 1978).

67. "Listening to the Voice of the Marketplace," *BusinessWeek* (February 21, 1983); Bill Abrams, "More Firms Use 800 Numbers," *The Wall Street Journal*; "Lauder's Success Formula," *BusinessWeek* (September 26, 1983); Peters and Waterman, *In Search of Excellence*; "Marketing: The New Priority," *BusinessWeek*.

68. *Technology Review* (January 1978); Robert E. Vanderbeek, "Social Responsibility Can be Profitable Too," *Response*, Vol. 9, No. 3 (May 1980).

69. McFarlan, "Information Technology Changes the Way You Compete," *Harvard Business Review* (May-June 1984).

70. Theodore Levitt, "After the Sale Is Over," *Harvard Business Review* (September-October 1983).

71. Quoted in Jean-Jacques Servan-Schreiber, *The World Challenge* (New York: Simon & Schuster, 1980), p. 186.

72. Severyn T. Bruyn, *The Social Economy* (New York: Wiley, 1977), p. xi.

73. Kenneth Wilson, *Prospects for Growth* (New York: Praeger, 1977). For a good survey, see John Applegath, *Human Economy: A Bibliography* (Amherst, MA: The Human Economy Center, 1981).

74. George Steiner, "An Overview of the Changing Business Environment," *1979 AACSB Conference* (AACSB, 1980). Fuller is quoted from Barbara Marx Hubbard, "Critical Path to an All-Win World," *The Futurist* (June 1981), p. 35.

CHAPTER 4

1. John Kenneth Galbraith, *The New Industrial State* (New York: Signet, 1967).

2. "A New Era for Management," *BusinessWeek* (April 25, 1983).

3. *Ibid*, p. 54.

4. "A New World Dawns," *Time* (January 3, 1983).

5. For an excellent assessment of the impact of the automobile, see Edward Cornish, *The Study of the Future* (Washington, DC: World Future Society, 1977), p. 7.

6. Lester Brown, "The Automobile's Future," *The Futurist* (June 1984).

7. Peter Drucker, "Managing the Information Explosion," *The Wall Street Journal* (April 10, 1980).

8. Alvin Toffler, *The Third Wave* (New York: Bantam, 1980), p. 194.

9. Robert Guenther, "Office-Building Values Fall," *The Wall Street Journal* (March 16, 1983); "Office Glut," *The Wall Street Journal* (October 7, 1983).

10. See John Naisbitt, *Megatrends* (New York: Warner Books, 1982) p. 100; "The Mass Market Is Splitting Apart," *Fortune* (November 28, 1984); and *BusinessWeek* (November 21, 1983).

11. Beer, *Platform for Change* (New York: Wiley, 1975).

12. Russell Baker, "What Did You Do Today," *The New York Times*.

13. Beitzel's comments were made to the U.S. Senate Committee on Rules and Administration (December 8, 1983). Also see Daniel Bell, *The Coming of Post-Industrial Society* (New York: Basic, 1973), p. 137.

14. Douglas Davis, "The Soft Sell," *Newsweek* (July 23, 1973).

15. "Business is Turning Data Into a Potent Strategic Weapon," *BusinessWeek* (August 22, 1983), and "Information Power," *BusinessWeek* (October 14, 1985).

16. Adam Osborne, *Running Wild: The Next Industrial Revolution* (Berkeley, California: Osborne/McGraw-Hill, 1979), pp. i, ix.

17. See Daniel Bell, *The Coming*, Ch. 31. Sinclair is quoted by Peter Osnos, "Hi-tech Wizard Sees Brave New World in '90s," *The Washington Post* (March 6, 1983).

18. The quote is from the Berkeley Independent Gazette, and was reprinted on the Electronic Information Exchange System (EIES) by Bill Spencer on October 31, 1979.

19. "A New Era for Management," *BusinessWeek* (April 25, 1983), p. 53.

20. See Alfred Chandler, *Strategy and Structure* (Cambridge, MA: MIT Press, 1962). C. West Churchman, "A Philosophy for Complexity," in Harold A. Linstone and W. H. Clive Simmonds (eds.), *Futures Research: New Directions* (Reading, MA: Addison-Wesley, 1977), p. 83.

21. Jay Galbraith, *Designing Complex Organizations* (Reading, MA: Addison-Wesley, 1973); W. R. Ashby, *An Introduction to Cybernetics* (New York: Wiley, 1952); Alvin Toffler, *The Third Wave* (New York: Bantam, 1980), p. 167.

22. "A New Era for Management," *BusinessWeek* (April 25, 1983), p. 61.

23. Marilyn Ferguson, *The Aquarian Conspiracy* (Los Angeles: J. P. Tarcher, 1980), p. 213; John Naisbitt, *Megatrends*, p. 198.

24. See Herbert S. Drobnick et al., *The Emerging Network Marketplace* (Norwood, NJ: Ablex, 1981); Jessica Lipnack and Jeffrey Stamps, *Networking: The First Report and Directory* (Garden City, NY: Doubleday/Dolphin, 1982). Starr Roxanne Hiltz and Murray Turoff, *The Network Nation* (Reading, MA: Addison-Wesley, 1978), p. xxviii. James Ogle, "Will Computers Destroy the Soviet System?" *The Washington Post* (November 1, 1981).

25. Wriston is quoted in Stanley Davis and Paul Lawrence, *Matrix* (Reading, MA: Addison-Wesley, 1977), pp. 3, vi.

26. My study is reported in *Strategic Planning in Major U.S. Corporations* (General Motors Report, 1980); and "Strategic Management: The State-of-the-Art & Beyond," *Technological Forecasting & Social Change* (May 1984). GE is quoted from Stanley M. Davis and Paul R. Lawrence, "Problems of Matrix Organizations," *Harvard Business Review* (May-June 1978) pp. 131–2.

27. "An About Face in TI's Culture," *BusinessWeek* (July 25, 1982); "Texas Instruments Cleans Up Its Act," *BusinessWeek* (September 19, 1983), p. 57.

28. Levison, *The Decentralized Company* (New York: AMACOM, 1983), pp. 20–1.

29. Thomas J. Peters and Robert H. Waterman, *In Search of Excellence* (New York: Harper & Row, 1982), pp. 42–4.

30. "The Wisdom of Peter Drucker," *MBA* (October 1976), p. 62.

31. "A New Era for Management," *BusinessWeek* (April 25, 1983), pp. 55–6. James G. Affleck, "The Constructive Orchestration of Chaos," in Lewis Benton (ed.), *Management for The Future* (New York: McGraw-Hill, 1978), p. 3.

32. William Coggin, "How the Multidimensional Structure Works at Dow Corning," *Harvard Business Review* (January-February 1973), p. 142.

33. For a good example of the effectiveness of decentralized approachs, see Raymond Van Zelst, "Sociometrically Selected Work Teams Increase Production," *Personnel Psychology*, Vol. 5, No. 3 (Autumn 1952). These studies are summarized in Jay Galbraith and Daniel Nathanson, *Strategy Formulation* (St. Paul, MN: West, 1978), pp. 56–7. Also see Karl E. Weick, "Organization Design: Organizations as Self-Designing Systems," *Organizational Dynamics* (Autumn 1977); and Russell L. Ackoff and Fred E. Emery, *On Purposeful Systems* (Chicago: Aldine-Atherton, 1972). Peter B. Vaill is quoted from, "The Purposing of High Performing Systems," *Organizational Dynamics* (Autumn 1982).

34. Richard Cornuelle, *Demanaging America* (New York: Random, 1975), p. 87.

35. "A New Era for Management," *BusinessWeek* (April 25, 1983), pp. 50–54, and (Sept 16, 1985), p. 34.

36. Herbert Simon, "The Corporation: Will It Be Managed by Machines?" in Melvin Anshen and George Leland Bach (Eds.), *Management and Corporations 1985* (New York: McGraw-Hill, 1960); Warren Bennis, *Beyond Bureaucracy* (New York: McGraw-Hill, 1966); Peter Townsend, *Up the Organization* (New York: Fawcett, 1978).

37. The DEC example was reported in my study, reference No. 26. The Dow Corning example is described by Coggins, *Multidimensional Structure at Dow Corning*, p. 142.

38. These examples are draw from "The Silicon Valley Style," *Newsweek* (June 8, 1981); "Defying the Recession," *BusinessWeek* (March 22, 1982); "TRW Leads a Revolution in Managing Technology," *BusinessWeek* (November 15, 1982), pp. 126–7; "A New Era For Management," *BusinessWeek* (April 25, 1983); Levison, *The Decentralized Company*; "A Xerox Cost Center Imitates a Profit-Center," *Harvard Business Review* (May-June, 1985); and my study reported earlier.

39. Alvin Toffler, *The Third Wave*, Ch. 19; Jerome Rosow and Robert Zager, "Punch Out the Time Clocks," *Harvard Business Review* (March–April, 1983).

40. "The Potential for Telecommuting," *BusinessWeek* (January 26, 1981); Alvin Toffler. *The Third Wave*, p. 196.

41. "The Potential for Telecommuting," *BusinessWeek* (January 26, 1981), p. 68; "Communications is Dealing Business a Potent Hand," *BusinessWeek* (October 24, 1983; Charles Norris, "Office Automation," *Computer Decision* (April 1981); Jeremy Main, "Work Won't Be the Same Again," *Fortune* (June 28, 1982); Robert Johansen and Christine Bullen, "What to Expect From Teleconferencing," *Harvard Business Review* (March-April 1984).

42. Murray Turoff's comment was sent via the EIES system (January 13, 1979). The Bell Labs experience was reported in Hiltz and Turoff, *The Network Nation*, p. 144. John DeButts, "The Management of Complexity," in Lewis Benton (ed.), *Management for the Future* (New York: McGraw-Hill, 1978), p. 82. Deal and Kennedy, *Corporate Cultures* (Reading, MA: Addison-Wesley, 1982).

43. Peters and Waterman, *In Search of Excellence*.

44. Examples are from "The Silicon Valley Style," *Newsweek* (June 8, 1981); Frederick C. Klein, "Manageable Size," *The Wall Street Journal* (February 5, 1982); Alvin Toffler, *The Third Wave*, p. 258; Erik Larson and Carrie Dolan, "Thinking Small," *The Wall Street Journal* (August 19, 1983); Marilyn Wilson, "Smokestack America," *Dun's Business Month* (July 1983).

45. "Small Is Beautiful Now in Manufacturing," *BusinessWeek* (October 22, 1984); Joel Kotkin and Don Gevirtz, "Why Entrepreneurs Trust No Politician," *The Washington Post* (January 16, 1983); Ann Hughey, "New MiniLabs Are Shaking Up Photo Business," *The Wall Street Journal* (August 19, 1982); Liz Roman Gallese, "New Little Breweries Cause Some Ferment in the Beer Business," *The Wall Street Journal* (March 15, 1983).

46. "The New Entrepreneurs," *BusinessWeek* (April 18, 1983); "Making a Mint Overnight," *Time* (January 23, 1984).

47. "The New Entrepreneurs," *BusinessWeek*.

48. *Ibid.*

49. *Ibid.*

50. Larson and Dolan, "Thinking Small."

51. Macrae, "Intrapreneur Now," *The Economist* (April 17, 1982), and "The Coming Entrepreneurial Revolution," *The Economist* (December 25, 1976). The GE executives are quoted in Laura Landro, "Electric Switch," *The Wall Street Journal* (July 12, 1982).

52. "Here Comes the 'Intrapreneur'," *BusinessWeek* (July 18, 1983); Jay W. Forrester, "A New Corporate Design," *Industrial Management Review* (July 1975), p. 824.

53. See Gifford Pinchot, *Intrapreneuring* (New York: Harper & Row, 1984). Examples are from Peters and Waterman, *In Search of Excellence*, p. 224; Robert Wood, "Every Employee an Entrepreneur," *Inc.* (March 1983); Sharon Nelton, "Finding Room for the Entrepreneur, *Nation's Business* (February 1984).

54. Geert Hofstede, "Cultural Dimensions for Project Management," *Proceedings of the 7th International World Congress on Project Management* (Copenhagen: The Danish Technical Press, 1982).

55. Peters and Waterman, *In Search of Excellence*, pp. 114, 205.

56. "Self-Employment: Promise or Threat?" *Goodmoney*, Vol. 1, No. 1 (January/February, 1983). Quotes are from "Worksteaders Clean Up," *Newsweek* (January 9, 1984); and "It's Rush Hour for Telecommuting," *BusinessWeek* (January 23, 1984).

57. Bill Huckabee, "New Retailer Competition Lurks in the Briarpatch Network," *Business Tomorrow* (June 1980).

58. Dean Robart, "Husband and Wife High-Tech Businesses Start Springing Up as the Industry Booms," *The Wall Street Journal* (September 17, 1982).

59. "IBM and Intel Link Up to Fend Off Japan," *BusinessWeek* (January 10, 1983); "IBM to Offer Version of an AT&T System," *The Wall Street Journal* (January 13, 1984).

60. Alvin Toffler, *The Third Wave*, p. 236.

61. J. Kenneth Benson, "The Interorganizational Network as a Political Economy," *Administrative Science Quarterly*, Vol. 20. No. 2 (June 1975), p. 229; William Evans, *Interorganizational Relations* (Pittsburgh: University of Pennsylvania Press, 1976), p. 12.

62. Lipnack and Stamps, *Networking Newsletter* (May 1984); Also see, Toffler, *The Third Wave*, pp. 322–6. Teilhard de Chardin, *The Phenomenon of Man* (London: Collins/Fontana, 1955). Marshall McLuhan, "Automation: Learning a Living," in Alvin Toffler (ed.), *The Futurists* (New York: Random, 1972), p. 62. Alvin Toffler, *The Third Wave*, p. 326.

63. William Ouchi, *Theory Z* (New York: Avon, 1981), p. 24. DEC is quoted from Peters and Waterman, *In Search of Excellence*, p. 16. See Thomas J. Allen and Stephan Cohen, "Information Flows in Research and Development Laboratories," *Administrative Science Quarterly* (March 1969); Arch Patton, "When Executives Bail Out to Move Up," *BusinessWeek* (September 13, 1982).

64. Stanley M. Davis and Paul R. Lawrence, *Matrix*.

65. Susan Helm, "A Review of Intrapreneurialism" (unpublished paper, George Washington University, 1982).

66. Earl C. Gottschalk, "Blocked Paths," *The Wall Street Journal* (October 22, 1981); "Baby Boomers Push for Power," *BusinessWeek* (July 2, 1984).

67. Peter Drucker, "Squeezing the Firm's Midriff Bulge," *The Wall Street Journal* (March 25, 1983).

68. Phavann Chhuan, Robert Lasken, Michael Mitchell, and Nancy Simmons, "A Study of Grapevine Communications Within Organizations" (unpublished paper, American University, 1976).

69. Linda Grant and Lois Timnick, "A Nightmare: Working for a 'Crazy' Boss," reported in *The Wall Street Journal* (September 19, 1980).

70. Schrank, *Ten Thousand Working Days* (Cambridge, MA: MIT Press, 1978).

71. Peters and Waterman, *In Search of Excellence*, p. 113.

72. Ouchi, *Theory Z*, p. 90; John Sears, "A Matter of Timing," *Washington Post* (October 9, 1980); Lewis Lapham, " . . . and a Feeling of Hope," *Washington Post* (January 1, 1983).

73. Virginia Hine, "Networks Empower Social Change," *Leading Edge Bulletin* (July 20, 1981).

74. "TRW Leads a Revolution in Managing Technology," *BusinessWeek* (November 15, 1982).

75. Harlan Cleveland, *The Future Executive* (New York: Harper & Row, 1972). p. 13.

76. "Break-Up Value," *BusinessWeek* (July 8, 1985), "The Urge to Unmerge," *BusinessWeek* (May 2, 1983).

77. Drucker, "Playing in the Information-Based Orchestra," *The Wall Street Journal* (June 4, 1985).

78. Michael Schrage, "McGraw-Hill Blends Print, Computer," *The Washington Post* (October 8, 1984).

79. "A New Era For Management," *BusinessWeek* (April 25, 1983), p. 70; Jeremy Main, "Work Won't Be the Same Again."

80. Michael Maccoby, *The Leader* (New York: Simon & Schuster, 1981), pp. 220–1; Harlan Cleveland, *The Future Executive*, p. 68.

81. See Marilyn Ferguson, *Aquarian*.

82. "A Catholic Bill of Rights," *Newsweek* (January 31, 1983); Naisbitt, *Megatrends*, p. 97.

83. "The Revolution in London's Financial Markets," *Fortune* (May 14, 1984); "Headhunting in Japan," *Newsweek* (November 7, 1983).

CHAPTER 5

1. David Vise, "The Japanese Style Is Catching on in Tennessee," *The Washington Post* (July 25, 1982).

2. "Eastern's Revolutionary Treaty," *BusinessWeek* (December 26, 1983).

3. "San Francisco Has Put Its Heart Into Electing Women to Office," *The Washington Post* (July 9, 1984).

4. See Anthony Jay, *Corporate Man* (New York: Random, 1971).

5. Stanley Milgrim, *Obedience to Authority* (New York: Harper & Row, 1975).

6. Quoted from Milton Derber, *The American Idea of Industrial Democracy* (Chicago: University of Illinois, 1970), pp. 6, 89, 374.

7. John M. Roach, *Worker Participation: New Voices in Management* (New York: The Conference Board, 1973).

8. See David Jenkins, *Job Power* (Baltimore: Penguin, 1977).

9. See *Work in America*, Report to the U.S. Secretary of Health, Education, and Welfare (MIT Press, 1973).

10. "The Reindustrialization of America," *BusinessWeek* (June 30, 1980), p. 82.

11. Zaleznik, "Power and Politics in Organizational Life," *Harvard Business Review* (May-June 1970). McClelland, "Power Is the Great Motivator," *Harvard Business Review* (March-April 1976).

12. Robert Greenleaf, *Servant Leadership* (New York: Paulist Press, 1977), p. 102; Zaleznik, *Power and Politics*, pp. 53–55.

13. Chalmers Johnson, "Yesterday's Loyalty and Today's Japan," *The Washington Post* (March 17, 1974); Nicholas von Hoffman, "White on Nixon," *The Washington Post* (June 25, 1975).

14. Fyodor Dostoyevsky, *The Brothers Karamazov* (New York: Airmont, 1966), pp. 228–230.

15. See Chester Barnard, *The Functions of the Executive* (Cambridge, MA: Harvard University, 1968). Vance's comments are from a speech reported in *The Washington Post* (August 2, 1979).

16. William E. Halal, "Toward a General Theory of Leadership," *Human Relations* Vol. 27, No. 4 (April 1974).

17. Riesman, *The Lonely Crowd* (New Haven: Yale, 1950).

18. William E. Halal, "The Legitimacy Cycle: Long-Term Dynamics in the Use of Power," in Andrew Kakabadse and Chris Parker (eds.) *Power, Politics, and Organizations* (New York: Wiley, 1984).

19. Bennis, *Beyond Bureaucracy* (New York: McGraw-Hill, 1966).

20. Michael Maccoby, *The Leader* (New York: Simon and Schuster, 1981), p. 23; Rosow, "Changing Attitudes to Work," *Journal of Contemporary Business* (Fourth Quarter, 1979); Greenleaf, *Servant Leadership*, pp. 71, 137.

21. Haire is quoted in David Jenkins, *Job Power* (Baltimore: Penguin, 1977), p. 311.

22. William E. Halal, "Participative Management: Myth & Reality," *California Management Review* (Summer 1981). Townsend, *Further up the Organization* (New York: Knopf, 1984).

23. For examples of these views, see *Work in America* (MIT Press, 1973) and Robert Flanagan et al., "Worker Discontent and Workplace Behavior," *Industrial Relations* (May 1974).

24. Studs Terkel, *Working* (New York: Pantheon, 1974). Stanley Seashore, *Quality of Employment Survey* (University of Michigan Survey Research Center, 1977). Frederick Herzberg, *Work and the Nature of Man* (Cleveland: World, 1961).

25. Relevant studies are Arnold Tannenbaum et al., *Hierarchy in Organizations* (San Francisco: Jossey-Bass, 1974), as well as classics like Robert Blauner, "Work Satisfaction and Industrial Trends in Modern Society," in Walter Galenson and Seymour Martin Lipset, *Labor and Trade Unionism* (New York: Wiley, 1960); Arthur Kornhauser and Otto Reid, *Mental Health of the Industrial Worker* (New York: Wiley, 1962).

26. *Work in America*, p. 13.

27. Productivity data are from U.S. Bureau of Labor Statistics. For productivity gains see *Work in America*, p. 27. Comparisons with Japan are from William Ouchi, *Theory Z* (New York: Avon, 1981) pp. 49–51. Industrial disputes and accident rates are reported in Arthur Elkins and Dennis W. Callaghan, *A Managerial Odyssey* (Reading, MA: Addison-Wesley, 1981), p. 272.

28. These studies were conducted by the AMA and reported by Alfred T. DeMaria, "Is This the Decade Managers Unionize?," *MBA* (November 1972); and "The Changing Success Ethic," (American Management Association, 1973). The Opinion Research Corporation surveys are reported by Judy Mann, "Life at Work," *The Washington Post* (February 25, 1983), and Thomas Boyle, "Loyalty Ebbs at Many Companies," *The Wall Street Journal* (July 11, 1985).

29. Townsend, *Further Up the Organization.*

30. James O'Toole, *Making America Work* (New York: Continuum, 1981), p. 5.

31. Warren Bennis, *Beyond Bureaucracy*, p. ix.

32. "Stonewalling Plant Democracy," *BusinessWeek* (March 28, 1977). The executive is quoted from James O'Toole, *Making America Work.*

33. Peter Drucker, "The Coming Change in Our School System," *The Wall Street Journal* (March 3, 1981).

34. See Janice Klein, "Why Supervisors Resist Employee Involvement," *Harvard Business Review* (September-October 1984). Robert N. McMurry, "The Case for Benevolent Autocracy," *Harvard Business Review* (January-February 1958).

35. Etzioni, "The Reindustrialization of Vocational Education," *The World of Work* (Washington, DC: World Future Society, 1983). William Winpisinger "Job Enrichment: A Union View," *Monthly Labor Review* (April 1973), Vol. 96, p. 56.

36. See Arthur Schlesinger, Jr., "Does Father Know Best?," *The Wall Street Journal* (September 25, 1975), and Alvin Toffler, *The Third Wave* (New York: Bantam, 1980), p. 399.

37. The survey was conducted by the Work in America Institute, and reported by James T. Yenckel, "The Rating Game at Work," *The Washington Post* (March 25, 1981).

38. Geraldine Brooks, "TRW Pushes to Raise White Collar Productivity," *The Wall Street Journal* (September 22, 1983).

39. Daniel Yankelovich, "New Rules in American Life," *Psychology Today* (April 1981), p. 51. Gordon Lippitt, "What Really Motivates People?," Paper presented at the International Council of Industrial Editors (Pittsburg, 1970).

40. John B. Miner, *The Human Constraint: The Coming Shortage of Managerial Talent* (Washington, DC: The Bureau of National Affairs, 1974); Daniel Yankelovich, *The New Morality* (New York: McGraw-Hill, 1974) p. 49; Jerome M. Rosow, "Changing Attitudes to Work and Life Styles," *Journal of Contemporary Business* (Fourth Quarter, 1979).

41. Jones, "What Is the Future of the Corporation?," in Lewis Benton (ed.), *Management for the Future* (New York: McGraw-Hill, 1978), p. 190. "Baby Boomers Push for Power," *BusinessWeek* (July 2, 1984), p. 52.

42. Ann Howard and James Wilson, "Leadership in a Declining Work Ethic," *California Management Review* (Summer 1982).

43. These views are from *BusinessWeek* (May 11, 1981), p. 85; "Can Labor and Management Form a More Successful Partnership?," *The Wall Street Journal* (August 3, 1982); U.S. Department of Labor press release (September 2, 1981).

44. "Young Top Management," *BusinessWeek* (October 6, 1975).

45. Rachel Flick, "The Gender Game and the GOP," *The Washington Post* (August 24, 1983).

46. Elisabeth Nickles with Laura Ashcraft, *The Coming Matriarchy: How Women Will Gain the Balance of Power* (New York: Seaview/Harper & Row, 1981).

47. See James O'Toole et al., *Employee Entitlements in the Eighties* (Center for Futures Research, 1979). The quote is from *Work in America*, p. 110.

48. "Reducing Human Resource Costs During Difficult Times," (Hay Associates, 1982). Macrae, "Intrapreneur Now," *The Economist* (April 17, 1982).

49. "Loggers Tie Pay to Productivity," *BusinessWeek* (November 29, 1982), p. 35.

50. "Europe Breaking the Grip of Wage Indexation," *BusinessWeek* (June 21, 1982).

51. *BusinessWeek* (May 16, 1983), pp. 148, 100.

52. See Lawrence Ingrassia, "Blue Collar Blues," *The Wall Street Journal* (February 4, 1982).

53. Pestillo is quoted in Hobart Rowen, "Ford, UAW Jump on Wave of the Future," *The Washington Post* (February 21, 1982).

54. Geoffrey Latta, *Profit Sharing, Employee Ownership, & Savings* (Philadelphia: University of Pennsylvania, 1979); Warner Woodworth, "Workers as Bosses," *Social Policy* (January-February 1981).

55. *BusinessWeek* (January 1, 1983, and November 12, 1984).

56. See "ESOPs: Revolution or Ripoff?" *BusinessWeek* (April 15, 1985); Thomas Lippman, "Firms Owned by Employees Multiplying," *The Washington Post* (March 8, 1982); Colman McCarthy, "The Benefits of Bureaucratic Sin," *The Washington Post* (November 11, 1979).

57. See Alasdair Clayre, *The Political Economy of Cooperation and Participation—A Third Sector* (Oxford: Oxford U., 1980). The examples are from Roy Harris, Jr., "Western Airlines and Unions Near Accord in Shadow of Ailing Industry," *The Wall Street Journal* (October 7, 1983); Paul A. Englemayer, "Worker Owned and Operated Supermarket Yields Financial Success," *The Wall Street Journal* (August 18, 1983); "Capital City Co-Op," *The Social Report* (June 1983); *BusinessWeek* (April 15, 1985).

58. Daniel Zwerdling, "Where the Workers Run the Show," *The Washington Post* (September 2, 1973); Daniel Zwerdling, "Workers Turned Owners Find They're Still Just Workers," *The Washington Post* (May 11, 1980).

59. Ted Mills, "Europe's Industrial Democracy: An American Alternative," *Harvard Business Review* (November-December 1978). John Hoerr, "A New Friend for Quality of Work Life," *BusinessWeek* (September 27, 1982).

60. Examples are from *BusinessWeek* (April 25, 1983), p. 74; James O'Toole, *Making America Work* (New York: Continuum, 1981); Heywood Klein, "Interest Grows in Worksharing," *The Wall Street Journal* (April 7, 1983); "The Key: Learning to Work Together," *The Washington Post* (April 12, 1981); "A Japanese Import Comes Full Circle," *The Wall Street Journal* (February 2, 1983); "Management and Workers Team Up to Combat Cheap Foreign Labor," *BusinessWeek* (August 29, 1983); William Batt, "Canada's Good Example with Displaced Workers," *Harvard Business Review* (July-August 1983).

61. David W. Ewing, "The Corporation as Public Enemy No. 1," *Saturday Review* (January 21, 1978). Examples are from *BusinessWeek* (January 11, 1982); James Bolt, "Job Security," *Harvard Business Review* (November-December 1983); "Beyond 'Equal Pay for Equal Work'," *BusinessWeek* (July 18, 1983); "Curtailing the Freedom to Fire," *BusinessWeek* (March 19, 1984).

62. Examples are from "Bureaucrat Need Not Be a Dirty Word," *The Wall Street Journal* (November 7, 1983); "Teamwork Pays Off at Penney's," *BusinessWeek* (April 22, 1982); Fred Gibson, "A Management Proposal Uniquely Suited to Education," *Phi Delta Kappan* (June 1982); "More Pay for Less Crime," *Newsweek* (April 1, 1974); "Calif. Judge Lets Jurors Question the Witnesses," *The Washington Post* (June 2, 1977); Marjorie Hyer, "Looking Back on 20 Years of Vatican II's Revolution," *The Washington Post* (October 20, 1982).

63. Quotes from *BusinessWeek* (May 11, 1981); Newsletter, Massachusetts QWL Center, Vol. 1, No. 1; Douglas Fraser, "Labor's Voice on the Board," *Newsweek* (May 26, 1980); "Bureaucrat . . . ," *Wall Street Journal*.

64. As reported by Stephan Klaidman, "Coal Miners Doing Their Own Thing," *The Washington Post* (January 25, 1976); Ward Sinclair, "At Staley, Management Loves Worker Takeover," *BusinessWeek* (April 26, 1981); "Steel Listens to Workers and Likes What It Hears," *BusinessWeek* (December 19, 1983).

65. David Jenkins, *Job Power*, Ch. X.

66. *BusinessWeek*, "Corporate Culture," (October 27, 1980). Quotes from Peters and Waterman, *In Search of Excellence* (New York: Harper & Row, 1982); William Ouchi, *Theory Z* (New York: Avon, 1981); Terrence Deal and Allen Kennedy, *Corporate Cultures* (Reading, MA: Addison-Wesley, 1980), pp. 33, 35, 238, 260, 261; Peter Vaill, "Toward a Behavioral Description of High-Performing Systems," in Morgan McCall (ed.), *Leadership* (Duke University Press, 1978).

67. Examples drawn from Charles Hillinger, "Big Bonuses at Lincoln Electric Get Big Results," *Professional Trainer* (Winter 1983); Joel Kotwin, "Management Techniques—Made in Japan," *The Washington Post* (June 2, 1979); Hobart Rowen, "Management a Family Affair," *The Washington Post* (April 12, 1981); Margaret Loeb, "Some Happy Employees at Delta Want to Buy a Big Gift for

the Boss," *The Washington Post* (September 28, 1982); Peter Nulty, "A Champ of Cheap Airlines," *Fortune* (March 22, 1982); Ritchie Lowry, "Social Investing," *The Futurist* (April 1982); David Oates, "Lessons from the Volvo Experience," *International Management* (February 1978), p. 43.

68. Sidney Harman, "A Peace Plan for Workers and Bosses," *The Washington Post* (April 15, 1979).

69. Herzberg is quoted in Jenkins, *Job Power*, p. 169.

70. "Where Being Nice to Workers Didn't Work," *BusinessWeek* (January 20, 1973).

71. Robert Greenberger, "Worker's Larger Corporate Roles Portend Big Shift in Labor-Management Relations," *The Wall Street Journal* (September 20, 1983).

72. Kathy Sawyer, "Court Faces Issue of Equal Pay for Comparable Work," *The Washington Post* (June 4, 1981); "Why Clerical Workers Resist the Unions," *BusinessWeek* (May 2, 1983); *BusinessWeek* (April 25, 1983), pp. 50, 60; Martin Carnoy and Derek Shearer, *Economic Democracy* (New York: Sharpe, 1980), p. 3.

73. Sherwin, "Strategy for Winning Employee Commitment," Harvard *Business Review* (May-June 1972).

74. James Burns, *Leadership* (New York: Harper & Row, 1978).

75. Douglas Fraser, "Labor's Voice." Jack Falvey, "To Raise Productivity, Try Saying Thank You," *The Wall Street Journal* (December 6, 1982).

CHAPTER 6

1. George A. Steiner and John B. Miner, *Management Policy and Strategy* (New York: Macmillan, 1977), p. 870.

2. *General Motors 1980 Public Interest Report*, p. 1.

3. Blumberg, "The Politicalization of the Corporation," *Boston University Law Review*, Vol. 51, No. 3 (Summer, 1971).

4. Ansoff et al., *From Strategic Planning to Strategic Management* (London, Wiley, 1976), p. 43.

5. Irving Kristol, "Business and the 'New Class'," *The Wall Street Journal* (May 19, 1975). The study was conducted by John L. Paluszek, *Will the Corporation Survive?* (Reston, VA: Reston Publishing/Prentice-Hall, 1977), p. 7.

6. Results of these surveys are from: Lipset and Lipset, *The Confidence Gap* (New York: Free, 1983); George Steiner, "An Overview of the Changing Business Environment and Its Impact on Business," in Lee Preston (ed.), *Business Environment/Public Policy-1979 Conference Papers* (St. Louis, MO: AACSB, 1980); the Hart poll was reported in a 1976 press release; Opinion Research Corporation data is in a press release (October 19, 1983); the Union Leader survey was reported in a 1983 release; Roper data is summarized in CEO Newsletter #5 including polls from 1981–83.

7. Ralph E. Winter, "High Corporate Profits are an Embarassment," *The Wall Street Journal* (April 13, 1979). "Profits and Oil," *The Washington Post* (May 12, 1982).

8. Bunke, "Anti-Business Sentiments and the Intellectual Community," *Business Horizons* (September/October 1981).

9. "Rendering Unto Ceasar," *Newsweek* (January 17, 1983).

10. Donna Cord, "Diary of a Mad Housewife," *Newsweek* (February 18, 1974).

11. Peter Drucker, *Preparing Tomorrow's Business Leaders Today* (Englewood Cliffs, NJ: Prentice-Hall, 1969), p. 77.

12. Bradshaw and David Vogel (eds.), *Corporations and Their Critics* (New York: McGraw-Hill, 1981), p. xxvi.

13. Lee Preston and James Post, *Private Management and Public Policy* (Englewood Cliffs, NJ: Prentice-Hall, 1975), p. 53.

14. See Prakash Sethi, *Private Enterprise and Public Purpose* (New York: Wiley, 1981) p. 106.

15. Frank Allen, "Big Companies Blame Public's Ignorance for Bad Image," *The Wall Street Journal* (August 21, 1981).

16. Nick Kotz, "Youngstown's Tragedies," *The Washington Post* (June 17, 1979). Jenkins, *Job Power* (New York: Penguin, 1974), p. 305.

17. Carol Hymowitz, "Mellon Bank Embarrassed in USW Protest," *The Wall Street Journal* (June 10, 1983); Jeremy Rifkin et al., *The North Will Rise Again* (Boston: Beacon, 1978); Jeffrey Kaye, "Unions Map Investment Guidelines," *The Washington Post* (March 9, 1980); "The Picket Line Gives Way to Sophisticated New Tactics," *BusinessWeek* (April 16, 1984).

18. "Where Consumers Want Their Own Electric Companies," *BusinessWeek* (May 23, 1983), p. 184; Jonathan Dahl, "Consumers Gain Unlikely Victory in Antitrust Action," *The Wall Street Journal* (June 5, 1984); "Why More Corporations May Be Charged With Manslaughter," *BusinessWeek* (February 27, 1984).

19. "Dow's Bad Chemistry," *Newsweek* (July 18, 1983); Doug Bandow, "Games Politicians Play," *The Washington Post* (April 25, 1984).

20. "A Move to Make Institutions Start Using Their Stockholder Clout," *BusinessWeek* (August 6, 1984); Carrington, "The Annual Nightmare," *The Wall Street Journal* (April 9, 1983); Knight, "Annual Meetings a Capitalist Farce," *The Washington Post* (February 6, 1984).

21. Kraft, "Greed at the Top," *The Washington Post* (October 24, 1982).

22. Forrester is quoted in "A Technology Lag that May Stifle Growth," *BusinessWeek* (October 11, 1982). For evidence of the congruence between economic and social goals see Robert Kuttner, *The Economic Illusion* (Boston: Houghton Mifflin, 1984).

23. Will, "The Limits to Thatcher's Success," *The Washington Post* (September 29, 1983).

24. C. Jackson Grayson, "Emphasizing Capital Investment Is a Mistake," *The Wall Street Journal* (October 12, 1982).

25. Peter Drucker, "Coping With Those Extra Burdens," *The Wall Street Journal* (May 2, 1979); John Ryan, "Costly Counsel," *The Wall Street Journal* (April 13, 1978); "The Tough New Faces on Corporate Boards," *U.S. News and World Report* (October 6, 1980).

26. Mary Ann McGivern, "Church Intervention in Corporate Management," in Lee Preston (ed.), *Business Environment*. Bell, *The Coming of Post-Industrial Society* (New York: Basic, 1973), p. 373.

27. Silk and Vogel, *Ethics and Profits* (New York: Simon & Schuster, 1976); also see Paluszek, *Survive*; and N. R. Kleinfield, "The Chief Executive Under Stress," *The New York Times* (November 7, 1982).

28. Sethi, *Private Enterprise*, pp. viii, 7, 157.

29. John Gardner, *Leadership* (University of Minnesota, 1981).

30. William E. Halal, "The Corporation Evolving."

31. Bok, *The President's Report* (Harvard University, 1977–78).

32. The history of measuring social impacts is described in Daniel Bell, *The Coming of Post-Industrial Society*, pp. 282, 330.

33. William E. Halal, *A State-of-the-Art Survey of Corporate Social Reporting* (General Motors Corporation Report, 1978), also published as "A Survey of Social Reporting Methodology," in Lee Preston (ed.), *Business Environment*.

34. "Manipulating Profits," *Fortune* (June 25, 1984).

35. *Science and Technology: A Five-Year Outlook* (San Francisco: Freeman, 1979), p. 441.

36. Steiner and Miner, *Management*, p. 67.

37. Thomas Watson, *A Business and Its Beliefs: The Ideas That Helped Build IBM* (New York: McGraw-Hill, 1963).

38. *Business & Society* (U.S. Department of Commerce, 1980), p. v.

39. William E. Halal, "A Return-on-Resources Model of Corporate Performance," *California Management Review* (Summer 1977); "Beyond the Profit Motive: The Post-Industrial Corporation," *Technological Forecasting & Social Change* (June 1978), Vol. 12, No. 1; "An Open-System Model of the Corporation," George Klir (ed.), *Applied General Systems Research* (New York: Plenum, 1978).

40. Merrill Brown et al., "Conglomerate Facing Asbestos Lawsuits Files for Bankruptcy," *The Washington Post* (August 27, 1982); Dean Rotbart and Raymond A. Joseph, "Upbeat Ads From Manville Anger Some," *The Wall Street Journal* (November 15, 1982).

41. Daniel Bell, *Post-Industrial Society*, p. 289.

42. *The Wall Street Journal* (April 17, 1972). Dahl is quoted in William Capitman, *Panic in the Boardroom* (New York: Anchor/Doubleday, 1975), p. 255.

43. Byrom is quoted in Silk and Vogel, *Ethics*, p. 160; Shapiro's comments are reported by Art Pine, "Du Pont's Irving S. Shapiro: Summing Up a Lifetime In Business," *The Washington Post* (February 8, 1981); O'Toole, "Corporate Leadership in Cooperation," *Business Horizons* (July-August 1983).

44. Bell's comments are reported by Peter Behr, "Business Confronts Social Issues, Public Policy Questions," *The Washington Post* (January 21, 1982).

45. Theodore Levitt, *The Marketing Imagination* (New York: Free, 1983). Also see Herbert E. Simon, "On the Concept of Organizational Goals," *Administrative Science Quarterly* (June 1964), Vol. 9.

46. See William Abernathy et al., *Industrial Renaissance* (New York: Basic, 1983).

47. "The Reindustrialization of America," *BusinessWeek* (June 30, 1980), p. 86.

48. See Michael Moch and Stanley Seashore, "Managing Relationships Between the Corporation and Society," in Sethi, *Private Enterprise*, pp. 385–6.

49. Jones is quoted in Weidenbaum, "Public Policy: No Longer a Spectator Sport," *The Journal of Business Strategy* (Summer 1980).

50. Jones, *Business and Society*, p. 75.

51. Andres, "Creative Corporate Philanthropy," in Bradshaw and Vogel (eds.), p. 143. Morita is quoted by Hobart Rowen, "Management a Family Affair," *The Washington Post* (April 12, 1981); the conference was the European Societal Strategy Project, held in Dublin, June 1982, and reported in *International Management Development* (Autumn, 1982); Sholl's comments appeared in J. Y. Smith, "Evan Sholl, 83, Founder of Sholl's Cafeterias, Dies," *The Washington Post* (March 3, 1983); McNamara is quoted in "Reconciling Management and Welfare at the World Bank," *The Washington Post* (October 12, 1980); James Emshoff, *Managerial Breakthroughs* (New York: AMACOM, 1980), pp. 141, 172; Wendy L. Wall, "Helping Hands," *The Wall Street Journal* (June 21, 1984).

52. Lehr is quoted in "Enlightened Self-Interest," *The Washington Post* (September 7, 1981); Danzansky's comments are from Robert Samek, "Danzansky: Business Is Not Just Profits," *Northwest* (Fall 1978); Filer, "The Social Goals of a Corporation," in Bradshaw and Vogel (eds.), *Corporations*, p. 271; Rouse is quoted in "Money Is Fine, But," *The Washington Post* (May 27, 1984); Kapor is quoted in "A Bit of the '60s Lives on at Lotus," *BusinessWeek* (July 2, 1984).

53. Erik Calonius, "Factory Magic," *The Wall Street Journal* (April 29, 1983); "Concerns Rush to Improve Quality," *The Wall Street Journal* (September 20, 1983).

54. See O'Toole, "Corporate Leadership"; Haynes Johnson, "A Success Story in the Industrial Cradle," *The Washington Post* (October 31, 1982); R. Emmett Tyrell Jr., "Urbane Renewal in Indiana," *The Washington Post* (September 6, 1982); Mayor Hudnutt's comments appeared in *The Washington Post* (November 5, 1982); Severyn Bruyn, "A New Direction for Community Development," *The Social Report* (February 1985).

55. See Richard Lowry, "Social Investing: Doing Good While Doing Well," *The Futurist* (April 1982).

56. R. J. Aldag and K. M. Bartol, "Empirical Studies of Corporate Social Performance and Policy," in Lee Preston (ed.), *Research in Corporate Social Performance and Policy* (1978), Vol. 1. John Gardner, *Leadership*.

57. Joseph Monsen, "Directions in United States and European Corporate Governance," in Lee Preston, *Business Environment*, p. 124; Joann S. Lublin,

"Outsiders In," *The Wall Street Journal* (May 26, 1978); *Business and Society*; "Labor's Voice on Corporate Boards," *BusinessWeek* (May 7, 1984); Jerry Knight, "VEPCO Customers Get a Piece of the Rock," *The Washington Post* (July 25, 1983); James Robertson, *The Sane Alternative* (St. Paul, MN: River Basin Publishing, 1979); Henry Mintzberg, "Who Should Control the Corporation?" *California Management Review* (Fall 1984).

58. Warren Brown, "Labor Member on Board Bad Idea, Says GM Chief," *The Washington Post* (November 11, 1982); "The Role and Composition of the Board of Directors of the Large Publicly Owned Corporation," (The Business Roundtable), published in Sethi, *Private Enterprise*, p. 212.

59. Fraser, "Labor's Voice on the Board," *Newsweek* (May 26, 1980).

60. Quoted in Paluszek, *Survive*, p. 135.

61. *Impact*, Newsletter of the Public Affairs Council (October 1978).

62. Matsushita's comments are from Mike Tharp, "A Talk With a Famed Japanese Entrepreneur," *The Wall Street Journal* (September 21, 1979); The Hewlett-Packard Philosophy; Andres views are in *Business and Society*.

63. Charles F. Kiefer and Peter M. Senge, "Metanoic Organizations in the Transition to a Sustainable Society," *Technological Forecasting & Social Change* (October 1982), p. 122.

64. Finn, "Public Invisibility of Corporate Leaders," Harvard *Business Review* (November-December 1980), p. 102.

65. Whitehead is quoted in Daniel Bell, *Post-Industrial Society*.

66. Harris's comments appeared in "For the Record," The *Washington Post*; Yankelovich, *New Rules* (Reprinted in *Psychology Today*, April 1981), p. 85.

CHAPTER 7

1. Peter Hall, *Great Planning Disasters* (Berkeley, California: University of California, 1982).

2. Sam Sieber, *Fatal Remedies* (New York: Plenum 1981).

3. *The Study of the Future* (Washington, DC: The World Future Society, 1977), Ch. 1

4. Peter Drucker, *Managing in Turbulent Times* (New York: Harper & Row, 1980), p. 1.

5. See *The Study of the Future* (Washington, DC: World Future Society, 1977), and Paul Dickson, *The Future File* (New York: Avon, 1977). Toffler, *The Futurists* (New York: Random, 1972), p. 3.

6. Irving Kristol, "Business vs. the Economy?," *The Wall Street Journal* (June 26, 1979).

7. See Wendell French and Cecil Bell, *Organization Development* (Englewood Cliffs, NJ: Prentice-Hall, 1978). John Poppy, "It's OK To Cry in the Office," *Look* (August 7, 1968).

8. Edwin Fleishman, "Leadership Climate, Human Relations Training and Supervisory Behavior," *Personnel Psychology*, Vol. 6 (1953).

9. Daniel Katz and Robert Kahn, *The Social Psychology of Organization* (New York: Wiley, 1966), p. 449

10. See Kenneth R. Andrews, *The Concept of Corporate Strategy* (Homewood, IL: Richard D. Irwin, 1980); J. Argenti, *Systematic Corporate Planning* (New York: Wiley, 1974) p. 1; Susanne Wood, "A Survey of Strategic Planning in Government Agencies" (Unpublished paper, George Washington University, 1984); "Now Academia is Taking Lessons from Business," *BusinessWeek* (August 27, 1984).

11. For further details, see the study report, William E. Halal, *Strategic Planning in Major U.S. Corporations* (General Motors Corporation, 1980), or the published summary, "Strategic Management: The State-of-the-Art & Beyond," *Technological Forecasting & Social Change* (May 1984).

12. See Walter Kiechel III, "Corporate Strategists Under Fire," *Fortune* (December 27, 1982); "The New Breed of Strategic Planner," *BusinessWeek* (September 17, 1984). The quotes are reported in: "The Future Catches Up With a Strategic Planner," *BusinessWeek* (June 27, 1983); D. E. Hussey, "Strategic Management: Lessons from Success and Failure," *Long-Range Planning* (February 1984); and Mitchell Ford, "Strategic Planning—Myth or Reality?—A Chief Executive's View," *Long-Range Planning* (June 1981).

13. See Robert Hayes and William J. Abernathy, "Managing Our Way to Economic Decline," *Harvard Business Review* (July-August, 1978).

14. See David Finn, "Public Invisibility of Corporate Leaders," *Harvard Business Review* (November-December 1980). Kirk O. Hanson, "Strategic Planning and Social Performance," in *Business and Society: Strategies for the 1980s* (Washington, DC: U.S. Department of Commerce, 1980), p. 149.

15. Quoted in Kiechel. "Corporate Strategists."

16. "The New Breed of Strategic Planner," *BusinessWeek*.

17. See Harold Linstone, *Multiple Perspectives for Decision-Making* (New York: North-Holland, 1984).

18. J. Quincy Hunsiker, "The Malaise of Strategic Planning," *Management Review* (March 1980).

19. See James Brian Quinn, *Strategies for Change* (Homewood, IL: Richard D. Irwin, 1980); Henry Mintzberg, *The Nature of Managerial Work* (New York: Harper & Row, 1973).

20. The problem was well stated by Reginald Jones, as described by Laura Landro, "Electric Switch," *The Wall Street Journal* (July 12, 1982).

21. H. Igor Ansoff et al., *From Strategic Planning to Strategic Management* (London: Wiley, 1976), p. 76.

22. Frederick Gluck et al., "Strategic Management for Competitive Advantage," *Harvard Business Review* (July-August 1980). For a definition see Dan E. Schendel and Charles W. Hofer, *Strategic Management* (Boston: Little, Brown, 1979).

23. George Steiner, *Strategic Planning* (New York: Free, 1979).

24. For good descriptions of this circular nature of the strategic decision-making process, see Herbert A. Simon, *The New Science of Management Decision* (New York: New York University Press, 1960), and Henry Mintzberg, "A General Model of Strategic Decision-Making," *Administrative Science Quarterly* (June 1976).

25. "America's Restructured Economy," (June 1, 1981).

26. James Thompson, *Organizations in Action* (New York: McGraw-Hill, 1967).

27. John Platt, "How Men Can Shape Their Future" (unpublished manuscript, Kyoto, 1970). The examples are from Cornish, *Future*; Keith A. Bea et al., *The States Look to the Future* (Report of the Library of Congress, 1975); Catherine Meschter, "San Francisco: A City and a Strategic Plan," *Public Administration Times* (February 15, 1983). The CWA and the AAAS cases were reported to me in personal interviews.

28. Joseph Bower and Yves Doz, "Strategy Formulation: A Social and Political Process," in Schendel and Hofer, *Strategic Management*, p. 165.

29. James R. Emshoff, *Managerial Breakthroughs* (New York: AMACOM, 1980); R. Edward Freeman, *Strategic Management: A Stakeholder Approach* (Pittman, 1983). William Dill, "Strategic Management in a Kibitzer's World," in Ansoff et al., p. 126.

30. James K. Brown, *This Business of Issues* (The Conference Board, 1979); Graham T. T. Molitor, "Environmental Forecasting: Public Policy Forecasting," in Lee Preston (ed.), *Business Environment/Public Policy* (St Louis, MO: American Assembly of Collegiate Schools of Business, 1980).

31. Grady Means, *Integrating Public Issue Analysis Into Corporate Planning* (Washington, DC: Sage Associates), p. 2; Peter Drucker, "Coping With Those Extra Burdens," *The Wall Street Journal* (May 2, 1979); William Renfro, "Managing the Issues of the 1980s," *The Futurist* (August 1982). The examples are from Howard Chase, *Issue Management: Origins of the Future* (Forthcoming), and from cases reported to me during interviews.

32. Igor Ansoff, *Understanding and Managing Strategic Change* (Amsterdam: North Holland, 1983), p. 2.

33. Reported in Halal, *Strategic Planning*. Computer applications are described by Starr Roxanne Hiltz and Murray Turoff, *Network Nation* (Reading, MA: Addison-Wesley, 1978), and "A Tool to Give Meetings More Focus and Speed," *BusinessWeek* (November 27, 1978). Organization Transformation is described by John D. Adams, *Transforming Work* (Alexandria, A: Miles River Press, 1984). The Volvo example is in "Putting Planners on the Shop Floor," *The Economist* (November 5, 1983).

34. Peter Vaill, "Fostering Strategic Management in a Turbulent World: A Crucial Challenge for OD," presented at a meeting of the OD Network (Los Angeles, Fall, 1983).

35. Kiechel, *Corporate Strategists*.

36. Russell Ackoff, *Creating the Corporate Future: A New Concept of Corporate Planning* (New York: Wiley, 1981).

37. Capra, "The Turning Point," *The Futurist* (December 1982).

38. Thomas Peters and Robert Waterman, *In Search of Excellence* (New York: Harper & Row, 1983), p. 12.

39. Michael, "Competence and Compassion in an Age of Uncertainty," *World Future Society Bulletin* (January-February 1983).

CHAPTER 8

1. Andy Pasztor, "Reagan Goal of Easing Environmental Laws Is Largely Unattained," *The Wall Street Journal* (February 18, 1983).

2. See John Palmer and Isabel Sawhill, *The Reagan Record* (Boston: Ballinger, 1984).

3. Guy Sorman, "France Relearns the Meaning of Entrepreneur," *The Wall Street Journal* (October 19, 1983).

4. Walter W. Heller, "The Disarray in U.S. Economic Policy," *The Wall Street Journal* (December 28, 1982).

5. Schnitzer, *Contemporary Government and Business Relations* (Chicago: Rand McNally 1978), p. 500.

6. *Economic Report of the President* (Washington, DC: U.S. Government Printing Office, 1980). Murray Weidenbaum, "Public Policy: No Longer a Spectator Sport for Business," *The Journal of Business Strategy* (Summer 1980), and *Business, Government, and The Public Interest* (Englewood Cliffs, NJ: Prentice-Hall, 1981).

7. John Quarles, *Cleaning Up America* (HM, 1976). Also see John Paluszek, *Will The Corporation Survive?* (Reston, VA: Reston Publishing, 1977), p. 111.

8. Fred Barbash, "High Court Refuses to Yield to Ease Laws on Job Safety, Health," *The Washington Post* (June 18, 1981).

9. Sven Rydenfelt, "Sweden's 'Meidner Plan' for Industrial Takeover," *The Wall Street Journal* (December 23, 1981); Thomas W. Lippman, "Proposals Before the EEC Alarm Multinationals," *The Washington Post* (March 3, 1982).

10. Al Senia, "A Political Pendulum Swings to the Left," *The Washington Post* (April 13, 1982); the Hart poll was reported in a press release, "Results of a Nationwide Public Opinion Poll," (September 1, 1975).

11. Byrom's comments appeared in, "The Faked Case Against Regulation," *The Washington Post* (January 21, 1979).

12. Koch is quoted in "Are American's Businessmen Cutting Their Own Throats?" *The Wall Street Journal* (Sept 18, 1979).

13. See John Dunlop, "The Limits of Legal Compulsion," *The Conference Board* (March 1976), and George Steiner, "An Overview of the Changing Business Environment," in Preston (ed.), *Business Environment/Public Policy* (AACSB: 1980). For a view of the accomplishments of government, see John Schwartz, *America's Hidden Success* (Norton, 1984).

14. Felix Kessler, "Mitterand's Programs Anger French on Both the Left and the Right," *The Wall Street Journal* (February 4, 1983). Drucker, *The Age of Discontinuity* (New York: Harper & Row, 1969), p. 213.

15. See Susan and Martin Tolchin, *Dismantling America* (Boston: Houghton Mifflin, 1984).

16. George Steiner, "Business Environment," p. 15.

17. Friedman, "Election Perspective," *Newsweek* (November 10, 1980).

18. "What Hath Thatcher Wrought?," *BusinessWeek* (June 6, 1983), p. 44; Leonard Downie Jr., "Britain's Pain is Sign of Progress, Thatcher Asserts," *The Washington Post* (June 29, 1980); David Stockman, "Avoiding a GOP Economic Dunkirk," *The Wall Street Journal* (December 12, 1980).

19. Cody, "Mitterand, Reagan Share Fiscal Goals, Not Methods," *The Washington Post* (September 20, 1981); Ellen Goodman, "The Three-Piece Jerry Rubin," *The Washington Post* (August 4, 1980).

20. Revzin, "Toughing It Out," *The Wall Street Journal* (May 2, 1980).

21. "What Hath Thatcher Wrought?," *BusinessWeek*.

22. Paul A. Samuelson, "Margaret Thatcher's Trials," *Newsweek* (June 6, 1980); Leonard Downie, Jr., "Britons Deflate U.S. Economist," *The Washington Post* (March 4, 1980).

23. Molly Sinclair, "Retired Managers Say Regulation Needed," *The Washington Post* (May 16, 1983).

24. Haynes Johnson et al., "America Today: Rich People, Poor Services," *The Washington Post* (September 18, 1983); David Broder, "Will the States Get the Short End Again?," *The Washington Post* (August 5, 1984); the European is quoted in, "The Welfare Crisis," *Newsweek* (July 25, 1983).

25. Lou Cannon and David Hofman, "At Mid-Term in Reagan Presidency, the Problems Seem Less Simple," *The Washington Post* (December 19, 1982); Gordon Crovitz, "Blueprint for a Second Thatcher Term?," *The Wall Street Journal* (June 9, 1983).

26. "Are Americans Getting the Government They Want?," *Common Cause* (May/June 1983); Tolchin and Tolchin, *Dismantling America*; John J. Fialka, "Reaganites Find Plans for Deregulation Stall After EPA Revelations," *The Wall Street Journal* (June 6, 1983); Mayer, "Regulatory Campaign Falters," *The Washington Post* (August 2, 1982); "Will the New Federalism Create 'a 50-headed Hydra'?," *BusinessWeek* (September 19, 1983); Claybrook, "Reagan's Rulebook Is All Wrong," *The Washington Post*.

27. See the articles in *The Washington Post* by Leonard Downie: "364 British Economists Assail Thatcher's Policies," (March 31, 1981); "British Businessmen Pressuring Thatcher to Ease Austerity Plan," (June 2, 1980); "Economic Woes Fuel Dissent Across Britain on Thatcher's Policies," (November 15, 1980); "Heath, Ex-Leader of Tories, Joins Criticism of Thatcher," (November 29, 1980).

28. "The President and the Polls," *The Washington Post* (May 20, 1983); "Studies Say Reagan Reverses Redistribution," *The Wall Street Journal* (December 6, 1982); Kathy Sawyer, "Reagan Industrial Policy Assailed," *The Washington*

Post (April 29, 1983); William Raspberry, "An Executive's Plea for the Poor," *The Washington Post* (December 4, 1981); "The Reagan Revolution: What If It Fails?," *The Wall Street Journal* (December 21, 1981); Thomas Edsall, "Reaganomics Is Target of Marshall Group," *The Washington Post* (January 8, 1982).

29. Leonard Downie, "Britons Deflate U.S. Economist," *The Washington Post* (March 4, 1980).

30. See James O'Toole, "What's Ahead for the Business-Government Relationship?," *Harvard Business Review* (March-April 1979); Leonard Silk and David Vogel, *Ethics and Profits* (New York: Touchstone, 1976), p. 213.

31. See Kevin P. Phillips, *Post-Conservative America* (New York: Random, 1982). *Business and Society: Strategies for the 1980s* (Washington, DC: U.S. Department of Commerce, 1980), pp. v, 48, 61.

32. Leonard Silk and David Vogel, *Ethics*, p. 37.

33. Graham Molitor, "Getting Out in Front of Impending Issues," *Through the '80s* (Washington, DC: World Future Society, 1980).

34. The Hart Poll appeared in a press release (Sept 1, 1975); Mark Green et al., *The Case for a Corporate Democracy Act of 1980* (An unpublished report); Congressman Rosenthal's comments appeared in a letter to the editor of *The Wall Street Journal* (June 2, 1980); Ralph Nader et al., *Taming the Giant Corporation* (New York: Norton, 1976), p. 1; Martha Hamilton, "Corporate Accountability," *The Washington Post* (March 8, 1981); the Hill and Knowlton study is from the Newsletter of the Congressional Clearinghouse on the Future; the ADA statement is from a news release "Statement on Big Business Day" (December 12, 1979); Helen Dewar, "Coalition Eyed to Curb Corporate Power," *The Washington Post* (March 4, 1979); Courtney Brown, "A Corporate Dilemma," Max Ways (ed.), *The Future of Business* (New York: Pergamon, 1979), p. 14.

35. William E. Halal, "Big Business vs. Big Government—A New Social Contract?," *Long-Range Planning* (August 1984).

36. Ouchi, *The M-Form Society* (Reading, MA: Addison-Wesley, 1984), and "Let's Emulate Japan's Interest-Group Competition," *The Wall Street Journal* (April 7, 1984).

37. Mitterand's ideas are from Guy Sorman, "France's Socialists: All Power to the Towns," *The Wall Street Journal* (August 11, 1982). Reagan's comments appeared in Herbert H. Denton, "Grassroots Activists Meet Conservatives," *The Washington Post*.

38. Naisbitt, *Megatrends* (New York: Warner, 1982), p. 175; Robertson, *The Sane Alternative* (St. Paul, MN: River Basin, 1978), pp. 71, 48; Toffler, *The Third Wave* (New York: Bantam, 1980), pp. 354, 235. Also see, John E. Fleming, "A Possible Future of Government-Business Relations," *Business Horizons* (December 1979).

39. Karson, "An Appeal to the Presidential Candidates," *Response* (January 1984).

40. "A Bipartisan Budget Appeal," *The New York Times* (June 23, 1985); Sorenson, *A New Kind of Presidency* (New York: Harper & Row, 1984); Neils I. Meyer et al., *Revolt From the Center* (Salem, NH: Marion Boyars, 1981); David Broder, *Changing of the Guard* (New York: Penguin, 1981).

41. See Michael Useem, *The Inner Circle* (New York: Oxford Press, 1984); Thornton Bradshaw, *Business and Society*, p. 109.

42. Amitai Etzioni, *An Immodest Agenda* (New York: McGraw-Hill, 1982); "The Neo-Liberals Push Their Own Brand of Reform," *BusinessWeek* (January 31, 1983).

43. Arthur Schlesinger Jr., "American Politics on a Darkling Plain," *The Wall Street Journal* (March 16, 1982). The quotes are from "The Neo-Liberals Push Their Own Brand of Reform," *BusinessWeek*; "Industrial Policy: Yes or No?," *BusinessWeek* (July 4, 1983); Bruce Bartlett, "The Old Politics of a New Industrial Policy," *The Wall Street Journal* (April 19, 1983).

44. Asao, "Myths and Realities of Japan's Industrial Policies," *The Wall Street Journal* (October 24, 1983).

45. See James O'Toole, "Corporate Leadership in Cooperation," *Business Horizons* (July-August 1983).

46. Timothy Wirth, "A Democratic Policy Agenda for the Future," *The Wall Street Journal* (October 19, 1982); Howard J. Samuels, ". . . And What the Republicans Should Reject," *The Washington Post* (January 2, 1981); Norman Jonas, "Why the Democrats Need to Come Up With an Industrial Policy," *BusinessWeek* (Nov 21, 1983); *The President's Commission for a National Agenda for the Eighties* (Washington, DC: U.S. Superintendent of Documents), p. 76; "Industrial Policy: Yes or No?," *BusinessWeek*; "A Cautious Nod to Industrial Policy," *BusinessWeek* (March 19, 1984).

47. Warren Brown, "Michigan's Battered Economy on the Mend," *The Washington Post* (July 29, 1984); Joann Lubin, "States Expand Enterprise Zones," *The Wall Street Journal* (July 31, 1984); Walter Olson, "Industrial Policy From the Grass Roots?," *The Wall Street Journal* (June 12, 1984); Guy Sorman, "France's Socialists," *The Wall Street Journal* (August 11, 1982).

48. Michael Pertschuk, "Listening to the Little Guy," *The Washington Post* (June 26, 1979). Susan and Martin Tolchin, *Dismantling America*, Ch. IV. Eugene Bardach and Robert Kagan, *Going by the Book* (Philadelphia: Temple University Press, 1982).

49. Dan Morgan, "Carter Unveils Plan to Aid Auto Industry," *The Washington Post* (July 9, 1980); Peter Behr, "Auto Pact: Historic Industry Policy Shift," *Washington Post* (July 10, 1980). Lindley H. Clark, "Is the Administration Re-Regulating Transportation?," *The Wall Street Journal* (July 27, 1982); Mark Andrews, "Stop the Air War—We Want to Get Off," *The Washington Post* (April 18, 1983).

50. Howard Kurtz, "A 'New Idea' Fizzles on Launch," *The Washington Post* (July 15, 1984).

51. Charles L. Schultze, *The Public Use of Private Interest* (Washington, DC: Brookings Institution, 1977).

52. Eugene Bardach and Robert A. Kagan, *Social Regulation: Strategies for Reform* (San Francisco: Institute for Contemporary Studies, 1982).

53. "Business Tax Seen Causing Social Change," *The Washington Post* (March 27, 1978); James O'Toole, "What's Ahead for the Business-Government Relationship," *Harvard Business Review* (March-April 1979).

54. "Want to Buy a Fire Department?," *Newsweek* (April 25, 1983).

55. Examples are from "Fire Department," *Newsweek*; Kathy Sawyer, "As Government Realigns, Scramble Begins to Bridge the 'Charity Gap'," *The Washington Post* (October 11, 1981); E. S. Savas, *How to Shrink Government: Privatizing the Public Sector* (Chatham, NJ: Chatham House, 1982); Jack Meyer (ed.), *Meeting Human Needs: Toward a New Public Philosophy* (Washington, DC: American Enterprise Institute, 1982); "When Public Services Go Private," *Fortune* (May 27, 1985).

56. "The Corporate Warden," *BusinessWeek* (May 7, 1984).

57. Gordon Crovitz, "Blueprint for a Second Thatcher Term?," *The Wall Street Journal* (June 9, 1983).

58. "Fire Department," *Newsweek*.

59. See Jacob Javits, "Government's Role in Economic Management," in Lewis Benton, (ed.) *Management for the Future* (New York: McGraw-Hill, 1978).

60. William Nordhaus and James Tobin, "Is Growth Obsolete?," (A 1972 monograph).

61. Weidenbaum, *Business, Government, and the Public Interest* (Englewood Cliffs: Prentice-Hall, 1981), Ch. 3; June Kronholz, "Consumerism European Style," *The Wall Street Journal* (November 20, 1979).

62. Daniel Bell, *The Coming of Post-Industrial Society* (New York: Basic, 1976), p. 326.

63. Rohatyn, "America in the 1980s," *The Economist* (Sept 1981); "Industrial Policy Divides the Democrats," *BusinessWeek* (May 14, 1984).

64. "High-Tech Companies Team Up in the R&D Race," *BusinessWeek* (August 15, 1983); Dan Balz, "Texas Rounds Up a Hi-Tech Prize," *The Washington Post* (May 18, 1983); Mark Potts, "Incubator Plan Helps Firms Hatch," *The Washington Post* (October 23, 1983).

65. "Business Tackles Hard-Core Unemployment," *BusinessWeek* (September 20, 1982); Kathy Sawyer, "Job Training Program Draws Donovan Praise," *The Washington Post* (July 27, 1984); John P. Blair et al., "The Market for Jobs," *The Futurist* (April 1984).

66. William Reilly, "Cleaning Our Chemical Waste Backyard," *The Wall Street Journal* (May 31, 1984); Savas, *How To Shrink Government*; Davis Garvin, "Can Industry Self-Regulation Work?," *California Management Review* (Summer, 1983).

67. Steiner and Miner, *Management Policy and Strategy* (New York: Macmillan, 1977), p. 46.

68. Daniel Bell, "The Cultural Contradictions of Capitalism," in Bell and Kristol (eds.), *Capitalism Today* (New York: Mentor, 1971); Robert Reich, *The New American Frontier* (New York: Times, 1983), Ch. 1.

69. See Jean Jacques Rousseau, *The Social Contract* (Chicago: Gateway, 1954).

70. Warren Bennis, "Democracy is Inevitable," *Harvard Business Review* (March-April 1964).

71. For instance, see Michael Novak, *The Spirit of Democratic Capitalism* (New York: Simon & Schuster, 1982).

CHAPTER 9

1. Reagan's comments appeared in "Hardening the Line," *Time* (March 21, 1983), and Andropov's were in Dusko Doder, "Soviets Offer to Cut Warheads," *The Washington Post* (May 4, 1983).

2. Richard Barnet, "We Need New Rules, Not Military Risks or Nuclear Bluffs," *The Washington Post* (January 20, 1980).

3. Alexis de Toqueville, *Democracy in America* (New York: Random, 1981).

4. Richard Nixon, *The Real War* (New York: Warner, 1980).

5. See Albert Szymanski, *Human Rights: USSR/USA* (Westport, CT: Hill, 1983), and Charles Lindblom, *Politics and Markets* (New York: Basic, 1977), p. 271.

6. Stephen Sternheimer, "The Soviet Economy," *Harvard Business Review* (January–February 1982).

7. John W. Kiser, III, "Technology: We Can Learn a Lot From the Soviets," *The Washington Post* (August 14, 1983).

8. For a discussion of the workings of one-party systems, see Jerzy J. Wiatr, "Political Parties and Interest Representation in Poland," *American Political Science Review*, Vol. 64 (December 1970). The quote is from Pat Derian, "Talking to Russians," *The Washington Post* (June 9, 1983).

9. Jonathan Yardley, "Russian Revenge," *The Washington Post* (July 20, 1983); Michael Kernan, "The Russians are Here," *The Washington Post* (June 13, 1983).

10. "Taking Drugs on the Job," *Newsweek* (August 22, 1983); "Use of Cocaine Grows Among Top Traders in Financial Centers," *The Wall Street Journal* (September 18, 1983); "The Executive Addict," *Fortune* (June 24, 1985). The papal encyclical is described by Dr. Gregory Baum, "Laborem Exercens," in *The Priority of Labor* (New York: Paulist, 1982).

11. The Roper Report (1984). The quote is from Forrest Miller, *The Washington Post* (April 15, 1984).

12. The quote is from Gregory Welter, *The Washington Post* (April 15, 1984).

13. See *The Global Economy* (Bethesda, MD: World Future Society, 1985).

14. Marjorie Hyer, "Bishop Laments U.S. Image," *The Washington Post* (September 9, 1985).

15. Daniel Bell, *The Coming of Post-Industrial Society* (New York: Basic, 1976), p. 68; Alvin Toffler, *The Third Wave* (New York: Bantam, 1981), pp. 99, 115.

16. See James Robertson, *The Sane Alternative* (St. Paul, MN: River Basin, 1979), p. 62; and Christer Danielsson, "Business and Politics," *California Management Review* (Spring 1979).

17. Muzafer Sherifs, *Groups in Harmony and Tension* (New York: Harper & Row, 1953); Jeremy Stone, "It's Time the Superpowers Discover Each Other," *The Washington Post* (March 27, 1983).

18. George Kennan, *The Nuclear Delusion* (New York: Pantheon, 1982). Daniel Yankelovich, *Voter Options on Nuclear Arms Policy* (Public Agenda Foundation, 1984). Michael Dobbs, "Fascination, Hostility Color Soviet View of U.S.,"

The Washington Post (October 23, 1983). Lewis Lapham, "Intercontinental Ballistic Images," *The Washington Post* (December 4, 1982). Arthur Schlesinger Jr., "Russia Revisited," *The Wall Street Journal* (August 17, 1982).

19. *Intercom* (Washington, DC: Population Reference Bureau, 1983).

20. See John Naisbitt, *Megatrends* (New York: Warner, 1982), Ch. 3. Paul McCraken, "The Fading American Importance," *The Wall Street Journal* (June 17, 1980).

21. Jean-Jacques Servan-Schreiber, *The World Challenge* (New York: Simon & Schuster, 1980).

22. James L. Rowe, Jr., "Distress of Poorest Nations a 'Time Bomb,' Clausen Says," *The Washington Post* (September 28, 1983); Charles William Maynes, "If the Poor Countries Go Under We'll Sink With Them," *The Washington Post* (September 18, 1983).

23. Henry Kissinger, "Saving the World Economy," *Newsweek* (January 24, 1983). *International Commission on International Development Issues* (MIT Press, 1980).

24. The World Problematique is described by Aurelio Peccei, *The Human Quality* (Oxford: Pergamon, 1977).

25. Marjorie Hyer, "World's Wealth Should Aid Poor, Encyclical Says," *The Washington Post* (March 16, 1979).

26. Robert D. Hormats, "Talking With the Third World," *The Washington Post* (September 3, 1982). OECD comments are reported in Jean-Jacques Servan-Schreiber, *Challenge*, p. 129.

27. Donella Meadows et al., *Groping in the Dark: The First Decade of Global Modelling* (New York: Wiley, 1982).

28. Theodore Levitt, "The Globalization of Markets," *Harvard Business Review* (May-June 1983); Dennis Kneale, "New Foreign Products Pour Into US Market in Increasing Numbers," *The Wall Street Journal* (November 11, 1982); Harry Freeman, "If America Were Allowed to Sell Its Services to the World," *The Washington Post* (January 25, 1983).

29. Peter Drucker, "The Rise of Production Sharing," *The Wall Street Journal* (March 15, 1977).

30. See Richard Barnet and Ronald Muller, *Global Reach* (New York: Simon & Schuster, 1974). H. Anton Keller, "Behind WHO's Ban on Baby Formula Ads," *The Wall Street Journal* (June 29, 1981).

31. Howard Perlmutter, "Super-Giant Firms in the Future," *Wharton Quarterly* (1968); Barnett and Muller, *Global Reach*, p. 13.

32. Kurt Waldheim, "Global Economic Problems and Transnational Corporations," in Lewis Benton (ed.), *Management for the Future* (New York: McGraw-Hill, 1978).

33. Orville Freeman, Paper delivered to the World Future Society (1980).

34. Casey, "Regroup to Check the Soviet Thrust," *The Wall Street Journal* (April 22, 1983).

35. The work of Phillips Corporation is described by Barbara Ward, *Progress for a Small Planet* (New York: Norton, 1979), pp. 211–2. Gulf & Western and Castle & Cooke cases are from Orville Freeman, "The Farmer and the Market

Economy," in *Creating a Global Agenda* (World Future Society, 1984), and Oliver Williams, "Who Cast the First Stone?" *Harvard Business Review* (September-October 1984). Jerry McAfee, "The Role of the International Oil Companies in the Less Developed Countries," An address to the National Association of Petroleum Investment Analysts (March 3, 1977). "Sears Tries a New Role as Wheeler-Dealer in World Trade," *The Washington Post* (April 9, 1984). Matsushita is reported by Kenichi Ohmae, "Rethinking Global Strategy," *The Wall Street Journal* (April 29, 1985).

36. John Kenneth Galbraith, *The Voice of the Poor* (Cambridge, MA: Harvard University, 1983).

37. "Greece Concocts a New Cure," *BusinessWeek* (April 16, 1984); David Ignatius, "Egypt Mixes Capitalism, Socialism," *The Wall Street Journal* (August 2, 1983); "The Future of Hong Kong," *BusinessWeek* (March 5, 1984).

38. "China Walks the Edge of the Capitalist Road," *BusinessWeek* (October 18, 1982); "Michael Parks, "China to Begin Sweeping Economic Change," *The Washington Post* (April 16, 1984); Michael Weisskopf, "China's New Capitalists," *The Washington Post* (February 6, 1982); Hobart Rowen, "China Pushes Industrial Modernization Through Deals with Capitalist Nations," *The Washington Post* (November 19, 1978); "Deng's Quiet Revolution," *Newsweek* (April 30, 1984); Elizabeth Becker, "Hanoi Tries Profits in Bid to Boost Economy," *The Washington Post* (February 27, 1983); Bradley Graham, "Hungary Plans Major New Moves Toward Free-Market Economy," *The Washington Post* (June 22, 1984); Frederick Kempe, "Modified Marx," *The Wall Street Journal* (March 26, 1982); Dan Morgan, "East Europe Tries Modified Capitalism," *The Washington Post* (May 24, 1982); Dusko Doder, "Soviet Study Urges Economic Changes," *The Washington Post* (August 3, 1983).

39. See articles by Dusko Doder appearing in *The Washington Post*: "Soviet Leader Calls for Economic Reform," (August 16, 1983); "Soviet Law Enlarges Workers' Role," (June 19, 1983); "Gorbachev's Vigor Raises Expectations," (June 4, 1985); and "Gorbachev Sets Shift in Economy," (June 12, 1985). David Ignatius, "Soviet's Course," *The Wall Street Journal* (May 23, 1985).

40. Clark Kerr, *The Future of Industrial Societies* (Cambridge, MA: Harvard, 1983).

41. The report by the Central Committee appeared in *The Global Economy* (Bethesda, MD: World Future Society, 1985). Loeser, "Communism Won't Change Until the Party Machine Goes," *The Washington Post* (August 19, 1984).

42. Kerr, *Industrial Societies*; P. R. Lawrence and J. W. Lorsch, *Organization and Environment* (Cambridge MA: Harvard, 1967).

43. Kerr, *Industrial Societies*, pp. 107, 126.

CHAPTER 10

1. "Industrial Policy and Autos," *The Washington Post* (July 2, 1983).

2. Alfred P. Sloan, Jr., *My Years With General Motors* (Garden City, NY: Doubleday,

1963). Also see, Peter F. Drucker, *Concept of the Corporation* (New York: Day, 1946), p. xx.

3. See Brock Yates, *The Decline and Fall of the American Automobile Industry* (New York: Empire, 1982).

4. Iaccoca is quoted by Amanda Bennett, "Down in the Dumps," *The Wall Street Journal* (August 16, 1982).

5. *The Future of the Automobile* (Boston: MIT, 1984). Caldwell is quoted in "Detroit: Hitting the Skids," *Newsweek* (April 28, 1980).

6. Drucker's quote is from James Flanigan, "U.S. Industry in Transition" *The Wall Street Journal* (November 7, 1980).

7. William E. Halal, "Strategic Planning in Major U.S. Corporations," (A report prepared for General Motors Corporation, November 1980). "The New Breed of Strategic Planner," *BusinessWeek* (September 17, 1984).

8. Douglas R. Sease, "X-Cars, Once GM's Pride, Getting a Shoddy Reputation With Owners," *The Wall Street Journal* (March 3, 1983); Amal Nag and Robert L Simison, "With Three New Cars, the Japanese Outdo U.S. Move Into New Market," *The Wall Street Journal* (May 17, 1983); Charles W. Stevens, "European Luxury Cars Capturing a Growing Share of the U.S. Market," *The Wall Street Journal* (May 6, 1983); Malcolm Salter, "Don't Be Fooled by Those Auto Profits," *The Washington Post* (May 22, 1985). The businessman's quote was a letter to the editor, *Fortune* (September 2, 1985).

9. Warren Brown, "GM Plans High-Tech Strategy," *The Washington Post* (July 4, 1984).

10. Larry Kramer, "Peterson Claims Detroit Ignoring Big Opportunity," *The Washington Post* (October 26, 1978); "Ripoffs in Auto Repairs," *U.S. News and World Report* (December 1, 1980); Frank Allen, "Bosses Tout Quality of U.S. Goods, but Single Out Autos for Criticism," *The Wall Street Journal* (October 12, 1981); William M. Bulkeley, "'Lemon Laws' Gaining Popularity," *The Wall Street Journal* (July 12, 1983).

11. John Schnapp, "America Breaks Off Its Romance With the Car," *The Wall Street Journal* (February 28, 1983); Ishihara's comments appeared in "Detroit Hitting the Skids," *Newsweek.*

12. John M. Berry, "A Chastened Auto Industry on the Rebound," *The Washington Post* (March 27, 1983).

13. See *Increased Automobile Fuel Efficiency* (U.S. Congress, Office of Technology Assessment, 1982); Barbara Hildenbrand, "Automotive Technology—On the Move," *Transportation Quarterly* (January 1982); "Solar Car to Cross America," *The Futurist* (June 1981), p. 3; Lester R. Brown, *Running on Empty* (New York: Norton, 1979); *Transformation of Transportation* (State of California, Office of Appropriate Technology, 1981); Krish Bhaskar, *The Future of The World Motor Industry* (London: Kogan Page, 1980).

14. "Detroit's Merry-Go-Round," *BusinessWeek* (Sept 12, 1983).

15. John DeLorean's experiences are described by J. Patrick Wright, *On a Clear Day You Can See General Motors* (Grosse Pointe, MI: Wright, 1979), pp. 108, 209, 234.

16. See William J. Abernathy et al., *Industrial Renaissance* (New York: Basic, 1983), p. 62. David Jenkins, *Job Power* (Baltimore, MD: Penguin, 1973), p. 57.

17. Wright, *On a Clear Day*, Ch. 3.

18. "GM's Boss Toughs It Out," *Newsweek* (July 19, 1982).

19. "Brock Criticizes Auto Firms," *The Wall Street Journal* (April 26, 1984).

20. Barry Bruce-Briggs, *The War Against the Automobile* (New York: Dutton, 1977). Peter Behr, "U.S. Halts Effort to Standardize Use of Air Bags," *The Washington Post* (October 24, 1981).

21. Walter Brown, "Records Show GM Knew About X-Car Defects," *The Washington Post* (October 21, 1983). Drucker, *Concept*, pp. 305, 307.

22. From a letter to the editor by Kirk A. Wickersham, *BusinessWeek* (November 30, 1981), p. 8.

23. Murphy's quote is reported by James B. Quinn, "General Motors Corporation: The Down-Sizing Decision," (Unpublished case study, 1978).

24. General Motors Public Interest Report (1980), pp. 2, 56.

25. Walt Bogdanich, "Long Delays Face GM Car Owners," *The Wall Street Journal* (July 12, 1985). *Ibid*, p. 62.

26. Wright, *On a Clear Day*, p. 223.

27. Quoted by Robert Simison, "Car Trouble," *The Wall Street Journal* (November 1, 1983).

28. The National Research Council, *Science and Technology: A Five Year Outlook* (San Francisco: Freeman, 1979), p. 242. See "Electronic Banking," *BusinessWeek* (January 18, 1982); "Telecommunications," *BusinessWeek* (October 11, 1982).

29. "The Giant Takes Command," *Newsweek* (July 11, 1983).

30. Thomas J. Watson, Jr., *A Business and Its Beliefs* (New York: McGraw-Hill, 1963), p. 3.

31. James Lardner, "The Campus Race for 'Computer Literacy'," *The Washington Post* (1983).

32. Watson, *Beliefs*, p. 9.

33. *Ibid*, pp. 15, 16; "Telecommunications," *BusinessWeek* (October 11, 1982), p. 63; "Chip Wars," *BusinessWeek* (May 23, 1983).

34. Watson, *Beliefs*, p. 19.

35. Kathy Sawyer, "Communications Workers Act to Ease Impact of Future Shock," *The Washington Post* (March 29, 1983). Marvin Cetron, "Getting Ready for the Jobs of the Future," *The Futurist* (June 1983), p. 21.

36. Sawyer, "Communications Workers."

37. *CWA Newsletter* (June 29, 1984). Watts is quoted by Claudia Ricci, "Once Secure Phone Union Faces Loss of Power," *The Wall Street Journal* (March 12, 1984).

38. Sawyer, "Communications Workers."

39. See Arthur Shostak, "Tomorrow's Technical/Communications Labor Force," *The World of Work* (Washington, DC: World Future Society, 1983).

40. "Pinpointing the Source of Air-Traffic Disputes," *BusinessWeek* (April 5, 1982); Albert R. Karr, "Tower Turbulence," *The Wall Street Journal* (October 4, 1982); Suzzane Garment, "PATCO's Strike," *The Washington Post* (August 14, 1981).

41. Louis Harris, "Americans Dislike Controller Strike," *The Washington Post* (August 20, 1981). Glenn E. Watts, "An Attempt to Crush PATCO," *The Washington Post* (August 22, 1981).

42. "Controllers' Strike Could Alter Airline Industry," *The Wall Street Journal* (August 7, 1981); "Rehire Air Controllers," *BusinessWeek* (November 9, 1981).

43. Douglas B. Feaver, "When Computers Crash and Controllers Curse," *The Washington Post* (August 8, 1981); John Burgess, "Air Travel is Found Safe, With a Caveat," *The Washington Post* (December 9, 1981); Warren Brown and Carole Shifrin, "Concern Mounts on Controllers," *The Washington Post* (October 15, 1981).

44. "New Priority on Employee Relations," *The Washington Post* (May 20, 1983); "Air Controller Problems Resurfacing," *The Washington Post* (April 18, 1982); Howard Kurtz, "Poll Shows Some Controllers Think Air Travel Is Less Safe," *The Washington Post* (March 15, 1983); Douglas Feaver, "Panel Finds Air Traffic System Ailing," *The Washington Post* (May 20, 1983); "Tower Turbulence," *The Wall Street Journal*.

45. John Mintz, "FAA Seeks Hearings on Bids to Organize Air Controllers," *The Washington Post* (July 24, 1984); Lee Hockstader, "Controllers Seek New Union," *The Washington Post* (August 1984); "Why Controllers Are Talking Union Again," *BusinessWeek* (May 27, 1985).

46. See Paul Von Ward, *Dismantling the Pyramid*, (Washington, DC: Delphi, 1981).

47. Hobart Rowen, "Airline Deregulation Comes Back to Haunt," *The Washington Post* (March 14, 1982).

48. Douglas Feaver, "Airlines Agree on Congestion Relief," *The Washington Post* (September 13, 1984).

49. *Money* (December 1982).

50. Salter, "Don't Be Fooled," *The Washington Post*.

CHAPTER 11

1. Blumenthal is quoted from his speech, "An Ethics Code for Business," reported by *The Washington Post* (December 19, 1976).

2. The prototype was invented by Clark Kerr, *The Uses of the University* (Cambridge, MA: Harvard University Press, 1963).

3. Quoted from Charles Griswold, "Can Howard Take the Heat From Within," *The Washington Post* (February 15, 1983).

4. See *Involvement in Learning*, (National Institute of Education, 1985); Lansing Lamont, *Campus Shock* (Dutton, 1979); Edward Wynne, "The College Testing Controversy," *The Wall Street Journal* (February 14, 1980); and *The Chronicle*

of Higher Education (Novmber 8, 1976). Robert S. Greenberger, "An Oversupply of College Graduates Forces Some Into Lower-Level Jobs," *The Wall Street Journal* (February 25, 1982).

5. *A Nation at Risk*: Report of the Commission on Excellence in Educational Reform (1983).

6. James Lardner, "The Campus Race for 'Computer Literacy,'" *The Washington Post* (1983).

7. "The 'Wired University' Is on the Way," *BusinessWeek* (April 26, 1982).

8. Andrew Hacker, "The Shame of the Professional Schools," *Harpers* (October 1981).

9. See Samuel Dunn, "The Changing University," *The Futurist* (August 1983); and Sharon Rubin and Amy Thomas, "Current Models for the Future Education of Workers," *The World of Work* (Bethesda, MD: World Future Society, 1983).

10. From a speech by Lloyd Eliott, President of George Washington University (October 21, 1983).

11. The quoted is from a letter to the editor by Marc Stein, *The Washington Post* (October 3, 1985).

12. Lawrence Feinberg, "Education by Industry Is Booming," *The Washington Post* (January 28, 1985).

13. These comments appeared in *The Hatchet* (The student newspaper of the George Washington University, January 21, 1980).

14. Drucker, "Our Entrepreneurial Economy," *Harvard Business Review* (January-February, 1984).

15. S. E. Berki, "Health Care Policy in America," *The Annals of the American Academy of Political and Social Science*, Vol. 468 (July 1983). "Corporate Rx for Medical Costs," *BusinessWeek* (October 15, 1984).

16. Paul Starr, *The Social Transformation of Medicine* (New York: Basic, 1982). Joseph Califano, "What's Wrong With U.S. Health Care." *The Washington Post* (June 26, 1977). "The Big Business of Medicine," *Newsweek* (October 31, 1983), p. 62.

17. See The National Academy of Sciences, *Science and Technology* (San Francisco: Freeman, 1979).

18. Richard Totman, *Social Causes of Illness* (New York: Pantheon, 1980); Ivan Illich, *Medical Nemesis* (New York: Pantheon, 1976).

19. Page, "Why Patients Lose Their Patience," *The Wall Street Journal* (April 14, 1975). The patient is quoted from a letter by Josephine Gimble to *The Washington Post* (February 20, 1976).

20. Robert V. Pattison et al., "Investor-Owned and Not-for-Profit Hospitals," *The New England Journal of Medicine* (August 11, 1983).

21. The patient's comments are from a letter by Marion Wolff to *The Washington Post* (March 19, 1984). Rassman, "Why Health Care is a Costly Disgrace," *BusinessWeek* (January 26, 1981).

22. C. Panati, *Breakthroughs* (New York: Houghton Mifflin, 1980), p. 216.

23. "Beyond Medicine," *The Futurist* (August 1982).

24. See "The Corporate Rx for Medical Costs," *BusinessWeek* (October 15, 1984); "Upheaval in Medicine," *BusinessWeek* (July 25, 1983); and "The Big Business of Medicine," *Newsweek*, p. 65.

25. "The Big Business of Medicine," *Newsweek*, p. 64; "Doctors are Entering a Brave New World of Competition," *BusinessWeek* (July 16, 1984). Laurel Sorenson, "Hospitals and Doctors Compete for Patients," *The Wall Street Journal* (July 19, 1983).

26. "The Corporate Rx for Medical Costs," *BusinessWeek*.

27. Gellhorn, *The Wall Street Journal* (June 7, 1984).

28. Philip M. Stern, *Lawyers on Trial* (New York: Times, 1980). Fred Barbash, "Burger Warns About Overloading Courts," *The Washington Post* (November 19, 1982).

29. Jerald S. Auerbach, *Unequal Justice* (New York: Oxford University, 1976). Burger's comments are from a speech made to the American Bar Association, February 3, 1980. The survey was reported in "Against the Law," *The Washington Post* (September 2, 1984).

30. *Deskbook on Organized Crime* (U.S. Commerce Department).

31. Alexander Cockburn, "Of Cocaine, Capitalism and the Martyred DeLorean," *The Wall Street Journal* (October 28, 1982); "Guns, Grass—And Money," *Newsweek* (October 25, 1982); Hugh A. Mulligan, "Serpico, A Cop Not on the Take, Is Still on the Run, *The Washington Post* (November 10, 1974).

32. Richard Shaffer, "Computers Are Transforming Traditions of Law Profession," *The Wall Street Journal* (August 19, 1983).

33. *Ibid.*

34. Al Kamien et al., "Judge Provides Rare Glimpse at Judicial Decision-Making," *The Washington Post* (October 25, 1982).

35. Fred Barbash, "Burger Urges Mediation to Ease Court Burden," *The Washington Post* (January 25, 1982).

36. Solly Zuckerman, *Nuclear Illusion and Reality* (New York: Viking, 1982).

37. George C. Wilson, "MX: How a Missile Got a Life of Its Own," *The Washington Post* (December 12, 1982).

38. Jeffrey Record, "Why Our High-Priced Military Can't Win Battles," *The Washington Post* (January 29, 1984). The plan to free two executives of Electronic Data Systems Corp. is described by Ken Follett, *On Wings of Eagles* (New York: Morrow, 1983).

39. Sally Quinn, "Lord Louis, Ever Undaunted," *The Washington Post* (October 14, 1975).

40. David Broder, "Ike on Man Against War," *The Washington Post* (September 7, 1983)

41. The quote is by William Kelly and appeared in *The Washington Post* (November 26, 1983).

42. See Jonathon Schell, *The Fate of the Earth* (New York: Knopf, 1982). Bill

Peterson, "Colby View of 'Macho' Atomic Issue Warms Hearts of Freeze Advocates," *The Washington Post* (June 4, 1983).

43. *Congressional Record* (September 21, 1982). Also see the newsletter *Checkpoint* published by Howard Kurtz.

44. *Ben Bagdikian, The Media Monopoly* (Boston: Beacon, 1983).

45. Haynes Johnson, "The Business of Communication is in Danger of Bankruptcy," *The Washington Post* (May 9, 1982); Schorr, "We're Not the Good Guys Anymore," *The Washington Post* (June 9, 1983).

46. James Dickenson, "Americans Question Credibility of Media," *The Washington Post* (April 13, 1985).

47. Goldstein, *The News at Any Cost* (New York: Simon & Schuster, 1985).

48. George Gallup Jr. and David Poling, *The Search for America's Faith* (Nashville, TN: Abingdon, 1980).

49. Marjorie Hyer, "Holy Spirit Parish in Dispute Over the Proper Role for Laity," *The Washington Post* (June 26, 1982).

50. "An Acute Shortage of Priests," *Newsweek* (April 11, 1983); Judy Mann, "Conflict," *The Washington Post* (May 20, 1983).

51. Raspberry, "What's Wrong With a Minute of Silence?" *The Washington Post* (October 26, 1982). The quote is from Barbara Bedolla and was reported in the Shalem Newsletter.

52. Cox, *Religion in the Secular City* (New York: Simon & Schuster, 1984).

CHAPTER 12

1. Dennis Farney, "Lamm, Colorado's 'Governor Gloom,' Fears National Disaster Looms Ahead," *The Wall Street Journal* (September 12, 1985). Stein is quoted in "Economists See Votes in Reaganomics," *The Wall Street Journal* (October 10, 1983).

2. Martin Feldstein, "Why and How to Contain Red Ink," *The Wall Street Journal* (July 15, 1983).

3. Greenspan's comments are from an interview in *The Washington Post* (August 4, 1985). Rohatyn and Kaufman are quoted by John M. Berry, "Bush Denies Staff Disarray Over Deficits," *The Washington Post* (February 6, 1984).

4. See "The President's Home is a Castle," *Common Cause Magazine* (July-August, 1984), and Haynes Johnson, "The Upper Crust Grows Ever More Remote," *The Washington Post* (February 26, 1984). The letter to the editor is from Andrew C. Teeter, *The Washington Post* (October 24, 1982).

5. For instance, George Cabot Lodge, *The American Disease* (New York: Knopf, 1984).

EPILOGUE

1. Hesse, *Steppenwolf* (New York: Holt, Rinehart & Winston, 1970).

2. See John Applegath, *Human Economy: A Bibliography* (Amherst, MA: The Human Economy Center, 1981); Willis Harman, "Humanistic Capitalism," *Fields Within Fields* (Winter, 1973-1974); and Alvin Toffler, *The Third Wave* (New York: Bantam, 1980).

3. Peters is quoted from *Fortune* (May 31, 1985), p. 20; Kristol's comments appeared in "The New Populism," *The Wall Street Journal* (July 25, 1985), and in Daniel Bell and Irving Kristol, *The Crisis in Economic Theory* (New York: Basic, 1981), p. 215.

4. John D. Rockefeller, *The Second American Revolution* (New York: John Day, 1973). Burnham, *The Managerial Revolution* (New York: John Day, 1941). J. F. ter Horst is quoted in John Paluzek, *Will the Corporation Survive?* (Reston, VA: Reston, 1977).

5. National Council of Catholic Bishops, *Catholic Social Teaching and the U.S. Economy* (November 11, 1984).

6. See Mark Satin, "The New Populism," *New Options* (July 28, 1984), and Kristol, *Economic Theory*.

7. Greenleaf, *Servant Leadership* (New York: Paulist Press, 1977).

8. Toffler, *The Third Wave*, p. 11.

Index